MW00533081

CRIMINOLOGY True Crime Podcast Presents:

THE CASE OF THE
GOLDEN
STATE KILLER

MICHAEL MORFORD

MICHAEL FERGUSON

WILDBLUE
P R E S S

WildBluePress.com

THE CASE OF THE GOLDEN STATE KILLER published by:

WILDBLUE PRESS
P.O. Box 102440
Denver, Colorado 80250

WILDBLUE PRESS is registered at the U.S. Patent and Trademark Offices.

ISBN 978-1-947290-55-6 Trade Paperback
ISBN 978-1-947290-54-9 eBook

Interior Formatting/Book Cover Design by Elijah Toten
www.totencreative.com

THE CASE OF THE
GOLDEN
STATE KILLER

TABLE OF CONTENTS

SEASON TWO, EPISODE ONE

The East Area Rapist, Original Nightstalker, Golden State Killer committed perhaps more than 100 home break-ins and burglaries. He committed at least fifty rapes and a dozen or more murders in the state of California over a ten-year period. As this monster evolved, his crimes became more horrific. When we made the decision to make Season Two of the *Criminology* podcast about this case, we wanted to make sure that we gave the listeners a true understanding of the level of terror this perpetrator brought on the state of California. For well over forty years this monster would go uncaptured. In fact, when we started Season Two this was a case without an arrest. That would all change around Episode nine of Season Two of *Criminology*. That arrest shook the world, and we'll cover that in detail later.

For this season of *Criminology*, we interviewed both current investigators on the case as well as the investigators who handled it back when it all began. We also interviewed victims and family members of victims to tell the stories of the survivors and to give a voice to the victims who died. In researching this case, it was mind boggling that despite the sadistic nature of the crimes and the sheer numbers, there were many people who had never heard of this serial killer. This includes many in California where the crimes occurred. Much of this is due in part to the confusion around the many different names given to this individual over the years.

The story begins in June of 1976 in the town of Rancho Cordova, California. Rancho Cordova is in Sacramento County in the northern part of the state. It was an unincorporated area of Sacramento County back in 1976, but it was a town during that time that was experiencing a lot of growth. There was a lot of new home construction, and residents were adding in-ground swimming pools which were really becoming popular. Rancho Cordova was a blue-collar town in 1976 made up of many military families. Many of these individuals worked at nearby Mather Air Force Base or one of several other Air Force bases in the surrounding areas. Mid-June of 1976 was a busy time for the residents of Rancho Cordova. School was letting out for the summer, and the Fourth of July holiday was around the corner. This would be a big one – the bicentennial of America. People in this area as well as many areas across the country were excited for the two hundredth birthday of the United States. They were busy living their lives and enjoying the summer. But, normal life for this town would change on June 18 of that year. There was no way for residents to know it at the time, but Rancho Cordova and many towns all over Sacramento County were about to change. They would become the hunting grounds for a ruthless and cunning predator, one who would go on to terrorize the residents of these towns repeatedly.

On June 18, 1976, a 23-year-old woman was feeling uneasy. She had recently moved back in to her father's home on the 2600 block of Paseo Drive in Rancho Cordova. She had been receiving odd phone calls for weeks. Her phone rang on multiple occasions, and when she answered it, she would hear nothing but silence. She tried to dismiss these calls as harmless pranks. Her father, a retired Air Force man, had been out of town for several weeks. All alone in an empty house, the calls weighed heavily on her mind. She had also noticed in the preceding weeks that a dark green car would drive by her on multiple occasions, and the driver always seemed to look away as he passed her. She didn't know what to make of this, but it made her feel uneasy.

This was a nice section of town on a quiet street. The only problem in the area recently had been in the yard of a resident on Del Rey Court, a few houses away. Someone had repeatedly cut through the fence that surrounded his yard. Whoever it was had damaged the fence on more than one occasion. The resident assumed that it had been done by kids wanting to make a shortcut through his yard. Besides that, incident, this area of Rancho Cordova was a peaceful section. This was in stark contrast to busier sections of the city, which were more densely populated and had a higher crime rate.

The 23-year-old woman settled in for bed on the night of June 18. Everything seemed normal; it was quiet, and she fell asleep. She woke up startled around four a.m. from a deep sleep. Her bedroom light was on, and there was a man standing in her doorway wearing a mask. He was tapping a knife on the door frame. It took the woman a second or two for her eyes to adjust, so she could clearly see the figure standing in her doorway. When her eyes did adjust, she was shocked at what she saw.

We interviewed many people connected with this case for Season Two of *Criminology*. Paul Holes was a Contra Costa County cold case investigator who worked extensively on the East Area Rapist case. He was instrumental in the eventual arrest of the suspect Joseph J. DeAngelo, but we'll get to that later. Paul had the following to say about this first attack: "He's showing up for the first official attack, in Sacramento, in Rancho Cordova. That victim is in bed, and she sees the East Area Rapist in her doorway. He's standing in her doorway, he has a t-shirt on as well as a ski mask. He's carrying a knife, and he is nude from the waste down. And he's standing there with an erection, but she sees his entire physique. And she describes him as having a very slim, athletic, well-proportioned build."

A masked man with an erection and holding a knife is standing there. The woman was stricken with fear, and she pulled her blankets over her face. The masked man walked over to the bed and yanked the blankets off the woman. He pushed the tip of his knife against her head and began to speak, "If you make one move or sound, I'll stick this knife into you. I want to fuck you, take it off." His voice was a hoarse growl or whisper through clenched teeth. The woman was defenseless, and she complied with his demands. Terrified, she took off her nightgown. He tied her hands behind her back using bindings he had brought with him. Then, he sexually assaulted the woman.

After the assault was over, the man got up from the bed and asked her if she had any money. As soon as she began to answer him he snarled at her, once again through clenched teeth, "Shut up." He rummaged through her room and then tied her feet with the cord from a blow dryer and a bra. He also gagged her. Before he left the room, he held the knife to her head once more, warning her that he would kill her if she tried anything. The attacker left her on the bed bound and unable to move. He told her, "You better have money in the house." Then he left the bedroom. She could hear him rummaging through her drawers and walking around the house. She then thought she heard the whispering of two separate and distinct voices. She clearly heard one voice say in a whisper, "I told you to shut up." She got the impression that he was alone and that he was the only one whispering.

When the young woman no longer heard any sounds coming from the house, she decided to try to free herself before he came back. She struggled to get herself free and was eventually able to untie the bindings on her legs. She crept quietly through the house with her hands still behind her back, hoping that the intruder was no longer in the house. Luckily, for her sake, he wasn't. She saw that the back door was open and tried to kick it closed with her foot, but the deadbolt was extended. This prevented the door from closing. She made her way to the phone and managed to dial the operator. Once connected with the operator, she pleaded for the police to be sent to her house. The police responded quickly to the home on Paseo Drive.

Upon entering the home, they found the victim nude and still partially bound. Police quickly searched the home to make sure the intruder was not still hiding inside. They removed the bindings from the victim's hands. They could see that her hands had been bound so tightly they had started to turn black from lack of circulation.

The investigation into this attack was officially started. Authorities had no way of knowing at the time that they were dealing with the first confirmed attack by the East Area Rapist. This would be a series of attacks that would touch a 400-mile stretch of California over a ten-year period. The pieces to that puzzle would not be put together until later.

The victim was asked to replay the events of what happened to her in her mind to be able to provide police officers with the information and details they needed. She recounted for them what happened. She detailed how the knife was about three or four inches long. She described how the mask seemed to be homemade out of some sort of white coarse material. The only holes in the mask were for the intruder's eyes. She remembered that he had also been wearing gloves. When the police checked the bathroom, they found balled up towels and baby oil. They theorized that the attacker had lubricated himself prior to waking the victim. The house was a mess with the contents of drawers strewn out all over the floor. The woman felt that her attacker was in his mid-twenties and between 160 to 170 pounds. She estimated his height at five feet, nine inches. She was able to give police some amazing details of her attacker. She said that he had dark hairy arms and legs and that he held the knife in his left hand. Then she told police something that would be a common detail given by many victims of this monster; he had a very small penis.

Police turned their attention to the outside of the home. They quickly determined that the back door had been pried open. The lock had been "slipped", meaning that a tool or object had been used to release the deadbolt from its locked position. The victim's purse was found in the yard with its contents scattered. Next, they discovered that the attacker had attempted to cut the phone line leading in to the house. Police began questioning neighbors. A few of them had heard dogs barking around three a.m.

After the police had finished combing through the house, they realized that the only items taken by the intruder were fifteen dollars in cash and two packs of Winston cigarettes. Why would the intruder take items with such minimal value when he had the opportunity to take items with much more value? This was a question that police were left to ponder. They concluded that the sexual assault was the primary motive, the theft of a few small items was almost an afterthought to this perpetrator.

Police removed items from the house to log as evidence, including the balled-up towels from the bathroom. This was 1976, years before DNA technology would be something at the disposal of investigators. Any semen left at the scene could provide vital clues including the suspect's blood type. After the police had gone, and in the days after the attack, the victim was left to deal with what had happened to her. But, as it turned out, her ordeal wasn't over. Over the next couple of weeks, the 23-year-old woman began receiving more hang-up phone calls. She received about six calls in total. And while the calls she received prior to her attack bothered her, these new calls would raise an entirely new level of concern.

Eventually these phone calls subsided. In May 1977, almost a year after she was attacked, the rape kit analysis came back. The results showed something interesting about the man who had raped her. He was a non-secretor, which is a medical condition in the body that does not allow a man's blood type to be determined from a semen sample. This condition is not overly common, in fact, roughly only 15 percent of the population are non-secretors. At this point, it had been almost a year since this woman had been attacked, but she had been trying to move on with her life with each day that passed. But, if things were starting to get back to normal, they wouldn't last. In late 1977, she started getting phone calls again. She contacted the Sacramento County Sheriff's Department to let them know she had been getting upsetting phone calls. The police didn't want to miss an opportunity to get the upper hand on the caller, especially if this turned out to be the man who had attacked and raped her. They put "traps" on her phone which would record any incoming phone call. The authorities monitored every call that came in for weeks but nothing out of the ordinary happened. But then, on January 2, of 1978, a phone came in from someone who apparently had the wrong number. In this short-recorded call, you can hear a man asking, "Is Ray there" and the woman, who is 24 years old by this time, simply tells him he has the wrong number. The call seemed innocent enough. The caller was a very soft-spoken man who apparently had the wrong number. But, just a little bit later that day another call came in. And this call would not be innocent, it was extremely sinister. This recorded phone call, which you can hear on the second season of the *Criminology* podcast, starts with the woman saying hello a few times. On the other end of the line there is silence followed by hissing and heavy breathing. Toward the end it sounds like the caller is whispering through clenched teeth, "gonna kill you" three times, followed by "bitch" several times, then finally "fucking whore" before he hangs up.

Unfortunately, this call was not traced, but it is still extremely valuable. It does sound like the caller on the second call made a concerted effort to disguise his voice on the call. But this was not the case on the first call, which sounded like a man's natural soft-spoken voice. There was no way to know whether both calls were made by the same person, but if they were, they had the attacker's voice on tape in that first call. And that soft-spoken type of voice is going to come up again in future attacks. In our interview with Paul Holes, he shed light on these calls:

There's one recording that is the East Area Rapist. And that is the recording that was made to victim number one who was attacked in June of 1976. He called her in January 1978 and that is the recording that everyone who is familiar with the case has heard. There is no question that is the East Area Rapist.

By the time this call was made to the first victim, this man had attacked over two dozen times in Sacramento County, and he was just getting started. Known originally as the East Area Rapist, then later as the Original Night Stalker or Golden State Killer, this predator would go on to rape more than fifty women. He would also murder at least a dozen people. Season Two of the *Criminology* podcast was dedicated to the victims who survived this monster (they collectively call themselves thrivers!), and those who sadly did not.

Carmichael is a town on the other side of the American River from Rancho Cordova. It is not very far as the crow flies but getting there requires a trip over one of several bridges. The fastest route is to take the Watt Avenue Bridge. But, there was such a serious drought in California in 1976 and 1977 that much of the American River had dried up so that you could almost walk across it. Carmichael boasted a variety of parks and bike trails. The town of roughly 37,000 residents was a tight-knit quiet town. But in the early hours of a mid-July morning, something terrible would occur in Carmichael. On the 4700 block of Marlborough Way, two teenage sisters were home alone after their parents had gone away to a church function for four days. The sisters were fifteen and sixteen years old. Their parents felt secure leaving them home alone. They were good girls, not the type who got into trouble. The parents were also comforted in the fact that they had an FBI agent as a nearby neighbor. The two sisters had an uneventful Friday night and went to bed around 10:30 p.m. That's early for two teenagers home alone, and it speaks to what type of girls these were. They were not the type to throw a wild party or get into trouble.

Around 2 a.m., the sixteen-year-old sister woke to the feeling of something heavy on top of her. It didn't take her long to realize that there was a masked man straddling her, and he was holding a knife. The intruder must have sensed that she was about to try to fight him because he began to punch her several times. He told her that if she made a move, he would stick the knife he was holding through her neck. He told her that he just wanted to steal some stuff and he would be gone in thirty minutes. He talked through clenched teeth. He then proceeded to bind her hands and feet using shoelaces, gagged her with a stocking and then tied a belt around her mouth.

Once the intruder was satisfied she was secured, he made his way to her sister's bedroom. The intruder crept quietly into her room. He was about to wake up the younger sister when she jumped out of bed and tried to hit the man. Her attack missed its mark, and she ran out into the hallway. Defiantly, angrily, the young girl yelled, "Goddamn it, what's this queer doing here"? She didn't make it far in her escape attempt as the man caught up to her and struck her on the back of her head with his fist. He dragged her back to her bedroom and laid her on her bed. He warned the girl that he had a knife and that he could kill her. It was at this point, fearing for her life, that she stopped struggling. He tied her up with shoelaces and then left the room to rummage through the house.

He went through bedroom closets and drawers in different rooms of the house. Periodically, he checked in on each of the helpless girls. He threatened the older sister, asking her where her money was. He also asked her where the doctor kept his drugs, mentioning that he had checked the fridge but didn't find them. It was then that he did the unthinkable. He repeatedly raped the younger of the two sisters. At one point, the intruder lubricated his penis and placed it in the victim's hands and ordered her to play with it. This would be a detail that many later victims would recount as well. During one of the assaults, he told her, "When I saw you at the junior prom, I knew I had to fuck you." The two teenage sisters endured two agonizing hours of brutal assault at the hands of this predator. And then the man was gone, and the house was quiet. A moment later, the two girls heard a car start up and drive off.

The younger of the two sisters had suffered the bulk of this violent intruder's aggression. She was afraid to move even after she thought he was gone and stayed in place for about thirty minutes. When she finally felt that she was safe to do so, she started to move around to free herself.

Meanwhile, the older sister had freed herself and made her way to her younger sister's bedroom. She grabbed a pair of scissors and was able to cut her sister's bindings. It was around four in the morning at this point, and the two girls raced to the phone to call police.

Police and emergency medical personnel responded quickly. They determined that the two sisters needed medical attention, and they rushed them to the Sacramento medical center, which was only a few miles away. The authorities notified the girls' parents who immediately rushed home. At the crime scene, police began their investigation. They determined that the sliding glass door in the rear living room of the house was the point of entry. Pry marks on the door, door jam, and latch were clearly visible.

Police eventually were able to question the two teenage girls. It was then they discovered that only the fifteen-year-old had been sexually assaulted. But, there was no doubt that both girls had been terrorized. Neither girl recalled their attacker wearing gloves, but the police found no prints from the intruder. They described their attacker as being white and sounding like he was young, perhaps between eighteen and twenty years old. They said he was about five feet, ten inches tall with a muscular build. He had worn a mask with eye holes, blue corduroy pants, and what they referred to as "waffle stompers" or hiking boots.

The two traumatized girls relayed some very interesting information to police. The younger sister told authorities that the man had said to her, "When I saw you at the junior prom, I knew I had to fuck you." But, she also told police that she felt as if the man was making this up. She had a photo of herself with her junior prom date next to her bed. In fact, the words "junior prom" were prominently displayed. She felt as if the man made up this statement after seeing the photograph.

The older sister told investigators what the man had said to her about wanting to know where the drugs were kept, and he had checked the refrigerator. It turned out that their father was indeed a doctor. Was this an indication that the intruder knew the family in some way? Or, was it simply that he had uncovered this fact while he was going through the house? It was of interest to the police that this individual knew enough about prescription drugs to know that some of them needed to be refrigerated. However interesting this information was to police, it was not much for them to go on. They would not be able to come up with a motive or develop a strong suspect in this case.

This attack shared some strong similarities to the one that occurred a month earlier in Rancho Cordova. The victims lived in a single-story home. They were all attacked as they slept by a masked man. There were no parents home at the time when the attacks happened. We can look back now and see the connections between these two cases, but back then, authorities did not immediately link the two together. But for Carmichael, this was the second incident that occurred in the span of a few days in the normally quiet community.

-

The day before the attack on the two sisters, a homeowner in his sixties named Harvey Rehrer, walked into his garage just before five a.m. He discovered a man he didn't know looking through his tools. Before the startled man could even process what he was seeing, the man in his garage started to beat the homeowner with a club. The victim suffered several severe blows from the club. He tried to escape, but his attacker kept beating him until the homeowner ultimately fell to the ground. While he was laying on the ground, his attacker unholstered a gun. The helpless homeowner scrambled under his car to keep from being shot. The attacker exited the garage and disappeared. This attack happened on the 300 block of Claydon Way in Sacramento, only a mile or so from the attack on the two young sisters the next day.

During the questioning of Harvey Rehrer, the police were particularly interested in the weapon used in his attack. Based on the description he gave, they felt the club was an older style military training club or baton, with one of the ends covered in white padding. There was no way to know if this attacker was a military man or if the club had been stolen from another garage or home nearby. The interest in this club would resurface later related to a subsequent attack. Being a day apart, and only a mile away, police were interested in a possible connection between the two cases. But, they were not able to find anything solid that connected the two events. Harvey's son Larry Rehrer interviewed for the podcast:

> *This incident happened to my father, Harvey Rehrer, who has since passed away. He was hit from behind, and he was hit hard, which knocked him to the ground. The guy started hitting him in the body. And my dad was rather small in stature, and he pulled himself under the car, grabbing onto the driveshaft of the car and held on for dear life. The guy was swinging some type of club, and the blows were severe enough that my dad required hundreds of stitches. And when he couldn't get to my dad's head anymore, he started pulling my dad's pants off to get to his wallet. He did finally get the wallet, and then he ran off leaving very little evidence behind of himself. My dad crawled over to the next-door neighbor's house, yelling, 'Bill, Bill,' which was the name of the man who lived there. They came out to find my dad basically clinging to life. The police and the ambulance were called, and my dad was transported down to Mercy.*

It had been over two months since the Paseo Drive rape had occurred, and the phone calls to that victim following her attack had ended. Neighbors, who had received similar calls before the attack, did not receive any calls afterwards. It seemed like an isolated incident. Perhaps the attacker singled out the 23-year-old victim, and calls to the neighbors were nothing more than a coincidence.

On August 28, around ten p.m., the homeowner on Del Rey Court who had previously had someone break his fence, once again had someone cut through the fence. The owner had earlier put up brand new boards to keep people from cutting through his yard, but on this night, whoever cut through the yard broke the fence again to access the shortcut. The homeowner heard someone possibly climbing the fence. Another neighbor had earlier complained about someone frequently cutting through his yard as well as leaving his side gate open. This neighbor went so far as to nail the side gate shut. Around ten-thirty that night, a homeowner on the 10000 block of Malaga Way walked out of his house and started his car to leave for work. The 46-year-old Sacramento Municipal Utility District employee had just switched from the day shift to the night shift the previous day. SMUD, as it is known, is the primary electricity provider for Sacramento County. The homeowner left his family inside the house when he left for work, including his 41-year-old wife, and two daughters, twelve and fifteen.

The mother and her two daughters were on only their second night alone in the house. It was hot that time of year in California with temperatures that day reaching 100 degrees. The youngest daughter decided to sleep with her window open hoping to catch some relief from the night air.

Around three-twenty in the morning, something woke her. It was the sound of the wind chimes hanging from her curtain rods rattling. She opened her eyes and looked towards the window. It was then that she saw the unmistakable outline of a masked man outside of her window, and a gloved hand trying to pry the screen on her window loose. The 12-year-old didn't hesitate bolting to her mother's bedroom. She woke up her mother in a terrified panic. The two of them ran back into the daughter's bedroom, and the mom looked outside for any signs of the prowler but didn't see anything. But, she did pick up the scent of what smelled like aftershave in the still night air. The anxious pair hustled to the older daughter's room to wake her up and make sure she was okay. The older girl was fine, and she barely woke up as they were describing to her what happened.

The mother was about the call the police, but before she did she wanted to take another look in the backyard to see if there was anyone out there. She and her younger daughter went back into her bedroom to get a good look out the window. They were terrified to see a masked man staring at them through the bedroom window. The man, after seeing the pair, turned and ran off. The mother grabbed her young daughter, and they both made their way to the kitchen. She grabbed the phone and crouched down on the floor and started to call the operator. Before she could dial, they heard a smashing sound coming from the youngest daughter's bedroom. Then, they heard her wind chimes dropping to the floor. Almost instantly, the masked man was running down their hallway towards the kitchen. Paul Holes shed some light on this attack:

> Attack number three occurred right around the corner, you have a teenage girl and a mom who see our offender nude from the waist down. Their description is very similar to the first victim's East Area Rapist's description.

The attacker was brandishing two weapons: a gun he held in his left hand, and a club he held in his right. The mother and daughter had to have been in shock seeing a masked man armed with weapons who was nude from the waist down. The masked man said in a low growl through clenched teeth, "Freeze or I'll kill you, hang up the phone." Then he asked the mother who else was in the house, and she replied that her other daughter was asleep in her bedroom. It was at this point that the mother made a desperate and brave decision. Thinking only of her daughters, she leapt at the man and attempted to grab at his gun to either gain control of it or knock it out of his hand. During the scuffle, this mother sensed that this man was weak, and she started to get the upper hand in the fight. But, the man pulled back and smashed her in the head with the club he had in his other hand. While this is happening, the daughter was screaming hysterically. The man hit the mother repeatedly, and, when she finally let go of the gun, he pistol whipped her with it.

Once the intruder was back in control, he told the pair, "Don't worry all I want is your money, I won't hurt you if you cooperate." That was a tough statement for the mother to accept since the man was nude from the waist down. She knew in her heart that he was not telling the truth. As the man attempted to get them both down on the floor to tie them up, she decided this was her last chance to make a move. She jumped up and caught the attacker off guard while he was in the act of trying to tie them. They started to struggle again, and the mother once again began to overpower the man. She quickly grabbed her daughter and headed straight for the door. As she made it to the door, she felt blows to the back of her head. The man had caught up with her and was reigning blows down on her head with the club. This woman was determined that the man was not going to get her daughter, and she pushed the 12-year-old out of the front door. After a short struggle, the mother was able to make it out the front door herself. They ran off screaming toward a neighbor's house. The neighbor heard their screams and opened the door quickly to let them.

At this point the older daughter was still in the house. There's no way that she could have slept through the entire ordeal and it turns out that she didn't. While her mother and sister were running to the neighbor's house, she was making her escape out her bedroom window. She saw the pair running and followed them in the same direction.

At this point, the attacker had lost any semblance of control. He attempted to attack a house with three females, and they were all able to get away from him. This guy didn't run off to get away quickly. He simply walked to a yard nearby. The homeowner whose yard he had crept into got a good look at him. She thought that he was wearing white shorts because the skin of his naked body was so white. The man hid in this homeowner's bushes for a few minutes. Then, he stood up and walked, not ran, down Malaga Way.

The neighbor who let the girls into their house called the police. The call to police came in at 3:28 a.m., which was about eight minutes after the daughter was awakened by the sound of her wind chimes. This would have been an extremely terrifying eight minutes for the residents of that household. Although the mother was hurt badly, she did what any parent would hope they would have the strength to do to keep their kids from being harmed.

Police arrived at the scene a few minutes later. When they assessed the mother, they discovered just how badly she was hurt. She was bloody from the blows she received to her head. Although badly shaken, both the mother and younger daughter were able to give details of their attacker to police. They described him as having a mask, some type of stocking, with slits for eyes. They also said that he was wearing black gloves, a light-colored shirt, and interestingly, a black lineman's belt on his waist. This is the type of belt that people wear who have jobs that require climbing. They said he was about five feet, ten inches tall, thin, and about 160-170 pounds. One other thing that caught their attention was that he had a noticeably small penis. They described the man's voice as almost timid, or nervous, and he spoke through clenched teeth. They felt that he sounded like he was between eighteen and thirty years of age. They also described that he smelled strongly of aftershave. The gun he carried in his left hand, a revolver, was small, with maybe a two-inch barrel. The description of the club that he used to hit the mother was very similar to what had been used in the garage attack on Harry Rehrer in Carmichael. Police thought the attacker was left handed since he carried his gun in his left hand. Also, when he started to beat the mother with the club, he switched it into his left hand. This lined up with what the victim in the June 1976 attack on Paseo had told police, that he held his knife in his left hand. The ambulance arrived and took the injured mother to the hospital. She was badly hurt but, after medical care and stitches, she would make a full recovery.

The police combed the crime scene inside the house for clues. They found out first hand how brutal the fight was; blood covered the floor and the walls. They made their way through the house. They found broken picture frames, the phone yanked from the wall, and a black shoelace lying neatly on a chair. The intruder had planned to use this to tie up his victims. Police also found torn pieces of a towel. Outside the youngest daughter's bedroom, they found a chair that the intruder had used to stand on to get into her window.

While police were out searching the neighborhood, they discovered a possible suspect. They encountered a mother looking for her 21-year-old son. She said he had not come home. They lived within a two-minute walk of the victims. They also lived close to the victim of the attack earlier that June. Police found the son quickly, questioned him, but he was evasive and shifty with his answers. He was brought into the station and police questioned people who knew him. An ex-girlfriend who was questioned described this man as very odd, and she told police he had a small, extremely thin penis. Police were very interested in this guy as a suspect. Later, though, it was determined through investigative measures that he was not the rapist.

On August 31, just two nights after the Malaga Way attack, the woman who saw the attacker make his get away had her own unsettling experience. Her home was broken into, but she was not attacked. But, this is a lot of activity in a small section of a normally quiet area. There had been two attacks, a little more than two months apart, only separated by 456 feet. Even if the police weren't aware of a connection to the July Marlborough Way attack in Carmichael on the two sisters, they had to have put together quickly these latest two attacks. The same physical descriptions were given of the attacker. Both attacks happened around the same time of the early morning. In both attacks, females in single-story homes were targeted. The biggest link between the two was the fact that both attackers had shown up and possibly left nude from the waist down. As it turned out, this latest attack was reminiscent of an attack that occurred the previous October in 1975, just a quarter of a mile away.

On October 21, 1975, a woman and her two daughters were attacked in the area of Dawes and Dolecetto in Rancho Cordova. A masked man broken into a home and repeatedly raped the 36-year-old mother and both of her daughters, aged eighteen and seven. The man entered the home through the garage and then through an unlocked door leading to the kitchen. He threatened the family with a knife. He tied up the mother and oldest daughter in one room and the youngest daughter in another room.

After committing these brutal rapes, he left the house, and the mother was able to free herself and her children and get to a neighbor's house to call the police. They described their attacker as a black male, between twenty and twenty-five years old, wearing a fatigue type of shirt. They said he was about 5 feet, six inches, weighed about 150 pounds, and had short hair. Police investigated the house and found that the man had ransacked it before leaving. The victims would later tell police that they thought the man was white and not black. We don't know for sure whether this was the work of the East Area Rapist, but the targeting of a woman and her two daughters so close to the other attack makes it very possible that it was.

There were several incidents in 1974 and 1975 that occurred in and around the area of Dawes and Dolecetto. There was a cluster of home burglaries and prowlings. In one incident, police officer Richard Shelby was called out to respond to a break-in at a home where the owners were away. Richard Shelby did an interview for Season Two of *Criminology* and said this about the incidents during that timeframe:

> *Neighbors saw someone prowling around in that house and called us. We got there and saw nothing. And as*

soon as we left, we got a call a call to come back. The neighbor said that as soon as we left, the guy jumped off the roof and hit the ground running. I had only seen that one before and it in a video of a Seal training tape. This guy jumped off the roof and ran right to the fence and jumped over it. He was about sixteen years old, wearing military fatigues, 5'9", blond hair and thin.

There were multiple incidents of dogs being bludgeoned to death around the Dawes and Dolecetto area. Shelby felt strongly that the youth who had jumped off the roof was on a prowling and burglary spree and had likely killed the dogs when confronted by them during his crimes. With so much crime occurring in a normally peaceful area, residents would have been on high alert after the Malaga Way attack on the mother and her two daughters. People in Carmichael were on edge as well after the details of Marlborough Way attack came out. People may have thought this was just an isolated incident, but sadly that would turn out not to be the case. In the middle of August, about two weeks after the attack on the sisters, a man in another part of Carmichael reported a prowler in his yard. This occurred on the 4800 block of Crestview Drive. A couple days later, a nearby home was broken into, but the owners didn't find anything missing.

On Saturday September 4, 1976, a 29-year-old woman decided to stop by her parents' home on the 4800 block of Crestview to do some laundry. Her washing machine was not working, and since her parents weren't home, this seemed like the perfect way to get her laundry done. The recently divorced woman and young mother pulled up to her parents' home around 6 p.m. She entered the home through the garage and carried her laundry in with her. She didn't bother to shut the garage door behind her. She spent about five hours doing laundry, and then around 11 p.m., packed it all into her laundry basket and carried it to her car. As she was loading the laundry into the trunk of her car, she felt a hand on her shoulder. Before she could look up, she was yanked around and saw a man wearing a mask standing in front of her. Before she could react, the man punched her in the face breaking her nose. She was knocked out for a moment and fell to the ground. When she came to, the man said, "Don't look at me, if you look at me, I'll slit your throat." It was at this point that the man picked her up off the ground and dragged the dazed woman through the garage and into the house. Once they were inside, he assured the woman that he just wanted her car and money because he was trying to get to Bakersfield. But he did tell her again that he would slit her throat if she looked at him. He pulled out white shoelaces and tightly tied her hands behind her back. He forced the woman to walk through various rooms of the house, as if he was seeing who else was there. Along the way, he asked her if anyone else was due to come home.

After feeling confident that they were alone, he pulled the bound woman into a bedroom and threw her onto the bed. He tied her feet together, and then blindfolded and gagged her. He left the room, and the woman could hear him going through drawers in other rooms of the house. She then heard him in the kitchen, and she could tell he had sat down to eat something. He came back every few minutes to check on the bound woman and told her repeatedly that he would kill her if she moved. At some point, she thought she could hear the man whispering, perhaps on the phone, but she wasn't sure. The man entered the bedroom, and she could hear the unmistakable sound of him lubricating himself. Then, she felt the man sit down on the bed next to her, and she felt his penis in her bound hands. "Do it right or I'll kill you," the masked man hissed at her through clenched teeth. He cut off her clothes with the knife, and then he held it to her throat and told her she had a nice body. The woman endured over two hours of sexual assault at the hands of his masked man.

Sometime after midnight, the masked rapist dragged the woman back outside and tied her to a patio post. The terrified woman heard the man get in her car and drive off. Her night of terror was finally over.

The police were summoned to the house, and eventually, so was the victim's sister. The 29-year-old woman was in bad shape. She had been beaten, raped, and tortured for hours. Her hands were black from the tightly tied ligatures. She was immediately taken to nearby Kaiser hospital.

Police made their way into the house to search for clues and evidence. All the lights in the house were off except for one. They found the back door had been propped open, and the air conditioning unit had been unplugged. Two empty Coors Light beer cans were found in the kitchen.

Later that morning around 7 a.m., the victim's car was found on Oakgreen Circle, which was about a quarter mile west of the crime scene and just a few minutes drive. It turns out, the attacker could simply have walked through a few yards and reached the location where the car was discovered. So, it's a bit odd that he decided to steal her car in the first place.

Police were able to question the victim, and she gave them some good information. She told them that the man who attacked her was white, had a slim build, and was about five feet, eight inches or five feet, nine inches. She went on to describe the mask he wore as being homemade, from gray flannel material with holes for the eyes and mouth. She said that he had spoken to her in a whisper through clenched teeth.

It's important to examine the events in the days leading up to this brutal attack. A few different homes on the 4800 block of Crestview had been the scene of suspicious activity, this included the prowler in the yard and the home that was broken into but appeared not to have been robbed. Then this attack and rape occurred, and there are some similarities to previous attacks. But, there are also some differences as well. This rape victim was attacked outside of the home and forced back inside. The other attacks occurred in the middle of the night while victims were asleep. Also, this attack was far more brutal than others before it in terms of the physical violence that occurred. It would have been difficult for police to link these rapes, which span a three-month period and crisscross the towns of Rancho Cordova and Carmichael. It's easy to sit back now and analyze everything and see that it's likely these cases are related. But the police investigating these crimes at the time had to sort through all the evidence, clues, and modus operandi to see if they had a serial rapist on the loose. If they were thinking that, they had to wonder when and where he would strike next. As it turns out, they wouldn't have to wait long to find out.

SEASON TWO, EPISODE TWO

On October 5, 1976, Jane would be the fifth victim in a series of brutal home invasions and rapes. While the reports give details of what happened to Jane, we thought there'd be no better way to share her story than to have Jane tell it herself.

My husband was stationed at McClellan Air Force Base and he would leave every morning, maybe around six-thirty a.m. to go off to McClellan. This one particular morning, I heard the garage door close, and I knew he had just left for work, and the next thing I knew there were footsteps running down the hall with a flashlight coming toward my bedroom. My son had just gotten into bed with me, and we were snuggling when I thought, wait a second. I yelled out my husband's name, and I said, "What's the matter? What did you forget?" And then when I looked up, there was a flashlight in my eyes, and a man stood there with a ski mask on, a leather jacket, leather gloves, and he was holding a large butcher knife. The first thing he said was, when I started to say something he said, in clenched teeth, "Shut up, shut up, shut up, or I'll kill you."

He then proceeded to tie both my son and I up with shoe laces. He gagged us. He blindfolded us, and then he started tearing sheets or towels. I wasn't sure what they were, and I could hear him opening my dresser doors and closing them. But I'll never forget the tearing and the fear, thinking, what on earth is he going to be doing with those strips of cloth? I thought, well God, is he going to hang us. What is he going to do?

Fear was the main emotion that I felt this whole time. Then he would leave and go around the house and then come back again. And again, his behavior was very bizarre. He picked up my son, and he moved him, and this is when the fear really began because I had no idea where he was putting him, what he was going to do with him, and that was just so terrifying.

He then untied my ankles and raped me. I do not recall much about the rape because the whole time I was just in a panic about where my son was. My heart was beating so fast, I thought it was going to come through my chest, so I wasn't really paying much attention to the rape. And the next thing I knew, I felt my son next to me again, so he put him back, which was such a tremendous relief.

Then he told me, told us again not to move, or he'd come back and kill us. He went into the kitchen and I could hear him; I don't know if he was cooking or what, but he was rattling pots and pans in the kitchen, and then he would come back again, and it was just so scary, so frightening. I didn't know what his next move would be. I still didn't know what he was doing with the cloth or the towels that he had torn.

It was about, oh, I don't know, maybe about fifteen minutes after he had left the bedroom for the last time. We didn't hear anything, but I could see. I was able to get my blindfold down a little bit, and I can see that it was getting light outside. I decided to take a chance and escape. I woke my son who had fallen asleep, so I woke him up, and I said, "We've got to get out of here. We've got to get out of here."

So, we basically hobbled down the hall and tried to get out the front door, but he had taken a chair and propped it up under the door. We went back to the sliding door, going out to the back patio, and that was opened and hobbled around to the left, to the front fence, and screamed. A neighbor from across the street came over and took us into her home, called the police, called my husband, who were both there right away.

The last thing I wanted to do was talk to a male policeman. Then my angel Carol Daily showed up. She was the female detective that was assigned. She took me to the emergency room and sat with me there for I would bet over an hour. Then I had my rape exam, which was also not a very pleasant experience. I had a male doctor. After the rape exam, I had to have a morning after pill to be sure I wasn't pregnant. I had to have a shot of penicillin to be sure I didn't have a venereal disease.

One minute I was laughing just so thrilled to be alive, and then the next minute I was crying and sobbing, just thinking about what we had just been through. But again, I was just so thankful to the Lord that our lives were spared.

At this time, there was no news about a serial rapist in Sacramento; nobody knew that this had been going on. But it was right after my rape that they put two and two together and figured out that there was a rapist that was breaking into people's homes prior to coming back and raping them. It had been probably, I would say maybe two to three weeks prior to my attack, I was robbed. Someone had come in my son's bedroom window and taken all my rings out of my jewelry box. That was bad, but we didn't know that in a couple of weeks he was going to return and rape me.

But what he did, I guess when he was in the house the first time is he was able to look at photographs in the house, and he could see that I was in the military, maybe my husband was in the military. He got a lot of information about us, and where he saw me to begin with I have no idea. Nor do I have any idea why he moved my son. Did he move him to be a nice guy, or did he just move him, so we had more room on the bed when he raped me. Those are two questions that I hope to sit across the table and ask him at some point.

Jane went on to describe her attacker.

I do remember that he had on black high-top sneakers and again he was holding this large butcher knife. He had this brown or black leather jacket on and gloves. He had on the ski mask, of course. I don't remember the color of his eyes. I'd say he was maybe six-foot-tall with a moderate build, not heavy at all. I was 30 at the time, and I would say he was maybe a couple of years younger.

Jane was also able to estimate how long her attack went on and shared some of the things that really stood out to her.

Maybe forty-five minutes to an hour. One thing I want to tell you about him too, he spoke through clenched teeth. I'm sure he was a white male. He was a white male, but he spoke through clenched teeth, with no voice recognition. Again, I do not remember the color of his eyes. But I do remember the size of the knife. He took the knife a couple of times and scraped my chest. He didn't cut me with the knife, but he scraped me to the point that I did have some blood on my chest, and of course, I didn't know what he was going to do with that knife.

Jane's ordeal didn't end when this man left her home after the attack.

I had phone calls afterwards where he would hang up, which was again, very, very, very terrifying, because I just completely hated my home. When I returned from the hospital, I wanted to move as soon as I could because I just felt so violated. Then I felt so violated by the fact that he kept going in and out of my drawers and looking through my underwear drawer. But we couldn't move for another year, we had to wait for my husband to get orders.

As you can imagine, picking up the pieces for Jane after her attack was not an easy thing to do.

You couldn't talk to people about this. I only told one close friend, and, of course, my husband knew because back 41 years ago, you didn't talk about rape. That was something to be ashamed of. That was something that people didn't discuss. That was really very difficult. My saving grace was going to the Rape Crisis Center in Sacramento and meeting other women that had been raped as well.

Then I realized I wasn't going crazy because of my feelings. There were other women who shared the same results: that they were scared, they were eating more, they were biting their fingernails, just unusual behavior normally one wouldn't have. But when I met with these other women, I realized that everything that I was experiencing, they had experienced as well. That was certainly a saving grace for me.

Jane went on to talk about the aftermath of her attack for her personally and for the community.

When they finally realized there was a serial rapist, and I was number five, it seemed every day in the paper there was another rape, another rape, and this just went on and on and on 27, 29, 31 and every day. Sacramento completely shut down. All the stores were sold out of all their locks, people were buying guns, and the hardware store shelves were empty.

One thing that I'll never forget that was so frightening was at night when my husband and my son and I would sleep together in our king size bed in our bedroom. We didn't know if he was going to return. Every night

*it seemed that there was a helicopter flying overhead
with a spotlight in the area trying to find this guy.
That's one thing I don't like now is to hear a helicopter.
It always brings me back to lying in bed and listening
to the hovering sound of the helicopter.*

*Of course, too, whenever I see someone with black
high-top sneakers that always reminds me of the rapist.
Also, watching anything or watching anyone with a ski
mask on. I haven't skied because it's very scary to me
to see a ski mask. Anytime I'm watching a television
program, and someone's got a ski mask on, which they
do a lot of times, I have to shut off the television.*

Jane hasn't dwelled on what happened to her over forty years
ago, if anything, she pushed through it to become the person
she is today.

*I am very fortunate that I was number five because he
became much more violent after my attack with other
women, and then of course with men in the home as
well. Then of course the rapes led to the murders. Now
I call myself a thriver. I've gone from being a victim to
a survivor to thriver.*

*I read this book by Rick Warren. It was called The
Purpose Driven Life. I thought back about my attack,
and I thought I've got to do something positive with
this. That was when I started to do public speaking
about it, and I realized if I keep this a secret, then how
can I help anyone else that's experienced something
similar. I started doing public speaking. I wrote a book
called Frozen in Fear. I started doing some interviews.*

*My first one was Dark Minds with Matthew Phelps on
his program. I would speak to women's groups and talk
about the backpack that I was carrying for so long,
full of hate and revenge and anger. It was just getting
heavier and heavier. I had to forgive the rapist and let*

that go because he wasn't the one hurting. I was. There was such a freedom in not having any more secrets.

My message that I had really received from reading Rick Warren's book is to take this terrible experience and turn my pain into power and make my mess a message, reach out and do what I can to help other women. That's really what I've been doing and that's very fulfilling for me, and only through the grace of God have I been able to do that.

A couple of years ago, I met Debbie Domingo whose mother and her mother's boyfriend were brutally murdered. I met Michelle whose sister was brutally raped and murdered. I met Carol Daily, who was the detective that took me to the emergency room forty-one years ago. So, oh my gosh, what a reunion.

We're all like sisters now. We keep in touch. It's just amazing. They are so special, and you know, I'm not sorry I was raped because I look at all the good that's come out of that. I keep my pain, I guess, compartmentalized in some part of my brain, but when Debbie started talking about the death of her mother, then I really teared up. It was so emotional. But these women are just amazing, and I just feel honored to be a part of their life. My dream is for all of us to all be there when they bring him in.

My fear is that one of us is going to say, "I know him. I know him," and that is just such a scary thought. Years ago, after he raped me, if I had been able to get to him after the rape, I would have had him, you know, tied up on a pole. I would have had him gagged, not blindfolded, and then I would take a knife, and I would walk very slowly toward him and unzip his fly, even though he has a very small penis. I don't even know if I could find it. I would unzip his fly, and I would just cause him fear because that's what he caused me, fear.

I wouldn't do anything to harm him physically, just mentally, emotionally.

Now, today, I don't feel that way. I just want to sit across from him at a table and ask him my questions. Why did you move my son? You know, where did you see me? Why me? Why was I one of your fifty rape victims? So that's my dream: that he will be caught, and I will get a chance to sit with him and to question him.

Jane's case was different than the ones that occurred before. Her attack started around 6:30 a.m. and in the first four attacks, the assailant was gone before the sun even came up. Jane's attacker didn't leave her house until almost 8:30 AM.

Police didn't want to waste any time, so they quickly brought in some tracking dogs. The dogs immediately seemed to pick up the assailant's scent, tracking him around the back yard and up close to Jane's son's bedroom window. Jane mentioned her home had been broken into in the weeks before the murder. At the time, police thought it was probably kids since nothing valuable was taken. It was obvious at this point, that wasn't the case, and this bedroom window had been the entry point for that burglary.

From there, the dog raced through the backyard, and to a fence. The handlers lifted the dog over the fence and continued the search on the other side. The dog tracked the scent through a partially overgrown field, and into a part of the field that was being developed and cleared. This field came out to the edge of a road named Shadow Brook Way. Later questioning of neighbors revealed that a woman had seen a strange man in that area in her driveway on Shadow Brook Way just a few days before Jane's attack. When she made eye contact with the unknown man, he stared at her for several seconds and then walked to a dark green car parked nearby, got in, and drove off. She thought the car was possibly a Vega.

This woman described the unknown man as being about five feet, ten inches with dark hair, around 170 pounds, and possibly being in his thirties. Interestingly, neighbors told investigators that they had seen an unfamiliar dark car parked in the same spot as the Vega on the very morning of Jane's attack. Neighbors had noticed that there around 7 a.m., but when they left for work sometime after 8 a.m., it was gone. Police theorize that Jane's attacker had parked in this spot and walked through the field before climbing Jane's fence and entering her home.

Back in Jane's house, further investigation revealed that two black shoe laces had been tied together and used to bind Jane. They also found white shoelaces in the home that didn't belong to Jane.

After Jane received treatment, she was able to provide other details. She specifically mentioned, as you heard her say, that her attacker was very poorly endowed. He had been wearing dark clothes and a ski mask with eye holes only. Jane was also able to detail how the attacker held the knife in his left hand, and he only spoke through clenched teeth.

In late August or early September of 1976, the street Jane lived on, Wood Parkway, started to experience some unsettling incidents. Several neighbors had reported prowlers, burglaries and hang-up phone calls. While it was concerning, these incidents didn't seem to be of major importance until after Jane's attack, it was at this point that police knew they had a serious problem on their hands.

It seemed like the entire neighborhood was being targeted for abuse, whether that came in the form of phone calls, the prowling burglaries, or the rape. Jane mentioned just how happy she was when detective Carol Daly got involved in investigating her attack. This is something that we heard time and time again from several people who we reached out for the podcast, just how well they were treated by Carol, and how she helped them cope with what had happened to them. Here's Carol herself.

My name is Carol Daly. And at the time that this case started in 1976, I was a detective with Sacramento County Sheriff's Department in Sacramento, California. At the time that these cases started I was assigned to the homicide detail, and once they realized that they had three or four of the cases that were alike they called me in to start interviewing the victims of these cases. One of the reasons that they did is, when I came on the department in 1976, women weren't used in patrol. So, when we hired on we either went to detective or we worked in the courthouse, and I was assigned to detective.

For several years prior to that, I had been involved in investigations of sex crimes, basically child molestations, incest, all crimes against children. And then I had also worked rape cases. They pulled me out of homicide because of my background of working sex crimes to start interviewing the victims. And I think Jane Carson, she was number five, and she was one of the first victims that I interviewed when we realized that we had a series going. The task force was formed of crime scene investigators, patrol officers, detectives, anybody that was associated with the crime. They were on the taskforce, so every time a crime or a rape was committed that we attributed to the East Area Rapist, this taskforce came out. It was the same people responding to the scenes each time. We kind of knew what to look for and what to ask because we were more familiar with that case.

A rape investigation is a real sensitive issue, and I always explain to the victims when I'm talking to them, I'm going ask you very, very personal questions about things that the rapist may have done to you. I want you to tell me everything. I tell them the reason that we need to know absolutely all the details is that each thing that he did could be a separate felony. We're going to stack the felonies; we're going to stack the charges against the rapist whenever he's identified. That also helps when you explain to them why you're asking so many detailed questions, and why you're trying to extract from them everything that the rapist did.

These are very embarrassing things that the rapist did. You just have to kind of get them into your confidence. I do think they were able to open up maybe a little bit more with me. Even at that, there may have been some little intimate thing that they wouldn't share with anybody.

We asked Carol just how much involvement she wound up having with the victims in this case.

Oh, I talked to all of them that were in Sacramento County. We had a total of twenty-seven cases in the Sacramento County. We had four cases, three of the cases, in fact, in the Sacramento Police Department jurisdiction, which is just bordering our county. Then I traveled to Stockton when they had their first rape there and interviewed that victim. From the time that I came on we went back through the cases, and so I've had contact with every one of the victims that occurred in Sacramento County.

From talking with so many victims it was much easier for investigators to gather a lot of information about this predator's M.O., throughout the series.

Basically, his MO, was entering the house and it was either through an unlocked door or sometimes he had preplanned the raid, gone into the house before the people came home, and then waited for them to come home. He made his entry sometimes through unlocked doors, unlocked windows, or he confronted them outside, and on one of them he kicked in a front door.

But he was always dressed in a ski mask, always had gloves on, and his body was covered.

When he came in he would immediately shine a flashlight into the victim's eyes, have her or the couple turn over on their stomach, tie the male, and then he would tie the female up. He would bring shoestrings or ties with him, and he would tie them up. He would always talk through raspy clenched teeth when he entered and confronted them. It was do as I say or I'm going to kill you.

Then if the victim was alone in the home he would say, "I'm not going to kill you I just want your money. I'm not going to hurt you I just want your money." Of course, that ended up not being the case because they all ended up being victims of rape. It was the way that he entered the house, the way he was dressed, and the length of time he was there. I have never, in all the sex crimes and rape cases that I worked, been involved in a case where the rapist stayed in the house as long as he did.

Usually, rapists will come in and his goal is to rape and then get out and get away as fast as possible. Because he came in and he secured his victims, he had total control over them with the threats that he was making with a gun, with a knife pressed against the skin. He had total control over them. Even when they thought that perhaps he had left, and they would start to move around, he would come back and say, "Don't move. I'm still here. I'm going to kill you."

He would wander throughout the house and rummage through things. He would go into the kitchen; he would eat some of the food. In one case he went out on the patio and sat and consumed food and drank a beer. He knew that he had total control over the victims, and he wasn't worried about anybody coming in and finding him. It was the length of time that he spent.

And then when enough time had gone by and they again started to move and realized that perhaps he had left or maybe they heard a car leave, then they would try to get free. It was so much different than any of the other rape cases I had ever worked.

Shortly after I became involved in the investigation, we did a sheet for the victims to fill out. Where do you shop? Where do you go to church? Where do you go for your entertainment? Who are your friends? Where do you travel? What kind of car do you drive? Where have you lived? Where does your family live? Where did you go to school? We researched the background of every victim to find something common. We looked at, are they all blonde? Are they all tall? Are they all short? There was no common denominator. We didn't find anything.

I think in just about every case he at least rummaged through the refrigerator, rummaged through the kitchen. It was a cavalier attitude with him like you know this is my domain. I'm in charge. I personally don't think rape was his goal. I think his goal was to cast as much fear and terror in the woman and in all the victims that he could. I think the rapes were just secondary.

However, the rapes were brutal, and some of them were more brutal than others. I saw a pattern of accelerated aggression in his anger. As the cases went on, our biggest fear was that our next call was going to be to a homicide.

It was clear that Richard Shelby was on the same page as his partner Carol Daly following Jane's attack.

My name is Richard Shelby, Sacramento's Sheriff's Department. I became introduced to the East Area Rapist October 5, 1976. A home invasion, sexual assault report came out one morning about, I think eight o'clock is when I got to work. Myself, Carol Daly and John Irwin responded to it, and then we worked the case having no idea who this serial rapist was or even existed, and then went on from there.

I picked up on this early, his entire life focused on how to prowl, how to burglarize, how to sexually assault people. I'm not exactly sure what he had in mind, what he was doing, but that's all he ever done. Carol Daly and I thought he was going to kill. He was getting more and more deranged, his actions when he was assaulting his victims. We told several people that this guy is getting more violent. I personally felt that he really wanted to hurt somebody out there bad.

On that one victim, Jane Carson, she had about a one-inch wide abrasion on her shoulder where he held the knife. She said he just accidentally cut her, well bull, it was a serrated knife. You don't get abrasion with a serrated knife or any kind of knife. You have to wiggle it back and forth. I thought that's what he wanted to do was hurt her, and in several victims after that, it became obvious each and every one of them has some kind of a little cut.

It seemed police didn't want to start a panic in Sacramento County. At the time they tried to keep things quiet, thinking that they would quickly catch this guy, but that didn't happen. It was only a matter of time before the public got wind of what was going on, and you can imagine the terror as Carol Daly pointed out.

I have not experienced any fear in this community before or since the serial rapist and part of that is because when the rapes first occurred Sheriff Lowe wanted to keep it very quiet in the community. He didn't want the word to get out because he was sure that we were going to catch this guy. Then a couple of the high influential people through the media got wind of these rapes and went to him and said we must know about these, and so he promised them that every rape that we would have they would know about.

I think that was good because it alerted the community, but it also put more and more fear in the community because sometimes it was every day or every other day that a rape was coming out, and it always made front page headlines. There was a tremendous amount of fear in the community. We saw gun shops selling out and hardware stores were out of stock on a lot of their locks. People were doing everything they could to protect themselves.

There was so much fear in the community that PG&E workers and SMUD workers would not even go into people's backyards because people were confronting them with guns. Burglary rates went way down, because burglars knew that you know they would face a gun if they went into a home. In fact, we did have one case where a burglar was shot and killed, and the guy was exonerated. The citizen was exonerated because a judge said there was so much fear in the community that at that time anybody would have taken the same steps.

And so, yes, there was a tremendous amount of fear. There were a lot of rumors in the community as to what the rapist was doing and what he wasn't doing. When we got wind of the rumors that were going around, and, one of them was that he was cutting the nipples off the breast of the victims, we said we must do something to make sure, just to allay some of the fears in the community.

So, we set up group community meetings, where we talked about the rapist's M.O., how he would get into the houses, and we did a lot of safety education classes teaching groups, talking to the schools trying to educate the community as much as we could. Once we realized that we had a series of rapes going, we organized the response team, and we started using patrol officers in plainclothes who rode bicycles in and around the Rancho Cordova area because that's where the rapes started and along the American River Drive. Of course, they started in Cordova and then he moved east.

We had officers on bicycles in plainclothes riding around. There were sometimes when we know that the rapist was spotted, but he was so quick, he was so agile, he was gone before anybody could even locate him. At the time that we were doing the investigation, the daughter of the assistant director of Lawrence Livermore Laboratory, they were probably the world's best computer system at that time, and his daughter was attending Cal Tech University during the rapes. She lived in an area where some of the rapes took place, and so he consequently offered the use of all their computers which were the largest in the free world at the time.

The parameters were established; we set up parameters for the age and the description of the suspect. The DMV was contacted for assistance. Computer tapes of all males with California driver's licenses were taken in to the computers, and a list of all males matching the description were established. Also, a list of males was turned over to the task force which were prioritized by description and everything. We had a full-time district attorney that was assigned to work with us. We had members of the Department of Justice who were doing intelligence and investigations.

The Sacramento crime lab at that time didn't have a full-time serologist, so all that blood, saliva, semen, and sperm that we collected on the rape cases were sent to the Department of Justice. As a result, the Sacramento County crime lab hired a serologist who worked exclusively with the task force in helping us with the evidence. And in the beginning, we knew that we had a type A blood with a PGM factor of one dash one and a nonsecretor.

So, we were able to eliminate 98 out of 100 people, men that we stopped just by doing the blood testing. At that time over 1,000 suspects freely gave their blood type, and we checked their PGM factor to see if they were a secretor or not. We were eliminating a lot of our suspects at that time that way. Because everybody said, "Oh he must be a law enforcement officer, he must be military because he was so agile and the different things he was doing, and he seemed to know what was going on."

We had officers that willingly came forward who matched the description and would give their blood type and everything. One of the victims saw a car drive by when she was washing her car. And we took that information description of that car, and we sent it to Livermore Laboratories, and there were more than 400,009 Pintos registered in the state of California. We narrowed it down, and there were 500 vehicles that were checked out in Sacramento County.

To what lengths did we go on this investigation to try and identify this guy? There was no end to what we tried to do. We checked out all the UPS workers. We went to the start of shift and employees willingly chewed on the gauze and willingly gave up their blood type. We had 100 percent cooperation. We had an ongoing list of suspects that couldn't be eliminated by blood. So, at the time of a rape, we had officers that went immediately to their homes to try to figure out where they were, and we eliminated a lot of them that way.

There were ten police agencies at the time that we were working with that got involved in this investigation, so there was confusion with cross-jurisdiction. We took

aerial photos by the CHP helicopter of all the victims'
residences, so that we could track his path of escape.
We eliminated 6,000 suspects that were checked out.
There are still a lot of suspects being eliminated. At the
time the size of his penis was a real issue. We checked
with a medical specialist to see about men who were
treated for abnormally small penises, but that didn't
go anywhere.

We used dogs to try to track him. It seems like he
always went to a car. At the time that we were doing
these investigations a new technique came out where
we could fingerprint a victim's body. You kind of blow
through a pipe with iodine fuming, and you put it on
the victim's body, and it'll bring up fingerprints. Well,
it really must be done quite quickly. I would get a call
at the house. I'd probably drive 80 - 90 miles an hour
to get to a crime scene, so I could run in and let the
victim know what we were doing.

I only did it twice. It was embarrassing for me,
and it was embarrassing for the victim. She was
standing there undressed, and we were trying to take
fingerprints, and in one of the situations, we both
ended up giggling because it was just ridiculous. We
didn't do it anymore after that, and now they don't use
that technique anymore because it could cause cancer.

We tried everything that we could. We worked with
more than fifty psychics, so we had people calling
us saying that they knew that they could help us. We
served more than twenty search warrants during that
time, but there were many, many people who gave
us consent to search, and the suspects were stopped
on the street. And if they had a ski mask, they did a
consent to search, we would check for fibers in the ski
mask, and we took hair samples. I don't think there
was anything at the time that we did not do.

One gets a full understanding of the length that investigators went to try to get an upper hand on this rapist, from using psychics to checking with doctors to try to identify patients with penis disorders, to attempting to pull fingerprints from the victims themselves. And this is way before DNA, way before many of the techniques that investigators have at their disposal today, but this is what investigators had at their disposal back then.

One of the things that law enforcement tried to do was hold town hall meetings to let the public know what was going on and how to be vigilant in protecting themselves. It was at one of these town hall meetings that a male in the crowd stood up in disbelief.

At one of the public meetings, we were talking about the rapist coming in, and there was a man and a woman in the house, or there were two women, or there's more than one person, and he was able to secure them all and get them tied up and commit the rape and be in the house for such a long time. A gentleman in the audience stood up, and he said there is no way that that could happen, that some man in the house would be able to overpower him or do anything. He was calling us liars.

It was several weeks later that he and his wife were victims of the East Area Rapist and let me tell you, they became our biggest supporters. They understood, and they knew what we were talking about, and it was really helpful. I've been in contact with them, and they're still married. They relocated to another home, and they said they didn't want to go public about anything, but they were able to put it behind them. It did not define who they were. They were very strong people, and I just admire them so much. It was interesting because we know the rapist was at that community meeting. We know that he probably followed them home.

What Carol Daily had to say was nothing short of shocking. To think that the predator that had been committing these attacks would be at this town hall meeting and target the very man that had stood up in disbelief. Carol Daily also told us about how the case has weighed on her over the years and just how upsetting it was that they weren't able to catch this predator.

> There was so much notoriety in the community, and even as an investigator, you would be in the community, and, of course, people knew us because we were on television. We were at the public meetings, and the question was, "How haven't you caught this guy yet?" Even then towards the end, coming into the Sheriff's Department, I'd come to work, and patrol officers would say, "How haven't you caught that guy yet?" It was frustrating to everyone, and, of course, the fingers were pointed at us, "What are you doing? What are you not doing?"

> Let me tell you we did everything possible in trying to investigate this case, and I have three pages of things that we did, that we had never done to this extent in any investigation. When he left our jurisdiction and went into another jurisdiction, there was not good communication between the agencies because they said, "You couldn't catch him. We're going to catch him," and of course now history shows that no matter who was involved in this investigation, no matter how much work has been done over the years, the case still has not been solved.

> I formed a victims' support group. We had a psychologist come in and talk to the ladies that came forward. I tried to set up a support group for the men, none of them would come. They didn't want anything. It was very difficult for the men, and, of course, out of all these rapes, probably 97 percent to 98 percent of the relationships ended. After I left the case, I didn't stay on top of it. I wasn't a part of it, all I did was answer

questions. Then when we heard that the DNA matched up and our rape cases up here were meshed up with homicides down south, it was a very sickening feeling because I knew that's what was going to happen here, that somebody was going to be killed.

Just the tragedy of it all, and knowing so much hard work, so much effort went into these investigations, still, we didn't solve the case. You know it was interesting as all the publicity came about again, going back out to a couple of the areas where the rapes had occurred, and it was surprising how close-- because you forget. After forty years I can drive to a neighborhood, and I remember a rape here or a murder there.

I went back to one of the rape victims' homes, and I looked at that home, and it was a nice neighborhood. But her house, it was a house tied to that rape. It was scary. I'm sitting there, looking at the house, and I had a media crew with us, and the next-door neighbor came out. He was a probation officer, he's retired, was a probation officer working probation at the time of the rapes, and he said, "Oh yes, I remember the East Area Rapist, I remember the fear in my community."

And he said, "We were watching it on television," and he said, "My wife said, that's really a nice neighborhood. We should try to live in that neighborhood," because it was a lovely neighborhood, and I think they were in an apartment at the time. When they bought, they ended up buying the house next to where one of the rapes occurred in that neighborhood, and he said, "Look, the screen to the bedroom that was torn where the rapist got in is still on. They had never replaced that screen."

For over forty years, Carol Daily has been a part of this community, and this case, and I personally think, hearing from her allows us to have a real understanding of just what happened with this case, over forty years both inside the investigation and within the community itself.

Going back to the attack on Jane Carson Sandler, she didn't seem to have any enemies. She was a respected nurse in the military. There was seemingly no reason why anyone would have targeted her. Jane did have one encounter prior to her attack that made her feel uneasy. In early October, shortly before her attack, Jane had been to a club on Travis Air Force Base to meet up with some friends. She went to the restroom and down the dark hallway to the restroom, a man approached her. She felt uneasy.

He began talking to her and mentioned that he hadn't seen her there before, and he asked her for her name. Jane didn't want to make eye contact with him, and she hurried by him saying that she was with friends and that her husband was a Captain. As she went by, she could see that the man was short and thin. She heard him say, "Sorry, I didn't mean anything." There was no way to know if this brief encounter was related to Jane's attack, but one specific thing that Jane's attacker had said to her during the attack on her was, "Do it like you do with the Captain." The timing and the fact that Jane specifically told the stranger that her husband was a Captain, seemed interesting.

As we mentioned before, Jane Carson Sandler was the fifth in what would become a long line of victims. Jane's attack happened on October 5, 1976, and phone calls came to her after she was raped. The phone calls alone were not going to satisfy this guy. He needed to terrorize in person, and it turns out he didn't wait long before attacking a sixth victim.

Back in Rancho Cordova, the word was slowly getting around that there had been some sexual assaults in the normally quiet part of town, and, while very concerning, it had not reached a full panic mode yet. On October 4, the day before Jane was attacked, a resident on the 2600 block of El Segundo Drive witnessed a prowler in their backyard, but at the time the incident didn't seem overly important, and the prowler vanished into the night. A few days after this prowler was seen, only a couple houses away, a 19-year-old woman had the house to herself.

It's not known if the young woman knew of the prowler or of the other attacks in the area, but her home had previously been broken into three years earlier on March 7, 1973. A burglar had pried open the home's sliding glass door. Nothing of substantial value had been taken. In fact, it didn't seem like the break-in had even been worth the burglar's time. All he had gotten were some coins and a single earring from a set that the young girl had owned when she was 16.

On Saturday, October 9, 1976, this 19-year-old girl went to bed just after midnight. At about 4:30 a.m. she heard someone whispering her name. She thought she was dreaming but she wasn't. Before she was fully awake a gloved hand was on her mouth. She then felt something sharp pressed against her neck, and she heard a low hissing voice say, "Don't scream or I'll kill you." A man then forced her over onto her stomach at which point he tied her hands tightly behind her back with shoelaces. He then blindfolded and gagged her using cloth material and towels.

At this point all the 19-year-old had seen was a flash of a man in a ski mask before she was quickly turned on to her stomach. He asked her for money and told her that he needed a fix, an indication that he possibly was a drug user. The man was taking quick rapid breaths like he was overly excited. He then dragged the young woman from the bed and marched her blindly out of her room.

Terrified, she had no way of resisting, and she helplessly walked with him. It was then that she realized that the intruder had walked her out of the house and onto the patio. He then ordered her to lie down. He leaned over her, and she could feel his breath on her face. He told her, "I've been dreaming of you," and added, "I've always wanted to fuck you."

At this point, her assailant tied her feet together. She heard him walk into the house and then returned a moment later.

Then he walked out into her yard. She wasn't sure what he was doing or what he planned to do. After going into the home and coming back out again, he came over to her and asked her for money. He told her, "You better have money." As he stood by her very closely, he stopped talking. It was then that despite being blindfolded she could tell he was masturbating.

The man then whispered to the helpless woman, "You better let me do this." He turned her onto her stomach and placed his penis into her hands, they were still tied behind her back. After a moment, he untied her feet and then he sexually assaulted her. This would begin a cycle, where he would intermittently return to the inside of the home before returning and raping her multiple times.

The terrified and helpless victim laid there on the patio on top of a carpet. She could hear her attacker rustling bags. Then he came over and drug her and the carpet she was lying on to a spot on the patio where there was a post, and he tied her to it. She felt his hands grab hers, and he started pulling out the rings that she was wearing. He then told her that he was leaving and not to scream.

He warned her that he lived right down the street, and he would know if she screamed. Then there was silence. After she felt her assailant had left, she started wiggling to try to free herself. She was able to get her blindfold and gag off and remove herself from the patio post. Her hands remained tied tightly behind her back, and she couldn't free them, so she decided to make her way back into the house.

Once back in the house she made it to the kitchen phone but quickly realized that the phone line had been cut. She tried a second phone in the bedroom and found that it too had been cut. At this point, she was feeling defeated, to the point where she collapsed and decided to wait for someone to find her. Luckily about two hours later a friend came to her house and discovered her still partially bound.

The friend got the victim free and then brought the 19-year-old back to their house to call the police. While they waited for the police to get there, the victim couldn't help but want to clean herself up, and she took a shower. Who knows what physical evidence she may have washed away, but her reaction seems totally understandable.

Police arrived at the victim's home, a single-story house, a little after 9:00 a.m. They quickly determined that the point of entry was the dining room window. The screen covering it was found discarded in a bush. They found a candy dish on the ground, but it was discovered that it belonged to the victim's family, and the attacker had moved it as he made his way in through the window. They also found torn strips of towels and signs of ransacking in the home.

The police talked to the victim and tried to get some more information out of her, but she couldn't add much. She had been awakened so suddenly and didn't have much time to gather details. She was able to tell them the man who had raped her was wearing a ski mask. She felt he was white and sounded like he might be in his mid-twenties. He stood about five-feet, ten-inches. In the end, it seemed as if the assailant had gotten away with very little, not much more than a metal box with some cash in it and some jewelry.

But there was one very interesting clue found inside the home. The assailant had taken clothesline from the victim's yard and had used it to tie several bedroom door knobs together, running it across the hallway back and forth from door knob to door knob. This may have been done, so if others were home and tried to exit their bedroom, they wouldn't be able to. But there was no one else home that weekend. This may have been a clue that the attacker had not been watching her home closely leading up to the attack.

While police were finishing up at the crime scene, something odd happened. A young male neighbor of the victim walked up to investigators. He made it a point to tell the police on the scene that from his elevated bedroom window, he could clearly see down into the victim's bedroom window. He asked if the victim was all right. Police immediately were suspicious of the young man and questioned him more.

As they questioned this young man, they noticed that he seemed more interested in trying to peek into the victim's home to see what was going on than he was in talking with them. The man explained that his home had been recently burglarized, and it was at this point that he produced a small bag of cheap jewelry and rings and stated that his parents were out of town, and he had found it in his mother's room but didn't think it belonged to her.

The police listened to what the man had to say, but they were interested in him as a suspect. He was about the right age as the victim described and had the same physical stature. The odd mention of being able to see into the victim's room just seemed weird to police. They decided that this young man had to be looked at further.

It didn't take them long to find out that this young neighbor owned a dark green Vega. And a dark green Vega had been spotted near the scene of Jane's home in attack number five. This man was put under surveillance and watched very closely. But as later attacks would happen, this man would still be under surveillance, and police would have a record of him being at home at the time the attacks occurred.

But to play it safe, the police also had a tracking dog approach the young man, but the dog didn't hit on this young man. Even through all of that, police were still very interested in this guy. It wouldn't be until years later that they would use DNA to actually rule him out, but one can definitely understand why they were interested in this man to begin with.

The 19-year-old victim was left to wonder why she had been attacked. Had her rape been committed by the same burglar who had broken into her family's home three years earlier? Was he a neighbor or a friend? Had he been a schoolmate at Cordova High School where she had graduated from just a couple of years before? After all, the rapist had awakened her by calling her name. One interesting possibility was that she had been going to dances frequently at nearby Mather Air Force Base. To get on base, she needed to provide her name and address. Perhaps somebody from the base had tracked her. The possibilities were endless, and maybe she was just in the wrong place at the wrong time.

We have to recap, up to this point we have six attacks on women with no men present in the home. The homes were primarily single-story homes. For the most part, the victims were all awoken in bed or were awake in bed when attacked. That's the time when one is most vulnerable. In most of the attacks, a knife was used, but in the first attack, he also had a small gun. In the third attack, he used a baton, possibly a military training baton.

Another thing we see here is that in attacks one, two, and six, the victims have been left alone while their parents had gone away. This is going to be something seen again and again in these cases, which is this guy striking repeatedly when victims are left alone for a stretch of time. Is he getting lucky in catching them alone, or does he know somehow or have advance knowledge that the victims will be alone?

We also have to consider a possible military pattern with these early victims. The first victim was the daughter of an airman. Jane, victim number five, was in the military, and the sixth victim had frequently gone to dances on the base.

At this point, the Sacramento Sheriff's Department knew they had a problem and now the problem was expanding. He's crisscrossing the county and had struck three different towns at this point. For investigators, they didn't know where he might strike next.

It turned out the next attack, number seven, would happen back in the town of Carmichael, a little over five miles from the previous Carmichael attack. On October 18, 1976, sometime around 2:00 - 2:30 a.m., a young boy on the 4900 block of

Kipling Drive awoke to the sound of his dog barking. The 10-year-old boy made his way to the sliding glass door opened it and let his dog out. As he let the dog out, he flipped on the outside light. He was still groggy, but it's at this point that he saw something terrible when he looked out into his backyard.

Standing in front of him was a masked man. The boy's dog raced out the door heading right towards a dark figure. The masked man retreated and raced towards the fence, and he climbed to the top of it. The man sat on top of the fence for a second looking at the small dog barking below and the horrified 10-year-old just inside the sliding glass door. At this point, the man decided that neither the dog nor the boy was going to stop him from carrying out what he had planned, and he jumped back down into the yard.

The dark figure started casually walking back towards the 10-year-old boy, and this kid did not waste any time. He slammed the sliding glass door shut and locked it before racing into his mom's bedroom screaming. The boy was hysterical by the time he got to his mom's room, and he did everything he could to wake her up. When he finally did, she thought that he just had a bad dream.

This actually sounds like the scene from a horror movie, like it came straight out of Halloween, but this really happened. They say that truth is scarier than fiction, and this is proof of that. In a horror movie what one thinks would happen next, happened here in real life. She picked up the phone and started to dial the operator when suddenly they heard a loud thump in the kitchen. This guy had just gotten inside through the kitchen window.

The mom had dialed the operator, but it just rang and rang. She had just hung up the phone and started to call her friend when she heard footsteps coming down the hallway, and when she looked up, the door busted open. Standing there in front of her was the masked man, and he was nude from the waist down. This situation was about to go from bad to worse very quickly.

The intruder moved into the room quickly holding a short thick bladed knife. He quickly raised the knife to the 32-year-old mother's throat, and in a hissing growl through clenched teeth told her, "Shut up." He then warned her that if she didn't do exactly as he told her to, she would die. He added that her son would die too, and they would be butchered to pieces

While this was going on the family dog was barking, and this made the masked intruder a little bit nervous. He told the victim he was going to kill her if she didn't shut the dog up. He forced the woman to move the dog into another room, and at this point, he asked her who was in the house. She told him that it was just her, her 10-year-old son, and a 4-year-old daughter who was asleep in another room.

She also added that her husband was out of town. At this point, the masked man seemed to relax a little bit. But even so, he walked over and yanked the phone cord out of the wall. He then walked out of the room and returned a few seconds later with a towel. At that point, he ripped the towel into strips and during the tearing of the towel the woman sensed that the intruder was becoming angry again.

As soon as he was done tearing the towel, he yanked the woman up by her arms and spun her around so that her back was to him. He tied her arms behind her back tightly at the hands using a string that he had torn out of her window blinds. At this point, he tied the woman's 10-year-old son to the headboard of her bed using towel strips and a necktie. Somehow, whether purposely or accidentally, the man caused a deep cut on the boy's foot.

Once feeling the boy was secured the man scooped the bound mother up and started to drag her out of the room. At this point, the young boy helplessly tied to the bed called out to his mother and told her he was afraid of dying. The masked intruder responded by throwing a blanket over the young boy's head and told him, "If you move, I'll kill you." One can't even imagine what this poor 10-year-old boy was going through at this point having this happen and then watching his mother being taken away.

It's clear that this man has no conscience whatsoever. To do something like this to a young child and to terrorize his mother in front of him tells us about the kind of man that's underneath that mask. Once he threw that blanket over the boy's head, he had something terrible in mind for the mother.

He once again started to remove the woman from the bedroom, and as he walked her down the hallway towards the family room, he warned her that if she tried to make a move, it would take seconds off of her son's life. The man warned her that if she cooperated, no one would be hurt, and he would be gone shortly. This man was nude from the waist down at this point, so she probably didn't believe what he was telling her. She would later recount for police that as he whispered through the mask, she thought he may have been stuttering slightly.

Once they got to the family room, he shoved her down on the couch and asked her where her money was. She responded by telling him that she had cash in her purse inside an envelope that was intended to be a donation for the Heart Association. She told him that she didn't have any other money. He then tied her feet together using strips of a towel and left her there on the couch before walking off into another room.

Once the man walked off, she could hear him going through drawers and cabinets, but it wasn't long before he walked back in and leaned down close enough to kiss her. He whispered, "You're beautiful." At this point, the 32-year-old woman sensed that things were about to get worse, and she blurted out the words, "Please don't hurt me, I'm pregnant."

But her plea got no response because he then blindfolded her with a strip of towel and stuffed a piece of cloth into her mouth as a gag. Later she would tell police that the rag had some unknown sweet taste on it, but she wasn't sure what it was. At that point, he lifted the woman off the couch and brought her into the bedroom throwing her on the bed next to her son.

She had to feel some relief being reunited with her son. But unfortunately, that relief was very short lived.

After throwing the mother on the bed, the man started to rifle through the dresser drawers. When he was done, he again grabbed the woman and forced her into the family room. This time instead of putting her on the couch, he took her down roughly onto the floor. The man leaned into the helpless mother and slowly unbuttoned her shirt. The man pushed the woman back on the floor and then removed the underwear. While he's doing this, he was telling her that she had a beautiful body, and he asked her if she had done a lot of sunbathing. This is pretty disgusting. Here, this man is undressing her, and she has to know what he's about to do, but he's making small talk and trying to compliment her.

She's tied up, blindfolded, there's not much she can do to stop him at this point. She then felt the man's mouth on her. He had removed his mask, but she would never get a look at the man underneath the mask. At this point, the woman was sexually assaulted, and after he finished he got up and walked out into the kitchen. When he returned, he placed the blade of his knife against the victim's face, and he angrily told her that she had lied about the money she had as he found more cash in a desk.

At this point, he sounded as if he was stuttering heavily. He pulled a knife away from her face but placed it on her body, running the very sharp tip of it up and down over her hips, stomach, and shoulders, finally winding up at her throat. He then warned her that if she didn't do exactly as he said, he would kill her and her two children. At this point, he rolled her onto her stomach, and he placed his lubricated penis in her hands, which were still tied behind her back. He told her to play with it. This was becoming a very clear part of this man's M.O.

After this happened the man became interested in the rings she was wearing. He started pulling on them, but they wouldn't budge, her hands and fingers had become so swollen from them being tied so tightly that he couldn't get them off. At this point, he told her, "I'll cut your fucking fingers off." She was now able to talk since the gag had been removed during a sexual assault, and she screamed out begging for him to use soapy water to get the rings off.

Evidently, she had no doubts this maniac really would cut her fingers off to get the rings. The man actually took her advice and ran over the sink to get soap and water. He came back and soaked up her fingers, but they still wouldn't come off due to the swelling in her hands. He finally decided to remove the bindings from her hands in order for the swelling to go down. After a bit of struggling the rings came off, but once he got them off, he once again tied her hands.

After she was secured again, the masked rapist once again sexually assaulted her. This woman would later recount for investigators that she was so desperate to get out of this situation that she blurted out something to the man that caught him by surprise. She told him that he was a good lover, and when she did this the man stopped the sexual assault on the spot. He responded by saying, "Nobody ever told me that before, most people laugh at me." Trying to keep the conversation going and put a stop to this assault, she carried on the conversation asking him if he liked to be complimented.

He replied, "Yes, but most people make fun of me, especially since something happened to my face." This went from the middle of a sexual assault to a conversation, and it really seemed to confuse the attacker and caught him off guard. He then asked her where her clock was, and she told him it was in the kitchen. At this point, the man walked away, and the woman could hear him rummaging through the refrigerator, and then she could hear him eating. Now so far in these first seven attacks, we've seen that this guy has some very odd traits in his M.O. Taking a break to eat at some point inside these victims' homes is one part of that M.O.

At this point, the house fell silent. The bound women felt as if the attacker had left and that maybe what she told him had caused him to lose interest in raping her, but she was wrong.

Without warning the man was back and was on top of her. Once again, she was sexually assaulted. Finally, after this round, he tied her legs to a table and walked down the hallway. She heard him talking with her son who was still tied to the bed, and she once again heard him tell the boy that if he moved his mother would be killed.

After talking to the 10-year-old boy, he walked back out and asked the mom when her husband would be home, and he warned her that if her answer didn't match her son's he would kill everyone in the house. She told the man that her husband would be back on Friday.

Once she answered, he raped her again. She was raped repeatedly. She was about to pass out from the assault in the shock. She told the man she was cold, and he threw a blanket on her. She lost consciousness for what only seemed like a moment. Suddenly she came to the house was eerily quiet. The next thing she knew, she could hear a car start up outside. It sounded like it was a large American car, and although she wasn't sure, to her it sounded like it may have been parked near a large open field in the back of her house.

The man had finally left. The attack was over, but it had lasted over two hours. After a while, the victim was able to free herself and then her son. Amazingly her 4-year-old daughter had slept peacefully through the entire attack.

The police were summoned, and they arrived at the house. They immediately questioned the dazed and horrified woman, and she was able to give them some pretty good details despite what she had just gone through. She was badly shaken, but she told police her attacker was about five feet, eight inches to five feet, ten inches and around 160 pounds. She said he had dark hair and blue eyes, and one other trait that immediately caught police attention, was that this man had an extremely small penis.

This attack reeked of the attacker who had been striking the east area of Sacramento County in the six previous attacks. In addition to the unusually small penis, there were a lot more similarities in M.O. The attacker had a mask, and he talked through clenched teeth. One thing the victim reported that was different was that he seemed to have a stutter, but other things continued to line up. The victim had a one-story home and like Jane's yard in attack number five, it backed up to a large field.

Once investigators looked around outside, they found empty beer cans at the crime scene that did not belong to the victim. One thing worth noting was that the victim had recently sold her house but had not yet moved out. A realty sign was noted in the report as being on her lawn. This is very important because houses being for sale where attacks occur is another theme that is seen again and again.

Next, police questioned neighbors. One neighbor told investigators they had heard dogs barking at about 2:30 a.m. Another resident told the police that they had seen headlights near the open field in back of the victim's yard, at about 9:00 p.m. the night before, about five hours before the attack. Still another witness recounted seeing a Lincoln Continental with a dent on one side. They described the driver as being a white male in his mid to upper twenties to early thirties.

Another area resident reported that somebody had opened the fence in his yard that led to the field. It seemed that a lot of activity was going on leading up to the attack on the mother and her 10-year-old son. Unfortunately, almost everybody in the area with the exception of the victim herself was aware of it.

Police determined after talking to neighbors and residents that the assailant had likely parked in the open field, walked about 100 yards across the field to the victim's backyard and then scaled her seven-foot tall fence. He likely left the same way exiting through her garage. Police were able to cast part of a tire track in the field, but all it told them was that the tire likely belonged to a large American-made car.

Police did come away with a couple of very promising clues in this attack, though. One of the neighbors had made note of the license plate on the Lincoln parked in the field. They thought it was TOR 505. There's been some confusion over the years as to the background of that plate number, but the common belief is that the plate belonged on a car that was owned by a man who died in February of 1976. There's been no clear answer as to how it came to be on the car that witnesses saw.

The other major clue found while processing this crime scene was a set of fingerprints found on a closet door inside the home. These prints have never been identified. It's possible that they do belong to this rapist because he did move around the home during the attack without gloves on. A few days later when the victim was cleaning her house in the aftermath of the attack, she found a bent spoon under her couch cushion. It wasn't hers. It was bent in the way that heroin user may bend a spoon, but tests revealed no signs of any drug residue on it.

In the early 1990s, well over a decade after this woman was attacked and after she had moved and changed her phone number several times, she received the phone call that she was sure was from the man who had raped her in 1976. The caller whispered into the phone, "Do you know who this is?" She could hear what sounded like a woman and children talking in the background, but she couldn't tell if the voices were coming from a television program or not.

Including this latest attack, the East Area Rapist as he was finally being called had attacked seven times. He had crisscrossed the eastern part of Sacramento County and was striking at will in multiple towns. On the same day of this attack, October 18, 1976, the following article ran in the *Sacramento Bee*.

> *Jill Bradshaw is angry. She is afraid. She's frightened because three women who live near her have been raped. Jill Bradshaw is not her real name, but like other women in the area, she's afraid to identify herself. Her once serene Rancho Cordova neighborhood is in the clutches of fear caused by a faceless man who*

wears hooded masks and rapes, despoils, degrades and sometimes robs. Law enforcement officers refer to him as the East Area Rapist. Since last year, the white man described as being between 5'8" and 6" tall, 25 to 35 years of age, clean with dark neatly-cut hair and a medium build has raped eight and attempted to rape two East Area women.

Last month alone, he raped four women and attempted to rape two others. Two of his victims were in Del Dale and two others in Carmichael. All the rapes have occurred between 11:00 p.m. and 6:45 a.m. There have been no men in the homes of the victims, although sometimes children were present. The rapist has entered the homes through unlocked windows in all the cases except one. This man is not the only rapist in Sacramento, but according to Sacramento County Sheriff's Department, he is a repeater with a high tendency toward violence.

As a result, the residents of the Sacramento communities have taken steps to protect themselves against the rapist. Some husbands have canceled overnight trips. One man is installing iron bars on his windows and doors, other men are instructing wives or girlfriends in the use of handguns, and still, others have installed burglar alarms and floodlights around their homes. Fear has tightened its grip on the communities of Del Dale, Carmichael, and Rancho Cordova. Rumors are rampant. Publicity about the rapes was minimized because the Sheriff's Department feared widespread panic would result, and because they hope to entrap the rapist.

In our interview with Carol Daly, she relayed the following information to us.

The reason we started calling him the East Area Rapist is, we had a Bee reporter named Holloway, and he came in like you see on TV shows, roamed the halls of the detective division and just was a great friend to law enforcement, and knew that we would share information, and if we couldn't share it, he would keep it confidential. He was a very trusted person. He's walking by, hears a group of detectives talking about some of the different addresses and looking at where the rapes occurred, and he said, "Oh, they're all in the East Area," and so he was dubbed The East Area Rapist.

SEASON TWO, EPISODE THREE

You would think that the attack on this mother and her 10-year-old son would have satisfied whatever kind of sick twisted urge was driving this guy, but unfortunately, it didn't. He had other ideas, and later that same day, October 18, 1976, he would seek out another victim.

Later on, that same day of October 18, 1976, he attempted another attack this time back in the town of Rancho Cordova. This second attack would come later on at night after 11:00 p.m. on the 10200 Block of Los Palos Drive in Rancho Cordova. This is very close to the previous Rancho Cordova attacks. Just after 11:00 p.m., a 19-year-old woman pulled her car into her driveway after coming home from her job at the Sacramento Army Depot. She put the car in park and then turned to look in the back seat at her dog who had gone for a ride with her. She opened the door and without any warning she felt hands on her trying to rip her from the driver seat. Terrified, she turned to see a man with what looked like a large gray sock on his face with only eye holes in it.

As the masked man tried pulling her out, this young woman instinctively went into fight mode, and she began to struggle with this guy, but he pulled out a knife and put it against her throat, close enough that it cut her. The assailant then hissed through clench teeth, "Stop fighting, I only want your car." At this point, the 19-year-old woman was at a severe disadvantage and stopped struggling. It was then that he warned her not to make a move or he would kill her. She then stayed perfectly still. He ordered the young woman out of the car. The attacker walked the woman to the side of her house where there wasn't much light and pulled her down on the ground. He then tied her hands tightly behind her back with clothesline from her yard. He then asked her if she had any money. At this point, she started to struggle, and he told her that he would cut her up if she didn't calm down. She replied to him by telling him that she only had $1.

She told him that the dollar was in her wallet, but he quickly told her to shut up. Like he didn't want to hear anything about the money. The man started to rummage through her purse which had fallen on the ground. He dragged the helpless girl over towards her car, and it was then that she could see her dog watching this whole situation unfold from the back seat. The man started to enter the car, and she cried out, "Please don't hurt my dog." This woman was tied up. She was being attacked, but she was also very concerned about her dog. He didn't hurt the dog, instead he riffled through the contents inside her car. After he didn't find anything in the car, he hoisted the helpless 19-year-old off the ground and forced her to walk out of her yard and past the neighbor's yard. He walked her to the street corner. At the corner, there was a yard with an open fence, and the house there appeared to be empty with no lights on.

Once they were in the yard and out of sight from the street, he threw her on the ground where she noticed several strips of cut up towels had been placed. She's still tied with her hands behind her back at this point, but then he decided that he wanted to tie her ankles as well. He set down the knife he was holding, and he pulled out a strip of white cord. He used one of the towel strips to act as a blindfold, and he also stuffed a piece of it into her mouth to act as a gag. She started to struggle, and her assailant told her to shut up and poked her rib area with the knife.

At this point something weird happened. He stood up over the bound victim and shook her car keys over her head. He told her he was going to leave for five minutes, but if she moved, he would catch her and cut her guts out. He quietly walked off and then a moment or two later, she heard her car start up. The assailant backed the car out of the driveway and drove off.

Of course, she didn't waste any time here. She quickly worked off her bindings, removed the blindfold and gag, and raced off to go get help. We have a masked man who was talking through clench teeth. He had strips of towel. Some of the threats that he made are very similar to the threats in some of the earlier attacks, but the strange thing here is, he let this woman go without any type of sexual contact. He clearly had her bound and controlled and could have pulled her inside to a home to assault her or could have assaulted her on the ground in that yard, but for some unknown reason he didn't.

A few hours later police located her car on El Segundo Drive, just over a quarter mile away. El Segundo Drive was where the sixth victim had been attacked just over a week earlier. The dog was locked in the trunk, but it was unharmed. In some of the previous attacks discussed, there were instances when the victims had been forced out into their yards, but there wasn't a time like this when they were ordered to walk a couple of houses away. This was a bit different in that regard.

Once the police got to the scene, they were anxious to talk to the victim to see what details she could share about her attacker. She told them that the man who attacked her was about six-feet-tall and perhaps 170 pounds. She recounted details of his mask, his gloves, and most importantly how he talked through clenched teeth.

Now, based on the M.O. and the location, it was pretty obvious that the assailant in this case was the same man who had attacked the other women before this. We have to consider that where this attack happened was very close to the area of Dawes and Dolcetto, which was previously mentioned as being the spot of several dog beatings, burglaries, and sexual assaults. These instances dated back two to three years prior to this. There's no doubt that compared to some of the other victims, this 19-year-old was extremely lucky because although she was assaulted and terrorized, she was not raped.

Despite this victim not being raped, the terror followed her after the night of her attack. Over a year later, in December of 1977, she got a threatening phone call, and she was sure that the caller was the same man who had attacked her. This is just a very short time before victim number one received her horrible phone calls. The first victim received her call on January 2, 1978.

Police were convinced that all of these attacks were committed by one person, The East Area Rapist. They felt that the phone calls to the victims had also been made by this person. Now after the phone call to the first victim was recorded, and this was known as the, "going to kill you call," police played it for this latest victim. There was no doubt in her mind, the voice that she was hearing on this recorded phone call was her attacker. Police were definitely worried at this point. They knew that they had a big problem, a serial rapist on their hands in Sacramento County but they were especially worried because the attacks were coming so close together.

A couple of weeks had gone by since the latest East Area Rapist attack when he unexpectedly drove off and the victim had escaped relatively unscathed. It was now November 1976 and residents of Eastern Sacramento County were on high alert. On the 6600 block of Greenleaf Drive in Citrus Heights, about a mile from where Jane was attacked, a family was dealing with a dilemma. It was November 10, and they wanted to go visit their son who was in the hospital. They didn't know if they should leave their 16-year-old daughter alone at home. They finally decided to let her stay home while they went to visit their son. They left for the hospital about 7:00 p.m.

This 16-year-old girl was a student at San Juan High School, and after her parents left, she sat on the couch, watching television in the den. It wasn't long before she was startled by a loud bang. It sounded as if it had come from someplace in the house. She paused for a second to try to pinpoint where the noise had come from, and out of nowhere a masked man charged into the room. The 16-year-old girl became immediately scared, and she started screaming. At that point, her dog also started barking loudly. The masked man wasted no time in blurting out a demand to her speaking through clenched teeth. He said, "Shut up or I'll kill you." The man then kicked her dog and told the girl to shut it up or he would stab it. This masked attacker was very close to her. Close enough to have what she would later describe as really awful breath and a very strong odor emanating from his body. The masked intruder told the young girl that he just wanted money. He forced the 16-year-old off the couch and then pulled out black shoelaces. He used the shoelaces to tie the girl's hands tightly behind her back. Once he had the girl secured, he forced her to walk out of the house and into the backyard where he forced her down on the ground.

While she was on the ground, she was next to her bike, and she saw several black shoelaces hanging from the handlebars. He would use these shoelaces to bind her feet. He warned her, "Don't move or you'll be dead, and I'll be gone into the night." While the girl stayed helplessly on the ground fearing for her life, the man walked in and out of the house returning every couple of minutes. After doing this several times she saw him come back out. He put the living room window screen, which had been his point of entry, back onto the window. He asked her where her money was and then asked her if her parents had any, but she told him that they had their money with them.

His response at that point was sort of, "Oh Geez, no money?" It didn't sound like he really was upset by the fact she didn't have any money. He went into the house one last time and on the way out, he locked the door behind him. It was then that this man made his intentions clear to the young girl. The masked intruder hissed through clenched teeth. "Do you like to fuck?" She ignored him, and he started to say things to her that were very sexual in nature. Suddenly, he grabbed her legs and untied her feet. He pulled her up and then forced her to walk to a canal area located behind her street. Once they were down in the canal area, he forced the girl to walk in the very shallow water at the bottom of the canal. There was a big drought in California going on, so it was probably much drier and much shallower than it would normally have been. As he moved her along the canal, nearby dogs started to bark. She started to plead with her attacker begging for him to let her go. Once again, he told her to shut up and that if she didn't, he would silence her forever, and he would be gone in the night. The man brought her to the base of a large weeping willow tree and told her to sit down. He then tied her ankles.

Once the man had the girl's ankles tied, he walked away for a short distance. He then returned a moment later only to once again untie her ankles. He repeated this untying and then retying her ankles and walked away, and this is some pretty odd behavior on the attacker's part. It's hard to know if he was nervous or just not thinking straight but to constantly be tying and untying her ankles just seems a bit off. When the man came back again, he showed the girl his knife and then once again and untied her. This went on for minutes, repeating the same steps almost as if he was building up to something. Finally, he made a blindfold from some sort of material, but when he put it on her, she could partially see around the material, and she watched him walking back and forth as if he was trying to think.

Even during the times where she could not see him through the blindfold, she could sense how close this man was to her because of how awful he smelled. He started cutting at her jeans, removing them in pieces with his knife, but he seemed to have problems getting her pants all the way off and at one point even said, "This isn't working right." Finally, he got her pants and underwear off, so that she was naked from the waist down. This is where the attacker's behavior would become even more bizarre because he started making small talk with her. He asked her if he knew her from somewhere. She said, "No." Then he asked her if she went to American River College. The 16-year-old again answered, "No." He held a knife to her throat, and she blurted out that she went to San

Juan High School. Then he said, "You're lying. What's your name?" She answered, but she didn't give her real name. The hooded man then became very nervous.

He was so nervous that he started pacing back and forth. Then he told her that he needed to wait for his parents to leave, so that he could go home. He said to the girl that he was going to take off in his car. He warned her again that if she made a sound in the next twenty minutes, he would silence her forever, and he would be gone in the dark. The man walked off into the darkness, and the 16-year-old girl was there left alone. She was so scared that she waited almost an hour in the same spot before trying to get away. During that time, she waited, she got her ankles untied and got the blindfold off, but the bindings on her wrist were very tight, and she couldn't get them off. Finally, after what must have seemed like an eternity, she climbed out from the ditch and started toward her house. Luckily, she saw a neighbor and ran to him. The neighbor was able to get her wrist bindings off. From his house, they called her house to see if her parents were home yet. It turned out they had gotten home at 8:30 p.m.

Once police arrived at the family's home, they started to piece together the events of that night starting from the time the family left their 16-year-old daughter. The authorities knew that she was attacked soon after the family left for the hospital. The attacker had come in through a screen but had put the screen back on the window for some reason. Authorities figured out that while the 16-year-old was bound outside of her house, her attacker had gone back in and locked up and turned things off to make it look like she had simply gone out. In fact, when her parents returned home, and she was gone, that's exactly what they thought happened.

The frightened 16-year-old was able to give the police a pretty good description of her attacker. She told them that he was white with a light complexion. She thought he was possibly 18 to 23 years old. He stood about 5 feet, ten inches and weighed about 165 pounds. She also thought he had brown hair. His hood was made of leather and had slits for the eyes and mouth. She was also able to see that he wore black square-toed shoes. He wore military-style clothing or fatigues. She stressed how bad this man smelled, both his breath and his body odor, which really stood out to her. She told police that when she first saw the man in her house, he had a knife. When he brought her outside, he threatened her with what she thought was possibly a different knife similar to the ones in her kitchen. She stated that he had a flashlight. Then she also recounted for police the shoelaces that she had seen hanging neatly from her bicycle. She pointed out that for certain things, he used his left hand, but for others, he used his right. This girl was definitely able to tell police about some of his very odd behavior. The pacing, the indecision, the untying and the retying of the shoes, and the small talk all seemed extremely strange.

One possible theory is that he actually targeted a different victim and wound up attacking this young girl by mistake. It turned out a female neighbor of the 16-year-old girl did, in fact, go to American River College. It seems that with everything that happened in the attack this was definitely the East Area Rapist. The M.O. seemed to match. The method of entering and blitz attack was similar and the choice of a victim of a single-story home all matched up. If this was indeed the East Area Rapist who had attacked the 16-year-old, it was the second attack in a row in which he didn't sexually assault his victim.

Over the next month, police were on high alert for another East Area Rapist attack, but it didn't come. Things were quiet. Toward the middle of December 1976, there was one suspicious incident on Galewood Way in the town of Carmichael. A man entered a woman's house while she was on the phone. Before the startled woman even really knew what was going on, the man turned around and left. Around the same time, residents on the 4600 block of Ladera Way were dealing with hang-up phone calls. One home had received a few calls over one-week period, but another home had been getting these calls for weeks. They usually occurred three or four times a day.

The couple that had received these calls three or four times a day, went to a Christmas party on December 18, leaving their 15-year-old daughter home alone. Her parents left at about 6:15 p.m. She put some food in the oven and then sat down to play her piano while she waited for it to cook. She hadn't been playing the piano long when she heard a loud crashing noise from outside. She stopped playing to listen, but it was quiet. She started to play once again, but suddenly without warning, she felt a knife at her throat. Suddenly the girl heard a voice whisper, "Make a move and I'll kill you."

Feeling the man's breath on her, the young girl sat frozen in place at the piano. He hissed to her asking her if she had any money. She sat still and answered, "No." Then the man asked her when her parents would be back. He told her that he needed to know, so he would know how much time he had. She responded by saying she didn't know. At that moment, she heard the man say, "Get up. If you say anything, I will push this knife all the way in, and I will be gone in the dark."

Once she stood up from the piano, she was able to get a look at the man who had the knife at her throat. He was wearing a dark red ski mask. He must've sensed that she was afraid because he said to her, "You'll be okay. I won't hurt you." He added that he was going to tie her up to a post in the backyard but warned her that if she tried to look at him, he would kill her. The masked man forced her to walk out to her garage and into the backyard at which point, he pulled a white shoelace out of his pocket. He tied her hands behind her back and then he tied her to a post in the backyard that was next to a picnic table. He pushed her onto the table, and then tied her ankles together. He then pulled out a cloth and started to stuff it into her mouth to gag her, but she became resistant. He reminded her that if she didn't comply, he would kill her. She believed the man and then cooperated. After she was gagged, he also blindfolded her with a piece of cloth.

He had this 15-year-old girl's ankles tied together, her hands tied together, she's gagged, tied to a post. He had her totally immobilized. There was nothing she could do. He told her that he would check on her every ten seconds. She heard him walk into the house, but the door that he went into was not the same door they had come out of. Instead of walking into the garage area door, he had walked into a door leading into the family room. While she was tied helplessly to the post, she heard the man rifling through drawers and cabinets in the kitchen. It sounded like he was putting things in the paper bags. It wasn't long before she heard him walk back out of the house towards her. Suddenly he was at her side, very close. At that point, he asked, "Have you ever fucked a guy?"

This girl had to be scared to death, but she was able to answer him and said, "No." He became very stern with her and told her she had better not be lying or he would kill her. Then he asked her if she had ever felt a guy's dick and told her that he wanted her to play with his. This man placed his penis into her bound hands and hissed at her through clenched teeth, "Play with it." He did this for a few moments and then suddenly pulled her to her feet. He quickly pulled down her pants and fondled her, cutting her bra with the knife that he was holding. The masked man untied her from the post and order back into the house. Once inside, the man took her to the master bedroom and sexually assaulted her. After a short time, he brought her into the family room and sexually assaulted her again there. He left her there and wandered around the home for a couple minutes and then came back and raped her a third time. After this third sexual attack, he walked her outside to the picnic table and tied her to it, and after she was tied to the picnic table, he left, and it was over. She waited a few minutes to make sure that he was gone, and then she was able to get her bindings off and raced into the house to call her neighbor for help. Thankfully, they were home and they immediately rushed to her aid. They also contacted the police.

Police got to the house about the same time her parents came home. She gave a statement detailing her ordeal before being taken away to the Sacramento Medical Center. The 15-year-old Del Campo High School student had given police as many details as she could remember. She described the rapist as being about six-foot-tall with a regular build, and she noticed something very specific and that was that this man had a very small penis. This is something we have referred to multiple times so far in this case. One of the things she recounted for police was something that the man had told her during the course of the attack, and the words he said to her were, "I have seen you at school before, and you sure look good."

Police turned their focus to outside of the home. It was there they found that a part of the fence had been kicked down, which was likely the loud crash she had heard just before she first encountered her attacker. They also found some of the girl's clothing discarded in the next-door neighbor's yard. Some other interesting things they found scattered in the yard were shoestrings hanging from a tree, and they later discovered that the shoestring had been removed from shoes belonging to the victim's sister. At some point prior to the attack, the man had been in the house long enough to take the shoelace.

One of the most important items found at the crime scene was a bloody band-aid that was found close to the picnic table. Police knew it wasn't from the victim, they assumed it belonged to her attacker, but this was 1976, authorities couldn't get DNA at this point from a bloody band-aid, but what they could get was the attacker's blood type.

The parents of this 15-year-old went carefully looking through their belongings to see if they could ID things that had been taken by the masked assailant. They were able to determine that he had taken jewelry, a BB pistol, and most oddly a bottle of hand lotion. This is all part of the pattern of the East Area Rapist. The M.O. and the descriptions fit. There was little doubt that this latest attacker was he and another thing that we continue to see with this latest attack is that it's not just the victim who received phone calls prior to the attack. This is another instance where nearby neighbors also received phone calls. It does seem as if this guy got off in some form of fashion by targeting residents in certain sections of neighborhoods.

Only two days later, a woman would have a frightening encounter that led police to believe the rapist was back and active again. In the early morning hours of December 20, 1976, a woman came to a stop sign at the intersection of Oakcrest and Dewey, in the town of Carmichael. This intersection was about a mile away from the attack that occurred two nights before. As the woman looked around to make sure it was safe to proceed, she saw something that chilled her blood. She saw a man dressed in dark clothing, in a ski mask crawling on his hands and knees towards the front door of a residence. She had no intention of trying to investigate further and wanted to get out of there. She looked one more time to the right before she drove out into the intersection and after she did, she snapped her head around only to find that the masked man she had seen crawling in the yard was now standing next to her window.

Imagine how terrified this woman was. Think about that shot of adrenaline when you are suddenly startled. The pair stared at each other for a few seconds, and then the man knocked on her window. The woman punched the gas pedal and was across the intersection very quickly. Once she got through that intersection, she slowed down to glance into her rear-view mirror and it's at this point that she saw this man reaching into some bushes, and she watched him take out a bike and jump on it. The first thought that would come to most people's mind is that the guy knows he's been spotted, and he wants to make his getaway. But, instead of making his getaway, he started racing towards her. She punched the car again and she was not looking back this time. She left this guy in the dust. She was terrified by this incident but didn't want to go to police, and it's not until a week later that she finally decided to report what had happened to her. There were no attacks reported on that date, perhaps if that man was the East Area Rapist, she had interrupted an attack and at the very least whoever it was that was crawling around, we could say for sure that guy was up to no good.

The last part of December 1976 seemed to pass by relatively quietly. Both the Sacramento County Sheriff Department as well as county residents hoped that the East Area Rapist would vanish along with the 1976 calendar year, but it turned out that wasn't going be the case. The East Area Rapist wasn't going anywhere. In fact, it would soon become apparent that he had stayed busy right up until the year's end. Not long after 11:00 p.m. on the night of January 18, 1977, a 25-year-old woman on Greenville Circle in Sacramento awoke from her sleep to find a bright light shining in her eyes. She yelled out, "Who's there?" She knew it wasn't her husband because he was away on business. From behind the glare of the light, a voice whispered, "Be quiet, I won't hurt you. All I want is your money and then I'll be gone."

This woman was just waking up from a deep sleep, her husband's not home and there's an intruder standing there. This had to seem like a bad dream to her, but it wasn't a dream. The man was already alongside her, and he started to bind her hands behind her back with pieces of electrical cord. He then blindfolded the helpless woman with a bandana. She blurted out to him that she was five months pregnant, but the intruder seemed unaware she was even speaking. He then placed a pair of panties over her head to keep her bandana in place. His only response to all of this was to tell her that she'd better shut up or he would slash or cut her. Bound and blindfolded, there was nothing she could do. The man walked off and was gone for a couple of minutes, then he walked back into the room and stood very close to her. She heard a popping sound. The intruder asked her what she thought that sound was, but she had no idea. He warned her that she had better guess.

She guessed and told the intruder that it sounded like he was shaking can of spray paint. He told her that was the wrong answer and to keep guessing. This time his voice was angrier.

She made a couple of guesses just to keep him calm. It took her only a moment to realize that the sound she was hearing was of the man masturbating with the aid of some sort of lubricant. It was at the point that this woman realizes what he was doing that he placed his penis into her bound hands and told her to massage it. After a moment the man turned the helpless woman onto her back, and although she was blindfolded, she knew there was something in front of her face. It turned out the man had his penis in front of her, and he forced her to orally copulate him, and as he forced her to do this, he warned her through clenched teeth that he would kill her if she bit him. Then this twisted intruder told the victim to put her legs up around his back, like she did with her husband. It was then that he raped her. After a few minutes, the man climbed off of the woman and walked out of the room. She could hear him ransacking her home. This went on for close to four hours.

At some point during this four-hour period, he came back into the room and raped her again. After this occurred, he asked her where she kept her car keys. After a while, this woman could no longer hear the sound of the man going through her house. It was then that she heard the garage door opening, followed by the sound of a car starting up. Her attacker was gone. The 25-year-old woman struggled to get her feet free, and then ran out of the house to a neighbor's and alerted them. They called police and an ambulance.

Police arrived on the scene, and this time they knew what they were walking into. Even though the East Area Rapist had never before struck in the city of Sacramento, authorities all over Sacramento County were on edge that any sexual attack was going to be his handiwork. This was another single-story home on a quiet street with no man in the home at the time. This was very typical of the East Area Rapist's M.O. The victim's description further backed up their suspicions; five feet, eleven inches, 180 pounds and a ski mask, a flashlight that the rapist held with his left hand, and a knife in the other hand. Then there was the talking through clenched teeth. Although they were pretty sure they knew who was responsible, they investigated the scene fully.

The police first noticed the extreme disarray the house was in. It seemed as if this burglar and rapist had searched every inch of the home. They were able to determine that the point of entry was a window on the backside of the house. The intruder had made a hole in the sliding glass and removed a dowel rod allowing him to open it all the way and climb in. The victim's car was missing. It seemed that when she heard the car start up after her attack, the car that she heard was her own. The fact that the man asked her for keys now made sense. Her car would be found later that day at around 5:00 p.m. on Great Falls Way, not quite two miles from her home. The car was found to be locked up, and the keys were missing. Investigators found a tennis shoe track close to the car that they thought belonged to the man who had raped the 25-year-old and then driven her car away from her home. One odd thing that investigators discovered was that a photo of the victim, and her husband had been removed from a frame, and the portion that included the victim had been cut out and was missing. This was reminiscent of something Richard Shelby had come across while investigating the East Area Rapist series.

Carol Daly and I got the phone call. They found a white envelope full of driver's licenses, photos of women. They were all in their twenties, they were all pretty and there's nothing else on it. They looked to me like somebody had cut the driver's license photos out. We got that and really had nowhere to go with it. It looked like someone had sat down with the razor knife and cut out the photographs.

It was the questioning of neighbors that really raised some red flags for investigators. It allowed them to learn just how much suspicious activity there was in the area prior to the attack. Police learned that one nearby neighbor had been robbed about a month earlier. Another neighbor reported that around that same time an unknown man walked out of his backyard.

When the homeowner asked the stranger what he was doing, the man responded by telling the homeowner that he was taking a shortcut. Next, police learned of the same man whose home was burglarized in mid-December had also caught a man peering into a window of a nearby house on January 11, a week before the Glenville Circle rape. The neighbor loudly called to let the person know he had been witnessed. The unknown man turned around and calmly walked north on Glenville Circle. He was described as being about six feet to six feet, one inch. He was white in his late twenties with a medium build and dark hair

Just the next day, January 12, a female neighbor walked out onto her front porch and saw a man in her front yard. The man took off running. He was described as being in his twenties about five seven, to five eight. The next day this woman walked out on to her porch and discovered that someone had removed the light bulb from her porch light. On January 17, the night before the rape occurred, multiple neighbors had seen a dark blue sedan parked on Glenville Circle, which none of them recognized. Earlier on the night of the Glenville Circle attack at about 8:30 p.m., a dog at a nearby home started to bark repeatedly. The dog's owner looked out the window just in time to see a man walking through her side gate and into her backyard. She raced into her garage to make sure that the doors were locked. Then she ran back into the house and looked out a different window to see if she could see the man. When she looked out of her window, she was standing face to face with the man who had cut through her yard. He was looking into her house. He immediately turned and ran off jumping over her back fence.

This is a point where there's a major missed opportunity. This woman immediately called police to tell them about the prowler. Since he had taken off, they didn't think it was a big deal. She described the man as a white male about 35 years old, five feet, eleven inches, 175 pounds, with a small waist but broad shoulders. The man had a neatly styled and combed hairstyle, and she went on to state that he was very athletic looking and agile based on how easily he jumped over her fence. In the days after the rape of the woman on Glenville Circle, this woman who had seen the prowler in her yard was asked to go to the police station and view various photos of men that resembled the man she saw. She picked out a handful of photos that resembled the man but none that she was confident was actually him.

There was a lot of suspicious activity going on around Glenville Circle from mid-December until January 18, the night of the attack. There were mystery cars, multiple unknown men prowling through the area described as different heights, different ages. Now Glenville Circle is just that, a circle. It had about six homes on it, but that circle was wrapped around by another circle called Mossglen Circle. This area was essentially a circle within a circle. Many of the homes in the area were only about six or seven years old at the time. This was an area of newer homes and this was a lot of activity for such a small area. This latest attack would lead to local police coordinating a meeting to come up with a game plan to try to stop the East Area Rapist.

On the night of January 22, 1977, one tenth of a mile from where a boy had seen a suspicious car, a resident had noticed the man walking through the front yards of some of her neighbors. He seemed to be creeping, she tried to watch him to see what he was up to, but somehow it seemed as if he knew she was there and turned around looking directly at her. She was about twenty feet away, and light from an overhead floodlight brightly lit up his face. They stared at each other for several seconds, but the woman got nervous and went inside of her house. She came out a few minutes later, but she didn't see the man. However, she did see a man on the corner where her street intersected with Primrose Drive. She couldn't be sure if this was the same man she had just seen. Later, she would describe the man she saw as being about six-feet tall and weighing about 175 pounds. A couple of nights later on

January 24, 1977, shortly after midnight, this same woman could hear her dogs in the backyard starting to carry on and making a lot of noise.

Just a few homes over on the 5800 block of Primrose Drive a 25-year-old accountant was settling down for the night after hosting a small party. The recently separated woman was in bed by midnight. She had only been asleep for a short time when around 1:00 a.m. something woke her from her sleep. As soon as her eyes opened, she could tell that someone was holding her shoulder tightly. She screamed and tried to pull away. From the darkness a voice hissed, "If you scream again, I'll kill you." He then held something sharp to her throat. She quieted down, and the intruder made her rollover onto her stomach. He then tied her hands tightly behind her back with rope. He blindfolded her, gagged her, and then tied her feet together.

The intruder had gained control very quickly, and while she was lying there, unable to see or move, she could smell him. Smelled his foul body odor that smelled like stale sweat. He then told her not to make a sound, or else he would use what he referred to as an eight-inch ice pick on her. He whispered that he only wanted her money and wasn't going to hurt her. Most horrifying of all was that he addressed her by name. Then he asked her where her purse was, she told the man where he could find it, and he got up and left the room, but quickly returned after finding it and said, "This can't be all there is."

The woman could hear the popping sound of a cap, and then she could hear the sound of this man masturbating with some kind of lubricant. It was then that he spoke out through clenched teeth, "Do you know what I'm doing?" We know that this is the M.O. of the East Area Rapist. Just like in the attack before this one, he was making the victim guess that he was masturbating. We know that the East Area Rapist got some sick pleasure out of a number of things that he did as part of his MO.

This was at least the second time that he had made a victim guess what he was doing. We've talked about another part of his M.O. a number of times and that is, placing his penis into the victims' bound hands and telling them to play with it. This was exactly what the East Area Rapist did next. It was then that the man raped her. He would tie and retie her bound feet multiple times, raping her, and taking breaks in between to go wander around the house. During one of his trips, the victim heard the rapist go into a refrigerator and open a beer.

During these attacks, he would start some different conversations with her. He asked her if she knew him, and when she said she didn't, he replied by saying to her that it must have been too long ago for her to remember. Then he told her that even though she didn't know him that he knew her. Now this attack lasted about ninety minutes, and after it was over, he removed the bindings and retied her with her bra. Then he picked up the original bindings, so he could take them with him. He walked out of the room and out of her house.

The victim waited a while until she was sure the man was gone. Then she started to try and wiggle free from the bra she was bound with, but she couldn't get free. Still blindfolded, she hopped off the bed and worked her way over to a phone, and somehow, she was able to call the police.

The police arrived at the single-story home pretty quickly and started assessing the crime scene. Inside the home, they found the now familiar signs of a house that had been gone through extensively. They found that the phone cord in the family room had been cut. The point of entry into the home was likely either the garage door or a sliding glass door. Both had been pried. In the kitchen, the police found a partially eaten block of cheese with teeth marks in it and two empty beer cans. The search outside revealed various shoe prints of all sorts in both the victim's yard and in the neighbors'. The victim's fence had been left open and, on her lawn, was a sign advertising her house for sale. When they questioned the victim about her assailant, she described him as being white, in his twenties and of a medium built. Of course, one physical feature she mentioned was a very small and very thin penis. Police already were sure who they were dealing with, and this information just confirmed it. One interesting thing in the report or perhaps not in the report, is the mention of a ski mask. It's not indicated any place. We don't know if he wore a ski mask, or if it was just not submitted in the report.

On January 27, 1977, the neighbor who had seen the unknown man near her yard and whose dogs had acted crazy on the night of the attack, found several Marlboro cigarette butts outside of her living room window. On the very next day, January 28, this same woman was standing outside of her home when she spotted a man jogging down the street. He seemed very out of place, like he really wasn't a jogger. In her mind, he looked like the strange man she had spotted near her yard. This woman was actually able to follow this man and got his license plate. When authorities looked into it, the plate came back to a neighborhood man who happened to be Asian, so he was ruled out pretty quickly.

On this same day, not far away on Warehouse Way, a resident spotted a man prowling near her new home construction that was up for sale. She made eye contact with the man and immediately called the police, at which point the man ran off. The best description that she could give was that he was white and about five feet, nine inches.

In and around the immediate area of the most recent attack, we have some familiar things going on: prowling, homes for sale, and just several incidents of things that seemed unusual. Just more of the same stuff that was becoming commonplace leading up to and following East Area Rapist attacks. After this series of prowling and strangers, and the twelfth confirmed attack by the East Area Rapist, this Citrus Heights neighborhood understandably went into high alert.

Back in Carmichael, a town which had already experienced its share of East Area Rapist attacks, residents had remained on high-alert since the last attack there. Things for the most part had been pretty quiet but anything out of the ordinary stood out. In mid-January of 1977 an odd incident occurred. A couple had been out for a walk on a quiet day, suddenly the sound of racing cars behind them caught their attention. They saw several police cars racing down the street near the intersection of Heathcliff and Crestview. It was at this point as the cars went out of sight that they saw something very strange, a man dressed all in black and wearing a ski mask stepped out from behind a bus and walked out into plain view of the couple. He saw them but ignored them and focused his attention in the area that the police had headed. He had his hands on his hips as if he was winded. The couple knew this was weird, but they walked on leaving the masked-man where he stood. Later on, they would describe him as being about five feet, nine inches and dressed in dark clothes, but other than that there really wasn't much more that they could add.

Just a week or two earlier, a home very close to the spot on the 6200 block of Heathcliff Drive had been burglarized. It wasn't long after that that the couple who lived there started to receive hang-up phone calls. During the first week of February, several prowling incidents were reported in this neighborhood, but there were no strong leads, and no one was arrested. This couple was living right in the area where all this prowling was going on and their home had been burglarized. They had to have been worried, and it was at nighttime that most of the prowling and suspicious activity and the East Area Rapist attacks had happened. It was the daylight hours that would seem to be when people would get some relief, because up till now, East Area Rapist attacks had been very rare during daylight hours. The exception being Jane who was the victim of the fifth attack which occurred around 6:30 a.m.

Unfortunately, for the 30-year-old housewife and Sacramento State College student, the daylight did not offer her any protection. On February 7, 1977, her husband left for work leaving his wife and their seven-year-old behind. As he was about to leave, he noticed a white van parked in the area that looked out of place. He told his wife to make sure everything was locked up. His wife listened to him and went around the home checking all of the locks and windows even locking the deadbolts. She had checked every door and window except for one, and this was the sliding glass-door on the back side of the house, and that would turn out to be a very big mistake.

As the woman stood at the sink washing dishes, she felt the presence of somebody in the room behind her, as she turned around, she expected to see her six-year-old daughter standing there but was horrified to see a man in the ski-mask holding a knife in one hand and a gun in the other. Through clenched teeth, he warned her not to move, he told her not to scream, and he just wanted her money. The man ordered her to sit down in a chair and told her he was going to tie her up. Then he said, "If you don't do what I say, I'll kill you."

At first this woman was defiant and said, "No." Then he told her he wanted to tie her to the bed and reminded her, he had a gun at which point she cooperated. He pulled out shoelaces and tied her hands tightly in the back of her. He then led her down the hallway and passed her sleeping daughter's bedroom.

When they got to the woman's bedroom, the man raised the knife to the woman's throat and ordered her on the bed throwing her down face first. Then he tied her ankles. She could hear the sound of cloth or towel like material being torn. Then her attacker spoke out from underneath the mask, again through clenched teeth telling her he was going to cover her head. At that point, the scared mother defiantly yelled, "Get the fuck out of here."

The family dog was nearby, and the woman ordered the dog to attack the man, but he didn't react. The masked intruder responded by placing his hand over her mouth and telling her to shut up. As he was pressed against her, she could feel the handgun in the front pocket of the jacket he was wearing, and she grabbed at it and pulled it out and was about to squeeze the trigger, but she couldn't even tell which direction the barrel was facing because her hands were tied behind her back, and it was this hesitation that allowed the man to realize she had the gun, and he started punching her in the back of her head. At this point, the man knew he had to do something to get her to comply, so he threatened her daughter. He said, "Shut up or I'll kill your daughter. I'll cut her ear off and bring it to you." As he warned her, he stabbed at the bed very close to the bound woman's head. It was then that she complied fearing her sleeping daughter would be hurt or even worse.

This woman knows what's going to happen. She's probably aware who's doing this to her from all the news coverage, but she has to protect her daughter and she complied. The man gagged and blindfolded her, then he left the room, but this was when that motherly instinct kicked in, and she began to fear that he had left to go to her daughter's room. This woman started to struggle and was actually able to remove her ankle bindings. She started to stand up but suddenly the man was there, pushed her back down telling her that he would cut a toe off every time she moved. The man started pulling her jeans off and then her shirt. She knew that she was about to be raped. The masked attacker once again through clenched teeth hissed, "Shut up." He put the tip of the knife against her stomach, then he moved back, and she could hear him masturbating with some sort of lubricant. As the horrified 30-year-old victim laid there trying to think of her next move, any move, she could smell the strong smell of sweet-smelling aftershave coming from the man, and then without warning, he was on her, and she was sexually assaulted.

After the assault the man wandered out of the room. A few moments later, the woman, still helpless on the bed was horrified to hear her young daughter's voice. This man had brought her into the room and tied her up with some cords. The young girl started screaming when she saw her mother lying there, and this caused the mother despite being gagged to also start to scream. The assailant threw the young girl on the bed and both her and her mother started screaming. The masked-attacker must have felt uneasy because he raced out of the room and ripped out two phone cords to different phones in the house. He raced back into the room and tightly retied the mother's ankles and her wrists as her young daughter laid helplessly on the bed next to her. The house was finally quiet and soon the mother and daughter realized the the man was gone.

They both climbed out of the bed and hopped and scooted as best as they could towards the closest door, which was the back door. They started calling outside to the yard, and a neighbor heard their pleas for help and called police.

The police got there quickly and started to investigate. The woman was badly shaken, and her daughter was crying hysterically. The police were finally able to calm the pair down and began to ask them what had happened. The victim recounted that her husband had mentioned a strange white van parked nearby. As it turned out, it was still in the same spot and when police walked over to investigate it, they actually found a white male in his twenties sitting in it. He was questioned and later ruled out as having anything to do with the attack. Next, police questioned the victim about her attacker and everything she told them was familiar, around five feet, eleven inches, weight in the 180-pound range, a man in his 20s talking through clenched teeth, she told authorities about the smell of his aftershave, and that he had an extremely small penis. Police quickly determined that the assailant had entered the home through the sliding glass door. The fact that the home had been burglarized a month earlier and had been receiving hang-up calls was just further indication that the East Area Rapist was responsible for this attack.

The investigators questioned neighbors and found lots of interesting bits of information. They started with a man who had heard the mother and daughter screaming. He had actually seen a man scaling a fence and going down into a drainage ditch at about 8:00 a.m. on the morning of the attack, that was right around the time the attacker left the home. The neighbor stated that the man who scaled the fence was young, maybe around 20, thin, white and about five feet, nine inches. He also told police officers that the day before, he and his wife had encountered a strange man in the park across the street. The man had kept looking at the witness's wife and every time she looked back he looked away. Another neighbor reported seeing a man running near the park on the morning of the attack. He appeared to be about five feet, nine inches and in his mid-twenties. Other neighbors reported seeing odd men in the area in the day or two before the attack and generally all of them were described as being thin, white men in their 20s and all about five feet, nine inches.

On October 26, 1984 over seven years after she was attacked, this victim contacted police to tell them about phone calls she was getting from someone she felt may have been her attacker. In her statement to police she detailed how she had received at least half a dozen calls over the years. These calls were usually about a year or a year and a half apart. In this latest call she received, a male caller said, "Hi, how are you? How are you doing?" The victim responded by asking the male caller who he was. He replied, "This is an old friend. You know me." She hung up on the caller and called police, but she was unnerved by this call. She was trying to get her life back together after what she went through, only to have these periodic calls over the next several years. It was frustrating to have so many witnesses seeing so many men that fit the description of the East Area Rapist. It was very possible that perhaps one or more of these sightings was actually of the East Area Rapist, but as frustrating and violent as these attacks were, none of the victims had been seriously wounded. Just over a week after the latest attack, that would all change.

SEASON TWO,
EPISODE FOUR

The East Area Rapist had just committed his thirteenth confirmed attack on February 7, 1977, in Carmichael, California. There were a slew of prowlers, burglaries, and phone calls in the neighborhood where this latest attack happened, and people all over Sacramento County were on high alert. They were very aware of anyone who seemed out of place. Just a little over a week after the last East Area Rapist attack, a young man on Ripon Court in Sacramento had his own violent experience.

On February 16, a prowler shot and seriously wounded an 18-year-old named Rodney Miller. Miller was shot in the abdomen and was taken to a nearby hospital in critical condition. He underwent surgery that saved his life. Rodney's father Raymond told investigators that he and his son heard a noise in their backyard. They went outside into the backyard and saw a man standing in the shadows. The man took off running towards the street, and the father and son gave chase. Rodney closed in on the man, but as he did, the man turned around and fired two shots at him.

18-year-old, Rodney ran cross country in high school, and he was quick. He caught up to this man as he was trying to scale the fence and grabbed onto the man's foot, dragging him down off the fence. At that point, the gun went off, and Rodney was struck. The man ran off. Police responded very quickly to this call and arrived on Ripon Court and found Rodney lying on his back, and he was very badly hurt. At the crime scene, police found evidence of the shooter's gun being a nine-millimeter, which included a spent shell casing and a live round. Within two hours of the shooting, the police had brought in the dog to see if they could track the shooter. The dog was able to pick up the scent and track the man to a neighboring street called Citadel Way before losing it near the parking lot of a nearby school.

Once Rodney was stable, police didn't waste any time questioning him on February 18, two days after the shooting. From his hospital bed, Rodney was able to tell police, how the first shot from the man's gun had hit him, but fortunately the second shot had missed. Rodney, due to the traumatic experience in the poorly lit area, was not able to give a detailed description of the man that shot him. A police canvas of nearby neighbors yielded some eyewitnesses who were able to provide a pretty good description of the shooter.

One witness thought the shooter was about twenty years old and had sandy blonde hair, five feet, nine inches, and around 170 pounds. A second witness described the man in a similar fashion but felt that the shooter was in his mid to upper twenties and that he had "heavy legs." Police theorize that based on the witness descriptions and the prowling, the shooter of Rodney Miller was likely the East Area Rapist. What this shooting proved was that when cornered, this man wouldn't hesitate to shoot someone. One very interesting note about where the shooting occurred was that it was within 500 feet of where the eleventh victim's car had been found after the East Area Rapist stole it, following that attack.

Although his wounds were extensive, Rodney Miller would eventually make a full recovery. A composite sketch of the man who shot him, who was presumably the East Area Rapist, was created and circulated soon after the incident, but it didn't lead anywhere. It wouldn't be until February of 2018 that the sketch of Rodney Miller's shooter would once again become relevant in the East Area Rapist case.

Very recently, Detective Sergeant Ken Clark of the Sacramento County Sheriff's Department was going back through some pre-East Area Rapist burglary incidents, looking for burglaries that might contain an M.O. similar to the East Area Rapist. In one 1973 incident, Ken found something that caught his attention and as it turns out, it might be related to the Rodney Miller shooting almost four years later in 1977. Detective Ken Clark of the Sacramento County Sheriff's Department had this to say about the incident:

It seems to me to be conduct that is very bold, and I would not expect any burglar to readily find himself involved in. In this case, September 13 of 1973 on the 2,500 block of Sarda Way, a 28-year-old mother and her 18-month-old son are in the residence alone, the husband is at work. She's described by her family who I've spoken to and the officers at the scene that dealt with her as a very attractive lady. She is at the home when somebody knocks on the front door. This is about 11:00 in the morning, give or take. She doesn't answer the door. She thinks it's a religious solicitor, and so she decides against it, and a few minutes later she has her son in bed in one of the other rooms to the back, and she hears noises coming from the back area of the house.

She walks down the hallway and as she gets to her master bedroom, which basically faces the backyard, she sees a man at the window, and he has already taken the window screen off, and he is prying at the window itself. They see one another. He ducks down and runs around the side of the house. She looks beyond and sees that the gate to a school yard right behind her is open and that gate is normally kept closed. She was a bit alarmed by that. She comes back around, and she begins locking the doors and windows of the home and she arms herself with a handgun from inside the house.

She looks around and does not see any more sign of this guy and contacts her husband. It's alluded to in the report but not directly stated that she kind of left it at that believing that it was over, that she'd surprised a burglar who probably thought that nobody was home and now he's running off. I'll tell you that 99.9 percent of the time this guy would have been gone. He would be gone from the neighborhood, he would be gone that day, right then that minute. We wouldn't see him again during this episode, but things take a strange turn with this guy because though she's locked everything up and she's armed herself, the door leading from the garage to the kitchen is forced open while she's standing there a few feet away. The suspect got the door open and then also smashed through a chain lock that she had secured at the top of the door.

He got it open a little over a foot, and she had pointed the gun at him and said, "If you come any further, I'm going to shoot you." The man stopped, and he turned around and walked out of the garage through the overhead garage door, which she had left open for lighting in the garage. It was the middle of the day, and she'd been doing laundry out in the garage. This time she decides to call the Sheriff's Department. The Sheriff's Department is on their way.

Now at this point, I would think based on the confrontation that just occurred and even if the guy had decided that he was going to take an opportunity to do something more horrible that he had potentially contemplated with the initial burglary, at this point, he's got at a weapon pointed at him. I'm thinking that he's going to see this as a good time to go. One would have to suspect that she called the cops, I'm thinking he would leave, but not this guy.

She's in the home waiting for law enforcement, and he forces his way into the exact same door and rushes her and grabs hold of her hands when she's holding the gun. He closed the distance so fast that she couldn't do anything, and they fight over this gun. She's five *seven, about 135 pounds. The guy is a five foot eight, about 140 to 150 pounds. She ends up wrestling over the gun with him. He gets the gun pointed at her and that's unnerving, but she uses all her might and pulls it away, and it ends up going off and over her shoulder in terms of how they're fighting.*

At that point, the suspect does run, and she's medically fragile based on some medical conditions that are going on in her life and she passes out. The cops arrive, and she has passed out and basically recounts this story. She describes the guy as being mid-twenties, and she settles eventually when she does a composite sketch at the age of 27. She said that he was neatly dressed, his hair was neat, but longer as was the style of the time. It was over the ears. He had some small pockmarks or some kind marks on his chin, and he had a small sore on the corner of his mouth.

She said that he appeared to be sick as in like physically ill, like maybe he is recovering from the flu or something. He had bags under his eyes, and she said that his eyes were deep set and intense. She said that he was wearing a shirt that was a nice shirt and that he had light colored pants on. He had a blue decorative scarf coming out of the pocket of the shirt, had white ladies' gloves on, which she found to be very unusual.

We're getting the picture of a guy dressed a little bit like a dandy for that period of time. It's just another unusual thing to take into consideration here. He wasn't seen again, and he disappeared from the neighborhood. The composite sketch which she produced got an immediate reaction from me because when I first saw it in the report, I actually believed there had been a mistake and that the composite from the Rodney Miller shooting case that occurred in the city in February of 1977 had accidentally been merged with this file. It took me just about three to five seconds to realize that wasn't what happened at all, that this was the actual sketch done by this victim.

This would have occurred three and a half years or even more years before the Rodney Miller incident even occurred. It piqued my interest, especially the behavior and the way he was described, and then adding to it, the composite made me think that again, this was another individual potential case that was a pre-EAR case. He was beginning to adopt some of the behaviors, but still not succeeding based on the plan, based on what he's doing at this point. It looked like an opportunistic crime, but it was unsuccessful and probably frustrating for him, and it was tremendously risky, and he could have gotten shot, yet he still did it.

This 1973 attack that resulted in a sketch of the attacker which closely matched the Rodney Miller shooter is still being investigated by the Sacramento Sheriff's Department. It was incidents like the Rodney Miller shooting on top of all the rapes that had people in a state of panic. Right around the same time that Rodney Miller was shot, one woman in an undocumented incident in Sacramento had a terrifying experience. She was so unnerved and on edge after all the attacks that she could no longer sleep at night. She sat up in the dark of her bedroom with a loaded handgun, convinced that the East Area Rapist would come for her. She did this for several nights in a row, and all she had to show for her trouble was a lack of quality sleep.

Then one night while she sat there in the dark, she heard something outside of her bedroom window. She immediately went into high alert. She could tell that someone was tampering with their window. She tried to steady her shaking hands. She raised the gun and leveled it at the window, and then a light, possibly from a flashlight, trickled in from the outside, and her window was raised open. A man climbed in through the window and started to put a foot down on her floor. It was then that he made eye contact with the woman who was in a shooting position with the gun aimed right at him. This woman wasn't planning on asking any questions or letting the man get the upper hand. As she started to squeeze the trigger, the thought race through her mind, what if I kill this man and I go to jail for murder? She raised the gun a bit higher into the right and fired off a shot into the area around her window. Now, this shot was far enough away from the man to miss him, but close enough to scare the hell out of him.

In a flash, the man jumped back out of the window and disappeared into the darkness. If this was the East Area Rapist at her window, it may have been the first time someone had gotten the upper hand on him, and it's understandable why this woman chose not to shoot, but if she had put that shot into his chest instead of the wall next to him, things might have turned out a lot differently. This man's evil legacy may have been cut short.

The Rodney Miller shooting itself had taken some of the focus off the rapes for a moment, but that wouldn't last. Residents on the 3800 block of Thornwood Drive in Sacramento were troubled by odd phone calls. In some instances, the caller would hang up after a second, but in other calls they would stay on the line without making a sound. One of the residents was a woman who is getting these calls along with her daughter. In late February, this woman's daughter answered the phone and an unknown woman asks for the girl's mother, before her mother could get to the phone, the unknown female caller hung up and never called back.

Now at this point, there have been over a dozen attacks in the East Area Rapist case, and while police are openly acknowledging that there is a serial rapist, the one thing they're not doing is telling the public that many of the victims were getting calls prior to the rapes. They were not putting that information out there. Just imagine the panic if the residents of Sacramento County had had that info and then one of these calls came in.

It seems like there were some missed opportunities here to alert the public. What happened in mid-February of 1977, would be a major fail by police. In the same section of Thornwood Drive that was being targeted with phone calls, neighbors found some things that didn't belong to them hidden in their bushes. They had discovered a cloth bag that contained a ski mask, a pair of gloves, and a flashlight. Obviously, the homeowners were disturbed by this, so they did what most people would have done. They called the police. Whichever police officer took that phone call, instructed the residents to throw all the stuff away. I just don't think you can understate what a major blunder this was. You think about all the things that was going on and then a police officer told these residents to throw this stuff away, but that was exactly what they did. The homeowners threw away the ski mask, the pair of gloves and the bag but kept the flashlight.

Strange things continued late February and into March. There were odd men seen in the neighborhood. Dogs barked at night. Something seemed to be happening on the 3800 block of Thornwood Drive, but nothing was really being done about it. Around this time, multiple witnesses saw an old-style yellow truck from the 1940s or '50s. Sometimes they would see it being driven, and sometimes it would be parked in between two houses as if the driver could have been a visitor to either house, but as it turns out, he wasn't. Nobody knew who the driver was, but one eyewitness account said that he was white, in his twenties, and under six feet tall.

On March 8, 1977, a recently separated woman on Thornwood Drive, who had received some of the calls in February, was asleep in her bed. Around 4:00 a.m., she heard some noise that jolted her awake. As she sat up, she saw man racing at her. Before she knew it, he had a knife to her throat. The intruder spoke in a clear hostile voice telling her that he had a butcher knife and that he only wanted her money. He warned her that if she moved he would kill her, but it was dark, and the woman was still groggy, so she couldn't see him very well. She thought he was wearing a mask, but she wasn't 100 percent sure. The man immediately forced the 38-year-old woman onto her stomach and bound her hands behind her back, and then he tied her feet. He also gagged and blindfolded her. Once she was secured, the assailant left her room apparently searching the home for money but return to check on her periodically.

During one of the trips back into the bedroom, the man placed his penis into the woman's hands, which were tied behind her back. He then ordered her to play with it. After a couple of moments, he flipped her over onto her back and ripped her night gown down the middle. The attacker then warned her by saying she had better fuck good, or he would kill her. He then raped the woman before throwing blankets over her.

The man had been in the victim's home for about two hours, and around 6:00 a.m., slipped out of the house. Right around the same time a neighbor saw an unknown man standing on her front porch looking into a window, the window he was peeping into was near the intersection of Thornwood and Montclair about eight homes away from the victim's. The neighbor would later describe the peeper as being white and about five feet, nine inches with a medium build.

Inside her home, the 38-year-old victim struggled to get free of her bindings. Once she was able to, she ran to a phone in the family room but discovered the phone wires had been cut. She then went to another phone in the house and called police. This call to police came in at around 7:00 a.m. and they arrived just a few minutes later. The first thing the police did was ask the victim for a description of the man who had attacked her. She recounted that she wasn't sure if he had on a mask. She described that the man wore what felt like some sort of rubber gloves and a jacket that looked shiny. Then she told them about one thing the man had done in the attack that was especially cruel. During the attack, he had squeezed a thumbnail on her right hand so badly that the pain was terrible.

It seemed like she hadn't even put up a fight, so this was odd as it was unprovoked.

Police were able to determine that a window on the backside of the house was the entry point for the rapist. The glass at the bottom had been broken, and it had been pried open. Police asked the victim if she had anything unusual happen before her attack, and this is when she told them about the phone calls. She also recounted for police that a man she did not know had come to her door a few weeks before the attack asking for her husband, and she thought this was odd because anybody who knew her husband would had known that he had moved out following their separation. A lot of things that happened during this attack, were very typical of the East Area Rapist's M.O., attacking a lone woman, the bindings and targeting a single-story house. There had also been those phone calls to the victims and other relatives on top of the prowlers in the area. There were also some differences in this attack.

She couldn't say for sure if this man was wearing a ski mask, which is what the East Area Rapist typically wore. She also described his voice as not being the normal low hissing, clenched-teeth voice that many victims had described, but rather a clear and hostile voice. This victim also did not mention that the man who had attacked her seemed to have a very small penis, but while there were some differences, the overall M.O., strongly matched, and her attack was officially listed as the fourteenth confirmed East Area Rapist attack. On April 6, 2001, twenty-four years after she was raped by the East Area Rapist, her phone rang. The victim, who by this time had moved and changed her name, got the call between 6:30 and 7:30 p.m. When she answered, a male caller asked for her by name, when she acknowledged that she was the person that caller was looking for, the man again referred to her by her first name saying, "Don't you remember? Don't you want to party again?" When she asked who the caller was, he hung up. The woman couldn't tell for sure whether the caller was the same man who had raped her twenty-four years earlier, but she did feel this call was directly connected to her rape because only a couple of days before she got this call, news about the East Area Rapist had made headlines across the state of California. The East Area Rapist's DNA had been linked to a series of shocking crimes in southern California, but we'll get to those crimes later this season.

On March 18, 1977, only ten days after the East Area Rapist last attack, three taunting phone calls came into the Sacramento County Sheriff's Department. These calls were not recorded, but in the first call received at about 4:15 p.m., the caller said he was the East Area Rapist before laughing and hanging up. Another call came in at around 4:30 p.m. in which the same voice repeated what he had said in the first call. Finally, at about 5:00 p.m., the third call from the same caller came in, and he told the dispatcher that he was East Area Rapist and that he had his next victim stalked, and that police couldn't catch him. Once again, he hung up and he didn't call back.

Later that same day on the 2600 block of Benny Way in Rancho Cordova, a 16-year-old Cordova High School student had just arrived home after her job at a fast food restaurant. She walked into her house at about 10:45 p.m. The house was dark and quiet because her parents had gone away, and her plan that night was to eat some food that she had brought home from her job and then call a friend. She planned to sleep over at the friend's house that night because her parents were not home.

As soon as she walked up to her front door, she noticed that her porch light was off, which was out of the ordinary. She dismissed it, thinking her parents had simply forgotten to turn it on for her. Once she got into her house, she walked into the kitchen and set her food on the counter before picking up the phone to call her friend. She dialed her friend and the phone rang one time when she was startled by a noise behind her, she turned around just in time to see a man standing there with an axe raised above his head. She started to scream, but he stopped her saying, "Don't scream or I'll kill you." He yanked the phone cord out of the wall. Then he warned her again, not to even look at him or he would kill her.

The man shoved the young girl into the family room and ordered her down onto the floor on her stomach. He pulled her hands behind her, took out brown shoe laces, and tied her hands tightly behind her back. He then tied her feet together. Once he had her secured, he opened the back door and made sure that the living room drapes were closed tightly. It was at this point that a phone in the bedroom started to ring. The intruder froze as he listened to the phone ringing. After it stopped, he moved closer to the young girl. He warned her that he had a car parked a block away, and he would kill her if she didn't comply. The man then started cutting up some towels using a pair of scissors. The 16-year-old started to plead with the man not to hurt her. At that point, he tied strips of towel around her eyes and mouth. After she was secured, the stranger walked away.

He came back a few minutes and opened and closed the scissors close to her ear, and then at one point pushed the axe against her neck. Then the phone in the other room started to ring again. It rang for a full minute, and the man seemed nervous. He pulled the strip of towel from the girl's mouth and asked her when her parents would be home. She told him that her parents were out of town and that her sister was sleeping over at a friend's. He then told the girl to shut up. Then this man asked the 16-year-old if she had ever fucked. It was at this point that the helpless girl likely knew what it was about to happen. He asked her again, calling her by her first name. She started to cry and pleaded with the man not to hurt her. He untied her feet. Then he pulled her pants and underwear off. He turned her onto her stomach and placed his penis in her bound hands and ordered her to play with it. His penis felt like it was covered in lotion. After a moment, the man turned her over and raped the 16-year-old. After he raped her, he got up and explored the house, but then he came back and raped her again multiple times.

She had been terrorized by this man for about an hour. By this time, the victim's friend had not heard from her and was getting worried. The 16-year-old was supposed to be at her house by 11:00 p.m. and now it was close to midnight. The friend had called the victim's home but didn't get an answer, so she decided to ask her dad if he would give her a ride over to check on her friend. They hopped in the car and a few minutes later arrived at the home on Benny Way. The friend's father knocked on the front door, and this knock startled the girl's attacker inside, and he immediately raced towards the open back door and ran outside. The victim's friend and her father were able to make their way inside, and they found the terrorized 16-year-old girl. They called the police who arrived on scene just before midnight.

Police started to investigate the scene and determined the attacker had likely gotten in through the garage door and then pried open the door leading into the home from the garage. Outside, they found the green-handled hatchet the man had used in the attack hanging from the fence. Curiously, in the yard sticking up out of the ground was a pen with a local real estate company's name printed on it. It was near this pen that footprints were discovered as well as two empty Dr. Pepper cans that did not come from the victim's home. The police were able to get a description of the attacker from the young girl. She described him as being around five feet, nine inches to five feet, ten inches and wearing a green jacket. In her statement, the girl told police that this man's penis was just a little bit larger than a hot dog. He wore a canvas mask of some sort with eye holes. He was wearing dark, soft-soled shoes that didn't have any heels, and police would determine that the man had made off with some cash and jewelry as well as the victim's driver's license and two of her rings. Her sister's ID was also stolen.

Next, police checked with neighbors. One witness had seen a dark gray, four-door car parked on the street that night that looked out of place. About an hour before the attack, a neighbor across the street from the victim saw a man moving around in the dark, but she couldn't give a detailed description. Another neighbor had reported that their dog started growling and reacting to something near the victim's fence between 8:30 and 9:00 p.m. Police tried to investigate anything that may have happened earlier that day, and later they would find out that the victim's sister, before going over to spend the night at her friend's house, had taken a phone call from a man who identified himself as a roofer. She told the man that her parents were out of town for the weekend. Other witnesses reported seeing an older, yellow truck in the immediate area that day.

It came to light that in the days and weeks before this attack, a nearby neighbor had a burglary, and another home had an intruder while the family was out of the house, but they couldn't find anything missing. One of the most interesting things was that the victim and her family had been receiving several calls for a couple of weeks before the attack. The caller usually said nothing, but on at least one of those calls, it sounded as if there was a female coughing on the other end of the phone. A nearby neighbor also had received similar calls. This area of Benny Way in Rancho Cordova was very close to the first and the third East Area Rapist attacks. The victim's home, once again, was a single-story home. She was a female alone at the house, so this seemed like an East Area Rapist crime to police, the fifteenth confirmed attack. It also seemed as if the phone calls made to police earlier that day from someone claiming to be the East Area Rapist may have really come from him.

After this latest attack, the fifteenth confirmed attack of the East Area Rapist, the case dominated the news. One couldn't live in Sacramento without seeing or hearing daily news headlines about this case. It really was front page news. Orangevale was an area of Sacramento County that had been spared any attacks by the East Area Rapist, but from January of 1977 until April that year, one street in that town started to experience some East Area Rapist-type activity. The street was Richdale Way and most of this activity occurred on the

9500 block. In January, a homeowner caught a stranger in the backyard of a single woman. He confronted the strange man and the man ran off. This person was described as white, in his late twenties, five feet, nine inches to five feet, ten inches with a stocky build.

Not long after this episode, in February, a home close to where the stranger was spotted was burglarized. By spring, multiple homes in this area were receiving hang-up phone calls for several weeks. All they could hear was heavy breathing. By March, there were reports of men claiming to be meter readers spotted in the area, but it turned out they were not meter readers. In late March, one man discovered an empty meat wrapper near the patio where he kept his dog. He also discovered a tennis shoe print near part of his fence as if somebody had climbed it and scuffed it. Starting on the night of April 1 and carrying over past midnight into April 2, several area dogs were reported barking steadily multiple times for about a half hour at a time.

The dogs' barking was very close to one of the homes that had been getting some of the heavy breathing phone calls. Living in this home was a 29-year-old woman who was a Kaiser Hospital pharmacy technician. She had been out late to a movie with her 26-year-old boyfriend who also happened to work with her at the pharmacy. The woman's young children had also attended the movie. They arrived home very late after midnight on the morning of April 2, the pair carried the kids inside and put them into bed. Since it was so late, the woman asked her boyfriend to stay over, and he decided that was a good idea. The pair were in bed and asleep by 2:00 a.m.

Just before 3:30 a.m., the woman woke up to a flashlight shining in her eyes. When she looked up, a masked man was standing in her bedroom doorway. He spoke out, "Don't make a sound. Do you see the gun in my hand?" The horrified woman told the man that she saw his gun. At that point, the man told her to wake up her boyfriend who was still asleep next to her. Once she woke up her boyfriend, he instinctively tried to get out of bed but was blinded by the flashlight. The masked man through clenched teeth growled at him to stop and to not make a move. He ordered them both to rollover on their stomachs. He then warned the couple that he was holding a 45-caliber and had fourteen rounds. He told them that he just wanted their money and he asked the 26-year-old man where his wallet was. The man told the intruder that his wallet was in his pants pocket.

It was then that the intruder told the pair that if they made any type of move, he would kill them like he did to some people in Bakersfield. The man assured them that he would get their money and go and be out of their home in a few minutes. He then instructed the woman to tie her boyfriend's hands behind his back. He shined the light on the bed, showing her some white shoe laces that he had thrown onto the bed. The boyfriend told the woman to do as the hooded man said, and it was then that the attacker barked out to the boyfriend to shut up. He told the female to make sure she tied him tightly.

As she tied her boyfriend, the masked assailant walked close to him and put the gun close to his head, warning him not to look up, or he would kill them. The man once again told the couple that he would be gone soon and heading back to his camp down by the American River. Their attacker then tied the male victim's feet together, and then turned his attention to the female victim. He tied her hands behind her back as she was faced down on the bed. The hooded attacker then walked out of the room, leaving the pair helpless on the bed. The couple could hear the intruder tearing through closets. Before long, he was back in their bedroom, and he was carrying several dishes. He stacked the dishes on the male victim's back and warned him that if he heard the dishes rattle, he would kill everyone in the home. He took the woman out of the room, telling her he was going to tie her up in the hallway.

Once he got her into the hallway, he stuck something sharp into her back and ordered her to walk down the hall and into the living room. It was there that he ordered her down on her stomach. The attacker then tied the woman's feet with shoelaces and blindfolded her with a towel. He walked out in the kitchen, and the woman could hear dishes rattling. When the masked man walked back into the living room, he was carrying more dishes. He asked the woman if she had matches, and she told him that she didn't. He then placed the cup and saucer on her back. At that point, the man walked back into the kitchen, and she could hear him eating food. After a few minutes, he walked down the hallway and checked on the man who was still tied up, lying on the bed.

After checking on the boyfriend and finding him still secure, the man walked by the female and told her he was going to go out to her car and get her purse. The woman wondered to herself how he knew that her purse was in the car. Once he came back from getting the purse, he straddled over her back and removed the dishes. He then placed his penis in her bound hand and told her to hold it gently. After a moment, he pulled back and untied her ankles and then removed her underwear. Then he asked her a question. He said, "You have to tell me the truth and if you don't, I'll find out and kill you both." The question was, "Did you fuck tonight?" The woman said, "No," but she was lying to the man. The couple had been intimate before they fell asleep. It was then that the man sexually assaulted her. After a couple of minutes and without any warning, he jumped up and walked off. A moment later, he was back, and he placed high heel shoes on her feet.

For the next hour, the masked assailant alternated between raping the woman, eating in the kitchen, and checking on the boyfriend. During the rapes, the man told the woman that he was in the army before and had sex with a lot of girls. When he went in for the last time to check on the boyfriend, he leaned over the man who is still tied in bed with dishes on his back and said, "Next place, next town." Then, suddenly, the man seemed to vanish. The house was quiet. The family dog who had been absent during the attack was suddenly walking around the house. Sensing that the attacker had left, the male victim was able to free himself. He then called police before checking on his girlfriend and freeing her. Police received the call for help just after 5:00 a.m. and they arrived very soon after.

One of the first things they found was that the assailant had cut the power to the lamps and clock and had lit a candle, which may have been why he was looking for matches. He also cut the power to the television and heater. Police were not able to determine a point of entry for the attack but discovered that the rapist had left the home through a sliding glass door. Next, the police asked the pair to describe the attacker. He was white, about five feet, ten inches and had a medium built. He had worn a white mask with eye and mouth holes. He talked through clenched teeth. The male victim felt sure that the man had a hint of a German accent. The female victim stated that the rapist had a very small penis. She then recounted two things that seem to stand out to her. She mentioned that the attacker knew she kept her purse in her car. The other thing she mentioned was that the rapist had placed high heels on her feet, which was something she would do when she was intimate with her boyfriend. It was as if the man somehow knew their secrets.

Police turned their attention to neighbors. They found that one neighbor between 4:30 and 5:00 a.m. had seen a small foreign car circling the block several times at around the same time the rapist left. Another neighbor thought she'd seen a large American car with a loud exhaust near the victim's home. Police learned that just a few weeks before the attack, the home next door had been put up for sale and a for sale sign was on the front lawn. Two different men who matched the rapist's description had come by in the days after it went up for sale to inquire about the home. One was alone and the other was with a woman. Neither of these men were ever identified.

There's so much activity here that's very East Area Rapist-like, stalking, prowling, dogs barking, and then during the attack, placing his penis into her bound hands. There were some things that were new. First, the town of Orangevale was struck, but one thing that stood out was that this was the first attack in which a man was present in the home, and while most East Area Rapist's attacks didn't involve a gun, this one did. Did he feel as if he needed to have a gun because there was a man in the equation? It seemed as if the East Area Rapist was not going to take any chances and after this attack it truly seemed like no one was safe, not lone women and not couples. The East Area Rapist could pop up any place at any time.

The next East Area Rapist attack would occur back in the city of Carmichael on the 6100 block of Sherilyn Way. This street had been experiencing unusual occurrences since February. Around dinner time on a day in late February, a resident and her daughter were inside their home when they saw a man outside jump their fence and land in their backyard and instead of leaving, the man just walked around in their backyard. Fearful, the mother called police, but the man left before they arrived.

About a month later in a nearby backyard, a residence spotted a fleeing prowler. The only description of this man was that he was white and in his mid-twenties, around five feet, nine and 150 pounds. Then in April, another home close by was burglarized. This pattern of burglaries and prowling was a signal that the East Area Rapist was about to strike there, but somehow police didn't recognize it. Another incident on this street happened on April 11, 1977. A young woman and her boyfriend caught a man in the backyard of her house. He appeared to be checking out their locks, but he raced off as soon as he realized they were watching him, they were able to describe the prowler as five feet, ten inches with dark blonde shoulder length hair. A few days later, a dog in a nearby residents was barking wildly at something or someone outside of the home.

On April 14, a woman saw a suspicious man drive by her. The car, a light-colored Valiant, drove by slowly, and the driver was staring at her. She felt uneasy. It may have been because she had been receiving a series of hang-up phone calls for two to three weeks prior. The 19-year-old clerk typist, who was separated from her husband, tried to dismiss the incidents, but later that night after going to bed, she would come to regret not taking the calls or seeing the man in the car more seriously. The 19-year-old and her boyfriend were asleep in her bed. Early in the morning of April 15 at around 2:30 a.m., they were awakened by the sound of someone in their bedroom and by a flashlight shining in their eyes. Suddenly a hissing voice came from behind the light, "Don't look over this way or I'll kill you." The young man looked anyway and could see a gun in the intruder's hand. Then he heard the hammer being cocked. It was then that the man asked the couple if they knew what a 45 magnum was.

The man walked closer to the couple who were frozen in place. Then the woman felt the blade of a knife at her throat. The intruder spoke through clenched teeth, instructing the young woman to tie up her boyfriend. He threw her some black shoelaces. After the woman tied her boyfriend's wrists, the assailant tied hers as well before retying the boyfriends more securely. Then he left the room and wandered around the house.

This was part of the East Area Rapist script; he would do certain things in a certain order, and we've talked about it time and time again. He would secure the victim or victims and then he would walk around the house.

In this incident, after several minutes, he came back in the bedroom and told the woman to get up and come with him. He told her that he could not find her purse. As he walked out with the 19-year-old victim, he warned the man that if he moved an inch, he would cut his girlfriend's throat. He walked out with the girl, but after a minute came back in and tied the male victim's hands even tighter. Then he tied his feet using some electrical cord.

It seemed as if this attacker did not want there to be even the slightest chance that the male would get loose. When the assailant walked the girl into the living room, she saw the lamp had been covered with a towel. At that point, he blindfolded her and tied her feet together. Then he left her there. Next, he walked back into the bedroom carrying plates, and he stacked them on the man's back and warned him that if the plates fell, he wouldn't hesitate to kill his girlfriend. The stacking of dishes on victims to use it as an alarm system of sorts now had become part of that script.

Sticking with his script, the next thing that the woman felt was the man place his penis in her bound hands. Then he put the gun to her head and told her to talk dirty to him, and he gave her certain phrases that he wanted her to repeat back to him. All the while, he was talking to her through clenched teeth. He then sexually assaulted the helpless woman.

Afterwards, he left her to go into the kitchen and then started to eat something. He went outside onto the patio for a few moments and then returned and assaulted the woman again. Right around this time, both the woman and the intruder heard the dishes fall off her bound boyfriend's back and the intruder went to check on him. The dishes had simply fallen off. The young man was not trying to escape. The attacker stacked the plates on his back once more and covered the man's face with a blanket and mentioned that he would kill his girlfriend. He then went out once again into the kitchen where he ate more food, and then once again he raped the woman who was still tied in the living room.

He started to rifle through the contents of her purse, and he found two bottles of generic medication. The next thing that he did was odd because he went back in to where the victim was and asked her where she kept her codeine, and it turned out that the two bottles of generic meds and her purse were generic codeine. She told the man that they were in her purse, and he went back into the kitchen and started to run water in the sink. Later, the two empty pill bottles would be found in the kitchen. The question is, what happened to the pills that were in these bottles? Was he running the water to flush the pills down the sink or did he take them with him when he left? After he started running the water, she didn't hear any more noise and after a while she sensed that he was gone. She started to try and free yourself. Both victims were able to free themselves, and then they tried to call police, but the phone lines in the kitchen and bedroom had been cut. They ran to the neighbors for help. From there, the police were called and arrived quickly on the scene.

Police found that the sliding glass door lock had been pried and broken open, so they determined that that was the point of entry, and for some reason the thermostat had been turned down low, and a small amount of cocaine that belonged to the couple was missing. In their description of the attacker to the police, they stated he was about five feet, nine inches to five feet, ten inches, had brown eyes and collar length, dark blonde hair. He was wearing a ski mask of some sort, but they couldn't describe the mask very well for police.

The female victim was taken to Sacramento Hospital for treatment and later she would be hypnotized. Specifically, police wanted to ask her about the strange car that she had seen hours before she was attacked and under hypnosis, she was able to provide police with a license plate number, but it turned out that the plate number she gave them had never been issued, so that was basically a dead end. The male victim recounted that the attacker sounded to have an Asian accent, but he felt that it might been faked.

The East Area Rapist was starting to get too comfortable attacking couples, and there would be no letup in sight for the residents of Sacramento. The next attack and the East Area Rapist case would come on May 3, 1977. This time it would occur on the 8300 block of La Riviera Drive in Sacramento, and, as in most East Area Rapist attacks, it was proceeded by some troubling events. Mid-April, various residents on this block started getting hang-up phone calls. One of the people receiving the calls would turn out to be the next East Area victim. She started getting calls in late April, about a week before she was attacked.

Shortly after midnight on May 3 at around 12:30 a.m., the 30-year-old housewife and college student heard a loud bang in her backyard. She instinctively ran to check all the locks and windows and found everything was secured. She looked out in the backyard but didn't see anything unusual. By 1:00 a.m., she decided everything was okay, and she went to sleep. Her husband, an Air Force serviceman at Mather Air Force Base, was already in bed.

Around the same time, a neighbor close to this victim heard someone walking outside on some gravel. The next day, this resident would find that her side gate was open.

At around 3:00 a.m., the 30-old-woman was awakened in her bed to the sight of a man standing in the bedroom doorway. He was shining a flashlight in her face. She reached over and immediately woke up her husband. The man quickly told them that he just wanted their money and that he had a 45-caliber handgun. He let the couple know that if he wanted to, he could easily kill them and get across the levee to his camp. He walked up to the male victim and placed the barrel of the gun against his head and repeated the threats before throwing a shoelace to the female victim and hissing at her to tie her husband up. He ordered her to tie him very tightly, or he would kill everybody in the house. The couple couldn't risk any type of heroics as they feared for the safety of their two young children who were sleeping in their bedrooms.

After the male victim was tied, the intruder ordered the female onto her stomach, and he bound her hands tightly behind her back. Then the intruder said that he needed money for cocaine to get his fix. Remember, in the last attack, the East Area Rapist had stolen a small amount of cocaine from the victims. In another attack, he mentioned to a victim that he had a camp near the river, so it seemed as if he was sticking to his script. Also changing it as he went along and incorporating specific things from his recent attacks.

The intruder tied the man's hands tighter, then tied his ankles. The male victim volunteered his wallet to the intruder telling him it was on the dresser. After the attacker looked through the cash in the wallet, he told the couple that they had better have more cash, or he would kill them both. It was then that the wife directed the man to her purse, which was upstairs. The man started to shake like he was having some withdrawal to drugs, but the couple would later report that the man seemed to be faking the shakes.

After this shaking, the assailant covered the husband's head with the sheet and placed the jewelry box on his back. He warned him that if the jewelry box fell off, he would kill everyone in the house. Sticking to the script that we've seen, he ordered the wife up, placed the gun to the back of her head, and told her to walk out of the bedroom. He ordered her to take him upstairs to find her purse. Once he found her purse, he threw her down to the floor and tied her feet together. He put what turned out to be a shower cap over her face, and then she heard him walk off and head down the stairs. The man had gone downstairs and placed dishes on the male victim's back in addition to the jewelry box that was already on it. Then he made his way through the house rifling through closets and cupboards. The victim could hear what sound like a zipper bag opening and closing.

Suddenly, the man was standing by her side, and he told her he wanted to move her and untied her ankles. He sat her up and left for a moment, going into the kitchen and opening the refrigerator before quickly returning to her side. She heard a wet slurping sound, and she knew that he was masturbating. In typical East Area Rapist fashion, he told the woman to guess what he was doing. Following his M.O., he placed his penis into the woman's bound hands. During this period, he talked with the woman and told her that she was very tall, and keep in mind this victim was six foot tall. After all this small talk, the intruder raped this woman.

After the rape, he secured the 30-year-old woman again and stacked plates on her back. He warned her not to move, then left the room and went downstairs. He started rummaging through the master bedroom closet next to the helpless male victim who was still tied up on the bed. The intruder asked the male victim if he was in the service, and he replied that he was in the Air Force, to which the attacker replied that he too had been in the service but had gotten kicked out. The man walked out of the room and went into the kitchen where he started eating. After he finished eating, he walked in to check on the female victim, who was still tied upstairs. He placed the gun to her neck and asked her, "You don't want to die, do you?" As soon as she started to tell the assailant, "No." He stopped her, and he said, "Shut up." She became very frightened and started to cry and once again, he told the woman to shut up. The man left her side and before long the house was quiet. After a while the victims freed themselves and called police.

Police got to the house sometime between 5:00 a.m. and 6:00 a.m. The attacker had stayed in the house for about ninety minutes. Police quickly found that the point of entry was a pried sliding glass door, a typical entry point for the East Area Rapist. The couple was able to describe their attacker as being white and wearing a light tan or beige ski mask. He seemed to be in his twenties and he was about 165 to 170 pounds. As usual, he was described as having a very small penis. When it came to the height, they felt the attacker was about five feet, eight inches to five feet, nine inches. The female victim was very specific because being six-foot-tall and walking next to him, she had looked down and could see the top of the attacker's head. They described the man's voice as articulate, but when he got nervous, he would breathe heavily. While most of the M.O. here was typical East Area Rapist M.O., choosing to strike a two-story home was not.

The female victim was taken to Sacramento Medical Center around 7:00 a.m. Police then brought bloodhounds in and tracked the assailant's scent to a levee behind the victim's home. A knife that came from the victim's home was found near the levee along with two empty beer cans, but there was no proof that the beer cans were left there by the assailant.

Several months after the attack, early on the morning of January 20, 1978, the female victim in this incident answered the phone. On the line was a man who said, "I haven't struck in a while, you will be my next victim, I'm going to fuck you in the butt. See you soon." Within ten minutes of this call, an identical call would be made to the twenty-seventh victim in the series. It's important to know that the pace of these attacks was picking up, and the time in between attacks was getting shorter and shorter. As we go through this, you're going to see just how quickly the frequency of these attacks escalate. It's not going to be a question of is the East Area Rapist going to strike again. The only questions were, where would he strike next, and who would be his next victim?

SEASON TWO, EPISODE FIVE

The East Area Rapist had committed his eighteenth confirmed attack on May 3, 1977, in the city of Sacramento. One day later on the night of May 4, in the city of Orange Veil on the 9500 block of Winter Burke Way, a 34-year-old man who worked for a brokerage firm had invited his 25-year-old female coworker to come by his new home for a tour and to discuss some business. The man had literally just moved in. He didn't have any shades or curtains on the windows yet.

The female coworker arrived at his house around 10:30 p.m. and brought along her two dogs. They thought it would be good for the dogs to run around in the backyard, so they opened the back door and let the dogs out. Both dogs immediately started barking at a big oak tree in the backyard. On the other side of the fence, a neighbor's dog was also barking at something in that same area. The pair didn't see anyone or anything going on in the backyard, and they discounted the dogs barking and headed inside to talk. Ultimately, they would begin to become intimate with each other.

The pair spent time together until just after midnight. At about 12:15 a.m. in the very early hours of May 5, the woman packed up her belongings and the dogs and headed outside to leave for home. Her coworker walked her to the front door. As she opened the door, her dogs went out ahead of her and started barking immediately. They were on high alert, and the hair on their backs was standing. Suddenly a hooded man jumped from the darkness, from the garage area of the home. He was holding a gun and told the pair to go back inside immediately, or he would blow their brains all over the house.

Once they got back in, they were ordered down onto their stomachs. The masked man threw black shoe strings to the female victim and instructed her to tie up her male companion. The dogs were barking, and the intruder threatened the woman, telling her that she had better shut the dogs up, or he would kill both the couple and the dogs. Once he had the male victim tied up, the man told her to take the dogs into one of the bedrooms and lock them up.

After she locked up the dogs, she returned to the living room, and the man ordered her to the floor next to the male victim. He tied her wrist very tightly but did not tie her ankles. After the woman was once again secured, the attacker turned off the lights in the home. He then walked into the kitchen and came back with some dishes and placed them on the helpless pair's backs. The male victim started to plead with the intruder to take what he wanted. The masked man told him that he would take their money and go, and then held a knife to the bound man's neck and ordered him to shut up, hissing through clenched teeth.

The attacker ordered the female victim to her feet and at gunpoint, directed her towards one of the bedrooms. This is typical East Area Rapist behavior: lie to the victims, get them to cooperate, tell them he just wants their money, and then separate them. Once he had the 25-year-old woman in the bedroom, he held the knife to her throat while he unbuttoned her shirt. He cut her bra open using the knife, and then blindfolded her with a towel. Sticking with his script, the next thing the woman heard was this man lubricating himself and masturbating close to her, and then finally sexually assaulting her.

After the initial rape, the masked man left the room and wandered through the home going through drawers, closets and the like. This home had just been moved into. There wasn't much there to rummage through. The man also visited the kitchen and ate some food that was in the refrigerator. He returned to the female victim and then raped her again.

This happened multiple times. In between the sexual attacks, the man would wander through the house. During one of the attacks, the rapist told the female victim, "You better swear to God that you didn't see a van down the street."

You must wonder why he would make this statement. Did he really have a van down the street? Because if so, why would he volunteer that info? Or as some investigators think, was he deliberately providing the victims with bogus info to pass along to police? Not long after mentioning the van down the street, the house fell silent. The female victim waited for a while and then was able to get to her feet and make her way out to the living room where the male victim was still bound. There was no sign of the attacker, and she was able to untie her male companion

Once the couple were free, they tried to use their kitchen phone to call police, but the cord had been cut. They decided to run to the neighbor's house for help. Police arrived on the scene around 3:00 a.m. They called in an ambulance to take the pair to Sacramento Medical Center. Before they were taken away, they were able to give the police some good information about their attacker. They described him as being white, around five feet, ten inches to six feet tall, and about 160 pounds. The female victim also described his penis as being small and thin, no more than five inches.

They described the assailant as having light colored eyes that they could see through the beige colored ski mask the man was wearing. His voice was low as if he was soft spoken, and it had a high pitch to it. The gun he carried was a large caliber, silver semiautomatic handgun. After the victims were taken to the hospital, the investigators focused their attention outside of the residence. They checked that area close to the big tree in the backyard where the dogs had been barking as if startled by something. They found scuff marks around the tree and tracks from a tennis shoe.

Also found in the backyard was an empty beer can, something found at other East Area Rapist crime scenes. After processing the crime scene, the investigators made their way to some of the neighbors' homes to question them. It was at that point that they discovered some troubling pre-attack incidents. Only about five hours before the attack, a full-size American made car, green or blue in color, was seen parked in front of the victim's home. Inside, the driver, a white male who looked to be in his thirties appeared to be reading a map, but he never exited the vehicle.

Only a week before the attack, a man posing as a plumber visited a nearby home on two separate occasions. The man was described as white, in his early twenties, five feet, eleven inches, with short curly brown hair, and a pockmarked face. His car was an older, rusty Ford or Chevy. The man was never identified. On May 2, only three days before the attack, a neighbor coming out of her garage saw a strange car parked across the street from her home. Something told her that the car did not belong there. She attempted to make her way over to get the car's plate, but as she did, the driver quickly drove off. The very next day on May 3, another neighbor saw a metallic gray Plymouth parked in front of her home. She called police to investigate, but by the time they arrived, the car was gone.

So once again, we have an entire section of a street with many residents experiencing people in cars who didn't belong there preceding an East Area Rapists attack. The East Area Rapist had struck twice within a two-day period, and it seemed as if these attacks were coming in rapid succession. The next East Area Rapist attack would happen on May 14, 1977, and would occur on the 6100 block of Merlindale Drive in Citrus Heights. This area of Merlindale Drive had been suffering serious East Area Rapist-like activity dating all the way back to December of 1976. That's when a woman found a plastic bag in her bushes containing gloves and a flashlight.

All through the spring of 1977, odd people canvased the neighborhood claiming to be doing work for organizations that didn't exist. Prowlers were witnessed. In one incident, somebody awoke to a flashlight shining through a window, and another neighbor scared off someone trying to pry open their sliding glass door. Now, this is a lot of activity going on around this street. It's hard to imagine how police we're not staking out this area with all these strange things going on over this extended period.

In February 1977, one resident was so unnerved by hang-up phone calls she was getting, that she decided to move. Once she moved to her new address, the calls picked up again. At her old house on Merlindale, a new couple had moved in, and they too started to experience trouble right away. It started with hang-up phone calls. In mid-May, after living there for a few months, they had scared a prowler out of their backyard. In the early morning hours of May 14, 1977, this couple would become the next victims of the East Area Rapist.

The husband was 30 years old and the wife was 22 years old. They were both in the restaurant industry. That morning, they went to bed around 3:00 a.m. Before she fell asleep, the woman heard something hit the outside of the house, and she immediately sat up in bed. She woke up her husband and told him what she had heard. He dismissed it as being a tree branch. This would turn out to be a big mistake because after a few uneasy minutes and not hearing anything else, the 22-year-old woman fell back asleep.

It was about five minutes later, just before 4:00 a.m., that the victims were awakened by a flashlight in their eyes, and a man standing in their doorway. He was wearing a nylon stocking on his face and holding a gun. The intruder spoke out, "You make a sound and I'll kill you. I have a 45 and I'll kill you if you move." He then told the startled couple, he would be taking their money and some food and, then he would be leaving in his van.

He ordered the pair to turn over on their stomachs, threw the woman shoe laces, and ordered her to tie up her husband. Once the woman had her husband tied, the intruder tied the woman's hands behind her back. When he tied her hands, he tied them very hard, violently. At this point, her husband pleaded with the man not to hurt her, but the assailant told him to shut up. The female victim then realized that her cat was in the bed, and fearing it would be hurt, she told the attacker that the cat was in the bed, but he told her to shut up as well.

The assailant then tied both victims' feet. He placed the gun against the man's head and asked him where his money was. The victim told the man that it was on his dresser. The masked man walked over to the dresser only to find a big bottle of pennies and smashed the bottle, breaking it. The man then went to the closet. The couple's pet dog was lying quietly on the floor, and the man picked it up and carried it into another room.

The intruder found a green file box in the closet and asked the couple if there was cash in it, but they told him no. They said that the box only contained insurance papers. The masked man told them that if they were lying, he would kill them. He pried open the file box and found the insurance papers just as the couple have told him, and he threw them down. After coming up empty with the file box, the attacker told the couple he needed to go outside and take a break. He walked out of their sliding glass door and into their backyard, before returning just a few minutes later.

Once the man walked back into the home, it was time for the next phase of the familiar script. The intruder asked the woman where her purse was, and she told him that it was in the family room. The man left the room and came back with some dishes and stacked them on the male victim's back. He told the woman he could not find her purse, and she needed to come with him to find it. He cut the bindings on her feet, and, as he walked her out of the room, warned her husband that if the dishes fell, he would slit his wife's throat.

Once they got into the family room, the woman pointed out her purse to the man, and he dumped it out, taking her cash. She was extremely afraid, and she pleaded with him not to kill her. The man said he wouldn't if she did exactly as he instructed. The attacker walked back into the bedroom and placed his gun to the husband's head and warned him not to make any moves. He told the husband that he was going to get a beer and rest. The helpless husband listened as the man rummage through the house. He eventually made his way back to the female victim in the family room.

The man walked up to the terrified woman holding a bottle of Vaseline lotion and a towel, both of which had come from the victim's bathroom. He ripped the towel and placed half of it over the television set that was turned on, slightly illuminated in the room. The other half was placed over the woman's eyes as a blindfold. Once she was blindfolded, right on cue, the man placed his lubricated penis into her bound hands and told her to play with it.

The man told the 22-year-old woman how beautiful she was as he removed the bindings on her ankles. He then removed her pajamas and underwear. The man told her that he was going to take her with him in his van and asked her how she'd like to be in the river. She took this to mean that he was going to kill her and throw her in the river, and she started sobbing. The attacker told her to shut up and then sexually assaulted her. After the attack, he told the victim that he was going to cut her phone cord. It was then that she heard a snip, just like the sound of a phone cord being cut.

After the assault, the attacker grabbed at the rings on the woman's fingers, but she made a fist, and he couldn't get them off. He put the gun to her head, and she stopped fighting. The man took the rings off her hand and walked away and out the back door. He had left just after 5:00 a.m., about ninety minutes after the attack started. At about the same time, a paper boy delivering newspapers, saw a blue van possibly sanded down, driving away from the area. The couple were able to quickly get free, and when they checked the phone, they found that had not been cut after all. They contacted police who arrived shortly after 5:30 a.m. The married couple recounted the attack for investigators. They described the assailant as being about five feet, nine inches to five feet, ten inches tall, with dark brown hair about shoulder length, and through the stocking mask, they could see a few days' worth of stubble on his face.

Police discovered the entry point to be a window on the north side of the house. The attacker had climbed in after removing the screen. His escape route, after fleeing through the back-door, led over the fence towards a nearby apartment complex close to where the paper boy had seen a van drive away. The victims detailed the items that were stolen, which included a wedding band and engagement ring and a class ring. In addition, the assailant had taken photographs and the female victim driver's license. The couple admitted to the police that they had some marijuana out in the open, but the attacker didn't take it. They had one other piece of information for police; not long before the couple had turned in for bed, they received a phone call that was a wrong number. The male caller had asked for a Mrs. Jones.

Only a couple days later, on the night of May 16, 1977, just after 11:00 p.m., a resident on the 5700 block of Haskell Avenue saw a man in his yard. We interviewed this resident that we'll refer to as Mr. Haskell. He recounted for us just what happened that night over forty years ago.

May 16, 1977, if I remember correctly, I was watching television and glanced up and saw like a shadow go by through the kitchen window. Of course, I jumped up because the kitchen window is next-- it's not out front, it's by the side yard. I jumped up and looked and saw this man. It looked like he had some sort of hat on or something. Think he had a ski mask on that was rolled up on top of his head. It wasn't a hat that had a rim on it. I ran to try to catch this guy, but he was like an athlete. I've never seen anybody like this. I'm six foot, four, and that time I was probably 280, but this guy was-- I'm saying probably five foot, ten. He had a dark jacket on, Levi's, and he's wearing tennis shoes, but he hit the fence with one arm and brought both feet over the top just like an athlete. It was unbelievable. Almost

*like he was military trained, or athletic trained, or
something like that.*

We asked Mr. Haskell just how close he had come to catching
the prowler.

*Right at the beginning, I was very close. If my arms
were six foot long, I probably could have had him. He
was skinny. I'm big, so I would have absolutely kicked
his rear. But because I had no idea what was going on,
it didn't click in my mind that it could have been this
guy. I know that everybody was nervous, the whole city
was kind of in a panic because of all this. Everybody
was locking their doors. But yes, he was pretty close.
I almost had him. I did not get a good look at his face,
I just got the right side. I could tell he was white, and
I'm guessing between five feet, seven inches to five feet,
ten inches tall, somewhere in there and very athletic.
Again, this guy one armed over the fence. This is like
you see in the movies. It's unbelievable. These are six-
foot-tall fences. It was very easy for him. It was like
he practiced it, or he was very athletic, or you know.
I talked to a friend of mine who was a Marine and
he said, "You know, we have to do that all the time. I
mean, that's how we're trained." And I thought, "Wow,
I wonder if the guy's a Marine or something."*

The prowler seemed to have lost Mr. Haskell. A police officer
showed up quickly in the area after responding to a prowler
call, and he found Mr. Haskell still trying to locate the prowler
near a SMUD electrical substation.

*The deputy looked up and saw something, and he
took off running. I remember, I don't know if he had
a walkie-talkie or what he had, but he kept yelling
something and took off after what looked like to be
the same guy. When he came back like thirty minutes
later he said, "You know, somebody just tried to run
me over. I was trying to flag the car down. Somebody
tried to run me over."*

The police officer witnessed the car pull away from the curb on Locust Avenue, just southeast of Mr. Haskell's home. He tried to flag the car down to ask the driver if he could assist by shining the car's headlights into a nearby field to eliminate it. Without warning, the driver accelerated and attempted to run down the officer. It appeared that the vehicle was driven by the suspect fleeing the scene. An extensive police presence was immediately brought in to keep the prowler who was possibly the East Area Rapist from getting out of the area.

I gave the description to them and boy, I'm telling you, it was like sheriff departments from all over showed up. There were cars everywhere. Helicopter, cars, all kinds of stuff.

Despite the all-out effort to capture this man, all the hard work proved fruitless, and the man seemed to vanish into the darkness. Mr. Haskell described the aftermath of the incident for us.

There was an empty house two from mine, that I think the guy ran to or through. The sheriff and I went over there, and it looked like somebody had been there. There's an empty house. It was brand new, just was sold, and it looked like somebody set up some sort of a little camp or something there, maybe, I don't know. There was no electricity, but there was a-- I don't even know if you'd call it an orange crate, some sort of box or something. They found some evidence there, and I don't remember what it was. We got an alarm system installed the next day.

Within a day of Mr. Haskell having the alarm installed, his home was broken into.

Looks like somebody came in through my bathroom window later. I can't remember what the police found. They found something to do with paint. Small paint particles or something. In the laundry room, there's an attic access, and it looks like somebody had stood on the washer and dryer to get up in the attic. I think that's exactly where they found those paint particles. It wasn't in the bathroom, I think they found them there. The alarm system is not as sophisticated as the ones we have today. It was just the front door, the garage door, and the back-sliding door. Then it had pressure pads. A few days later, I got a religious pamphlet on my door. Each page had something written on it, but it wasn't handwriting. It was like a stamp or something.

It was like somebody took an edge of something and put ink on it and then wrote. It wasn't real handwriting. It said, "You think you caught me, next time you die," or something like that. I think it was a word per page. Then the Sheriff's Department said-- I called them and they came over and got it, and looked at it and they said, "Wow." One lieutenant showed up at the house later and said, "I'd like to put a couple of deputies in your house because if this guy comes back, we'll be able to get him." I said, sure. My work was only a few miles away. Before I went home, they would show up. I would put them in the back of my truck and open the garage door, roll down the garage door and let those two deputies out for, I think it was two or three nights in a row. Nothing ever happened. We used to get phone calls, several phone calls a week with nobody on the other line, just dead line. It sounded like somebody stuck the mute button on. It was before, but we didn't really pay any attention to it, so I'm going to say maybe a month so. It went on for a month. My girl wouldn't even answer the phone, so I would answer it. I would answer it with profanity. Nobody said anything. So, I would say, "Come and get me you piece of crap. Yada, yada, yada."

The sheriff of the department said, "Hey, have you got any calls?" Of course, I put two and two together. I'm trying to entice the guy to come see me. It was *probably a few months, and it wasn't regular thing, it was very irregular. It wasn't like once a week. Before it was probably once a week, but after it started a few times and then it would not go for a month or so, and then a few times more. I would say, probably a few months afterwards, but none on a regular basis. It was very irregular.*

Mr. Haskell had been lucky. The prowler, who was likely the East Area Rapist, despite getting into his house and leaving a threatening note, never wound up attacking him. Despite escaping the police dragnet at that time, this predator was not done.

Then we heard that night that the East Area Rapist had-- Two hours later I think or three hours later from when I saw him, and when we all-- the police saw him, that he actually was at somebody's house.

While police were occupied that night trying to hunt Mr. Haskell's prowler down, Carl Michael, a resident on Sandbars Circle, five miles away, was feeling secure. He was confident and not worried about the East Area Rapist coming into his house. After all, he had been the man that stood up at the town hall meeting months earlier.

Perhaps he would have been more nervous had he known that some of his neighbors had been getting phone calls since early 1977, and many other had seen prowlers. Other neighbors reported packs of people claiming to be census workers walking through the neighborhood, but the census was not supposed to be conducted until 1980, three years later. In the months of April and May, this man and his wife began to get hang-up phone calls. At this point, if these hang-up phone calls didn't alarm them, it's because police had still not disclosed to the public that many of the victims of the East Area Rapist had received hang-up phone calls prior to being attacked.

In early May, somebody shot BB gun holes through this man's window. In another occasion, his garage door appeared to be pried. In mid-day, the man's wife noticed a stranger walk through a yard and towards the neighbor's home, but she didn't pay much attention to it. There was a lot of activity happening around on Sandbar Circle and much of it right around this man's house, the same man who had voiced his disbelief publicly of what the East Area Rapist was capable of doing. It turned out, this man and his wife would be the next victims of the East Area Rapist.

The male victim, a 31-year-old manufacturing employee, and his 26-year old wife, a college student, were home on May 16. They were joined by their children and the male victim's father who had been visiting from his home in Italy. The victim's father and the couple's children went to sleep around 10 p.m. The male and the female victims went to bed around 11:00.

Early in the morning hours of May 17 at around 1:30 a.m., a female victim awoke to a bright flashlight shining in her eyes. She could see the outline of the man holding it. The man hissed through clenched teeth in what sounded like a stutter and whisper, "Look at me. Do you hear me?" She did hear him, and she was scared. As if it was a bad dream, she pulled the covers over her head. The whispering voice warned her that he had a 45 magnum and ordered her to take the cover off over her head.

The man started to bang on their door to get their attention, and the male victim woke up. As he tried to get up, the intruder shined the light in his eyes and told him to stay in the bed. He then ordered the husband and wife to turn over onto their stomachs. He told the pair that he was going to take their money and jewels. He then threw shoelaces to the woman, ordered her to tie her husband's hands tightly behind his back. Then the intruder tied the female victim's hands behind her back.

Once the husband was secured, the intruder tied his hands even tighter and then tied his feet. He held the gun to the male victim's head, and the bound husband started to say something, but the intruder, who they could clearly see was wearing a ski mask, told him to shut up and warned him that if he said another word, he would kill everybody in the house. It was then after the attacker had both the husband and the wife tied securely that he opened the sliding glass door and stepped outside.

The assailant sounded as if he were throwing items into a metal box outside. After a couple of minutes, he returned to the bound couple and placed something on the male victim's back. He then started to open their drawers and looked in their closet. He stopped searching and told the couple he was going to get something to eat, and if he heard any noise while he was gone, he would kill everyone in the house.

The intruder was gone quite a while. It seemed as if he was gone perhaps thirty minutes. The victims thought that he might be gone before he once again started making noise, letting them know that he was still there. In sticking with his script, it came to the point where the attacker needed to remove the female victim from the same room as the male. He asked her where her purse was, and she told her it's on top of the refrigerator. The man ordered the bound woman up and told her she needed to go with him to get her purse.

At gun point, the woman walked with the intruder into the kitchen. The masked man then led her into the living room and ordered her on to her stomach. He tied her feet. She could see that a blanket had been placed over the lamp to make a softly lit area. The intruder went into the kitchen and got some dishes walked back to the husband who was still tied up in his bed. He placed the dishes on his back before once again threatening to kill everyone in the house if the man made a noise. He walked back into the living room towards the female victim.

The attacker walked past the victim, and into the kitchen where he ate food. After eating, he then went back to the female victim. He told the woman that he needed more money. She told him that they had a bunch of coins. She let the man know where he could find them, and he left the room. He returned a few minutes later and stood very close to her. She felt the man's lubricated penis in her bound hands. He instructed the woman to rub him and addressed her by a shortened version of her first name.

The man untied the woman's ankles, then he raped her. Not once but multiple times. He made this woman do some very disgusting things. In between the assaults, he would take walks back and forth to check on her husband. He seemed to be much angrier than he did in most of the other attacks. He took a break at one point. Told the woman he wanted to grab something to eat and a couple of beers. That he was going to go outside and enjoy them.

At one point, the attacker said to the woman that he had never killed before. Added that he was going to start. He told her, "I want you to tell those fuckers, those pigs. I'm going home to my apartment. I have bunches of televisions. I'm going to listen on the radio and watch television. If I hear about this, I'm going to go up tomorrow and kill two people. People are going to die." The woman agreed that she would tell the police to keep the man at bay.

After a bit of silence, the husband had had enough and figured the intruder was gone. He started yelling out as loud as he could in Italian to his father. Who was awakened by his screams. It's amazing more that this man's father and the couple's children slept through the entire attack. The father came in to find the couple tied up and removed their bindings. They then contacted police who raced to the scene.

Police immediately took a description of the attacker, who was described by the victim as being white, and about five feet, eight inches to five feet,ten tall. His voice sounded young in his twenties perhaps. Of course, the female victim also described him having a small penis. Both victims describe the rapist as talking through clenched teeth. The mask he wore was described as beige. They were able to determine the rapist had made off with an undisclosed amount of cash, coins, and one of the victim's wedding bands. It wasn't what he took that intrigued the investigators. It was what he appeared to have left behind. When looking through the female victim's jewelry box to see what was missing they had discovered a St. Christopher's medal that the victim stated did not belong to them.

Police discovered that the attacker had gotten in the home through the sliding glass door which had had the screws removed. Investigators also found that a phone line had been cut. The investigation turned to the outside of the home. In the backyard, they found some empty beer bottles and some cracker wrappers. Investigators wanted to question neighbors to see if they had heard or seen anything unusual. They quickly learned that some of the neighbors did have valuable information.

One neighbor saw a small brown car drive through the circle and turn around at 11:15 p.m., a couple hours before the attack started. Other types of vehicles that seemed out of place to the residents were also reported driving through the circle on the day of the attack before turning around and exiting. These included a newer station wagon and a brand new, brown El Camino that was seen behind the victim's home earlier on the day of the attack. One of the neighbors got a partial plate number for the vehicle, 366-T.

Police would later place the witness who saw the El Camino under hypnosis to learn more about the car or its driver. Under hypnosis, this witness was able to provide some detailed information. He described the driver as being a white male in his twenties with brown, collar length hair. They also said that he had deep-set eyes. One specific detail provided by this witness was a highly detailed description of a decal that the El Camino had on it. The decal appeared to show a parachute attached to a missile or rocket that included letters that were possibly a f c. The decal appeared to be somehow related to the military. Despite this detailed info about the decal, the car, the driver, and the license plate, none of those things have ever been identified.

One thing that came to light, which investigators had seen before in the history of this case, was a home for sale very close to the victim. In this instance, the home across the street had been for sale for a month. Numerous realtors and clients had been in and out of the home during the previous weeks. In the days following the attack, one neighbor found a towel hidden under bushes that appeared to be stained with semen. Police staked out this home in case the East Area Rapist came back to attack this woman, but he didn't.

Finally, on December 9, 1977, eight months after the attack, the victim's phone rang. When the female victim answered, a hoarse voice whispered, "Merry Christmas, It's me again." The woman immediately recognized that this was the voice of her rapist. The attack on this couple was interesting in many ways. First, these victims had been at a town hall meeting months earlier at which the male victim openly doubted that the East Area Rapist could attack in the way they were describing. The likelihood here was that the East Area Rapist had also been at this meeting, followed this couple home, and targeted them months later.

Of interest in the attack on this couple was the anger that the East Area Rapist seemed to have about the police. This was something he hadn't done before, calling them pigs and threatening violence. It's very possible that he was angry after the police and Mr. Haskell had pursued him earlier forcing him to change plans. Just when the East Area Rapist investigators seemed to have all they could handle, another wild card was added to the deck. This was a deck that was already stacked against them.

Investigators 200 miles away in Visalia, California felt that Sacramento's East Area Rapist could possibly be a serial offender in Visalia, known as the Visalia Ransacker. The town of Visalia was an agricultural community situated off Route 99 between Fresno and Bakersfield. Back in the mid-70s the southern half of the city was under siege by a burglar and killer known locally as the Visalia Ransacker. The Visalia

Ransacker, or VR for short, began his home intrusions in April of 1974.

There were several incidents in the years leading up to this day that he may have been responsible for. Usually operating on weekends, the Ransacker would enter several unoccupied homes in one night stealing very little, but usually engaging in activities that had a sexual undertone. Even though the VR restricted himself to a small geographic area, he remained elusive and the police were unable to predict when and where he would strike next. His burglaries continued at a steady pace escalating to a fateful night when he attempted a kidnapping and committed a murder. A few months later after an attempted homicide the Visalia Ransacker seemingly stopped offending and vanished. But there is some evidence that indicates he didn't stop at all. It's possible that he might have simply moved to Sacramento to become the East Area Rapist.

Keith Komos, co-author of *Case Files of the East Area Rapist / Golden State Killer,* commented on some of the things he and his co-author Kat Winters discovered while researching the Visalia Ransacker case.

> *The Visalia Ransacker was a very unique type of offender. He committed well over 100 burglaries, most of them over about a two-year period. Despite operating in a fairly small area, he was never caught or identified.*

The Ransacker generally stuck to the area south of Noble Avenue, east of Demaree Street, west of South Court Street, and north of West Whitendale Avenue. This was a very specific zone that this offender operated in, much like the East Area Rapist would do later in Sacramento County. The attempted kidnapping and murder happened on Whitney, and the attempted homicide happened on West Kaweah.

According to Keith Komos:

> *The activity all happened in that small area which was pretty brazen, and it was incredible that he was never*

caught, especially since that occasionally there were police stakeouts and special patrols happening during that time and in actual moments that he was offending. It wasn't bad police work, it was simply a careful elusive offender committing random crimes that were almost impossible to predict.

Becoming such a prolific and daring burglar was only one of the things that set the Visalia Ransacker apart from other criminals. His crimes were unique. Most burglars focus on breaking into a residence stealing whatever they can and getting out as quickly as possible. Not the Visalia Ransacker. The typical Ransacker crime saw him breaking into a home while residents were away often away for an extended period, like a vacation. He looked for unlocked doors or windows first, and if he didn't find any, he pried his way inside. Once inside the residence, he opened more windows removing at least one of the screens and usually leaving it out on the bed.

This was done, apparently, so he had an easy escape route if someone came home unexpectedly. Sometimes he placed some items against the front or back door that would crash down if it were opened, which could alert him if someone else entered the house. He then began rummaging through almost every room in the house, especially the bedrooms and in almost every scene he took women's bras, panties, lingerie nightgowns, or whatever they had. He took them out of the drawers and threw them onto the floor or folded them up on the headboards, or he laid them out on the bed.

This activity was fairly unique to him as was the opening of escape routes and placing items against doors. These things help differentiate a Ransacker burglary from a 'normal' burglary. He appeared to be sexually motivated and not motivated by personal gain. VR didn't take much from his crimes. Usually only taking a piggy bank, coins, or coin collection, loose cash, things like that, but very little else.

Blue chip stamps were stamps issued to customers when they checked out at participating grocery stores. It was essentially a loyalty program, and the more items bought the more stamps received. The stamps could be collected usually by licking them and placing them into books and then traded in at redemption centers for items like housewares, toys, merchandise, and even furniture. The Ransacker stole these at several crime scenes. Because the VR hit while victims weren't home, he was usually long gone by the time the police were called. This made him very difficult to track or catch.

Sadly, not every Ransacker event involved him stealing from homes while the residents were away. In the early morning hours of September 11, 1975, the Ransacker went from petty burglar to attempted kidnapper and murderer. The night of September 10 was normal for the daughter of Claude Snelling, a 16-year-old student at Mount Whitney High School. She was spending time at home with her family and her boyfriend. The windows were open that evening because the air conditioner had been acting up. Her boyfriend left around 10:00 p.m. and she went to bed shortly thereafter.

In the very early morning hours of September 11, the Visalia Ransacker approached her home and entered her backyard. He removed the screen from the large window at the rear of her house and deposited it across the street on top of a neighbor's camper. Then he went back to the Snelling residence. The window that he'd removed the screen from may have already been opened or left unlocked. It was situated right next to the back door, and he was able to reach in and unlock the back door. Leaving it open a foot or two, he entered the Snelling home.

The first thing he seemed to do was locate Mrs. Snelling's purse. He brought it outside and set it down on the other side of the house, as he did this he took a few dollars from the purse. Then he went back inside. The interior of the house was lit by a back-porch light and a bathroom light that had been left on. He was able to make his way silently through the house and into the teenage daughter's room. The girl was asleep, but the next thing she knew she was being suffocated by a heavy weight on top of her. One of her hands was pinned down and with the other, she pulled out whatever was suffocating her.

She felt bare hands covering her nose and mouth and saw angry eyes just a few inches from her face. She heard a quiet growl coming from the darkness. You're coming with me, "Don't scream or I'll stab you." He grabbed her arm and pulled her up from the bed. He produced the gun from his back pocket and pointed it at her and snarled, "Don't move or I'll shoot you." The girl began to cry, and then asked the man, "What are you doing? Where are you taking me?" He began pushing her through the house and towards the back door, which the daughter could see had been left open by the intruder.

She began to struggle against him, but his grip was very strong. He took a few steps in front and took the lead dragging her toward the door. She was doing everything she could do not to let this man take her outside of the house, and because of this, she was making quite a bit of noise. She cried as he led her out of the door, down the steps, and through the gate which had also been left open. They stopped briefly at the carport, and it was at that point they both heard a noise from inside the house, and it was her father Claude yelling, "Hey, what are you doing? Where are you taking my daughter?" He was shouting this as he was moving through the house and out the back door. The kidnapper turned around and looked at him.

As Claude Snelling began walking down the steps, the kidnapper let go of his daughter who fell to the ground. He then faced Claude Snelling and without hesitation, opened fire. The first bullet struck Mr. Snelling in the arm and he spun around. The second bullet went through his torso and into a window of the Snelling house. Mortally wounded, Claude Snelling went back into the house and ran towards the front door, most likely hoping that he could still head off the kidnapper. At that point, the shooter pointed a gun directly at the teenage daughter. He apparently reconsidered shooting her because he lowered the weapon, and then he kicked her in the face two or three times.

He turned and jogged down the driveway at a medium pace and disappeared into the darkness.

Police and paramedics were called to the scene. Claude Snelling was pronounced dead on arrival at the hospital. Responding officers searched for the suspect, but he was nowhere to be found. He had escaped. They canvassed the neighborhood thoroughly, and a few interesting pieces of evidence were found. They found a glass container that apparently had alcohol in it at the property next door. A neighbor one street overheard clicking and creaking sounds, a few minutes after the murder happened.

It was discovered that the sound was most likely from a bicycle that had been stolen a day or two before from a nearby residence on West Tulare. The missing window screen was found on the camper across the street, and a screwdriver was found wrapped in a clear plastic raincoat. As more and more evidence presented itself, the police were able to cleanly tie this event to the Visalia Ransacker. A gun stolen from a previous Ransacker crime was found in a ditch. It wasn't the murder weapon, but the timing of the find was significant. A flashlight was found that was linked to a previous Ransacker break-in. The most damning evidence came in the form of ballistics.

Police determined that the gun used to kill Claude Snelling was the same weapon that had been stolen during a ransack or burglary that had occurred two weeks earlier. They were able to recover some spent casings from this weapon that had been fired from the owner, and they were matched for the casings at the Snelling scene. This physical evidence tied the Ransacker to the abduction attempt and the homicide. Since the Ransacker was rarely seen, the description that the teenage girl gave to police was very important. She described him as wearing a black ski mask with white zigzag stripes. She described his voice as a growl, which she said seemed disguised.

He appeared to have a medium or slightly heavy build. Now, she couldn't give a good estimate of his weight and wasn't very sure about his age but described the killer as most likely being in his twenties or thirties. She thought him to be around five feet, nine inches. The search for the Ransacker intensified after the murder of Claude Snelling. It was now known that the Ransacker was targeting young women. The police hoped to use that information to help them apprehend him.

On Tuesday, December 9, the woman living at 1501 West Kaweah summoned the police to her residence. Once they arrived on the scene, they were shown shoe prints that had appeared in her yard. The prints were concentrated under the bedroom windows of her teenage daughter as well as the bathroom that the young woman used. Officers at the scene found the same shoe prints at the residence next door. After inspecting them, they noted that they were similar to other shoe prints that had been found at Ransacker crime scenes. A special patrol was already scheduled for the following day that involved six officers on foot staked out at various locations in the city, and a police car driving around the areas looking for suspicious persons.

Two officers decided to stake out the area where the footprints had been found hoping that the Ransacker would return to the scene. One officer was stationed across the street from the house at 1501 West Kaweah and a few hours after getting into position, he noticed a subject walking near the residence in a crouched position. This person was sticking close to the darkness. In the shadows of some shrubbery in the area, the subject crept toward the location where officer McGowan was stationed inside the garage next door to 1501 West Kaweah. At one point, the subject stopped and looked in the garage for a moment but did not discover the hidden policeman.

Then the subject began making his way to the back of the house. Officer McGowan left the garage and began silently following the suspicious man. He observed this man go up to the back gate and begin tampering with the lock. McGowan clicked his flashlight on. The suspect spun around and faced McGowan. Officer McGowan trained the light directly on the subject's eyes and the man screamed in a high-pitched voice,

"Oh no, oh my God, no." Officer McGowan shouted out to the man, "Police officer, hold it right there." The suspect who was apparently wearing a stocking cap or ski mask rolled up on his head, reached up, removed it and put it in his pocket. As he made this motion, he took off running.

He ran a few steps then made his way over a gate and landed in the yard at 1505 West Kaweah. McGowan jumped over the fence as well and screamed at the man, "Hold it, put your hands up." But the suspect didn't stop. He was running in the yard, almost in a zigzag or a circular-type pattern. He was still shrieking in this very high-pitched voice, which was described as a feminine voice. He was screaming things like, "Oh my God, please don't hurt me. Oh my God, no." McGowan fired his service weapon into the ground, far away from the suspect to act as a warning shot, but also to alert his partner across the street, but still the suspect did not stop.

He continued to run, and then he scrambled over the fence into the yard at 1501 West Kaweah. This is the house where the shoe prints had been found earlier. The whole time, McGowan is shouting at this guy, "Police officer, stop, I told you to put your hands up. Stop, I'll shoot." But he's on the other side of the fence at this point from the suspect. There were gaps between the slats and the fence wide enough that he could see this man easily. He continued to shine his flashlight on the subject holding it up and away from his body like he'd been trained to do. Even though they were separated by the fence, they were less than five feet away from each other.

The suspect continued pleading in a high-pitched voice with officer McGowan. The suspect turned to his side, so that McGowan could only see his profile. Then raised his right hand as if complying with officer McGowan's request for him to put his hands up, but his left hand began digging around in his jacket. The suspect said, "Look my hands are up." Then he quickly pulled a gun out of his jacket, turned and fired at McGowan. Officer McGowan was knocked to the ground and was lying motionless when his partner arrived to assist him.

McGowan's partner saw the suspect run through the gate. Inside the residence at 1501 West Kaweah, the homeowner and three other people were surprised to hear a gunshot so close by. The homeowner looked out his window just after a second shot was heard, and he saw a man run through his back gate.

This guy exited his house and followed the suspect. He caught sight of him and saw that he was walking not running next to the fence. The suspect turned and looked directly at this homeowner. He paused for a minute then got a running start and jumped over some hedges that ran alongside of the yard. Meanwhile, McGowan's partner was on the radio requesting back-up. As he spoke on the radio, officer McGowan got to his feet, and it turned out that the bullet didn't strike McGowan. It had actually struck his flashlight right on the lens. Some debris from the flashlight glass had cut McGowan near his eye and had left powder marks all over his face.

He was relatively unharmed. He was transported to the hospital where he was later treated and released. This was a golden opportunity to finally catch the Visalia Ransacker. Every available officer on the Visalia Police Department was called in. The California Highway Patrol was called, and the Tulare County Sheriff's Office was also called in. They had nearly seventy officers descend on the area. It was quickly learned that on his way out of the yard, the shooter had emptied his pockets of the loot that he had stolen at another ransacking that night.

He'd stolen a few pounds of pennies which were found tied up in a sock on the ground. They also found a few books of the *Blue-Chip Stamps* as well. It was definitely the Ransacker that they were dealing with. These officers were eager to make it right for, not only Claude Snelling, but for every burglary victim over the past two years. For these guys, the chase was on.

The Visalia department was besieged with burglary reports for several months. They wanted to end it and finally catch this guy. While hunting the Ransacker, police found a large amount of shoe prints throughout the town. Tracks were found to the west of the shooting on West Kaweah. From there they headed north up to Route 198. Then the prints doubled back and started heading east. Tracks were found heading east past the scene of the shooting. Just a block north of it, they vanished for a bit. Later, police determined that due to the pattern of broken branches and indentations, the suspect had hidden in some bushes to avoid police. Tracks were found in an alleyway still heading in the opposite direction. Because of this maneuver of doubling back, the VR eluded the perimeter that the police set up and he escaped.

Tracking dogs were even used at the scene, but to no avail. Officer McGowan described the shooter as a white male, twenty-five to thirty-five years of age, five feet, ten inches tall, and at least 180 pounds or more. He had a round face, short light blonde hair with no sideburns and no sign of whiskers or stubble. McGowan described the man as having large shoulders, large legs, large hips, big thighs and a large rear end. He was wearing tight pants that looked like blue jeans, and a brown or green camouflage jacket with elastic cuffs, Converse tennis shoes, low tops, and dark brown cotton gloves.

The cap he was wearing was very thick. It gave the impression of a ski mask rolled up. The neighbor who saw this guy and even chased after him. He described the man as having a large frame about five feet, ten inches and 180 pounds. McGowan described this man as running slowly, and running in a funny manner, like he was running with his knees together. After this incident, aside from some possibly related activity a few weeks later, the Visalia Ransacker was never seen or heard from again. What makes this case relevant to our discussion is that the Visalia Ransacker had several elements in common with the East Area Rapist.

We don't know for sure where the East Area Rapist was before 1976, and we don't know for sure where the Visalia Ransacker went after 1975. It makes sense to study the similarities to see if these two offenders might be the same person.

Keith Komos offered up some additional insight:

> *The way that both offenders navigated the neighborhoods bore some similarities. With the East Area Rapist relying on ditches and canals and the VR seemingly using ditches to traverse the neighborhoods. They both also stole bikes locally and ditched them nearby. That's something in my research I've seen a few other offenders do. So, it may not mean much. Stealing coins is an odd similarity because these are cumbersome to take low-value items, and they don't have any personal connection to the victims. Something else worth mentioning is that they both used dishes and household items in strategic places to alert them to know if someone moved or someone came home. The East Area Rapist usually used them on people. The Visalia Ransacker usually used them on doors. It's not the same thing but it's somewhat the same concept. One area where the two offenders diverge is in the physical description. McGowan and other witnesses described the VR as a stocky character with a very pronounced lower half.*

> *The age range generally fell into the late 20s which is a little high when compared to the East Area Rapists descriptions. Several witnesses including McGowan described a man who ran with an odd gait. It's tough to reconcile some of those things. On the other hand, the other similarities between the offenders are hard to ignore as well.*

During the investigation of the Visalia Ransacker, police discovered that more than once he had used lotion at the crime scenes to masturbate. In fact, both offenders had brought their own bottles of lotion to crime scenes. They both disguised their voices and used different techniques to do it. The Visalia Ransacker spoke in a low masculine growl during the Snelling incident and then in a frantic high-pitched feminine voice in the McGowen incident. The East Area Rapist typically spoke in a forced whisper through clenched teeth, often trying to sound as if he had a deeper voice than he actually did.

Rummaging though and ransacking the entire house is something that both offenders shared. While it's part of the MO of a common burglar, both the VR and the East Area Rapist spent far more time ransacking than a typical thief. While the MO ties are interesting, hard physical evidence of a tie between the Visalia Ransacker and the East Area Rapist remains elusive to researchers and investigators.

Keith Komos told us:

> The police found fingerprints at three dozen Visalia Ransacker scenes. None of them matched. It's assumed that they're all from visitors and friends of the victims. They didn't have any usable DNA evidence of the Ransacker, but there are some shoe impressions that they were able to match to a size 9 Converse. Those were common among the scenes. That's somewhat similar to an East Area Rapist shoe print. There's not really anything usable there either to tie the offenders together. Basically, any similarities found are through M.O.

The Visalia Ransacker is still wanted for the murder of Claude Snelling. If identified, he can still be prosecuted. There is no statute of limitations on murder. Law enforcement maintains an open file on him. Anyone who has any information on the Visalia Ransacker case is urged to contact the Visalia Police Department.

Debate has raged among investigators, in both the East Area Rapist and Visalia Ransacker cases. Some are open to the idea that both offenders could be the same. Based on the very similar M.O. Detective Ken Clark of the Sacramento Sheriff's Department told me that he was 50/50 on whether they might be the same offender.

Other investigators are sure in their minds that the two are indeed one and the same. On the opposite end of the spectrum is investigator Paul Holes of the Contra Costa Sheriff's Department, who by his own admission is one of the most outspoken critics of these two offenders being the same person. Paul sat down with us and shared his opinion on whether the two cases might be the work of one person.

The Visalia Ransacker was not very good at avoiding detection. He was seen by multiple individuals during his series. Most notably, there were two extremely reliable witnesses. You've got a 22-year-old anthropology student and then Officer McGowan. The 22-year old anthropology student is sitting in his car outside his girlfriend's house when he sees a man walking down the street. The man crosses the street in front of them, then gets down on all fours and crawls up to his girlfriend's living room window and starts peeping on her. He gets out, yells at the guy, and the guy gets up and runs away.

The student gives chase and ultimately corners the Ransacker at a fence. The Ransacker turns around. He doesn't have a mask on. The anthropology student gets a full head-to-toe visual of the Visalia Ransacker. Officer McGowan is at the end of the series. After this known homicide, there's been multiple burglaries. After that homicide, officer McGowan predicted correctly where the guy was likely to show up next. He is sitting in a garage and sees the Ransacker across the street at a house, near the fence line, and is able to approach the Ransacker.

McGowan lights the Ransacker up. The Ransacker turns around, he doesn't have his mask on. McGowan gets a full view of him head to toe, before the Ransacker pulls a gun and shoots McGowan. It really shoots McGowan's flashlight. The Ransacker is able to get away. Both those two witnesses describe the Ransacker as having this fat round face, almost juvenile looking very thick type of neck. They describe him as having hunched rounded shoulders, fat short fingers, fat hips, fat thighs, fat calves, fat short feet. The Anthropology student said he was almost mongoloid looking.

Then he talked like he was not somebody who was very coherent in terms of his speaking pattern and very almost womanish, girlish. He screams like a girl when he's being confronted by the 22-year-old student before he can walk off. Six months after McGowan sees the Ransacker, EAR is showing up for the first official attack in Sacramento in Rancho Cordova. That victim is in bed, and she sees the East Area Rapist in her doorway. He's standing in her doorway, he's got a ski mask on, he's got a T-shirt on, he's got a knife. But he's nude from the waist down, and he's standing there, he's got an erection, but she sees his entire physique.

She describes him as having a very slim, athletic, well-proportioned build. Attack number three, right around the corner you have a teenage girl and a mom who see our offender nude from the waist down and there is a prolonged period of seeing him in the kitchen. Their description is very similar to the first East Area Rapist victim's description. I have a serious problem resolving the Ransacker's description of fat hipped, fat round shoulders, this mongoloid appearance to a well-proportioned muscular, broad shouldered, slim to medium build.

Some people want to attribute that to weight loss, and I think it is an entirely different physique. At this point, I have decided there is too much of a difference physically between the Visalia Ransacker and the East Area Rapist. Then behaviorally, though there is some overlap, there are significant differences in terms of what these guys were doing. At this point I have moved away completely from Visalia Ransacker because that's where my confidence is. I know the East Area Rapist is in Sacramento starting June 1976. That is not in dispute.

SEASON TWO, EPISODE SIX

The East Area Rapist was on a torrid pace at this point and had attacked several times in the month of May. The frequent attacks had all of Sacramento County on edge and the result was a flood of letters to the editor of the *Sacramento Bee* voicing their concerns. The following two letters were printed in the May 26th, 1977 Sacramento Bee:

> *For the first time in my life, we have a loaded gun in our bedroom, the East Area Rapist has all of us so fearful that we're all becoming dangerous. The police alone cannot handle the situation, but private citizens should look to them for leadership. The police should organize neighborhood alert units. These units should consist of unarmed people who would patrol the neighborhood or in some other way would be more alert than usual. These people must be trained and guided by the police, or we will kill some innocent people and not capture the rapist. Perhaps some good can come out of this. The same patrols guided by the authorities could be retained after the crisis to increase the safety of our homes.*

> *Recently, as I sat reading my evening paper, I could not believe what I read. On the front page, I read of the 23rd rape victim. On another page, I read of parents picketing the police department because of the recent rape murder of a 15-year-old child. These parents are afraid for their own children. They want more protection. I then looked over to another column and I saw where Sacramento Vice Mayor Robert Matsui, "Suggested extra funds may be needed to beef up the*

police vice squad to combat street corner prostitution. On a one-year basis, I'd be willing to allocate extra funds."

I can certainly see that there are such pressing matters on the vice mayor's mind. As a parent and a woman afraid in my own home, I can see where extra funds should go, to protect our citizens from rapists and murderers rather than a street corner prostitute. Don't you think our priorities are in the wrong place? A concerned citizen, Carmichael.

I think you can tell by what those people wrote into the paper, just how worried they were. The very next day on May 27, an article ran in the *Sacramento Bee* detailing how fed up Sacramento residents were with the East Area Rapist not being caught. They were so fed up at this point that they had their own citizens' patrol working with police looking for this guy. More than 100 Sacramento residents armed with citizen band radios officially began nocturnal patrols of East Area streets. Members of the East Area Rapist surveillance patrol riding in vehicles plastered with EARS patrol stickers set out in search of the man who had raped twenty-three women and threatened to kill his next two victims. At the end of the first four-hour shift, all was quiet, and no incidents were reported. One set of volunteers slowly cruised the deserted streets in the area where the rapist had made his latest attack.

This was a lot of attention given to the East Area Rapist by this newspaper in just a two-day period, especially considering that the East Area Rapist had not struck in over a week before these articles ran. This time lapse was surprising considering how many attacks he had committed in May. It seems as if these articles and the mention of a patrol out looking for him may have motivated him to make an appearance.

He would strike next on May 28. Perhaps the East Area Rapist took it as a challenge, knowing the patrol was out looking for him. On the 7000 block of Fourth Parkway in Sacramento, a 28-year-old woman was home doing some chores on the night of May 27 when she noticed that her garage door was partially open. The married library clerk didn't think much about it, and she shut the door before going back to do her housework. She put her young son to bed before going to bed herself around 11:30 p.m. Then it was just after midnight on May 28, her husband arrived home after work. The 31-year-old man had just finished his shift working at the county water treatment plant.

Once the man arrived home, he sat down and watched a movie until about 2:00 a.m. Then got into bed, at which point his wife woke up, and the two began to become intimate with each other. While they were in the process of being intimate, the man heard a noise behind them coming in from their sliding glass door. As he turned around to see what he heard, he was shocked to see a man in a red ski mask walking through the door towards him. In a second, the man was almost on top of them and shining a flashlight in their eyes. Despite the light in their eyes, they could see him holding a handgun that looked to be a 45 caliber in his right hand.

The first words out of the masked intruder's mouth let the couple know that he meant business. He said, "Lay perfectly still or I will kill all of you. I will kill you. I will kill her. I will kill your little boy." The masked intruder told the terrified couple that he just wanted food and money and then he would be gone. It was then that he instructed the woman to bind her husband as he threw her some shoelaces. The attacker told the man that he needed to lay face down, and if he moved, his wife and son would be dead. The couple complied, and the woman started to tie her husband's hands behind his back. The woman planned to tie her husband loosely hoping that he might be able to escape. The man watched her closely, and he kept demanding that she tie her husband even tighter.

Once the male victim was secured, the assailant forced the woman down and tied her hands behind her back. The man again warned them to lay face down and not to move or they would be dead. He rifled through their drawers and their closets. Then he walked over to the male victim, placed the gun to his head and again warned him not to move. He then tied the man's hands very tightly and also tied his ankles. The masked man left the room and went to the bathroom. The couple could hear the unmistakable sound of him pumping a bottle of lotion. He returned to their bedroom and placed some glass items on the male victim's back and warned him that if he heard those items make a sound everybody in the house would be dead.

At that point, he tied the female victim's ankles as well, and then left the room and went to the couple's kitchen. A few minutes later, he returned with even more items that he stacked on the man's back. This time he held a knife to the bound man's throat, once again warning him not to move. The masked man reiterated that he only wanted food and money and that he would soon be gone.

Suddenly, the intruder untied the female's ankle bindings and removed her from the bed. He forced her to walk to the living room where the woman could see strips of torn towels spread on the living room floor. The assailant forced the woman to the floor and then used one of the strips of towel to blindfold her. The man walked back into the bedroom to make sure that the male victim was secure and then shut the bedroom door and walked back into the living room. At that point, he sexually assaulted the woman.

As the rapist sexually attacked the woman, he whispered in her ear that, "I have something for you to tell the fucking pigs," The cops got it wrong last time." Then he said he would kill two people if news of this attack was on TV or in the papers the next day. He made the woman repeat back to what he had told her, and she did. He warned her that he had TVs in his apartment, and he would be watching them. Then he said something really odd, which was, "It scares mommy when it's on the news." The woman thought the attacker was sobbing when he told her that.

After a few minutes, the house fell silent. The male victim thought he heard the sliding glass door open, but he didn't hear anything after that. He thought the intruder was gone. He decided to try and free himself, knocking the dishes off his back which made noise. The intruder was in fact gone, and the man was able to free himself, and then his wife. They called police. Luckily, the couple's son was unharmed and had not been disturbed.

Police arrived at the home before 5:00 a.m. and immediately took inventory of the crime scene. From the outset, they figured this was likely an East Area Rapist attack. The couple told the police that their attacker was a five feet, nine to five feet, ten, slender to medium-sized man who weighed about 160 to 170 pounds. The female victim added that the rapist had a very small penis. They also told investigators that the man talked in what sounded like a low whisper that was raspy and that he may have had a slight stutter.

They relayed all the conversation which included the talk about delivering a message to the police, and they added that the man also mentioned he would be eating the food in his van. It's unclear from the police report what if anything the attacker took from the home. The female victim was taken to the hospital for treatment and then outside of the house, police found food from the home on the patio; they found a wine bottle. Tracking dogs were brought into the property. Just after 5:00 a.m., the canine units began to work the scene.

The dogs followed the rapist's scent to the back fence and then picked up the scent on the other side of the fence leading down towards the freeway, and to another fence along the freeway that led to a cement drainage area or a canal. Remember this area because it's going to come up again. Around this area, tire tracks from a small car were found, but it's unknown if the tracks belong to the assailant. Police pieced together the events that led up to the attack. The couple had only moved into the home three weeks prior to the attack, and the home still had a realtor sign on the lawn. Police were interested to learn that the treatment plant where the man worked at was located very close to Sandbar Circle in Carmichael, the scene of the previous East Area Rapist attack. After questioning neighbors, it came to light that preceding this attack, there was a lot of strange activity on this block.

Several residents had received odd and hang-up calls in the days and weeks preceding the attack. There were reports of several people going door to door, everything from backroom salesmen, to men selling children's books, to Mormon missionaries. A man representing a fictitious organization called library educational system was handing out survey forms. Several suspicious cars were seen and at least one prowler was reported. A few days before the attack, a man described as being 25 years old, 5 foot 9 and 160 pounds with dark hair was carrying a camera case and asking neighborhood children if he could take their photos.

As we've seen in other East Area Rapist attacks, this kind of activity was common leading up to an attack, and you have to wonder if one or more of these people seen in the area was the East Area Rapist surveying the neighborhood. If he wasn't surveying the neighborhood, was he trying to slip in to some of these areas filled with activity to blend in? One very interesting event happened early in the month of May. While on patrol, police noticed a man in a small square shaped car, possibly a Datsun or Chevy watching a woman playing football at a park about a mile from the location of the attack.

As they passed the car, they noticed that the man was a blond male on his twenties and then a short while later, the same patrol car drove by and spotted the man in the same place still there watching the woman. This time they took note of the license plate and then drove past the car up the road. But they decided to turn around because they wanted to check this guy out. But when they got back to the spot where it'd been parked, he and his car were gone. They called in the plate number and discovered it had never been issued.

This most recent attack had been the twenty-second confirmed attack by the East Area Rapist and his fifth attack in the month of May alone. It seemed as if there would be no slowing down for this serial rapist but then without any warning, that's exactly what happened. Days went by, then weeks. There was not an attack in Sacramento County attributed to the East Area Rapist. Incidents of prowling seemed to almost be non-existent. May turned into June and then July, and August. The entire summer in Sacramento seemed to be East Area Rapist free. Theories abounded as to where the East Area Rapist was and why he wasn't attacking. The fear in the community was still there. But for police, it gave them a chance to catch their breath.

It wouldn't be until February 2018, over forty years later, that police would announce that they were investigating a lead that might be tied to the sudden stop in East Area Rapist activity. Detective Sergeant Ken Clark of the Sacramento County Sheriff's Department broke down this possible lead in great detail for us in an interview.

> One of the other leads that we featured on our media release for the fortieth anniversary of the Brian and Katie Maggiore murder was a lead we came across in files that we recently discovered that dealt with a visit to America River Hospital. It's an odd set of circumstances and that's what struck us as being something that we might need to look into further.

> Why we chose it to put out in the public was the only way we could possibly get information was to release it to the public. We had previously investigated everything we could about the lead and hit dead ends along the way, and so really, we as a long shot effort we're hoping that somebody might remember the incident enough to give us something tangible. In this particular case, as part of our work here, we obviously went several times but when we read these reports, we

went to all the crime scenes and looked at different features and factors that you would as a detective.

Sometimes we came up with thoughts that were not always represented in the case files. In this case, we had looked at the crime scene that occurred on Fourth Parkway in South Sacramento and that particular crime scene bordered Highway 99. It was believed by investigations at the time that the suspect had parked on the shoulder near the cloverleaf of Highway 99 and then jumped over the fencing that separated the freeway from this neighborhood, and had emerged to commit the crime, and then left via the same route.

When my partner and I over the years of being out there, and I went out recently, and one of the things I noticed was that, again, there's a lot of conjecture involved here because there was a dog track and some other things, and so I would give the caveat that this isn't a perfect science, so to speak. There's some supposition that goes into this type of analysis, and we can't know what did or didn't occur as we don't have an eyewitness to his escape from this scene.

But one thing that we were struck by was given the best information we had about how this man escaped, that he might have injured himself in the creek area and it's like a drainage canal. Right now, there's a sound wall that you wouldn't even be able to scale. It's many feet high, probably ten to twelve feet high that protects the neighborhood from the freeway noise, but at the time it was just two chain link fences and both those fences were on either side of this drainage canal.

It's kind of wide open but there is a small grove of trees that has some advantages if you're going to try to go over because there is a locked gate that has some footing where you can get your footing and get over the fence, and it has a top bar on the chain link fence. The remainder of the fence is open, and it's got that kind of pointy unfinished look on top, and it would be a little more difficult to get over the fence in that section. It's also opens to the view of the street. This grove of trees protected this little gate, and it appeared a good possible spot based on what we understood about the tracking that had been done, for him to have tried to get over.

But we were struck by the kind of sheer nature of this canal which was different than some that he would run in. This was literally a V-shaped bottom, so you've got on each side about four and a half to five-feet of canal below this six-foot fence. We didn't really see a good way because there was no footing or no place to jump where when you landed he would almost definitely fall, because when you went into this V-shaped creek, you can't-- there's no way to gain footing, you would definitely gain speed going down and then you end up, now we would think smashing on the other side.

From the other side of the fence, there is a bit of footing and our thought was that maybe when he came over from the freeway direction, he probably didn't realize that it was going to be a more treacherous jump coming back across, and especially in the dark. We think that- - we thought that there was a possibility that it was a rather dangerous jump, we made that observation. Fast forward to when we get these reports, and I had found this report that showed that a guy had come to American River Hospital on May 30, 1977, which was two days after the Fourth Parkway attack, and that during this time period he entered the hospital and basically requested treatment for a broken shoulder.

He told the medical staff that it had occurred on May 28, and he spoke to a clerk with the initials B.K. In fact, as of the release of this, I will let you know that we actually have identified the clerk with the initials B.K to a great deal of satisfaction that it is the person and unfortunately, she has passed away. We had a couple of potential candidates that were B. K's but this one is very clearly the name on the signature.

We had a signature of this person, but it was rather illegible, and then we had the definite initials of B.K. But in looking at the signature coupled with the information we had about this individual, we determined that that was the case. We got that information, it was actually some work done by Paul Haims who was a researcher for Michelle McNamara, and he's the one that basically approached us when he saw our press release and gave this information that he thought it was a woman who he had found that worked at the hospital, and then looking at it, it all made sense.

Unfortunately, that's a dead end for us, but the remainder of the lead is goes somewhat like this. The subject that's in the hospital arouses suspicion for an unknown reason from staff there and he basically leaves the hospital without receiving treatment. He indicated to them and is verified by the form that he was an individual by a certain name, and he provided the name and a birthday of May the 12th, 1946, which made him a 31-year-old male at the time of this incident.

He stated that he was employed by the Rice Growers Association and that this occurred on a fall from scaffolding on May the 28th in the morning hours. The person whose name he used, and all of this turned out to be fictitious. The name that he used, that individual did work at the Rice Growers Association. They went and visited him, and the result of that was that he had no injury to his shoulder and stated that he had had his wallet including identification cards and credit cards either lost or stolen sometime around two years prior to this incident.

In that particular time period, he thought it was stolen, but he figured it could have been lost because they never heard of any of the credit cards ever being used. But then all of a sudden, here we are a couple of years later, and his card has popped up as an identification card being used by a man, who according to the report, fled when nurses started to look at him with suspicion. That ended the lead for them at this point now because they didn't have too much to go on. You've got to bear in mind there had been a 13-week gap in crimes.

This is two days after an offense and after this particular offense, there are continued prowls and peeps going on throughout many of the areas that the East Area Rapist hit. This was a lead that I think they viewed as maybe not as valuable in that time period. Again, their judgment may prove completely sound in that, we don't know, but they took it as far as they felt that they could. The phone number that he provided was no good. I verified that in the modern era and the address he provided for an emergency notification was another individual that worked at the Rice Growers Association. He's been spoken to and knew the gentleman whose ID was used.

The only thing we can consider is that perhaps the individual who had the ID had some information with this guy, or he knew in some way that they were associated based on information in the wallet, and so he used that as an emergency contact and try to make the story better. The social security number he used is bogus. Basically, everything in this report that he did was wrong. We also spoke to and found out that the Rice Growers Association didn't have any scaffolding there during that time period. And that again confirmed that the original investigators' thoughts regarding this particular lead.

But knowing that there had been a thirteen week gap and knowing that there was a possibility, albeit again, it is possibility only that there was an injury that could have occurred on that particular egress from the crime in the Fourth Parkway case, we felt that it was worth getting it even forty years later into the media in the hopes that a B.K, the clerk, was identified and maybe had more information about this man or we got some more specificity on what made him flee the hospital. Of course, our big hope was, if that somebody was in the hospital, recognized him for a more concrete reason than just a resemblance to a composite or something like that, where he felt vulnerable enough based on their having seen him that he wanted to leave.

We do know one of the victims worked at that hospital, and she had actually been working that day, but it was in the graveyard shift, and she had heard about this going on at that time. But at that point, there was nothing she felt she could or should do. We have this guy showing up and we just really don't know why. The lead is largely played out now. Every angle we have been able to explore has reached a dead end. Now that we have the clerk B.K identified, it's going to obviously be much more difficult.

But we're still hoping that somebody might remember this specific visit and whether or not the East Area Rapist had a shoulder injury in the late spring or early summer of 1977 is a point of conjecture only, and we don't know for sure. But we still would like to get this individual even forty years later identified and be able to verify that they were not or in any way involved with the East Area Rapist crimes. The identification card that he took, the gentleman was older than that by several years. That raised a couple of thoughts for us. One is that the offender or whoever was in the hospital knew that it would be tough passing off his real age, vis-à-vis the age of the gentlemen whose ID was stolen. He got closer to it to where it was still reasonable. In other words, if he's born in 1952, this guy is born in the thirties. He backed it up a bit so that it was plausible. The other thought is he may have actually been born in or near 1946 and that he would state the age which he appeared so that it wouldn't raise any suspicion maybe knowing that they wouldn't have the identifying information on the age of the guy whose ID card it actually belonged to.

The other possibility is that some of this behavior is what raised the hackles of people at the hospital, and that that could have caused his flight because he thought that the gig was up regarding the fraud. But it just seems like an onset of circumstances coming together at once. Again, very strange that somebody within the hospital would believe for whatever reason, that this was the East Area Rapist among all of the many young men that come in to the hospital.

This was a time period of very heightened activity of the East Area Rapist. A lot of sketches were floating around back then and description of the suspect were out there, but it seems kind of a leap given the number of young white males in this age group and general description that was coming to the hospital that they seized on just a man walking in looking like the East Area Rapist and caused this much scrutiny to come onto this individual. That's why it's of interest to us. For some reason, they thought he was the EAR, and we want to find out why.

Ken detailed for us, how the dog had tracked the East Area Rapist into the area where they suspect he may have injured himself while fleeing.

There was no eye witness. This is coming from a dog track and where they believed, the freeway place where he had parked. This would be a logical place to go over. If he doesn't go over here, he's really going to spend a whole lot of time in the neighborhood, away from his car before he can get to his car. The most logical place is where they supposed back then that he went over and that was that particular location.

A lot of people after hearing about these new leads being looked into, had been under the impression that law enforcement has been sitting on these for years and just decided to release them now. Ken wanted to set the record straight about that.

One of the big considerations with the case of this volume is, and it's forty years old, most of these detectives have long since retired, and memories fade over time. And so, we've got this giant case that came to us in many boxes to begin with that we organized for the first time in 2005/2006 time period. When I first got these cases, they were in a closet, and they had been examined about four years prior with the DNA hit. Then again, it was really the leads kind of stopped coming. They went back into storage.

When I took them out and looked at them, we organized them and looked at everything, and did not know what we did or didn't have. We had what we thought were complete case files that contained a lot of the original investigation and certainly the case files for each individual sexual assault case. We had all of the files for the, the Maggiore double murder case, which was kept in homicide. We were largely convinced we had a more complete copy because it was among all of the other files that we have here.

But we had heard over the years, whispers that reports that were related to our case we're still outstanding that they were in other jurisdictions, in other allied, investigative agencies, etcetera. We did our best to run that down as best we could. We put our feelers out, we let them know that we believed that these additional documents may exist. We really didn't get too much back after that. When we put together the working group that we have with the southern California agencies, everybody uploaded all of their reports, so we could all view them.

We put everything that we had up at that time. It wasn't but a few years or just about a year ago, maybe a little bit more, that we got word that some reports had been located in one of the allied agencies that works this case, and that they look like original reports, and they were in the old original style folders that I was so familiar with from having seen the original East Area Rapist files when I first took the case on. These reports contained a lot of good information that had not yet been seen by us in the modern era.

They were leads that were worked and many of them were closed completely back in the time period, but we did not have knowledge of some of the results of these investigations. Some of these leads that were worked related directly to leads that we had also worked in the modern era. Then these leads were more complete than the ones that we had worked, because so much of the missing documentation we had didn't have some of this information in it. We were pretty happy to get these and when we went through this is where I found the American River Hospital lead.

At that time the investigators worked it as far as they could, and they didn't necessarily believe that it was a prime lead, if you will. How we choose what to release is going back through and looking through those things that the public truly can help on. I mean, we don't release every lead we get or as we're working on things and read reports and find something interesting. If it's something that we as investigators can flesh out and eliminate or include, we do so, but every once in a while, you get a lead like this, and you take it as far as you can, but it has some promise and some closed or loose end feel to it.

Even though it's been forty years, we've made a decision as an investigative team that the only way that-- If it was even a one tenth of 1 percent chance that somebody remembered something really specific, and it led us down a road that identified this individual or led us to the individual who this tip was actually about and we can exclude them, then it was worth doing. There's a lot of interest in this case, I think people when they read this type of thing they seem genuinely interested. We get a lot of passionate people that approached the investigation, they call, they send us email tips, and we're very gratified by that.

When things like this are put out, you would be surprised by the number of people who really try to help us through a lead like this, and they give us information. Again, that's how we ended up figuring out who the clerk was, sadly, she had passed away. That could have led somewhere, it could have led to a little more than we knew about this lead going in. While this particular lead isn't necessarily panning out for us, we feel that releasing some of this stuff, even forty or forty-five years later, in the case of the 1973 burglaries we've discussed has value. People aren't getting any younger. This case, as I've said before, is in the fourth quarter and we're on the two-minute drill now. Is there an argument to be made, that some of this stuff should have, could have been released back in that era? I really don't know. I wasn't part of that initial investigation. I know that the detectives I've spoken with did the best that they could, and they were dealing with a fresh and active rape series that was ongoing and in real time with a media demand that was voracious, with a city on the edge. There really wasn't a method for them to get out all of this stuff *without flooding the public with a bunch of potentially not just useless but misleading information.*

Here with the benefit of forty years of hindsight, we can go through and look at things that we know about somebody now and make some assessments as to whether we think it's valuable, whether we think this lead has any ability to solve the case, and it's a judgment call. I don't do it alone. I submit what I'm thinking to my partner, we submit it to other partners and people that we work with on this case and get their opinion on whether or not it's worth going forward. We got, basically, feedback that this was something that we should be getting out in the public with the slim chance that it was going to identify somebody.

We are very careful, we try to be very careful and not assert something that's not in evidence. Meaning we have no proof that the East Area Rapist suffered any injury at all during any day of the series. I wouldn't want anybody to assume that there's a shoulder injury here. This is a supposition, it is a possibility and that's all it is. But yes, if it includes-- If somebody remembers an individual that had a shoulder injury and may have been some circumstances that appear to fit in another way beyond that injury, and they want to approach with that information, we're certainly interested in that.

We don't exclude anybody that didn't have a shoulder injury in the summer of '77 if you understand what I mean. Unfortunately, the way these investigations work in something this mammoth, you have to sometimes look at possibilities that you wouldn't normally entertain on cases that are just easier to work. This is one where there's 'is it an explanation for the summer gap?' yes, it could be an explanation for the summer gap but there's many others as well. This just tied in with the American River hospital lead in such a way that we felt it was a possibility that it was worth getting out there.

During the East Area Rapist hiatus in August of 1977, a mysterious letter writer mailed a letter to the Sacramento Police Department. On August 18, the *Sacramento Bee* at the request of police, ran an article about the letter in an effort to get more information.

It turned out that the author of the letter provided information which police felt was possibly legitimate, and they asked publicly for the writer to come forward. The letter writer claimed to know who the East Area Rapist was and provided sketchy details, but the author did not give his name, and instead he signed off the letter with 'afraid'. Some have theorized the letter was a red herring sent by the East Area Rapist himself. However, in researching this case, I talked to multiple investigators that verified that the letter writer had been identified, and he had written the letter because they legitimately suspected somebody of being the East Area Rapist. Investigators ruled out both the author and the person they suspected as having anything to do with East Area Rapist case. At the time, it seemed as if this letter might be a viable clue but like so many other things in this case, it was really just another dead-end lead.

The summer of 1977 had come and gone without an East Area Rapist attack, but residents of Sacramento County were still vigilant. They hoped the East Area Rapist was gone, but they were very guarded. Meanwhile, in the town of Stockton, California, in San Joaquin County, that's about fifty miles south of Sacramento, residents had just wrapped up their summer. They weren't paying a whole lot of attention to the East Area Rapist crimes that were occurring in the state's capital of Sacramento. To them, Sacramento might as well have been another planet. Like many other areas of California, Stockton was building up, new homes and new development.

There was the Stockton Civic Auditorium, a huge theater perfect for concerts. In September of 1977, about thirteen weeks after the East Area Rapist had last attacked in Sacramento, he showed up in the city of Stockton. The 150,000 residents there would soon experience the fear that the communities back in Sacramento County had come to know. The East Area Rapist made his presence felt in Stockton prior to the attack, whether purposefully or not. In August, about three weeks before the attack, several residents in the area of North Portage Circle started to find footprints in their yards.

Dogs began barking at night for no known reason. People would hear noises in their yards, still, others began to receive hang-up phone calls. Towards the end of August, some people reported seeing an out of place white station wagon cruising slowly on local streets. In the first week of September, the strange activity increased with even more hang-up phone calls and more barking dogs. But the residents of Stockton didn't know to look for the signs.

After all, back in Sacramento County authorities had never even alerted residents there of these signs that often preceded East Area Rapist attacks. In the early morning hours of September 5, a woman was talking on her phone when she heard someone trying to get into her back door. She hung up her phone call and grabbed a handgun that she had nearby, and she was prepared to use it on whoever was going to come through that door, but the person on the other side was never able to get the door open.

The next day in the early morning hours of September 6 around 1:00 a.m. on North Portage Circle, neighbors heard a car driving on the circle, followed by the sounds of barking dogs. Just a short while later around 1:30 a.m., a 29-year-old woman on North Portage Circle was awakened by the sound of something at her sliding glass door.

This sliding glass door led directly into her bedroom. She opened her eyes and caught the site of a masked man nude from the waist down, coming through the door and carrying a handgun in one hand, and what appeared to be a doctor's bag in the other. The man saw that she was awake and warned her to be quiet, but she turned quickly, and started to wake up her husband. Her 31-year-old husband awoke to the beam of light in his eyes from the intruder's flashlight, the masked man and a low hoarse voice told the male victim he would kill him if he moved.

At that point, what had become a familiar script in the East Area Rapist case started to unfold. The intruder ordered the man to roll over onto his stomach. He threw shoe laces to the woman and had her tie her husband up, but unlike most of the other East Area Rapist cases, he didn't bring the shoe laces with him. He actually got the shoe laces by removing them from a pair of the male victim's shoes. Once the woman had tied her husband up, the intruder retied him even tighter, and tied his ankles as well. Then he tied the female victim.

The attacker told the helpless couple that he just wanted money and some food for his apartment. The assailant then asked if there was anyone else in the home, and the couple told him that they had two small children who were asleep in their rooms. It was then that the man told them something that shook this couple to their core. He warned them that if they gave him any trouble and didn't comply, that he would chop up their children and bring back their ears to the couple.

The couple decided then and there they were not going to risk any harm to their kids and they fully complied. The attacker left the room for a bit, and the couple was worried about their children, but the man came back after a couple minutes and held a knife to the male victim's throat and threatened him to cooperate. He then ordered the female victim out of bed. The woman was nude and uncomfortable, and asked the man for a robe. The attacker gave her a robe, placing it over her shoulders. At knife point, he ordered her to walk through the home with him. All the while he carried the doctor's bag with him.

When they got to the living room, the woman saw that a blanket had been placed over a lamp, giving off a soft glow to the room. He forced the woman to the floor and then walked away from her. He showed up back in the bedroom a minute later where the husband was still bound on the bed face down. The assailant placed dishes on the man's back and then he placed the gun to his head, and he cocked it, and he warned the husband, "If these rattle, I'll kill you." The attacker walked back to the female victim and approached her from behind. She was facing away from him, but she could hear him masturbating behind her.

He told her that ever since he had seen her in a store, he had wanted to fuck her. He then climbed on the woman and raped her. He stopped for a minute and pulled away from her. After a moment, he started the rape again, but this time something was different to the woman.

What had before felt like a very small, thin penis, now seemed large and firm, and she got the distinct impression that the man was using some sort of sex toy or dildo to assault her with. The rapist left the woman bound in the living room and walked through the home, once again, checking on the husband who hadn't moved. At one point, he went into the kitchen, made himself something to eat, after he finished eating, he talked to the couple one at a time mentioning things like, "I only live a few blocks away. I need stuff for my apartment, like soap, towels, and a portable TV."

During this conversation, one of the couple's young children walked out into the hallway and saw the man standing there, and he spoke to the child and he said, "I'm playing tricks with your mom and dad, come watch me." More of this is just further proof of how warped and demented this man was, but he didn't hurt this child. The child went on to the bathroom, then walked back to the bedroom, and went back to sleep.

After the child had gone back to bed, the man once again walked over the female victim and masturbated before raping her again. Once again, she felt he was using both his real penis and a fake one. He then climbed off the woman and walked away from her. After several minutes of silence, the couple, their young child, and a neighbor all heard what sounded like a loud VW startup and drive off. The couple scrambled to get free and called police. When the Stockton police arrived on scene, they found what looked like a random break-in and rape. They didn't know that this attack was the work of the East Area Rapist.

Now, Sacramento Police would have known that the single-story home, the use of both a gun and a knife, and the lines used by the assailant were all straight out of the East Area Rapist playbook. The victims describe the man as is being about five feet, eight inches to five feet, ten inches, weighing about 150 to 160 pounds and having a slender build. The female victim described the man's small penis. The couple described the attackers mask as being a brown ski mask, and one detail they added was that the rapist had a foul-smelling body odor. They told police that the man was naked from the waist down, but he did have a belt around his waist.

The entry point to the home was the sliding glass door that led into the couple's bedroom, but the victims felt that it was most likely unlocked. It was determined that the intruder had removed ketchup and peanut butter from the refrigerator. Outside, a Pepsi can was found in the yard. Police felt that the attacker had left by jumping over their back fence.

The attacker didn't get away with much. His haul included a few silver dollars and a money clip with the word missile carved into it. He also took the male victim's wedding band. It was yellow gold with the inscription, 'For my angel' on the inside along with the date the couple got married. He took some yellow gold cuff links with the male victim's initials on them and a few other odds and ends.

Most of the stuff that he took had more of a personal or sentimental value. There really wasn't a lot of monetary value to the things that he took off with. Police wanted to question the couple's child about what they remembered, and they actually later put the child on under hypnosis. While under hypnosis, the child recounted in detail about a tattoo that was described as being on the attackers left arm, a little bull similar to the Schlitz malt liquor bull, a black bull with white horns. She also detailed a distinct belt buckle with two pistols crossed toward each other.

In the days following the attack on this couple, their phone would ring in the late morning, but nobody would be on the other end when they answer. In fact, their phone didn't seem to work properly in general, and the couple had the phone company come out and fix it, but even after that it seemed to work intermittently. Sometimes during a conversation, the victims would hear a click, and they became convinced that someone was listening to their calls.

One day the police were at the home when a call came in and a young man on the other end of the phone told the female victim who had answered that his office had fixed her phone recently, but he needed for her to verbally tell him her phone number. She handed the phone over to the police officer who was there so they he could hear the man's voice. The officer asked the man to repeat what he had said to the woman, but the caller hung up. Police decided to place a phone trap on the line, so that incoming calls could be recorded, but once the trap was installed, no more odd phone calls came in, and the trouble with their phone lines seem to clear up.

Three months later, in December of 1977, the female victim received an obscene phone call. She was sure that the caller was the man who had raped her. In January of 1978, after victim number one had recorded a call from her attacker, investigators played that recording for many victims of the East Area Rapist, and this included this latest victim as well. She verified that the person on that recorded call was her attacker, so there was no doubt at this point. The East Area Rapist had come to Stockton, California.

The September 1977 attack in Stockton was confirmed to be an East Area Rapist attack, and it was a wake-up call proving that the East Area Rapist wasn't afraid to leave the confines of Sacramento County to commit his crimes. Back in Sacramento, residents weren't taking any chances. Self-defense classes were being offered, gun sales soared, and hardware stores sold out of locks and deadbolts. People wondered if the East Area Rapist was gone for good or if he would return. They wouldn't have to wonder for long.

On September 30, a young couple was arguing. A 17-year old maid and her boyfriend, a 21-year-old electronics representative had been fighting about personal issues that they were dealing with. This was occurring at the man's home on the 9100 block of Tuolumne drive in Sacramento. The fight escalated, and at one point got so bad that the young woman asked her boyfriend to drive her home to her apartment which was nearby. Once they were there, she started feeling ill from the effects of a medical procedure that she had undergone a day or two earlier.

Despite the arguing, her boyfriend didn't want to leave her there alone, so he decided to take her back to his house around 11:30 p.m. When they got back to his house, the couple went inside and went to sleep. About an hour or so later, just after 1:00 a.m. on the morning of October 1, the couple was awakened by a masked man holding a gun in his right hand and a flashlight in his left. The intruder warned the couple, "Shut up, don't move or I'll kill you." He added that he had a 357. He then told them that he wanted their dope, and he knew they had some, and he would look for it until he got it. The young man, still half asleep, looked over at the shotgun he had next to his bed and for a second thought about going for it.

The intruder shined his light on the shotgun, and then stared at the young man as if he is waiting for him to go for it. He decided not to, and the intruder sensed that and took a step forward. Speaking through clenched teeth, he told the pair to roll over on their stomachs, which began a very familiar script. He threw shoelaces to the female ordering her to tie up the male before retying the man tighter, then tying the girl's wrists. The intruder cocked the gun and placed it against both of their heads threatening them to comply.

The next act in the script fell into place as he left the room and started to rummage through the house. At one point, he was in the room with the bound couple, the male victim's pit bull jumped on the bed and growled at the masked man, but this pit bull was a puppy, and it didn't attack the man, didn't even scare him. He simply took the young dog into another room and locked it up. As expected, the intruder took the female victim out of the room, tied her ankles, and blindfolded her. He returned to the male victim with a tray and salt shaker, placing it on his back. As the attacker turned to walk away, the male victim started moving to see if the items on his back would make noise.

As he did this, the masked assailant turned and walked up to the man, and placed the gun to his head, and told him not to move again. After feeling that the male victim was secured, the intruder walked into the room where the female victim was located. He whispered to her through clenched teeth that if she didn't cooperate, he would slit her throat. The next thing she knew she could hear him masturbating using lotion. As we talked about frequently, he placed his penis in the woman's bound hands and ordered her to play with it, then he sexually assaulted the woman.

Afterwards, he went in to check on the male victim. Everything here was a normal part of the East Area Rapist M.O. but this is where things would take a strange turn. The doorbell rang. The two bound victims heard the intruder walk outside where he stayed for several minutes. The attacker then came back into the house and once again, turned his attention to the female victim, and raped her again. He held the cocked gun to her head in the process.

The man then made his way to their kitchen to eat. Outside of the house, they heard a car horn honk two times. After a couple of minutes, the doorbell rang several times, and then they heard a knock on one of the windows. The helpless pair could only listen, trying to determine what was going on. The female victim heard the rapist talking to somebody. The voices were muffled, but she thought that it was a female voice.

While the female victim was listening to the conversation, her boyfriend in the other room used this opportunity to roll over and free himself. He was able to get to his pants pocket and pull out a pocket knife and cut himself free. He then retrieved a loaded revolver that he had under his mattress, and he raced out of the room expecting to shoot the rapist but instead, he found that the home was empty. The young man stepped out into the yard and fired a round out of frustration. He freed his girlfriend and then called the police.

Police arrived at the home shortly after 3:00 a.m. They took statements and called an ambulance to take the female victim to the hospital. The victims described the assailant as being about five feet, nine inches, and 170 pounds with a medium stocky build. As usual, the female victim described the man's penis as very small. The pair also said that the attacker had very bad breath. The female victim added one more odd detail before she was taken to the hospital. She said that during the rape, the man called her by her sister's name. While searching the home, the young man's shot gun was found stashed under a couch. Pry marks on the sliding glass door indicated that the intruder had entered the house there and likely exited the same way.

Much of what the East Area Rapist did in this crime was normal for him, but some things were very different. One of those differences being that the home that the attack took place in was actually a duplex, and as we've talked about, the East Area Rapist typically attacked single-story, single family homes. Also, there was a lack of any prowling activity or odd events leading up to this attack. This was different in many ways, but the thing that really stands out is the possibility that the East Area Rapist may have had a willing accomplice with him and possibly a female accomplice at that.

The victim thought she heard a female voice but thought that the East Area Rapist was most likely talking to himself.

We have to wonder here if the doorbell, knocking, and car horn were part of some elaborate plan by the rapist to make this couple think he had help but the possibility of a female accomplice will come up again. There's evidence to suggest that it wasn't out of the question. One final note about this attack: five years later, October of 1982, this young woman would receive a call from her attacker described here by Contra Costa county investigator, Paul Holes.

> The 1982 phone call was made to victim number twenty-four. It was five years after she was attacked up in Sacramento, actually in Rancho Cordova, and at the time she's working at a diner in 1982. She's at her job when she receives a phone call. This phone call, based on the content of the phone call, I am convinced was the East Area Rapist and it's significant because it's in that 1981 to 1986 gap where we don't have any cases.
>
> It's also significant in that it is after all but one of the cases that occurred down in Southern California, and going to that diner today and taking a look at its configuration and how it sits off the street, and where the victim was living at the time, which was completely across town, I believe our offender was most likely a customer of that diner and saw one of his previous victims there. I believe that our offender was back in Rancho Cordova in 1982.
>
> That's after he's been down in California. Some people felt that that five-year gap could be accounted for by him being in custody, he got popped for a burglary and did a five-year stint at CDC. This was not a phone call which there is a collect call coming out of the CDC. He is not in custody in October of 1982, so he is out and about.

This most recent attack was the first committed by the East Area Rapist in Sacramento County in a four-month period. His return led to questions from citizens about what was being done to catch the East Area Rapist, and these questions prompted the police to respond in an October 8, 1977, *Sacramento Bee* article. More than 5,000 names had been offered to police and sheriff's detectives tried to track down the sexual terrorist known as the East Area Rapist. All but a dozen of the thousand names of possible suspects received by city police had been cleared.

Once the East Area Rapist was back in Sacramento, reports of odd activity, prowling and the like started to come in. On the 6700 block of Gold Run Avenue in Sacramento, several residents started to get hang-up phone calls that started in early October. One of the families receiving these calls had a teenage daughter who arrived home after school one day to find the door leading from her garage into the kitchen partially ajar.

She dismissed it thinking her parents or younger sister must have left it open, but a few days later, she noticed that the door was open once again. Earlier that year, they had arrived home to find their sliding glass door open but didn't find any signs of anybody entering the home or burglarizing it. On the morning of October 21, 1977, this home would be targeted by the East Area Rapist. Sometime after midnight, the youngest daughter had gotten up to use the bathroom. She heard movement in the house but dismissed the noise thinking that one of her family members had also gotten up, so she went back to sleep.

At about 3:00 a.m., the young girl's mother, a 32-year-old homemaker and her husband, a 35-year-old contractor, were awakened to a flashlight shining in their eyes. A masked man was pointing a gun at them, he growled in a harsh whisper through clenched teeth, "I have a 357 magnum. If you don't tie him tight, I'm going to blow your fucking head off." Then he proceeded to throw shoelaces to the woman. The intruder instructed the woman to tie her husband's hands tightly behind his back. After she tied him, the intruder tied her as well. He then left the room and started rifling through the home. After a short while, he returned with dishes that he stacked on the male victim's back. He then left the room again but returned swiftly after the dishes made a slight rattle.

He warned the victim not to move and that he would cut his wife's throat if he did. The attacker dragged the woman off the bed and forced her to walk to the family room. Once there, he raped the woman. After the rape, he walked to the kitchen and got some food, and started to eat. The female victim could hear the rapist crying in the kitchen. After a few minutes, the man walked to the bedroom to check on the male victim before returning to the female victim and raping her again. After the second sexual assault, he stepped away from the woman, and he seemed to be sobbing.

The rapist composed himself and returned to the woman's side. When he did, he told her that he had a buddy in the car outside waiting. He told her to give the police a message. "Tell the pigs I'll be back on New Year's Eve." It sounded as if he stuttered when he said the word pigs. Before he left he pulled the rings off her fingers, and then just like that, the house was silent. After a little bit of time, the couple felt it was safe and they called out to their children who had slept through the entire attack. The children came in and were able to free the couple at which point they called police. Police arrived at the scene close to 5:00 a.m. and immediately started the investigation.

First, they took a detailed description of the attacker. The couple concluded that he was about five feet, ten inches, not large and possibly in his twenties. They mentioned that the man spoke softly but was nervous and hyper at times. The woman added that his penis was fairly big around which clashed with many other statements made by East Area Rapist victims. She also said that despite raping her multiple times that the man had been very gentle with her. During the attack on this couple, the rapist had a lengthy conversation with them. They detailed for police very specific things that the man said. Some of the things he mentioned were that somebody had told him that there was a large amount of cash in the home.

He also mentioned that there was no money in this town, and he was going to have to leave town. He added that he wanted to fill his bag with food. As investigators moved around the house, they found a lamp with a sweatshirt partially covering it which resulted in a softly lit room. We've talked about this in other East Area Rapist attacks. This was a very common tactic that he used. The point of entry was determined to be through the garage and then through the door that led into the kitchen. Outside of the home, they found the victim's rings on the patio as well as three Miller beer bottles.

The only thing missing from the home seemed to be a baseball cap with a logo on it. Neighbors were questioned, and the only sign that the attacker had been in the neighborhood that night was the tell-tale report of dogs barking around the time of the attack. The police left the scene of the crime confident that this had been the twenty-fifth confirmed attack by the East Area Rapist.

The next attack by the East Area Rapist would occur just the very next day on October 29 and this would be on the 4400 block of Woodson Avenue in Sacramento. In the days and weeks prior, suspicious men had been seen walking through the area as if they were looking at houses. Multiple cars that didn't belong to anyone that lived on the street were witnessed.

The residents of one home had found on multiple occasions that their garage door was partially open. On October 27, a day after the same residents had new phone service installed at the home, the 22-year-old housewife who lived there answered the phone. On the other end was silence. This woman and her husband would become the next East Area Rapist victims. On Friday night, October 28, a woman and her 27-year-old husband who was a salesman went out to dinner at around 7:30 p.m. They arrived home at around 10:00 p.m. and were asleep just before midnight.

On early Saturday morning of the 29th at about 1:45 a.m. the husband was fast asleep when he felt something tapping his foot. He opened his eyes only to be blinded by a flashlight.

A voice from behind the lights said, "Don't move or I'll blow your brains out." The hissing voice went on to say, "I know you have a gun around here someplace." The husband motioned towards the nightstand and told the man that it was in the drawer. By now, the wife was awake too and was horrified to see the scene unfolding. The man warned the couple that he only wanted food and money for his van.

The intruder tossed shoelaces to the woman and ordered her to tie up her husband, but she was panicking, and she only tied one of her husband's hands and the attacker noticed this. He warned her that if she tried that again he would blow her brains out. He tossed her another shoelace and told her to tie both of her husband's hands tightly behind his back.

The woman tried to tell the man that they didn't have any cash and offered to write him a check, but he told her, "Shut your fucking mouth." Once the male was secured, the man retied him even tighter and then tied the woman before leaving the room.

The couple could hear the man going through their stuff. After a few minutes, he returned with dishes that he stacked on the male victim's back and brought the female victim out of the room at knifepoint. He led her to the living room threatening to kill her if she tried anything. When they got to the living room the woman saw strips of torn up towel on the floor. The man used these strips to blindfold her. He walked out of the room but returned a few minutes later and straddled her. He placed his penis in her bound hands and ordered her to play with it. He then sexually assaulted the woman.

As soon as the assault ended, the rapist stood up and started crying, and he said out loud, "Mommy, please help me. I don't want to do this mommy." The man walked across the room, and he was still sobbing loud enough that the male victim in the other room could hear him. "Mommy, I don't want to do this. Someone, please help me." Both victims would later tell police that they thought this crying, this sobbing was genuine. But after a few minutes, the man composed himself and snapped back into the predatory attacker that he was earlier. He called the female victim a bitch and said that he was going to watch TV and told her that she had better keep her mouth shut.

He returned later with a cup and saucer that he placed on the woman's back. He noticed that she was wearing a wedding and engagement ring. He grabbed her fingers and pulled off the rings. He then left the room and after several minutes of silence, the couple realized the attacker was gone. They worked to get free and then called police who arrived at the scene a little after 4:00 a.m. The couple detailed for police what they could about the man. They described him as being about five feet, eight inches to five feet, ten inches with average build and weight. The woman told police that the man's penis seemed bigger than she expected based on all the news account.

Police found that one of the telephone cords had been cut and like most of the other East Area Rapist attacks, the point of entry was a sliding glass door. Blood hounds were brought in to try to track the rapist's scent. They followed it to a cab on the 4400 block of Whitney Avenue not far from the scene of the attack, but it was there that they lost the scent. At this point, police were pulling out all the stops trying to apprehend the East Area Rapist. One of the things that they decided to do was to vacuum the areas in the home where the East Area Rapist had been. When they analyzed what they were able to vacuum, they found blue specks of some type of blue architectural paint on hairs that were collected.

This blue paint would also be found on shoelaces that the East Area Rapist had handled. It would be determined that this type of paint was associated with waterproofing. Throughout the East Area Rapist's investigation, lab work would continue to find specs of this blue paint. Later on, in Southern California, it would also result in a possible lead in the case. Later that morning, around the spot where the blood hounds lost the rapist's scent near Whitney Avenue, police found a woman who ran a beauty shop and often went to work very early in the morning to get started.

They questioned the woman to see if she had seen anything unusual that morning, and it turned out she had. She had arrived that morning for work around 4:00 a.m. At about 6:30 a.m. while looking across the street, she witnessed a man stand up in an open trailer that was attached to a dump truck. The man was wearing dark clothes and had a ski mask on. He pulled a bike up from the trailer and jumped down onto the bike and took off very quickly. Police were left to wonder if the man witnessed by this woman was the East Area Rapist and if it was, this was a missed opportunity to catch him.

They could only sit back and wait to see when and where the East Area Rapist would strike next. During late October and November of 1977, area residents on the 8100 block of La Riviera Drive were experiencing activity that was typical leading up to an East Area Rapist attack. One woman and her husband had received hang-up phone calls. Six months earlier, this same couple spotted a prowler shining a light into their bedroom window from the outside. On November 7, a message was found scrawled on a bathroom wall close to this area at the California State University. It read, "The East Area Rapist was here. Will rape my first black girl tonight. Dumb cops will never find me." Back on the 8100 block of La Riviera drive, people had prowlers in their yards at night on November 9, and early morning hours on the 10. Barking dogs broke the silence. Somebody was moving around in the darkness. One man put his outside light on but didn't see anything unusual. Only minutes later, his mother was awakened by pounding sounds coming from outside. Only a few houses away from this commotion, a 13-year-old girl was asleep in her bed with no idea that she would become the next victim of the East Area Rapist. That girl's name was Margaret and she joined us to share her story.

We won't lay out all the details of how the East Area Rapist got in, what he did and what he said, instead, we'll let Margaret tell you what happened in her own words and how it affected her over the years:

My name is Margaret Wardlow and I was the twenty-seventh victim of the East Area Rapist in Sacramento on November 10, 1977. I was the youngest victim, I was 13 at the time. For me, looking back on the day that it happened, I've had the benefit of meeting with Sacramento homicide and now it's been forty years, of course, and I didn't remember everything that I did as a kid that day.

Of course, it was a school day, and I met with the Sacramento homicide. They let me go over the case file, and I read that I had gotten home from school, and I don't think the dog—I had a big golden retriever that we kept in the garage during the day and the garage was open, so when I got home from school, I'd open up the garage door. The dog wasn't in the garage at the time, I believe, and so I waited around for the dog to come home. We lived right on the American River at a house-- A condominium that backed up to the American River.

When the dog came home, I got on my bike and rode across the river to a soccer game that was being held at a private school called Country Day and took the dog with me, met a girlfriend over there, and then came back after the game and met up with my mom. We went over to a neighbor's house, put the dog back in the house, but didn't lock our front door or anything.

We really were very lax about locking our house up even though we knew this prolific rapist was running around. My mom really thought that she was too old to be a victim. I was definitely too young and so we really-- I don't think we really thought of ourselves as being vulnerable to this guy. But anyway, we went to over to a single guy who was a neighbor in the area. We listened to an album, had dinner with him, and went back home about eight o'clock. In between this time, we left our front open when the dog was in the house. I was awoken very early in the morning by a flashlight shining in my face. He's telling me, turn over, I'm going to tie you up. I thought for sure it was this guy that we just had dinner with. It was a school morning, and I thought it was my mom who had let him in to joke around and wake me up for school because he was just a prankster. I refused. I said, no, no. I'm not going to let you tie me up and he said, this isn't a joke. I said, quit joking, quit joking. Numerous times he said this isn't a joke and finally, I just played along with it. Playing along with it, thinking that this is still a joke, and then finally once he got me tied up, I turned over and looked at the clock radio, and I thought it was about 2:30 in the morning, then I realized this isn't a joke.

I realized, yes, this is probably the East Area Rapist. My head went right to it. As a kid, we got the newspaper. I think we got The Afternoon Union, I believe it was. It was delivered in the afternoon or maybe The Sacramento Bee was delivered in the afternoon. My mom subscribed to the Bee. I was just an avid reader of anything related to the East Area Rapist. I was number twenty-seven and everything that had been written about this guy, every single profile, anything that came out in the news, I remember reading one particular article three times over and thinking, why can't I glean more about this guy? Why don't they write more about him? What is making this guy tick? Why is he doing this? Why is he attacking these people?

By that time, he had already started attacking couples in their homes and putting plates on the husband's back and taking the woman into another room and attacking her. This was even more of a reason for both my mother and I to believe that we weren't possible *victims of his. Anyway, he was very threatening. He spoke in a very harsh whisper, and it was usually in a question, like do you want to die, do you want me to kill you, do you want me to kill your mother. From what I understood from reading all of these articles is that this guy just really got off on scaring the bejeebers out of his victims. He would just really get off on frightening people, and I was just bound and determined not to let him get to me. Even as he started threatening me and threatening to kill my mom, I just-- I couldn't. "Do you want me to kill your mom? Do you want me to kill you?" I just told him I don't care. I just continued with I don't care. I don't care and as soon as you started to answer his questions, he'd tell you, shut up, shut up, shut up, in this really harsh-- A harsh whisper is just really the best way to explain how he spoke.*

You couldn't even get a word out when you started to answer him. It was really frustrating. It was almost like he had a script that he went by, and you weren't part of it. You didn't have anything to say in his script. It was all of what he had to say. You didn't have any role in the part. I remember not being scared, but just feeling so offended like what are you doing here. There's nothing here for you. He asked me a couple times if I had had sex, and I was a virgin and I told him no. I think he probably thought I was older than I was. I can definitely see why he chose me. I was very visible. I was very visible in the area. I was always outside. I was always running around in my bathing suit.

We lived in this condominium that my mom had waited for. They were very coveted. It was a real coveted real estate area. There were these condos that sat right up against the levee, on La Riviera drive in Sacramento. They butted right up to the levee, and they were unique in that you had your kitchen, your dining room, and living room area upstairs, so you had a view of the river and the trees and everything back along the river area. All the bedrooms were downstairs. The only thing about that was in the evening when all the lights were on in the house, anyone walking up along that levee could really look into the house. You could see exactly what was going on in that home. Anyone that was a victim of his, he was watching the home. He was in their home. He was familiar. I'm sure he was familiar with my dog. My dog was very protective of the house, and anyone that was outside of the home, my dog was always barking, but my dog didn't let out a sound. I know this guy was in the house. He had to have been there.

We weren't very vigilant about locking the house. Anyway, after realizing that of course, this is the East Area Rapist. I could hear him talking to my mom. I knew he was upstairs. He was in and out of the room. You never knew when he was in or out. I was blindfolded. I was tied up. I had gotten my feet untied at one point. I got my feet untied and he came into the room and was furious and I was debating like, "Should I get up, should I stand up and try to walk out the door, what should I do?" But then I thought, I can't see well because I was blindfolded. I thought where am I going to go.

How am I going to get out the door? My hands were tied behind my back. I just didn't know what I was going to do, but I could hear him. Once he got the plates, I could hear him coming down the stairs, and I just knew at that point, "Okay, he's coming downstairs with those plates. If he comes into my room, he's going to rape my mom. If he goes into my mom, it means he's going to rape me. I could hear him going into my mom's room, and I just prepared myself because I knew-- I just knew from everything I had read, everything I had known.

This is one thing you can't get yourself out of. You're the kid. You know you can get yourself out of a lot of things, but I knew this is something I was going to have to face up to. Just be tough and it's going to be over with, and it's almost like I had a little angel on my shoulder just telling me, "You're going to get through this. You're going to survive." I knew just by talking to him and telling him just refusing him the pleasure of showing fear, I knew that he wasn't going to hurt me, he wasn't going to kill me because he hadn't hurt or killed anyone as far as I knew. I knew he wasn't going to hurt me. He wasn't going to kill my mom. He wasn't going to hurt me.

That's what I based all of my actions on and my behaviors on with the fact that he hadn't hurt anyone, hadn't killed anyone. Once later on, I found that he murdered people. I thought, that's not the guy. He's not killing people. There's no way he's a murderer, but of course, I know that he became a murderer. It's very frightening to think that I tangled with this person like I did, but as a kid, you're immortal, right? That's what happened.

Once the attack was over, you never knew when he left. He turned on the fan upstairs. He turned the fan- - The kitchen fan. He ran the kitchen water. Once he departed, we just really didn't know when he had left. My mom started screaming for the next-door neighbor. The next-door neighbor came over with a rifle or a shotgun and came into the house. By that time, I had hopped all the way upstairs and my feet were tied still I climbed all the way upstairs and got up to the powder room upstairs and locked myself up inside there. The neighbor's wife came upstairs and untied me and then shortly after that, Sacramento Sheriff's Department came and questioned us. They asked me, what did you say to him? You said you didn't care? They couldn't believe the way I responded to the guy. I was just a tough kid, and I did the best I could, I don't think I could do it today.

We asked Margaret how much time the East Area Rapist was in her home.

I want to say an hour, but maybe it was as short as 45 minutes. As a kid, it's really hard to gauge, but I would say it was about an hour.

Margaret told us how it was that she was able to not only cope with the attack, but to also cope with the attacker not being caught.

Well, I was fearless, I remember just feeling indignant like, "What are you here for, why are you here." I was pissed. I don't really remember the fear so much like, "Well, there's nothing here for you not this I have nothing for you, this is not-- I'm not your victim." I don't know, it's such a weird thing. It's almost like I had some kind of predisposition that I had to know, that I had to read every single article, and know everything about this guy before the attack and then after the attack I didn't follow up on that.

I watched it, attack after attack, after the attack and after a while, I was just like so disgusted that you know they hadn't found them, and they couldn't get him. I had no ill will towards that the Sheriff's Department. I knew they were trying to find him, that they worked so well with me, and I knew they were trying their best to get him. They were out there, were stopping people, and they talked to numerous people that they had stopped. I understand that there was a lack of communication between jurisdictions because they didn't have Internet, they didn't have all the technology we have nowadays.

Margaret shared her opinion on what the East Area Rapist thought about his encounter with her.

He definitely was less interested in me because I wasn't sexually experienced because he asked me, "Have you fucked before?" He asked me that a couple of times, and he was more interested in girls that were experienced. Yes, he wanted girls that were more experienced because he wasn't getting that satisfaction. I wasn't playing along to his script, I believe he wasn't getting what he came for, that fear factor thing. The weirdest thing about it is you think he'd be really angry with me for not playing along. I was shivering at the end, after he attacked me, before he left. It was cold, and I didn't sleep with any clothes on and I was shivering, I didn't have any covers on me at that point and he said, "What's wrong why are you shaking?" I said, "I'm cold." He took a blanket and picked it up and covered me with it, and I thought that was weird. Why would he be compassionate towards me after I was such a little bitch?

We asked Margaret how she thought the East Area Rapist may have targeted her?

I was highly visible, my mom was not a protective mom, my mom let me do whatever I wanted, stay out after dark, I did whatever I wanted. Even after the attack, I never looked over my shoulder, I was never fearful after that, I knew he would never attack me again, I knew he never chased down his victims. I wasn't fearful of that. I know he called his victims, we had a recorder on our phone, whenever we answered the phone we had to turn on the recorder. I was waiting for the guy to call, I was going to give him an earful, I was ready for that, I couldn't wait to tell him to fuck off.

Despite what happened to her at such a young age Margaret didn't let this affect the rest of her life.

In Sacramento, people really reacted to it adversely, and I was not that affected by it and years would go by. Like a lot of the victims are going to tell you, "I get a bad feeling towards that time of year; I get kind of spooked, or I have a very uneasy feeling." I'll tell you years have gone by and I never thought twice about it and in fact, I had even mistaken the date I thought it was November 27. Well actually it's November 10, I was twenty-seventh victim. I had even messed up the date. I didn't even remember the exact date of the attack.

For me I only got tired of telling the story. I thought sometimes people got a different idea about me maybe or they felt sorry for me. I didn't want anybody to feel sorry for me, I really felt that it was a victory in my life rather than a tragedy. It was nothing that ever defined me. I can never be a rape advocate or something or help somebody else because I would have been like, "Hey girl, it's time to walk down that dark alley because you know you can't let somebody affect your life so adversely because they've done something terrible to you. You can't let somebody have so much power over you."

Margaret told us about how meeting other surviving East Area Rapist victims and family members of his murder victims changed her outlook on the case, and on the East Area Rapist himself.

For me, I never really felt like it could help anyone. I never felt that anybody really cared about my story to be quite honest. I never really cared if he would get caught to be honest with you until I met these other women. Within the last year I met Debbie Domingo, I met Michele Cruz, I met James Sandler, I met these lovely, lovely women and heard their stories. Their stories are incredibly moving, tragic, and horrific. For me, it's become very personal in the fact that I've met these people whose lives have been changed unimaginably. That's how I've been affected, with them just the last year of meeting some of the other victims and people who have been affected by this guy.

Now, I want to see justice done, not for me, but for others. The story that needs to be told is that this guy is still out there. The story that needs to be told is that we have his DNA. The story that needs to be told is that somebody has information about him, and somebody knows something about him, somebody was his girlfriend, somebody was his classmate, somebody in Sacramento knows something about him, and maybe in Visalia as well. Somebody knows this guy, but there's a few people out there probably that know this guy or may suspect who this guy may be, and he may very well be alive in Sacramento, still living his life for all we know.

If he is out there, he needs to be held accountable for what he's done to these people. That's where my story comes in, and that's where I think it's important that I contribute if I can. If somebody wants to hear my story, or if there's anything that I can do to help bring light to these crimes, or if I bring more interest to this piece, bring more people to the table and hear about what's going on with the history of these crimes, then that's what I want to be able to help do. And hopefully it will bring some results for the people that have lost their loved ones, that's the most important thing to me.

What's the most important part of it is that more people that are made aware of what happened with these crimes, and the fact that we're still looking for this guy, I think that's the most important story that needs to be told, is that we're still looking for this person, he's never been held accountable for these murders, and that we need to find who he is. I mean, he may very well be dead by now, but we need to find out who he was, and have some answers, give some answers to these families, because it's not fair and it's just not right. It's horrific what they've had to go through and not have answers to who he was and why he hasn't been brought to justice.

SEASON TWO,
EPISODE SEVEN

The few weeks following Margaret's attack were largely uneventful. There were no reported East Area Rapist attacks, one of the East Area Rapist's many victims mailed in a rather moving letter to the Sacramento Bee. This letter was in response to an article that the *Bee* had previously run about the East Area Rapist.

> *As a recent victim of the East Area Rapist, I read with interest your July 3 article: Rape Case Conflict on the disagreement between local police and the Rape Crisis Center. According to your article, the Rape Crisis Center and its supporters claim that police agencies too often are insensitive to the immediate emotional needs of a rape victim. In the immediate aftermath of my attack, the decency and tact of the uniformed officers played a large part in helping to keep myself glued together. I am deeply grateful to them all. A uniformed lady officer was summoned immediately and shortly afterward Detective Carol Daly.*

> *At no time was I made to feel that the need for police information was being put above my well-being or that the emotional pain of my experience was being disregarded. In the days after the incident, Detective Daly showed great concern for my well-being more than anyone else. She seemed to understand my feelings and I never spoke with her without feeling better afterward. On the other hand, I am still ambivalent about my talks with the women at the Rape Crisis Center.*

Several times they made the comment that other rape victims were feeling insignificant and out of the ballpark because their assailant was not the East Area Rapist and they were presumably not getting the same level of attention that I was after just being raped, robbed, terrorized, and having the lives of my husband and child threatened, it left me confused to hear from a counselor that other women were envious of the circumstances of my attack. However, innocently the comment was made, it hurt badly.

The women at the Rape Crisis Center are very well intentioned and I do not want to appear to bite the hand that tried to help me, but I do believe these women have some very ingrained political orientations that affect their attitudes toward victims and the police. These attitudes need to be reexamined. Regarding the anti-police comment of Ted Sheety, it is certainly a shame that a man could hold county office for so long and still be totally ignorant of the workings of his local law enforcement agencies.

If local politicians, TV commenters and rape counselors were half as dedicated and professional as our police, Sacramento would be in really good shape. But, until such a fine day arrives, here is my advice to any Sacramento woman who was raped, "Call the police immediately. Then call your two closest girlfriends." - Rape Victim Sacramento.

Almost a month since the last East Area Rapist attack on Margaret, on December 2, the Sacramento Police Department received the following call.

You're never going to catch me I'm the East Area Rapist, you dumb fuckers. I'm going to fuck again tonight. Be careful.

When this call came in, police didn't know what to make of it, and they had no way of knowing if the call was really from the East Area Rapist or simply just a prank call.

Later that night, a woman on the 900 block of Revelstock Way in Sacramento, settled in the bed for the night. Her husband had gone out for the night with some friends and her teenage son was sleeping at a friend's house. This woman decided to allow her six-year-old daughter sleep in bed with her. She went to sleep at about 11:30, but not long after falling asleep just before midnight, she was awakened by a noise that she assumed was her cat. She ignored it but heard it again, and then rolled over to the sight of a masked man shining a light in her eyes.

The masked man whispered to the woman telling her to get up. Almost defiantly, she asked him, "Why?" The man replied, "Get up and come with me or I'll hurt your little boy." This intruder had mistaken her daughter for a boy. Once the woman stood up, she saw that he had a black pair of shoe laces, but she didn't see a weapon. He forced her to walk down the hallway into the living room and then forced her to her knees before tying her with the shoelaces.

The woman started to cry, and he threatened to gag her. She begged the attacker not to and told her she would be quiet. She wanted to not be gagged, in case her daughter got up. That way she'd be able to tell her to go back to bed. The masked man agreed, and he didn't gag her, and he also did not blindfold her. Noise outside caught the attacker's attention. There was a group of teenagers playing in the street in front of the home. The man was distracted by them, and he kept peeking outside the window at them.

As she lay on the floor, the assailant walked by her a few times. He was talking to her or maybe to himself and said, "You think you're smart, but I'm smarter." After a few moments, the house was silent. Outside, the woman heard what sounded like a loud van start up and then drive away. She waited a few minutes, then she got up and went to her phone where she called a neighbor for help. Thankfully, as in some of the other East Area Rapist cases, the child slept through the entire event. Police were called, and they arrived after midnight on December 3, and started their investigation.

This woman compared to some other East Area Rapist victims had escaped relatively unharmed. The thinking is that the intruder had been so nervous about the teenagers outside that he decided to abort the attack. Police questioned the woman, and she told them that her attacker was white and sounded as if he was in his twenties. He was under sex feet tall and had a thin build. He spoke through clenched teeth. They were able to determine that the point of entry was the family room window, which had been pried. The victim was able to determine that the intruder hadn't stolen anything. She did tell police that in the weeks leading up to her attack, she had received several hang-up phone calls that almost always came after 2:00 p.m.

Police questioned neighbors, but they wanted to start with the group of teenagers who were gathered on the street out in front of the victim's home. After speaking with them, they verified that none of them had seen anything unusual. One person, however, spotted an out of place white station wagon with black tires that was parked across the street from the victim's home around midnight. Other residents close by reported that in the spring of that year, they had received a call from a man whispering, "You are next." One neighbor reported seeing an out-of-place blue van in the area with a Sacramento army decal on it and this was just a week or so before the attack.

Another neighbor saw a beige-colored station wagon in front of the victim's home a few days before the attack, and there were other unknown men and prowlers spotted in the area in the days leading up to the attack. All of this was typical activity leading up to an East Area Rapist attack.

Police learned that in late August, a nearby home had been burglarized. The thief had made off with two photos of the homeowners and their typewriter, not the typical things a burglar would take. The call placed earlier, the day of the attack, to police in which somebody claimed to be the East Area Rapist may have been legit. He threatened that he would attack that night and he did. Thankfully, this woman escaped an attack, which could have been a lot more serious. This aborted attack seemed to drive home the fact that the East Area Rapist was all about self-preservation. If things didn't go right or weren't going as planned, or something seemed off, then he simply aborted the attack. In this case, the noisy teenagers outside had made him nervous enough to take off. For weeks after this attack, throughout December of 1977 and in early January of 1978, the East Area Rapist focus seemed to shift away from attacking in person toward harassing people over the phone.

On December 9, the twenty-first victim of the East Area Rapist received a phone call from someone she thought was the same man who had raped her. The next day on December 10, a man called into the Sacramento Police Department and said, "I am going to hit tonight." Then he indicated that it was going to be on Watt Avenue but there were no attacks that night. The next day on December 11, very close to Watt Avenue, a man riding a bicycle and wearing a ski mask was witnessed by police and they chased after him. The man ditched the bike and outran police on foot. Police traced the bicycle and found that it had been stolen in Redding, California, 150 miles away.

On December 12, multiple copies of what may have been the first written communication from the East Area Rapist were received by the Sacramento's mayor's office, the *Sacramento Bee*, and a local Sacramento television station. The communication came in the form of a typed poem titled *Excitements Crave*.

> "All those mortals surviving birth upon facing maturity take inventory of their worth to prevailing society. Choosing values becomes a task. Ones self must seek satisfaction. The selected route will unmask character when plans take action, accepting some work to perform at fixed pay but promise for more

is a recognized social norm as is decorum seeking lore. Achieving while others lifting should be cause for deserving fame, leisure temps excitement seeking, what's right and expected seems tame.

Jesse James has been seen by all, and Son of Sam has an author. Others now feel temptations call. Sacramento should make an offer to make a movie of my life that will pay for my planned exile. Just now I'd like to add the wife of a Mafia Lord to my file. Your East Area Rapist and deserving pest. See you on the press or on TV."

Police searched these mailings for clues that might lead to the author of the poem, then recovered a palm print on one of the letters that has never been matched to anyone, and it would be determined that the typewriter used to create the poem was the same exact make and model of the typewriter we mentioned earlier as being stolen from a home leading up to the most recent attack. Also interesting was the fact that the poem mentioned, "Wife of a Mafia Lord," which may have been in reference to the twenty-first victim and her husband who were Italian.

Later in December of 1977, police got a good lead that they were interested in. A man who matched many of these East Area Rapist's descriptions had been coming into a 7-Eleven store located at 10721 Coloma Road in Rancho Cordova. He came in almost daily either late at night or early in the morning. He would walk to the back of the store and loiter as he read adult magazines. Police took it seriously enough that they decided to set up a stakeout. The officer at the head of making the stakeout happen was Ted Daly, who was Carol Daly's husband.

Ted Daly ordered two officers to go to the 7-Eleven. One was to sit outside in an unmarked police car, the other would go inside the store and wait in a backroom for the man to come in. Once the man came in, the police were supposed to approach the man, question him and learn his identity. However, things did not go as planned, according to detective Richard Shelby.

I talked to Ted Daly, the Sergeant. Today, they call it SWAT, then it was SCD, Selective Enforcement Detail. I ordered them out. Basically, he found out about this guy that hung out in 7-Eleven about two o'clock every morning. I understand he looked at the little dirty books back in the corner. Well, he put two officers out there and told them to go into the backroom and stake it out. Go in there in civilian clothes. One of them sat outside in the squad car which I thought was smart, the other one put a shirt on over his uniform I guess. I don't know what kind of shirt he had on.

But, the dumb shit, he was wearing his uniform pants, and he was back there in the backroom. He came out to get coffee on occasion. Then the clerk got a phone call from a man asking to talk to the cop in the back. The clerk said there's no cop. He said, "Don't give me that." When the cop came out and picked up the phone, the guy just laughed at him and hung up the phone. Then the suspect never turned up again.

This seemed like a really good lead but like many other leads, in this case, police couldn't capitalize on it. The man that they were looking for was thought to live very close to the 7-Eleven, maybe in one of the nearby apartment complexes on Coloma road. But he never came back in the store. During that month of December, another victim, the eighth victim, also received a call that they thought was from the East Area Rapist. Then Christmas passed, as did New Year's, but on January 2, 1978, that's the day that the very first victim received the sinister phone call.

Hello? Hello? Hello?

Gonna kill you. Gonna kill you.

Fucking whore.

Fortunately, this call was recorded, and it was later played for other victims of the East Area Rapist whohad received similar calls. They all agreed that this was the voice with the man who had raped them. Four days later, on January 6, a counselling service volunteer received a phone call from a man who claimed that he was the East Area Rapist. The caller claimed that he had been treated on and off at the Stockton State Hospital. He also accused the counselor of tracing his call and hung up.

Later, on January 20, at around 5:20 to 5:30 a.m., two different East Area Rapist victims received phone calls that were identical in nature. The caller said to each of them that he had not struck in a while. "You will be my next victim. I'm going to come over and fuck you in the butt. See you soon."

Now these calls, although frightening and terrorizing, they were just that. They were calls but assuming that they were from the East Area Rapist, it proved that he was still terrorizing but not in person. It had been two months with no East Area Rapist attack. That would change on January 28 when the East Area Rapist would strike on the 4300 block of College View Way in Carmichael. This attack would be one of the most despicable in the series because the East Area Rapist would attack and rape two teenage sisters.

Just a few weeks before, the mother of these two girls had witnessed a man running from their garage. When she investigated, she found out that some tools were missing. Over the next two weeks, these two girls who were La Sierra High School students aged 14 and 15, received odd calls from a man they didn't know. They described the man as having a funny voice and during these calls, he would ask if their mom was home. On January 28, at about 7:00 p.m., the girl's parents left to go to a concert. The sisters stayed at home and went to bed at around 10:00 p.m.

Between 10:30 and 11 p.m., the older sister was awakened by a thump followed by a voice in her room. The startled girl sat up, and she saw a man in a mask standing in her doorway holding a flashlight. The intruder told her to get all her money or he would kill her. As her eyes adjusted to the light, she could see that the man was holding a gun. She turned over to get some cash that she kept close to her bed. It was about sixty dollars. She handed the money to the man after he approached her. He then ordered her to go wake up her sister.

The older sister escorted the man into her younger sister's room. At which point the hooded man shook the younger sister waking her up. He told her as soon as she was awake, "Don't look at me or I'll kill you." He then ordered her to give him cash as well. He forced the girls to lie down on the bed face down. He bound their hands tightly behind their backs with shoelaces. He then asked the pair when their parents would be home. They told the attacker that they were to come home at midnight. The man threatened them with a knife telling them that if they were lying, he would kill them both and then kill their parents when they came home.

The attacker left the girls bound on the bed and went to look through the house going through several drawers in the process. He'd later returned, and this is when the unthinkable happened. He placed his lubricated penis into the older girl's hands and then moved to the younger sister doing the same exact thing. Again, we're not going to go into every detail of this attack, but the attacker raped both sisters while they laid next to each other. The East Area Rapist has done so many disgusting things up to this point.

Just when you think that this monster can't get any more depraved, he goes and does something like this. During the attack, he covered one victim's head with a sweater and the other with a pillow.

After the sexual attack, the man stood up and warned the girls not to talk to each other. He told them that he would kill them if they did. He asked them where their parents kept their money, and they told the man that it was on top of their dresser. The man went to their bedroom to grab the cash but came back very quickly, and he started to speak in a rather whimpering voice tongue that he couldn't find the money. Then in the same whimpering voice he told them. "I don't want to do this anymore. She's making me do it."

The man walked out of the room, and the house became quiet. The two sisters were not sure if he was still there, so they remained still until 11:30 p.m. when they heard their parents walk into the house. The parents freed the girls and immediately called the police. Police arrived just before midnight and started their investigation. They determined that the point of entry was the front door which had been kicked in.

Before being taken to Sacramento Medical Center for treatment, the sisters were able to describe their attacker as being five feet, seven inches to five feet, to nine inches, thin to medium build with a small penis. They thought he might be in his thirties. Police thought he may have been in the house for only thirty minutes or so and perhaps was scared off by the arrival of the girl's parents. The fact he simply kicked the door open to get to these two girls shows that this attack was more rushed and not calculated like some of the other attacks before.

Four days later on February 2, 1978 on the 10,000 block of La Alegria Drive, a young couple was shot and killed.

The Maggiore's were newlyweds. At the time of the murders, they had been married for about eighteen months. Brian was a young security policeman in the Air Force. He and Katie were awaiting orders to go overseas, something the young couple was excited about. The couple had taken their dog Thumper, a poodle, out for a walk.

The Maggiores lived in an apartment on La Verta court, just a short distance away from where they were shot. Their murder seemed random, but it also appeared that the killer had gone out of his way after shooting Brian to make sure that he also killed Katie. These senseless murders shocked their families. Katie's brother Ken Smith told us about how his family got the news and how it affected them not just immediately following the murders but for the rest of their lives.

I was in high school at the time. The Air Force actually sent somebody to his place of business and informed him and then they escorted him over to where my mom worked for Fresno Unified School District, and they picked her up and told her. Then they picked Keith up at school, and then they came to the high school where I was going to school and had to be pulled out and told me about it. That weekend prior to it happening, we had just seen them. They'd come down into town from Sacramento.

My sister turned twenty on January, 29, three days before it happened. They came down to celebrate her birthday, but we had talked to them on the phone the night that it all happened. When this all happened, they just moved like a week or so prior. The whole thing was just devastating to our family. Like I said, our family didn't talk about it much and almost withdrew probably from each other because of it. I think it put a heavy burden that all of us have been left to deal with for quite some time now. Kate and Brian were just a wonderful, happy, young couple.

Brian, you couldn't ask for a better guy, you know, he was a wonderful person. Katie was always a happy go lucky, outgoing personality, just was always just fun. I mean, her and I were really, really close, and so it was very difficult for me. I had a hard time with it even to this day. One of the things that bothers me the most is the fact that not only were we cheated out of a life together as far as, I mean, you know, her being 20 and I was 16, but her not getting to meet my family. I have three kids and two grandbabies, and they never met her.

Ken went on to detail for us what investigators were thinking at the time.

At the time, there was a lot of different information floating around out there. Probably 98 percent of it is very inaccurate, I would say. My family didn't speak about it much, so they would not come to me and tell me anything about what was going on. If I found out anything that was going on, it was kind of overhearing a conversation with somebody else. It was kept really hush hush. There were a lot of rumors that went around at the time.

One positive thing to come out of the investigation of Brian and Katie's murder was that there were multiple witnesses who filled in what happened at the time of the murders. One of those witnesses, named Carl, was 17 at the time, and he sat down with us to tell us what he could remember about the events of that night, events that occurred over forty-one years ago.

My name is Carl Nollsch. I grew up in Rancho Cordova, California, and I was involved with the East Area Rapist case when a shooting occurred two doors down from me when I lived in Rancho Cordova along La Alegria Street. I was one of the few witnesses of the perpetrator is how I got involved with the case. I've recently been contacted and I've been trying to help out any way I can, even though it's been forty years. I'd like to help any way I can to solve the case. It was a February evening, I think it was around 7:00 something at night. I was a 17-year-old teenager, lived with my folks on La Alegria Street. I had a bedroom that was in the back of the house.

In California, all the tract homes have wooden fences in their backyard. It's not uncommon to have a lot of fences blow down with a heavy storm and wind. I remember sitting in my room, and I heard some banging of fences like somebody was trying to break down a fence or something to that effect. I heard a couple of loud bangs not really knowing what it was. I walked out of the front of the house through the garage onto our driveway. As I was walking out there-- it was a winter night but it was clear.

It was dark, but there was enough light from porches that you could get a good look of what was going on. I remember walking out there, and I heard a couple more- two, three more shots and maybe a scream. I looked to the left, and then I heard a scrambling of somebody trying to try to climb a fence and then somebody falling into maybe some bushes and scrambling. The gate was locked, he had to climb the fence. The gate was right by the driveway, and there was a small alleyway between the fence next door and the house.

That's where he, I guess, shot the second person. He had to scramble that fence. Then I heard somebody running towards me and the perpetrator, he runs out down the street and across our neighbor's lawn actually next door to the left. I made my way up to the front of the house enough where I was near the front of the lawn area, and I was looking at him, and he ran up within five to ten feet of me next door onto the neighbor's lawn. It was dark enough where he didn't really see that there was somebody out there standing out there until they got within ten, twenty feet. He stopped because he was startled, looked at me, and then he turned around and ran back down the opposite side of the street as fast as he could to get away. At the same time my neighbor Don Morris on the right, he had he come out of the house also because he'd heard some loud booms. We both didn't know what was going on. We walked to the Otlinger's because I had seen him hopping over that fence. I had a direct line to the Otlinger's gate, and so we walked over there. We had heard somebody breathing that had been shot in that area. It is about that time we finally realized that there had been a shooting.

It's a nice quiet neighborhood in Rancho Cordova. To expect a couple of people that had been assassinated or murdered two doors down was pretty frightening. Then naturally the police came, and we did some interviews. I got approval from my mom to go downtown. The head detective Ray Biondi did an interview with me and then I was actually put under hypnosis. I recalled some details. I worked with a sketch artist also. I had some artistic talent, so I was able to give him some general features. He was more of a slender guy, longer legs, probably five feet, ten inches to six feet tall or something like that. I actually helped out with a few renderings. He had kind of a light brown bomber jacket type on that I recalled.

When he turned to run away, he had a large penis shaped stain on the back of his jacket. I recalled that from the hypnosis and helped sketch that out. I thought he was taller, slender, kind of athletic type of gait. There was a level of franticness for him to be escaping the crime scene and then running. He seemed to have a longer gait. Taller, slender guy and moved pretty quick. I thought he had deeper set eyes. I have a vision of some hair. I can't recall him having a ski mask. I think I said in one of my first interviews that he didn't have a mask on. When I went under hypnosis, I said he had a mask on. It's really hard to say.

Carl mentioned Ray Biondi as being the detective in charge of the Maggiore case. Detective Biondi may sound familiar to some. In the same year the Maggiores were murdered, he would go on to catch Sacramento's infamous vampire killer Richard Trenton Chase. He joined us to discuss the early investigation in the Maggiore murders. He even read aloud for us from the actual reports that he prepared forty-one years ago.

On February 2, 1978, around 7:00 in the evening, it was their nightly routine to walk their dog after dinner each night. They left their residence which was at an apartment complex within this suburban neighborhood. About that time, neighbors heard a screaming female and shots and then more shots. We were called to the scene and what we determined the victims had already been evacuated from the scene by the time I got there. What we were able to piece together was that Brian and Katie were walking on an adjacent street when they were confronted by a gunman.

This gunman chased them through the backyard of the residence and between this residence and the next residence on another street a fence had blown down because of a high wind in the area. Brian obviously ran around the side of the house that they went into the backyard, and he went to the blind side of the backyard. There was no fence. He was shot there. In fact, some of the shots fired by the gunman actually went through the glass door at that residence where the people were watching television. Katie meanwhile ran to the other side of the residence where there was the gate. It appeared that she tripped on a flower bed there, and that's where the gunman caught up with her and shot her.

That's where the screams could be heard from various neighbors. What was unusual about the crime is it was seven o'clock in the evening, and there was still light, the neighborhood was still very active, people were out and about. It wasn't late, middle of the night. Why would a gunman confront a couple walking down the street? The neighbors next door where the crime occurred and others in the area reported numerous sightings of an individual running. The one that seemed most interesting or at least was one of a comprehensive compilation of many sightings but *generally was a white male about six feet, six feet, two inches tall, probably medium build.*

He had a dark blue knit cap with only eyes and nose showing, more like a skier's cap, a light brown waist length jacket with a dark color stain on the lower right side. His jacket was interesting in that there were other sightings where people said that there was a military insignia or a patch on the side of the jacket. Some described it as a brown leather jacket. Most consistently, they were talking about a brown leather jacket. Probably had anywhere from five to seven different people that saw this male running. In one instance, their neighbor witnessed that he appeared to have a gun in his back pocket.

At the crime scene, what was interesting is the description with the ski mask on and then the backyard at the side of the backyard where Brian was shot, we found shoelaces that obviously had just come out of the package. They still had the new kinks in them. But they were tied in such a fashion as to make a pair of loops or bindings. That was interesting because the county had been suffering from a whole series of rapes called the East Area Rapist. The signature of this particular rapist was that he wore a ski mask, he used new shoelaces to bind his victims, and in some cases, had even confronted male and female victims outside of a residence and ordered them back in at gunpoint.

We had that going for us, but we have a lot suspects that developed initially. Brian worked in the administrative part of the security police at Mather. One of his jobs was to take care of all the tickets and the traffic situation on the base. Katie worked at a local gas station and had been bothered by at least one individual. There are several good suspects that surfaced initially. There was a security guard who worked in the area who that night carried a similar kind of and displayed some very unusual behavior following that night. His wife said he had locked himself in his room for two days.

There were several other Air Force males that were in the area. Many of these fit the description but as we kept going and going, none of these came to fruition. The first witness who was actually next door to the scene where they were murdered was coming out of his house and saw an individual run from the area of the bushes about where Katie was behind those bushes and fence and was shot. That is probably the most viable sighting. That individual was wearing a ski mask and had, again, the light brown jacket. There were witnesses throughout the whole area who were seeing this young guy running, had a jacket on, some had the two color stripes in the shoulders, others military patches, but basically it sounds like he was probably wearing a waist length brown leather jacket.

In the days following the murders, police release sketches of what appeared to be two different men. Weeks later, they revised the sketches and settled on one single man that they were looking for. Over the years, this has led to some confusion and speculation that there may have been two different gunmen involved.

We didn't have any evidence or information from the very outset from the scene that there was any more than just one gunman. Why there's two sketches, I'm not sure.

One of the possibilities that has been mentioned over the years is that the Maggiore's knew their shooter and that might explain just why the killer went out of his way to kill Katie after shooting Brian.

That was one theory but why? It's also why target them in the open, in a residential area right on the street somewhere where other people are present? Did he actually know him? We were never able to determine the why. The strongest evidence led towards maybe the East Area Rapist and I say maybe because up to that point, there had been a whole series of rapes, but no one had been shot or injured in any serious way. What was interesting is after this case, there was only one more case that was attributed to the East Area Rapist and that was in the city of Sacramento.

We asked Ray how long he worked the Maggiore case.

I worked it right up until 1993 along with other ones that we were trying to solve. Then there were other detectives that picked the case up and continued to work it. That's why there is additional information that's even if it's there, that's new to me actually.

We wanted to know if Ray and other detectives considered a possible connection to the East Area Rapist at the time of the murders.

Initially, I didn't even think of it until I was told I wasn't the one who found the shoelaces. I was suspicious about the ski mask because I was aware of the East Area Rapist but then the shoelaces really made it sound like a very viable lead. This is what it could be, but we continued on all the other avenues and there were many. It was a very high profile case, close to the Air Force base. The fact that this was a young couple, and there was nothing in their background to explain why anybody would target them.

Ray looked at hundreds of suspects during his handling of the Maggiore case. He told us about his favorite.

The security guard at first looked really good because he worked at that area. He was an individual who had been suspected and arrested for other rapes, a couple of rapes, nothing similar to the East Area Rapist, but he was a guy who was a suspected rapist, worked that area and had some real unusual behavior that night. He was worked really hard and even carried the right kind of gun. As far as I know, though, the gun did not compare.

As Ray mentioned, he retired in 1993 and other detectives would inherit the Maggiore case. Along the way, theories, confusion, and general misinformation have played the Maggiore murders. Rumors of Brian being silenced because he was involved in bringing down a military drug ring have been mentioned. A mysterious man who was supposed to give Brian and Katie CB lessons on the night of their murders has been discussed. Perhaps the most confusion has been in the several witness accounts following the shooting, which led to multiple sketches being released to the public.

For years, investigators with the Maggiore murders debated amongst themselves whether or not the East Area Rapist was responsible for the murders. The pre-tied shoelaces found at the crime scene was something that was held back from the public for a long time.

Detective Sergeant Ken Clark of the Sacramento County Sheriff's Department is one of the investigators who inherited the Maggiore case. He joined us to try and clear up some of the confusing aspects. In this lengthy and very detailed segment, Ken told us why investigators are confident that the East Area Rapist murdered the Maggiores. It's a pretty long segment but it's loaded with valuable information about the Maggiore murders and the ties to the East Area Rapist.

> *The case had been worked over the years by successive detectives that were in the Homicide Bureau, and it had by the time I got there, just had a pretty refreshed look. In 2001 the DNA was matched between the Northern California rape series known as the East Area Rapist and the Southern California murder series known as the Original Night Stalker.*
>
> *They've gone through and looked at it at that time and done some collating of files. There's a lot of stuff that had gotten separated over the years, and they requested*

full copies of reports related to East Area Rapist investigation. Homicide files are kept in homicide, so those were in much better condition than the East Area Rapist files which had been, unfortunately, spread around a little bit within the department.

They were initially investigated by our Sexual Assault Bureau and ended up coming over to homicide as a result of the murders, and there were some other places they went because allied agencies obviously had cases as well. It was there when I first arrived, but it needed some organization, and it needed to be checked to make sure that we had everything. The main issue we had was that you don't know what you don't have, so you go through a case and you're not really sure if you've gotten all the documentation. With this particular case, I had to do some rounding up of things and it is a process that took some years because of just the nature of a forty-year plus investigation.

Probably started all of this in early 2006, I was finishing up the training process in 2005 and had my plate pretty full with homicides, but I had pulled it, and then not too long after, I want to say, I just started reading it. There was a lead that came in related to the Maggiore case, and it was a fingerprint. I was able to research that fingerprint and it immediately piqued my interest obviously. You first get to a case and all sudden there's a fingerprint hit and there hadn't been one for twenty years. You can imagine I was pretty excited and then come to find out it was an innocently left fingerprint by somebody who we already knew had access to one of the areas that were fingerprinted.

In that respect, it was a lead that just kind of got me started, and I was able to resolve it within a couple of days. Then from there, I was off to the races. Well, I can't speak for all of the original investigators because there were a lot of people that worked on this case.

Inspector and Lieutenant Ray Biondi had probably the first initial investigative portion of it and, there was a lot of detectives working on his team that also were working on it. They probably had many theories on what they thought or didn't think was involved here.

I contacted many of them early on to get their take on the case. In my reading of it, and I cross read it a couple times, being able to look back over the entire forty-year investigation as it stood, I had developed some of my own opinions, but I wanted to hear from them. What I received was somewhat mixed. I got some people who were obviously pretty certain back then that the East Area Rapist was probably the culprit. There were others that thought, now in hindsight, in retrospect, after clearing out all of the leads that they did work, that there was clearly a chance the East Area Rapist was responsible, but they weren't as certain back then. Then there were investigators that just didn't know. Very few certainly indicated that they absolutely thought that the East Area Rapist was not involved, but there were individuals that had varying opinions on whether he was or wasn't, with some very strongly that he was and some not as strong. Again, if I can step back just a little bit, we actually did a program, as one of the first that we'd ever been asked to do in the modern era by a show called THS Investigates.

A man by the name of Todd Lindsay had come out and interviewed us about that case and about the East Area Rapist in general. I want to say it was 2008, but I'm sure it's easy to research when that program came out on THS Investigates, but in any event, that was, I believe, the first time, we publicly linked it in the modern era, to the possible series. If you go back and look at that, there's quite a bit of talk about the links and that was, I believe, the first time we also publicly acknowledged the finding of shoe laces in the backyard where the murders occurred. They were pre-tied.

The M.O. links in the Maggiore case are numerous, and that was probably a very strong one. It was one that many of the officers and detectives that were first on the scene, had noted and was definitely of interest to them. To me, it was adventurous because just the rarity of a pre-tied shoelace being found anywhere, that is simply not something you see lying around. Especially in the backyard of a murder suspect where the suspect emerges on the other side with a ski mask on. That was a fairly telling clue to me and though there had probably been talk to the media, I know there had been talk about bindings of victims and various things, it seems like the presence of pre-tied shoe laces was just a bit too much to ignore for me.

When I researched the knot that was used, it also was pretty clear that it was the knot that was favored by the offender. We know the East Area Rapist and he had used it most commonly, and there was a couple dozen or at least twenty events where he had used that very knot. That was a unique M.O. trait to me, but there were many others as well. One witness saw him with the ski-mask, and I believe that was released during the time period, but we will be re-releasing it, and by the time this airs it may well have already been released. At any event, there was several sketches done of people who thought the offender was running through the area, and they had seen individuals that they felt were behaving oddly or in some way had something with them and in one case a handgun that obviously alerted them that this was not a normal person in the neighborhood.

We did get different sketches from people along the route of his egress from that crime scene. There were also some sketches done prior to the crime scene. I should say it was sketches done by an individual who saw a couple of subjects prior to the crime scene and in the subsequent days of the investigation, though it took quite a while, she did identify an individual, the young girl, 11 years old. She identified an individual that was a match for one of the composites that she had done. Then she ended up having looked at about eight photos before she made that ID. It wasn't like she was picking the first guy she saw. She was patient and seemed very earnest to find the person she thought it was, and she picked somebody.

When detectives went back, they had looked at statements, they had taken statements and the individual that she selected had made a statement, indicating that he was in the area at the time and would have been passing very likely through that area. Though he doesn't mention that street specifically, it is on the route that he would have taken to get from his residence, which was at the time on La Loma Drive, north of Folsom Boulevard to the Cordova Meadows School grounds and what is now Taylor Park on West La Loma. He is with a second person, per the statements we received, and that second person also confirms the story.

Neither of these two individuals was very familiar with the street names and the Rancho Cordova Area. When you read the statements, you have to drill down a bit because there's some confusion based on the street names they give, but they wind up at the same destination which is Cordova Meadows School and Taylor Park to the west end of the school. If you look at the streets that they actually say they traveled on, it would have put them in a different place and the area even that they say they came back to their apartment is that from Cordova Meadows Park. Some of that *confusion, I think, is what led to the two suspects theory, I call it, continuing to be alive.*

That lead itself, in my mind was adequately cleared. You have each subject admitting they were present in the neighborhood and that particular area would have been the exact area we would expect that they would have traversed. Also, the young girl who saw them reported that they were walking from east to west towards West La Loma, and she saw them at a point about mid-block on La Gloria Drive and she last saw them essentially at La Gloria drive and West La Loma. With a slight trip to the north from that location, you would be at Cordova Meadows School and Taylor Park, which is where they said they were heading.

Both of those men said that by the time they reached the park and to give some perspective the girl said that there was about three to five minutes prior to when she heard the shots fired that she'd seen these two men. She described them disappearing at the corner as I said in West La Loma and La Gloria, but then the men say that when they reached the park, is when they first heard shots. They walked around the perimeter of the park to the north and came back down, met up with a Las Casas Drive and then down back to La Loma where they said that when they arrived on La Loma headed to their apartment, they saw the ambulance that had just arrived, which was there very quickly in response to the shootings.

The two suspects being seen together, only occurred one time and those individuals were eliminated. Though, from their statements, it's not clear that all of the individuals that were investigating the case were able to see right away that the explanation for these men being on the street as described by the 11-year-old was indeed these two men. To add to that, the individuals that were in the neighborhood and seen there to the north, when the shots get fired, the first we see of the suspect is he's alone. He's in the backyard of a residence on La Gloria Drive. We don't know how Brian and Katie came to be in that yard. There's many theories about that, but their dog ended up in a swimming pool in that yard and it was a small dog, a poodle.

When Brian and Katie end up leaving that yard, they're witnessed moving through that yard by a resident who is in an upstairs window, and he gets a pretty good look at least the activity going on. The subjects are running through the yard, and they end up going through a section of blown down fence. Apparently, there have been some storms and the fence between the backyard of the home on La Gloria and the backyard of the home to the south on La Alegria Drive was traversable just by walking directly over it because the fence was completely blown down.

The witness from the upstairs sees the subjects, all of them in the yard, the two clearly fleeing to try and get away from the man, and he just described the man as being a dark figure. A figure in dark clothing. He has no features of any of these subjects but he hears the woman screaming. When the first shots are fired, he actually sees the muzzle flashes. The male falls towards the patio area, and he can see this. Then he sees the arm of the offender extended, and it looks like he fires again at the male subject probably while on the ground. Though from the distance it was difficult for him to see and again it was dark.

He then saw the offender run around the east side of the residence which was the portion of the residence where there was a locked gate and a fireplace. The brick, the outside portion on the house of a fireplace. Katie, we know, was unable to get over the fence in time when the male subject shot her, and she unfortunately *passed away as did Brian. Both were transported, but neither one of them made it. The male subject is seen for the first time outside that yard jumping over that fence. At the time that he goes over the fence, he has a bit of trouble because he's caught by some bushes.*

A witness that was three houses away to the west hears the commotion, heard the first shots fired, exits his home; he is standing in his driveway, then hears the next volley of shots which are the shots we believe killed Katie. He hears the subject wrestling around in these bushes.

The subject rights himself, and the first our witness becomes aware of him visually as a man wearing a ski mask, a dark-brown leather coat with possibly jeans or similar kind of pants, and then shoes that don't make noise. He is running down the sidewalk to the west and passes the one resident that is next to the yard that he had jumped into, jumped out of and then into the front yard area. He ends up running up on the common area between the two homes onto the lawn, get to a probably about twenty to twenty-five feet from the witness.

He immediately changes direction runs across the street and then onto the side yard of a home that's on the south side of La Alegria Drive. He was seen running along that side yard by the residents across the street. One of who made a statement in the past in the crime report that was unaware of anything other than the suspect ran across the street after seeing the witness.

I spoke to another resident within the last few weeks that was in the house. She said, the suspect ran right by the window on the side yard, and she saw his shadow, and then she heard him hit the fence in the backyard, very consistent with the next witness. The witness that sees him jump the fence from the yard that I just mentioned, sees him emerge on to Capitales Drive.

She sees him running, and he runs right past her and then heads towards the intersection of Capitales and West La Loma. She describes him as a wearing like a ski-type coat, a heavier coat with epaulets, or some kind of different coloring on the top portions, she thought the color might be green. She just said that he had a pistol that looked like a revolver to her with wooden handles in his back pocket. He continued running, and he shielded his face from her both with his arm and jacket and then ran on to the next street over. I forget the name of the street, but he continues up towards Las Casas where he was seen by other people.

Some of the residents see him with an object in his hand that appears to be made of cloth but about the size of a football. This is a point of conjecture here but I think that could have been the handgun wrapped in the ski mask because again once he emerged out of the yard where he had run off of La Alegria on to Capitales, he no longer has that ski mask on. My thoughts on that, you probably don't want to be running around a neighborhood with a ski mask on once you've gotten out of the immediate hot zone. That is speculation on my part, but it makes sense that would draw more attention once you're away from the primary crime scene than you would want to do.

He continues up, and he ends up on Las Casas up near where it turns into, believe it's Las Palos. He is seen by several subjects there, and he slows down, and he kind of comes out from behind a bush after hiding for a little bit probably checking his six, so to speak, and looking behind to see if anyone's following him and realizing nobody is. He's been running for a while, so he probably takes a little bit of a breather. He realizes he's been seen because there's a male and a female, and he immediately rips his jacket up over his face, so he can't be seen and makes the comment, "Excuse me I'm trespassing," which if you follow this case our offenders seems to like phrases like that. He says odd things. That's an odd thing to say when you are a criminal that's running from a double murder.

That is the last sighting of him, and then he is gone. The descriptions are similar, but they had differences, some subtle. The reality is that as long as I've been doing this job as a homicide detective, and I've had no less than probably 200 cases that I've worked in the time period since I've been here. Witnesses frequently disagree on details, they're operating from a frame of reference, they're operating from a vantage point that may differ from a different witness. They have different experiences in life, different experiences with what they see and how to describe it.

You have to deal with the person whose questioning them may introduce some bias. Unintentionally, they may ask them a question that leads them to think of something else or answer in a certain way, things that they say can be misinterpreted. It's not something that we typically hang our hat on, these slight differences in description. In this case, it's no different, the general offender description remains the same. The most important thing about the description is only one man is seen in the yard shooting Brian and Katie, only one man is seeing coming over the fence after that shooting with a ski mask on. Only one man was seen running through that neighborhood for his life after committing this double murder. There are not two men and there never was.

That is something that I think hampered this investigation and made this case more difficult to solve because the two suspects were put out into the media and rightfully so because that's the best information they had in the portion of the investigation when you had to do these kind of releases. Unfortunately, it took a long time, many, many photos shown to the young girl who saw two men together. Many interviews to do and really it was a period of many weeks before they were able to come to the information that when interpreted holistically leads you to believe that the two individuals that were seen by the young girl had nothing to do with this.

One man was seen fleeing that scene, and one and only one man was ever involved in my opinion. The origin of that sketch was a woman who had seen the offender, reported what she had seen to the Sheriff's Department, but it was about a month later or a little bit more. I don't believe that. The reason I don't think she fully knew what she had seen until seeing some of the coverage, and she believed that she had seen the man based on everything that she was advised. She had an idea on the description of this man and then associated the event that she saw with him. She apparently got a clear look at him per her statement as he was moving past her house, and he was unaware of her presence because of where she was standing in her yard.

She got a bit of an unguarded look at him until he was out, realized that she was there and then of course, he started taking some countermeasures. We think that looking at the report, it appears as though they felt that since so few people had gotten a look at this guy's face, that she got the best look. Some of the other sketches were individuals that were seen in the area, but not as directly associated with the crime. As I said, all the witnesses that were on record said he was covering his face and doing other things. They were only able to make out the most general of features such as height and weight and that kind of thing.

When they did release that sketch, I want to note that he had not hit Sacramento sheriff's patrol jurisdictions since the murders. Though he was completely driven out of town or appears to have left town by mid-April of 1978, he had already left Sacramento Sheriff's Department jurisdiction.

His next attack was a Stockton attack following the Maggiore double murder, and then the attack following that. The last for the county at all was in the pocket area of Sacramento, which is a place he had never hit before and isn't really close at all to sheriff's jurisdiction. He was already showing different patterns of stalking and attacks on the very night of the attack on the Maggiores.

To me, I do think the sketch being released may have been a triggering thing, but we don't know which sketch because he's already changing his behavior as a result of the double shooting, and the stakes were high. He may or may not have killed before this event, but this event was a double murder, and that's a very serious thing. Whatever he had done before, though horrific, paled in comparison to this double murder, and he probably was well aware that all the resources that were already coming to catch him, now you can add to that an entire bureau of homicide detectives and numerous other officers that support the homicide unit. I'm sure he realized that the stakes just went higher.

The Air Force security police in such on Mather, was the unit that Brian worked. Our detectives spent a lot of time on the base, working with them and certainly the higher ups on the base to try to figure out if somebody that might have worked with Brian, could have been involved or had information about it. Their initial role with us was mostly cooperation because the murders of a service member and his wife took place off base, and so they didn't have jurisdiction over that crime, *the local agency did. They worked with us very closely during that time period, as best as I can tell based on the reports, it was a cooperative relationship.*

I know that in recent years, the Air Force's OSI or I believe that's what it's called, a special investigation office took a look at this case and realized that it was an unsolved murder of a military personnel off base. They came and offered some support and some additional documents that they didn't know if we did or didn't have. We had a couple of meetings with them, and they worked a couple of the angles that had to do with things going on and the base itself.

I'd like to talk a little bit too with the Maggiore murder about some of the incidents and activities going on in the neighborhood right around where they lived on LaVerta Court that also increased in my mind the probability that these cases are linked. At the time period that Brian and Katie were killed, there had been an absence of activity following the summer of '77 in the Rancho Cordova area. Though I think there was still small-scale things going on. There had not been a rape there since I believe the fifteenth rape of the series or around there.

In a couple of weeks to a month that led up to the murder, there are documented, in the report itself, and I also found other reports in the crimes associated with it. In that area several other cases, including LaVerta Court itself, there was a young female that lived there that had been receiving hang-up calls every night for a week prior to the murders. The person would say nothing and then hang up. These calls all occurred at the same time, which was 8:00 p.m. There have been no calls since the night of the murder to this woman. Then, she also didn't get a call the night of the murder.

In the 2700 block of La Loma Drive, there was a young couple living there and they moved in the fall of '77.

At night, they were suffering some significant prowler activity, and they actually had a burglary in the late winter. It'd be just maybe a month or so before the murders in 1977. In that burglary, undergarments that had belonged to the wife had been taken. They also found throughout the entire period around Christmas that the gates and doors of their residence were open.

This whole thing had led them to think someone had been entering their home, but they never found anything missing. We get over to the 2600 block of Capitales Drive, which is so far as you can see, this is a street that I've discussed as an area of eagerness for our suspect. In that block of Capitales, there was a young female that resided there and said that she had prowler activity for a steady two weeks before the murder and was receiving many phone calls where the caller would say absolutely nothing and then hang up.

In the 2700 block of Toro Court, which is a very nearby court, there's a 25-year-old female that experienced extremely heavy prowler problems, and these were going on just a little over a month before the murders and continued up to the point of the murder. She had found shoe prints outside her bedroom window and made police reports about it. Her gate was constantly being left open. Everything I'm mentioning, people familiar with the case will know what we would consider EAR activity.

She had this going on all the time in the month prior to these murders. She would try to secure the gate and the person, whoever it was, would actually damage the gate to gain entry. To try to fix the gate, and he just goes right through it or damages it in such a way that he can still use it. Then most interestingly, in the areas where she had found shoe prints under the windows, she also found drawings on one of the windows beneath where she had found footprints-- I'm sorry, above where she'd found footprints and the drawings were in bodily fluids, and I'll leave it at that. I spoke to her and interviewed her myself and confirmed this.

On the 2600 block of Sobrante Drive, which is also right there within a couple of blocks of the murder scene, there was a married couple in their early twenties and they reported that they had suffered a burglary about four months before the murder with nothing taken. They had seen an unusual subject in their backyard more recently. Also on the 2600 block of Sobrante, there was a male in his twenties and a couple of female roommates in their twenties that had heavy prowler activity throughout the summer of 1977.

They received numerous phone calls of a hang-up nature, received since that time up to the murder. Going back to the 2600 block of Capitales Drive again, a married couple in the early twenties reported that beginning a week prior to the murder, hang-up phone calls where the caller would say nothing and disconnect were going on constantly.

On the 10,000 block of El Torlito Drive, a female in her thirties was suffering a night-time burglary three nights before the murder where nothing was taken. She wasn't home at the time, so it's not a cat burglary, but it was yet a night-time burglary where she had been out and returned both leaving and coming after dark. Back to the 2500 block of Capitales, a female in her twenties, suffered another night-time attempted burglary on the night of the murder. The entry was thwarted to the sliding glass door because she had a secondary security device that kept the door from opening. She also had a lot of prowler activity in the area.

Then the most interestingly to me in the 10100 block of La Gloria Drive house right across the street from where the suspect and victims initially were in or encountered one another. A female in her late thirties and other females in the home reported numerous suspicious hang-up phone calls in the one week prior to the murder. They received all these calls at eight o'clock at night. Caller would say nothing. Just remained on the phone briefly and then disconnect. They got the final call from whomever was making those calls on the night of the murder at eight o'clock in the evening, just a little over an hour before Brian and Katie were killed. Those events are indicative to me of EAR activity. Those are all going on in the time period immediately preceding those two murders. I think that, that is something that can't be overlooked.

In addition, Katie Maggiore had worked at the Regal Gas Station on Folsom Boulevard and she reported a stalker. She had reported that a male in a blue VW Bug, was parked across the street from her and on Folsom Boulevard just watched her. He did it for a couple of hours and did it several times. Then one time she finally went to confront him, and she walked across the street, but before she could get all the way across Folsom Boulevard to confront him, he drove off.

She goes back to the business and in a couple of hours he'd returned to the location again and watched her. She quit her job two weeks after that stalking event. Her other coworker also were receiving phone calls from an unknown male at the business and the person would simply say, "Your turn is coming." A couple of the other workers had received phone calls from another male, unknown if it's this male or not, describing the rapes that had been occurring at other gas stations and asking what they knew about them. It was odd to them, and then of course after Katie passed and was murdered, these things started taking on a different possible meaning.

I think that's pretty much it for the Maggiore case, but it is possible again that because Katie had reported that she'd picked up this stalker. It was going on and it did scare her and that's always opened up a possibility for me that either she may have recognized the individual because she had seen him and maybe pointed him out to Brian. He's not even there for Katie on that particular night, but maybe he's in the neighborhood doing something he's not supposed to do and at about 9:00 PM, that was a prowler peak time for him and maybe a bad time but not usually a rape time.

Maybe he was doing some of those prowl peep-type activities, and Katie recognized and said something to Brian, "Hey Brian, I've been telling you about that guy. There he is." Well, Brian being everything we heard about him and it's not just his protectiveness of Katie, but the fact that he was a base policeman, would probably have confronted and then tried to at least identify the man for referral, or whatever he was going to do.

That is a possibility. It's one of many. I mean I've entertained several related to how that could have ended up in a confrontation in the backyard of a house that neither one of the parties involved in the confrontation lived, but that's something that I had considered. At the time period, the CB radio craze was pretty prolific and a lot of people were doing that.

Brian and Katie had apparently become interested in it and had met some of the CBers and had been talking to a couple of them about providing some instruction, and how to work the radios, and how to do that kind of stuff. It does appear that when this happened, that they were going to be meeting with an individual who was going to help them.

That individual was interviewed, and I'm pretty confident in the initial exclusion. They did not feel he was involved in the investigation. There's other subjects that were involved in that as well that were actually closer friends of theirs that came up over the normal course of the investigation. Then the CB angle was mentioned in their interviews as well.

One interesting thing that recently came to light was that Brian and Katie before moving to their apartment on Laverta Court in 1978, had lived at 10680 Coloma Road. This was across the street from the 7-Eleven where the botched 1977 stake out occurred. Katie Maggiore's brother knew the apartment well, and he remembered the 7-Eleven.

The fact that a man suspected of being the East Area Rapist frequented the 7-Eleven across the street from Brian and Katie's old apartment, opens up some interesting possibilities.

One of which is that they may have known the East Area Rapist from their time on Coloma Road, and perhaps he could have been one of their neighbors. If they caught him out prowling in the neighborhood and recognized him, it could explain the need for him to make sure that both Brian and Katie were dead.

The most accepted police theory is that Brian being an Air Force police officer may have confronted the East Area Rapist when he spotted him prowling, and Brian and Katie were just in the wrong place at the wrong time. Wherever the answer lies, it seems as if the stalking, prowling, and rapes that had plagued the eastern portion of Sacramento for so long ended with the Maggiore murders. The East Area Rapist wouldn't turn up again for over a month, and when he did, it would shock everyone when he struck back in the city of Stockton.

On March 18, 1978, police officer Sgt. Tom Spivey was on patrol in the city of Stockton. It had been six months since the East Area Rapist had struck there, but Stockton Police were on high alert knowing that there had not been another attack in Sacramento County in a month. Stockton Police didn't want to take any chances that the East Area Rapist would come back to their city. Stockton had their own East Area Rapist task force.

We started what we called the East Area Rapist task force, and we had people on stakeout, really undercover, under tarps and stuff in backyards where they could look around the lake with binoculars and see if anybody was walking because there were no fences in the backyard of these homes. That was going on for quite some time. I wasn't involved in that.

I was a patrol sergeant so we were running shifts about fifty or so guys on a shift, guys and girls. As time went by, I was thinking about well if he's ever going to hit in Stockton again, where would be a likely spot he would show up because he probably knows this task force is out there, and he would maybe avoid that. I just in my mind, just on my own, I came up with the idea that if he came back to Stockton, committed a crime or he lived here, who knew back then. I thought he might go to an area of town called Parkwoods, an older area of town, affluent area of older homes, tree-lined and very close to Interstate five and the major boulevards in Stockton to make an escape. Knowing I didn't have a beat responsibility because I was the North sergeant at the time, so I could go anywhere I wanted to go. I started just patrolling around in this area, this affluent area where we never had a police car hardly ever. I was doing that night after night after night for two, three hours when I could and then the next night.

This particular night we did have another attack, and it happened to be exactly in that area of town. I had been driving around that area for probably two hours and had the kill lights on the car, using those so there were no brake lights, no lighting of any kind and just coasting along. I remember the night was very still, might have been a little bit of haze in the air, maybe a little fog as I recall, but it was very still. I could hear dogs barking, I could hear everything with windows rolled down as you're listening if you're going to come up with anything.

I was going along and driving around, and I had been down to a particular street where this attack occurred I'll bet twenty times that night because it's a small area of town. I had pulled over and was sitting there with the engine still running, idling, with the windows down listening for any noise of a car starting or somebody walking. Sacramento thought maybe he came to the scene of these crimes on a bicycle, that type of thing.

Tom decided to park on the 1600 block of Meadow Avenue and watched the area. It was after 2:00 a.m.

I got a radio call and the radio call was just that we think there's been an attack, gave us the address and right where I am parked, I am parked in front of that house. I jumped out of the car, we had big kill lights, flashlights that we put under the arm back in those days.

I started towards the house trying to find an entry point, and I immediately saw that the side gate, which hadn't been more than thirty feet from me, the side gate was ajar, it was more than ajar. It was opened a couple of feet. I figured that was the way he probably went in or came out, and I would go in that way and I did. I'm sweating at this point because I'm thinking I might be right on top of this guy.

He might be leaving, and I might confront him but unfortunately or fortunately, I didn't. When I got in the backyard with the flashlight, I was looking around, I saw that the glass slider into the dining room area, as I recall was open. That was my entry point. As I came into the house, it was pitch-black, and I'm just moving very slowly and very cautiously to see what we've got. I started calling out, "Is anybody here?" I heard the female victim say, "Back here we're back here." I made my way to where they were. I don't think I turned any lights on which is kind of odd right now when I look back on it, but I was so fixated on what was surrounding me and where I was going in the house. I don't believe I did, but anyway I did get into the area, a bedroom area where the voice was coming from and sure enough, there was a male and a female, they were tied back to back on the bed. As I recall, it was like a shoelace material or something similar to a shoelace that she was tied to this man. I remember having the presence of mind to not untie the knot but to cut it loose so that maybe the knot would be important.

Of course, immediately I asked her if she can describe this guy, and she couldn't. It all happened too quick with the light in her eye and all but I put out what we had to the cars that were responding to that area. She related to me that they were awoken in bed with this man shining a light in their face, that he had taken charge immediately, and had her tie the male up. Then he moved her to another location where he put dishes on her and that type of thing on top of her with the idea of course if she started moving the dishes would fall off and he would know it.

Then he made sure he had him tied up and they did move him to another location in the house and did the same thing with dishes on him. Then subsequently, he forcibly raped the woman. The story she told me. She said that he laid her down after he raped her. He laid her down in another spot in the house, puts his hands on her and was just sitting there, and she said he removed his hand, and he got up and walked away. She said, "I waited about, she said fifteen minutes," but it was probably like five. She said, "I started to move, and he just put his hand on me again."

He had left, or he was seated next to her, gone out in some other part of the house, come back, and she felt him come back. She said it was just so frightening. Later on, we had detectives arrive at the scene, and it was going to get light pretty soon, so we had a chance to look around. We found in the backyard in the planting bed there were footprints where he was taking the window and he would move sideways. That's how the footprints were lined out.

This particular house they had removed their window coverings, and they had them sent out to be cleaned, so there was no drapes or anything like that on the window. Detectives believe that he probably came in the backyard, spend some time there looking around and looking into the windows and whatnot waiting for them to go to sleep and then made his entry into the house. It was very frightening to them. It was very eerie experience for them.

One of the things that was really interesting to me was we found that he had gone out on the front porch. Now, that's the porch facing the street that I had been parking in at one point and consumed two or three cans of beer from their refrigerator. Apparently, what he had done is he had gone outside after he tied them up at some point to see what's going on, anything to worry about.

He probably saw me drive by two or three times, and then I suspect, by the time, I park he probably had already left, 'cause they had to get loose to make a phone call, but he was in and out of as quick as he could be and as quietly as he could be. I remember thinking back, I didn't hear a car engine. I didn't hear anybody running. I didn't hear a motorcycle, nothing. He just disappeared.

As soon as I was able to get a description, male, twenties, I think, early twenties as I recall she said, but she didn't get a really good look at him and the man didn't either. But as soon they had that out and knew that other units were responding, right off the back nobody needed to come to the house. I was already at the house.

They were going to work the area, but as they did that for probably a half hour just to see if anybody was moving. Then, the next step would be to start canvassing in the neighborhood, did anybody see anything, anybody hear anything? Was anybody prowling in the backyard, did your dogs bark? That type of thing. It was a dead end.

I mean, he was like a ghost.

Once the detectives were on the scene, they were able to question the two victims. The 24-year-old woman, who was a sales manager, and her 29-year-old boyfriend was an attorney. The pair told the investigators that the intruder had woke them up at about 1:00 a.m. The woman described the rapist as being in his twenties, about five feet, ten inches and a 160 pounds. She said that he had a small potbelly and a very small penis that was no more than three inches erect.

The 29-year-old boyfriend gave a slightly different description of the attacker. He estimated him to be about six feet, one inch and thin, but both said that the man wore a black ski mask that covered his entire face. The victims recounted that the attacker had carried a flashlight in his left hand and a gun in his right that the attacker told them was a .357. The attacker's MO was the same as most East Area Rapist attacks. He gained control, told them he only wanted money and food and then bound the victim's hands behind their back before separating them and raping the female victim.

During the sexual attack, he called the woman by her first name. He also said to her that stood out during the rape, which was, *"This is how me fuck."* When the assailant talked to the male victim, he said, *"If I hear these dishes, then I'm going to kill your girlfriend."* The attacker knew that the pair was not married. The victims told police that only three days before there have been a prowler in their yard.

They also related that there had been a prowler in their yard in the month of January and the month of February as well as in the weeks leading up to the attack. They had come home to find that the locks on their doors were damaged. Additionally, they had been receiving phone calls where someone asked for people who did not live in the home and the couple just assumed that it was someone calling a wrong number. The victims had determined that their attacker had stolen cash, jewelry, and the female victim's driver's license. When the police questioned neighbors, they discovered that several had information about events in the area prior to the attack.

One woman reported seeing cars that didn't belong to the neighborhood parked in front of her house during the overnight hours. These included a faded VW van and green Ford. The same faded van was reported driving slowly through the neighborhood. The driver was described as white male in his early twenties with blond hair. Just two days before the attack, a woman on that street received a phone call from a man who asked her if she would talk to him while he masturbated, and just forty-five minutes before the attack, another neighbor woke up to see a man trying to open her sliding glass door, she quickly woke up her husband, but when they investigated, the person was gone.

SEASON TWO, EPISODE EIGHT

Despite being on alert Stockton PD was not able to stop the East Area Rapist from once again striking there. Back in Sacramento County police continued to investigate the Maggiore murders and debated whether they were killed by the East Area Rapist. It had been almost a month since the recent Stockton attack. On April 14 a couple who lived on the 1000 block of Casilada Way asked a 15-year-old girl who lived nearby to babysit their 8-year-old daughter for the night. The 8-year-old's father, who worked for the State Department of Water Resources, wanted to take his wife out to dinner.

The girl had babysat for them before without incident. This area was in the western portion of Sacramento County more than ten miles away from most East Area Rapist attacks. People in this section of County weren't dealing with the constant fear that eastern Sacramento County was dealing with. The teenage girl arrived at the home to babysit around 9:00 p.m. and the couple left for dinner right away. By 9:30 she had tucked the 8-year-old into bed and then started to watch a movie. The teenager had just gotten comfortable when a crashing sound startled her. She turned around and saw a masked man walking in from the back door, which had been dead-bolted.

The man ran towards her with a gun, not leaving her time to do anything. He talked softly but deeply and warned her not to move, or he would kill her. He immediately ordered her down to the floor face-first and tied her hands behind her back with shoelaces. As he tied the girl's hands, he warned her not to move, or he would stab her with his ice pick. He added that he just wanted food and money, and then he would be gone.

While the bound teenager was lying on the floor, the intruder made his way into the kitchen and started going through the cabinets and drawers. The attacker then went through the girl's purse, he picked the girl up and covered her face with a blanket to act as a blindfold.

He forced her to walk to another room. When they got to the room, he shoved the girl down onto the floor and tied her ankles together. He then left the room before returning a few minutes later and untied her ankles. He turned her over and unzipped her pants. The terrified girl started to struggle, and the masked man told her to shut up, or he would kill her. At that point he said, "I wanted to rape you for a long time." And he addressed her by her first name. He started to rape her, and the phone rang.

The assailant paused his attack as the phone rang several times. A minute later, it rang again, and the man paused again before the phone stopped ringing. The attacker didn't know it, but the caller was the 8-year-old's parents calling to check to make sure everything was okay. After not getting an answer twice, they were concerned. Then they called the babysitter's parents' home to let them know that they were worried. The attacker left the room for a moment and returned with some lotion that he applied to himself and then to the teenage victim.

He attempted to sexually assault her for a second time when the phone once again rang. This time, it was the young babysitter's parents who were now worried and wanted to call to check on her. The man pulled the girl up and made her walk to the phone to answer it. He forced her to hold on to his penis as they walked. He then ordered the girl to say hello, and then handed her the phone. The terrified girl said hello to her parents who were on the other line. But then the man swiftly hung up the phone. Her parents, sensing something was wrong, decided to go over and check on her.

They got dressed and walked up to the car to make the one-minute drive to the home on Casilada Way where their daughter was babysitting. The attacker made the girl touch his penis and then the phone rang once again. This time, it was an 8-year old's parents calling. The man ignored the call, and it finally stopped ringing. All these phone calls must have made the attacker uneasy because he scooped the teenage girl up and walked her outside to the patio where he once again tried to sexually assault her, but suddenly, a car pulled into the driveway, causing the rapist to pause. It was the teenager's father who immediately jumped out of the car and yelled out.

Hearing her father's voice, the 15-year-old screamed out to him, and her father raced into the yard, but the masked rapist had vanished. The girl still had the makeshift blindfold on, and she couldn't tell which direction he had left in. The father freed his daughter and brought her inside where they called police. The 8-year-old girl was safe in her room. Police arrived on the scene shortly after 10 p.m. The entire attack had not lasted very long, maybe fifteen minutes or less. The 15-year-old victim was able to tell police that her attacker was under six feet tall but couldn't pinpoint exactly how tall. She guessed he was in his twenties.

During the questioning of this young victim, she revealed that she had been receiving prank calls at her home on Piedmont Drive during the previous two months. In one of the calls, a man told her, "I fucked your sister." In other calls, the male caller would say things like, "let me sell you out." The most recent call had come only a couple days earlier. When police questioned the parents of the 8-year-old, they told police about something that had happened only a few nights before the attack. While the father was out of the house, the mother was watching TV with her 14-year-old daughter. It was then that they heard a bang outside their door on the patio, but the parent had been too afraid to look outside.

The police canvassed the neighborhood speaking with neighbors. One witness reported seeing an out-of-place blue Cadillac in the area in the weeks leading up to the attack. Another neighbor had found that someone had been prowling in her yard and had repeatedly left her gate open. Another resident on Rio Lane just a short distance away, had heard someone scratching at their window, but their dog started to bark and scared off the prowler. Earlier on the night of the attack, only about fifteen minutes after the parents had left, another witness saw the same blue Cadillac. It pulled into the driveway of the home where this attack happened, and then backed out and drove off. And then just prior to the attack neighbors heard their dog barking and thought someone was in their backyard but didn't see anyone, so they dismissed it.

In examining this attack, we must consider a lot of things. This was an area of Sacramento County that was not typically targeted by the East Area Rapist. Also, it was the second recent attack on young victims in which the rapist simply kicked the door open, as opposed to taking his time and trying to be stealthy. Perhaps he was growing impatient by this time. During April, police had released a revised sketch of the Maggiore shooter after closely talking with the witnesses of the shooting. One of the witnesses had gotten a very good look at him up close from her window.

When this sketch was released, the East Area Rapist left Sacramento and searched out victims in other Northern California counties. It appeared there was too much heat on him in Sacramento County, or perhaps, the revised sketch closely resembled him and forced him to leave. After April of 1978, Sacramento County residents would be able to breathe easier, but the rest of California wouldn't be safe. The East Area Rapist wouldn't appear again until June. But when he did, it would be in a rapid succession of attacks over a two-day period in two different counties.

Modesto is the county seat of Stanislaus County, and it's about seventy-five miles south of Sacramento. In 1978, the population of Modesto was just under 100,000 people. The town consisted of rich farm land, tree-lined roads, as well as a heavily used railroad system. It was vastly different from Sacramento County, and residents there never had any reason to fear the East Area Rapist, but that would all change on June 5, 1978, when he would strike in Modesto for the first time.

On the 3800 block of Fuchsia Lane, a 27-year-old woman, her 24-year-old husband, and their young child were fast asleep when a tapping sound woke the two adults at around 3a.m. The pair opened their eyes only to find a hooded man shining a flashlight at them. A voice reached out to them through clenched teeth, "Wake up motherfuckers." Once the couple was fully awake, and realize what was happening, the man, who was holding a gun on them, told them that he had a .357, and if they moved, he would blow their brains out. The intruder ordered the male victim to lie face down, then threw the woman a shoelace and ordered her to tie her husband's hands behind his back, and to do so tightly.

Once the woman tied up her husband, the assailant forced her to lie face down, and then he tied both her ankles and her wrists together before retying the male victim even tighter. He placed a barrel of the gun he was holding against the male victim's head and cocked it, warning him not to move. The masked intruder told the couple that he just wanted food and money for his van that was parked outside, and then he would be gone. He walked out of the room and started rummaging throughout the house. After being gone for a few moments, the intruder reappeared and warned the couple that if either one tried anything that there would be quote, "Two dead people."

The masked attacker turned his attention to the female victim and placed a knife against her neck, ordering her up. In the process, he cut the bindings on her ankles. Once again, he placed the gun against the male victim's head and warned him that if he moved, he would kill the child who was asleep in another bedroom. The masked attacker forced the woman to the living room, and then shoved her down on the floor. He then walked into the kitchen and gathered some dishes and took them back to the victim's bedroom. He stacked the dishes on the male victim's back. After stacking the dishes, he walked back out to the living room where he raped the female victim.

After sexually attacking the woman, he threatened her, and demanded money, and she gave the rapist approximately $1,500 in cash. The assailant then told her to remain still, not to move, and he walked away. Following a few minutes of quiet, the victims both freed themselves and checked on the young child, who was still asleep, before calling police who arrived a little after 4 a.m.

Now, by this point we know that this is classic East Area Rapist M.O. He gained entry, subdued the victims, separated them, placed dishes on the man's back, and so on. But this was not something that police investigating this attack were aware of, because the East Area Rapist had never struck in their county before. So, to them, this seemed as if it was a random home burglary and rape. The victims described their attacker as wearing a dark ski mask and clothing. He was white, about six feet tall, and fit with a medium build. They also told police that it sounded like he had a slight stutter and that he sometimes sounded as if he was speaking with a fake Spanish accent.

When the investigators asked the couple if they had had any previous problems, they reported that they had received several hang-up phone calls over the previous month, but the calls had ended a few weeks before. In one final call, a male caller said, "I want you on my lap," to the female victim. Police questioned neighbors who didn't have anything significant to add, although one did report hearing a car with a very loud exhaust starting up at about 3:50 a.m., and this was undoubtedly the attacker fleeing the scene. Investigators consulted with Sacramento County Sheriff's Department and it didn't take them long to conclude that this attack was indeed the work of the East Area Rapist. He had come to Stanislaus County.

Two days after the Modesto attack, the East Area Rapist would show up in Yolo County in the town of Davis, which is home to the large University of California Davis College campus. The city of Davis was about a hundred miles north of the Modesto attack and about fifteen miles west of Sacramento.

This time he would strike at an apartment complex on Wake Forest Drive, and this was highly unusual of the East Area Rapist, who typically targeted single-story homes.

At 3:55 a.m., a 21-year-old woman awoke to a hand clamped over her mouth. A voice whispered, telling her to relax and to cooperate, and she wouldn't be hurt. The man was wearing a black nylon stocking on his head. The woman felt something pressed into her back, and the man told her that he would blow her brains out if she did not cooperate. The assailant grabbed her arms, forcing them behind her, and then tied her wrists with a shoelace. He told the woman that he just wanted food and money.

The attacker held a flathead screwdriver to the woman just over her left eye as he threatened her. She resisted as he tried to tie her up, and he pulled her hair. She started to scream out, but the man stuffed underwear into her mouth to keep her quiet. When he moved down to her feet to tie her ankles, she kicked at him. When the attacker finally felt that the woman was secure, he turned his back and began to look through her drawers, but she continued to quietly struggle to loosen her bindings. The man must have realized this because he turned around suddenly and rushed towards the woman jumped on top of her and punched her in the face to try to get her to stay still, but this only made her fight harder, and she struggled against her attacker as he punched her again, multiple times. This was a violent struggle, one of the punches ended up breaking her nose.

Dazed and bleeding, the woman relented. Her attacker, who was out of breath by this point, told her that he would kill her, and she'd never see her friends again. The attacker then walked into the kitchen leaving her by herself. He was only gone a minute. When he returned, he used a nail file to stab her in the face, nearly missing her eye. She cried in pain, and the man held the file to her neck and told her to shut up. Then he straddled her from behind and placed his penis in her bound hands. He ordered her to play with it. After a moment, he climbed off her and stood near her, applying lotion to himself.

He then climbed back on her and raped her. In a few minutes, it was over. Without saying anything else, the man got up and walked out of the bedroom and out of her apartment.

The woman freed herself and tried to call police, but the lines were busy. Remember, this was back before many areas in California had 911. She stumbled into the stairwell outside of her apartment and cried out for help. A neighbor heard her and called the police, who arrived shortly after 4:30 a.m. This was an extremely brutal attack. She had been stabbed with a nail file that was about eight inches long. She was punched multiple times, receiving a broken nose in the process. So ultimately, she would be taken to the hospital, but she was able to give the police information about her attacker.

She said he was white, about six feet tall and weighed around 175 pounds, but she also was able to tell police that her attacker had an extremely small penis. During the attack, the rapist had touched her with his bare hands, and she could tell that the skin on his hands was quite rough, very callused, indicating that maybe he had some type of job as a laborer. She also told police that her wallet was missing. As police questioned apartment residents, they only heard one thing that was out of the ordinary. A resident had witnessed a man who seemed to be watching people, including the victim, in the complex pool about a week before the attack.

Another resident reported seeing an out-of-place black Camaro with a spoiler. The police officer detailed in his report that upon arrival at the scene, he had observed a black Camaro exiting the complex and turning north on to Wake Forest. A be-on-the-lookout was issued, but police never found the car or its driver. Davis was a lot closer to Sacramento than Modesto was. Police quickly figured this was likely an East Area Rapist attack. Now the East Area Rapist had struck in multiple counties, and it was anybody's guess where he might show up next. Back in Modesto, police had their eyes open. Although it seemed like a onetime attack by the East Area Rapist there, they didn't want to let down their guard.

On the night of June 22 at 11:15 p.m., a cab driver was parked at the United Airlines terminal in Modesto at 617 Airport Way. As he waited for a fare, he didn't notice someone walking up to the cab until the door opened, and a man got in. The driver asked the fare where he wanted to go, and the passenger told him to go to Sylvan and Coffee about five miles away from the airport.

When the cab got to the destination, the passenger told the driver to turn west on Sylvan. As soon as the cab driver did that, the man told him to stop. He paid for the ride, then gathered his belongings and stepped out of the cab. As the cab driver prepared to pull away, he looked just in time to see the man walking with his luggage towards a field. The only homes close to the field were homes that were under construction, and this cab driver felt uneasy about this man. He would later describe him as being white, about 30 to 35 years old, five feet, eight inches to five feet, nine inches tall, with light brown hair.

A few hours later around 1:30 a.m. on the other side of the field on the 1000 block of Grand Prix drive, a 24-year-old woman was awakened by her dog barking and growling. The woman sat up to see what was going on, and a flashlight flipped on blinding her. From behind the light, a voice said, "Don't move, or I'll blow your heads off." It was at that point that her 25-year-old husband also woke up.

The intruder sounded is if he were speaking through a forced whisper. He ordered the couple to rollover on their stomachs, the intruder then threw shoelaces to the woman and ordered her to tie her husband's hands behind his back. As she tied up her husband, the attacker warned them that he just wanted food and money and that if they kept quiet, he would leave. The woman tied her husband's hands, but the man hissed, "Tie him tighter." Once the male victim's hands were tied, the attacker sat on the bed near him and tied the man's ankles.

After the male victim was tied, the intruder turned his attention to the female victim and tied her ankles and hands. He warned them both again, if they made a sound, they were dead. He then walked out of the bedroom, and the helpless couple heard the man going through items in various rooms and closets. But after a few minutes, he came back into the bedroom and ordered the woman to come with him. He led her down the hallway into the living room. The attacker was carrying a knife in his right hand, and as she started to look up at him, he hissed at her, "Don't look at me." He made her lie face down on the floor before going into the kitchen and gathering dishes. The man made his way to the bedroom and stacked them on the male victim's back warning him not to flinch, or he would kill them both.

The attacker then headed back to the living room and turned on a TV set. He placed towels over the woman's head, the light from the TV set dimly illuminated the room. As the woman laid there, she could hear the attacker going through stuff in her garage. After rummaging in the garage, the man returned to the woman and straddled her. He placed the knife against her cheek and said, "Whisper to me if you want to live." The man then placed his penis into her bound hands. As he forced the woman to hold his penis he told her, "I've been watching you and every time I see you I get a hard-on." He then turned her over and untied her feet, he removed her underwear and pulled the straps of her nightgown down off her shoulders. He raped the woman and afterwards retied her feet.

After it was over, the rapist walked into the kitchen, and the female victim could hear him putting things into what sounded like a plastic container. Then the house fell silent, but the woman was so afraid to move that she stayed perfectly still for ten to fifteen minutes. She started working the towels off her face and then worked to get her hands and feet untied. She heard her husband hopping down the hallway towards her. Using a knife from the kitchen, they were able to cut off all their bindings. They called the Modesto Police Department around 3:15 a.m. and police were there by 3:20.

The police quickly determined that the intruder had gained entry to the house via an unlocked sliding glass door. The couple told police that their attacker was a white male with a thin build perhaps about six feet tall.

Later, the victims would discover that the attacker had made off with their gun, a .357 Magnum and two rings. Although their jewelry would never turn up again, their gun was later found a month later discarded near the previous Modesto attack just over a mile away.

Modesto police knew following this attack that they had a problem. The East Area Rapist had struck there now twice in less than a month. They would become very vigilant because of these attacks. But unbeknownst to them at the time, the East Area Rapist would never strike again in the city of Modesto. But barely twenty-four hours later, he would strike again in the city of Davis.

On the 2400 block of Rivendell Lane, the Davis family was fast asleep. A husband and wife, both 32 years old, were asleep in the master bedroom. Also in the house they had their two small children and a 10-year-old relative who was staying with them. The man and woman were awakened by a voice, they opened their eyes to find a masked man shining a light in their eyes. Through what they would later describe as talking through his teeth in a mean whisper the dark figure told them that he had a .357 Magnum and that he would kill everyone in the house if they didn't cooperate. The man said, "Don't move, or I'll blow your fucking brains out."

The intruder told them that if they cooperated, they would be fine, and he just needed money for food and gas. For a split second the male victim thought of springing from the bed and fighting the man. But he quickly realized that there were too many people's lives at stake, so he cooperated. The attacker then ordered the couple to lie face down on the bed. The woman was made to tie her husband's hands behind his back using black shoelaces that the man had thrown on her husband's back. The assailant then tied the woman's hands behind her back as well.

He then went through the victims' closets where he found additional shoelaces and bound the woman's ankles before retying her husband very tightly. The assailant then asked the couple where their money was. The male victim told the man that his wallet was in his pants pocket on the floor, but the attacker couldn't find it. And he stuck his gun into the woman's back saying, "Where is your husband's wallet?" The female victim told the man that she had about forty-five dollars in her purse that was in the kitchen. The attacker walked out towards the kitchen when he almost bumped into one of the couple's children in the hall, and this couple was horrified. They could hear the man talking to their child in the hallway, and they were frightened that the man would hurt their child.

Awful thoughts raced through the mind of the female victim. She thought of how they had failed to protect their children and the 10-year-old relative who was sleeping over. She wished the man would take what he wanted and leave. For a moment she thought about the little league game that they were supposed to go to in the morning. But as in many of the other incidents, the intruder did not harm the child. But what he did do was manage to lock him in the bathroom.

The assailant then went to the kitchen and returned soon after, walking into the master bathroom. The couple could hear him ripping and tearing towels. While he was in there, he grabbed the bottle of Vaseline Intensive Care Lotion. The intruder then stuck what felt like an ice pick in the female victim's back, poking the tip against her skin. He warned her, "That kid better stay in that bathroom, or I'll kill every person in this house." The man walked to the kitchen. When he did the couple whispered to one another, and the attacker raced back in warning them not to talk.

He told the woman to move away from her husband and to get down on the floor. The female victim who had been sleeping nude was afraid to move because the stranger would see her body. The woman tried to ease down out of the bed, but the man pulled her up forcefully by her arm. He told her to walk to the living room. When she got to the living room, he told her to lie face down near the coffee table. The TV was on but there was no sound. He covered her head with a towel or rope. The man walked around the room then suddenly, they heard what sounded like a cabinet door shut. The man froze and asked the female victim what was that? She told him that she didn't know. The man leaned down on her resting his hand on her buttocks as he listened.

After a few seconds he got up, and he walked around some more. When he returned she could hear him squirting lotion from the bottle that he had taken earlier. The man squatted down on her back and placed his penis in her bound hands and told her that she had better make it feel good. Right around this time it popped into the victim's head that this man was probably the East Area Rapist. Her attention turned towards the reports of him having a very small penis, and she found herself taking note of its size. He then raped the woman, and, in the process, he threatened her with an ice pick, telling her he would stick it six inches into her back. During the attack he spoke to her by her first name.

After the rape was over he tied the woman's feet together again. She could hear the man getting dressed and walking into the kitchen. He called out asking where there was more money. She told the attacker that there were rolls of pennies near the refrigerator.

The woman heard the rapist gathering up some of the pennies, and as he did some of the coins fell to the floor. She thought she could hear the attacker sobbing then it was completely quiet. She thought he was gone; she could feel a cool breeze on her skin, and she decided to wait thirty minutes before she tried to free herself. After just a couple of minutes, her husband who was still bound in the bedroom yelled out for her, and the woman was able to get her bindings and her blindfold off. When she was free she saw that the man was gone, and she also noticed that he had turned off the TV set. She freed her husband, and they called the police.

They also freed their son who was still locked in the bathroom but was unharmed. They checked on the other two children in the home and found them safe as well.

Police received a call from the victims at 4:18 a.m. This was about an hour after the couple were awakened by the predator. Police arrived on the scene at about 4:30.

The victims described the attacker as being around five feet ten and thin, wearing dark clothes, and a dark ski mask. The female victim thought the rapist penis was very thin, but not abnormally short. She couldn't give many more details other than saying he smelled very clean but had sour breath.

Police determined that the rapist had come in through an unlocked door or window. Outside the home there was a deck, where police found a footprint that they thought belonged to the rapist. It was very distinct with three circles near the toes and three circles near the heel. Police decided to bring in a bloodhound. The dog immediately seized on the man's scent, and it took off steadily following the scent for almost two miles before losing it at the UC Davis private airport.

Police questioned neighbors of the victims to see what they might be able to add. One resident on nearby Shire Lane reported that just two days prior, on June 22, they had spotted a man looking into windows of houses.

Another neighbor saw a man peering over their fence the day before the attack, but he quickly disappeared. Perhaps the most interesting event leading up to the attack was told to police by a female neighbor. She said that about a week prior to the attack, she spotted a man standing between her yard and a neighbor's yard. The woman yelled out to the man asking him what he was doing, he told her that he worked for a developer, and they were doing some research for solar power. She asked the man a few questions about solar power, but he didn't seem to know very much about it, so this stuck with the homeowner as being extremely suspicious.

Something else that was interesting was that in the hours following the attack, this same homeowner found a navy-blue jacket on her sidewalk that was not there the previous night. Police learned that the jacket was a brand known as Golden Bear sportswear, and this jacket was only sold in select stores in Northern California.

The timeline is staggering if you consider the possibility that some of these prowlers are also the East Area Rapist. You'd have them attacking in Modesto and exiting at 3:15 a.m. on the morning of the twenty-third and arriving at this scene in Davis on the morning of the twenty-fourth at about 3:15 a.m. But in between you also have the mystery guy looking into windows on Shire Lane and Davis on the twenty-second and we can't forget about the man who that arrived from the cab driver of the same night at around 11:15 p.m. in Modesto. This is a whole bunch of bouncing around for this guy in a little over twenty-four hours.

Now one possibility that Contra Costa County investigator Paul Holes thought of was that the East Area Rapist may have had access to a plane and that seems like a theory that could explain him being very mobile and covering so much ground back and forth during that period which was less than forty-eight hours. The cab driver picked up a guy who may very well have been the East Area Rapist at the airport in Modesto and the bloodhound tracked the scent in this recent attack to the UC Davis Airport.

We also need to consider what would make him need to be back and forth during this two-day period in both Modesto and Davis. Did he have some business function or event that he needed to travel to? It's very unlikely he randomly picked places on a map and just traveled to them with no plan. After all, we know that the East Area Rapist had stalked and prowled most of his victims prior to attacking them. Perhaps he had reason to be in these areas and did recon while he was there, or a more frightening alternative might be that perhaps he had not chosen these victims randomly, but that he knew them somehow.

Paul Holes even told us that it wouldn't be out of the realm of possibility that the East Area Rapist targeted the couples in the attacks not because of the female but because he was angry with the male victim due to some perceived wrong that the East Area Rapist felt had been done to him by the male. The possibilities seemed endless for investigators now. Just like Modesto, Davis was on high alert, but unlike Modesto the East Area Rapist would strike again in Davis and it would only be about two weeks later when he did.

On July 6, 1978, just after the Fourth of July holiday, the East Area Rapist would strike on the 2000 block of Amador Avenue in Davis. The victim would be a 33-year-old woman who was home with her two small children. She was a Sacramento State College student who had just completed her summer session the day before. She was separated from her husband who was a doctor. She returned home from a date just after midnight and immediately went to bed. At about 2:50 a.m. the woman woke up to the sight of a flashlight being shined in her eyes.

A voice shattered the silence, "Don't move, or I'll blow your fucking head off, and I'll kill your boys." The woman later recounted that the voice sounded like it contained a slight stutter. The intruder told the woman, "Do you see this? Do you see this gun?" The terrified woman looked into his hand and noticed he was holding a small handgun. He told the woman that he needed food and money for his band. She told the intruder that she had cash in her purse, the assailant ordered the woman to turn over on her stomach, and then he tied her wrists and ankles very tightly using brown shoelaces.

The man then placed some material or towel over her head to act as a blindfold. After she was secured the man left the room, and she could hear him going through the drawers in the house. He came back in periodically, and upon one of these returns, he tapped her head with something heavy and hard that felt like a gun. He was angry about not finding much cash in her purse. She told him that she had more cash in the checkbook in a desk. The man didn't seem to understand what she meant by desk, she repeated, "It's in the desk." This seemed to confuse the man.

During one of the times that he returned to the bedroom, the man placed his lubricated penis into her hands. He asked her if she knew what it was, and she told the attacker that it was his penis. After a moment he turned the woman over and raped her, she could smell cigarette smoke on his breath. During the assault or just as it ended the man started to sob, it sounded to the woman as if he was saying, "I hate you Bonnie" or "I hate you mommy." He left her alone and again wandered around the house. She heard him go in and out of the sliding glass door that led to the patio.

The man told her at one point that he was going outside on the patio to eat. Around 4:00 a.m. the rapist left the home without the victim knowing. After a period of not hearing any noise, she was able to free herself. She woke up her children, and together they made their way to a neighbor's house to call the police, and this was around 4:30 a.m. When police arrived, the woman recounted for them what she had seen and heard. She was very shaken and didn't remember if he had a mask on or not. It happened so quickly, and it was dark that the events were just a blur to her. She did recall that the man was wearing a plaid shirt, that was white with red, blue, and green plaid on it. She told them that the man's actions were robotic, which as we know in East Area Rapist cases is sort of like a script.

What he did and said was all just part of his process during these attacks, and he usually didn't deviate from the script. She added that the man was about five feet, nine inches tall. The victim was taken to Davis Community Hospital arriving there just after 6 a.m. After she was examined at the hospital, she was able to speak more calmly and detail the events of her day leading up to the attack. It was unremarkable. Nothing really stood out to her. Her babysitter and the babysitter's boyfriend had watched the children from 9:00 p.m. the night before until she arrived home later that night. Neither the babysitter nor the boyfriend saw or heard anything unusual while they were there.

When the woman arrived home and the babysitter left, she checked all the doors before going to sleep to make sure they were locked. Although police didn't initially see an obvious point of entry, it was determined that a small hole had been punched through the lock in the kitchen window using a tool, or possibly a screwdriver; the screen was removed and discarded in bushes on the property. Investigators felt that the way in which this hole was punched, made it possible that this offender had some specific skill, or tools that helped him in entering in this manner.

Looking right outside the victim pointed out that the patio furniture had been rearranged. Investigators also found a herringbone pattern shoe print in the yard, and the same print was found inside on the kitchen counter.

Police turned their efforts towards questioning neighbors to see if they had seen or heard anything unusual leading up to or following the attack. One neighbor told them that they had seen a man, who appeared to be in his twenties riding around the street on a ten-speed bike a few nights before the attack. The neighbor thought that this man looked out of place. Another neighbor saw an unusual man walking around on the night of July 4. He appeared to be around thirty years old and about five feet, nine inches and the neighbor said the man wore a poncho and had a beard that looked to be fake. He walked with a cane and was not someone that they recognized from the area. Police were called that night about this man, they came out to investigate, but by the time they got there, the man had vanished.

This was just another example of odd and out of place people being seen proceeding an East Area Rapist attack. Davis PD reached out to Sergeant Jim Bevins of the Sacramento County

Sherriff Department, and after speaking with him, there was no doubt this was the work of the East Area Rapist.

On July 14, a little over a week after the attack, the victim had to go out of town and asked someone to house sit, while house sitting, this person discovered a knife that was used in the attack hidden inside boxes that were with the cheese in the refrigerator. While it didn't provide any clues, it was proof that the East Area Rapist's actions had effects that lasted beyond the actual attacks.

After these attacks outside of Sacramento County, the East Area Rapist once again seemed to disappear. Over the next three months, they were no confirmed attacks in any place in Northern California that are attributed to the East Area Rapist. Sergeant Bevins and his team believed that the East Area Rapist was not done terrorizing people, was moving south, and would show up in other counties. Bevins reached out to some of these counties to warn them, but his fears were met with doubt and skepticism from some police in these other counties.

One of the counties that was warned was Contra Costa County, which was over sixty miles south-west of Sacramento County. Larry Compton shared his thoughts with us:

I'm Larry Crompton, I'm a retired Lieutenant from the Contra Costa County Sheriff's Department. At the time that the East Area Rapist hit our area, I was a sergeant, and I was put on the task force once it was formed. Prior to that I was working in the crime lab, so when he did hit, I was sent out to do some work on it. I knew nothing about the rapes that were happening in Sacramento until August of 1978. I learned about the EAR from a Lieutenant Root and Sergeant Bevins from Sacramento Sheriff's Office. I was contacted by the Sherriff, and he said that they were coming down to have a meeting in Concord, and he wanted me to go to that meeting.

When I was there, and they started talking about the East Area Rapist, like I said we knew nothing about it, even though this was going on in Sacramento, and they had already had 37 attacks by then. Back in those days, if you didn't live in the town or if you didn't get the newspaper from that town, a lot of times you didn't hear anything, so it came as a real shock to us that that was going on. They said that they wanted to talk to us about it because they believed that the East Area Rapist was coming down to our area and that we should be ready for it. And unfortunately, we didn't look at it that way, we looked at it as this is Contra Costa County and things like that don't happen.

Unfortunately, in October, it did happen, Lieutenant Root and Sergeant Bevins contacted us again, and we looked at it, and we looked at the reports, went over it with Sergeant Bevins. I became very close with Sergeant Bevins in working this. We looked at it and said yes, this is your East Area Rapist, because of the way that it was done, and then from there on it just got worse.

In the early morning hours of October 7, 1978, an attack occurred around 2:30 a.m. on Belann Court, this was in the town of Concord in Contra Costa County. A 26-year-old woman and her 29-year-old husband woke to a man shining a light in their eyes. The man was wearing a ski mask and holding a flashlight in his left hand, and a revolver in his right. The man whispered through clenched teeth. "I just want food and money, I'll kill you if you don't do what I say," The man warned the couple not to look at him, or he would kill them. In typical East Area Rapist fashion, he threw shoelaces to the woman and ordered her to tie her husband's hands behind his back as he lay face down.

She complied and when she was finished tying her husband, the intruder tied her hands as well as her ankles. He then took the shoelaces from the victim's shoes and tied the male victim's ankles before tying his wrists even tighter. Once the couple was secured, the attacker asked the couple where their purse and wallets were. They instructed him on where he can find them, and the man left the room. A few minutes later, he returned asking the couple if that's all they had, and they assured him that it was. The attacker left the room and proceeded to ransack the house going through drawers and closets. He returned to the bedroom carrying plates, which he stacked on the couple's backs warning them that if the plates made noise, he would blow their fucking heads off.

The intruder wandered off into the house where he continued rummaging. The couple estimated that he was gone for about thirty minutes. When the man returned, he ordered the woman from the bed and told her, "Don't look at me or I'll cut your fucking head off." He forced the woman at knifepoint to walk out of the bedroom towards the living room. He then forced her to the floor, in front of the fireplace, and warned her that if she didn't do everything he said, he would kill everyone in the house. The female victim was terrified, and immediately thought of her baby that was sleeping in another room. The assailant turned on the TV and turned the volume all the way down, and he threw a blanket over it which dimly illuminated the room. He went to get more dishes in the kitchen, carried them into the bedroom, and placed them on the male victim's back, warning him that if the plates fell, everyone will be dead. The attacker walked back to the living room to the female victim who was lying in the same spot. He cut her nightgown in several places and then tore it off piece by piece. While he did this, the man threatened to kill everyone in the house and to cut off her baby's ear, promising her that he would bring it to her. She could feel the man's breath behind her. She heard him lubricate himself and masturbate behind her. She knew what was about to happen. As he masturbated he called the victim by her first name and told her that he had been seeing her for a long time. He raped the woman doing very disgusting things in the process.

After the rape the man walked to the corner of the room and paused there, it sounded as if he was crying. After composing himself the man walked out into the kitchen and was talking out loud. He said, "My main man wants gold and silver." He walked in and out of the garage and in and out of the sliding glass door a few times. Then the house was completely silent. The woman laid perfectly still without making a sound. Eventually, she hopped up and made her way to the sliding door and was able to get it shut and locked. Still bound, she managed to reach the phone and call police at 4:42 a.m. They were on the scene by 5:00 and began their investigation.

The woman stated that a few minutes after the rapist had left, she heard a car drive by outside, but did not hear it start up. This indicated that perhaps the car was not parked very close to their home. The couple described the rapist as being white, in his twenties or early thirties, and standing about five feet, eleven to six feet tall. They were able to determine that the attacker had made off with cash and jewelry. The point of entry eventually was determined to be a front window. As in the recent attack, the intruder had demonstrated knowledge and skill using a tool to somehow cut a small hole in the window and then disengage the locking mechanism.

Police found evidence that the side garage door had also been tampered with, finding a rectangular hole about four inches by two inches in the door. Investigators also noted that the side gate in the fenced in backyard was wide open.

Police went on to question residents and neighbors. A resident on Hollis Court, very near to the victim's home, had reported hearing a prowler at her door and windows just a few hours before the attack. When police examined her windows, they found scratch marks on both the windows and screens that were similar to those found at the victim's home.

Other neighbors shared similar stories with police. One of them told police of a very detailed encounter he had with the prowler just a few nights before the attack. His teenage daughter had seen a prowler in their yard around 1:30 a.m. and woke up her father who had been asleep. Once he was awake, he heard noises in the backyard, and he grabbed their shotgun. He ran to the back window and quickly opened it pointing the shotgun at the startled intruder. The man yelled out at the stranger asking him why he was in his yard, and the prowler stated that he was there looking for a friend. The homeowner felt that the man was lying and yelled to him to get out of his yard, or he would blow his head off. The prowler ran off towards the front yard and the homeowner raced towards his front door and out in the yard, but the prowler was gone.

The prowler was described as five feet, nine, white or Hispanic, and weighing perhaps 175 pounds. Around midnight, just ninety minutes before this incident, a different neighbor was awakened by someone entering their home. The man woke up and scared off the intruder. When he looked out of his window, he saw two young men in their twenties run off. Several neighbors and residents on nearby streets reported prowlers, out-of-place cars, dogs barking, and obscene phone calls in the days and weeks prior to the attack. But despite all this activity, not many clues were found, but on the day after the attack, one neighbor found a badge in her yard. The seven-pointed star badge that was found contained the words special officer on it and contained the California seal in the center of it. This was most likely a security guard's badge of some sort and not one that would have been issued to anyone in law enforcement. This opened the possibility that this rapist, assuming he may have been the one who dropped this badge, could have been some sort of security guard, but there's no way to know for sure. After the attack in Concord, Contra Costa County would become part of the investigation into the East Area Rapist. Larry Crompton provided us with additional details:

> We did get involved and Sergeant Bevins from Sacramento had got the reports and went over it and told us that yes, there is no doubt this is him. This is the way that he did it. He wore the ski mask. He tied them up very, very, very, tight, and threatened them.

The one thing about the East Area Rapist right from the very start, he threatened to kill, and he wanted to kill. Because of the way that he went through this when we met with the victims, and you can see the fear in them, and the tremble in their voices when they were talking. You knew that they really did think that they were going to die.

Once I got on the task force, and I went to the Vacaville Medical Center to talk to one of the psychiatrists there that work with rapists, and I gave her a couple of reports and asked her if she'd look at them. Then said I'd come back the following week and talk to her. I did, she said, "Yes, I met with my rapist. I went over these, and they say you had better catch him. He wants to kill, and he will kill." I said, "Why hasn't he?" She said, "Well, he just hasn't found the justification yet." In going over all the reports one of the things that I found was that in his first ten attacks, six of them were teenagers.

The youngest two were fifteen years old. Looking at the Northern California victims, fourteen were teenagers, and in looking at their reports and talking to Sergeant Bevins, we felt that he had a hatred towards women. His first fifteen attacks were single women. There was no male in the home. In his sixteenth attack, there was a man in the house and still the threat to kill. He would show them a gun. He would place a gun against the man's head, threaten to kill him, threaten to kill his wife, threaten to cut off the ears of their children if they had them.

No one saw his face because he always wore a mask. When there was a man in the house, he started putting dishes on their back, and he threatened him, "If I hear the rattle, I'll kill your wife. I'll come back and I'll kill you." We knew right from the start, that he wanted to kill, that was his number one priority. The sex and the rape were not, it was the terror that he put in them that was it for him. It just got worse as it went on. I think that what was going on in Sacramento he knew that they were getting close to him. During that time, he was hitting other places like Stockton, Modesto, Davis. It seemed like he was heading down our way, especially when he was hitting Davis.

Davis was on our route. In talking to Sergeant Bevins, he said he really thinks that he is coming down our way and felt that he was going to come to Concord. Mainly because that's one of the major cities in our area, and it fit the kind of areas that he was hitting in Sacramento, and their thoughts on it were true. I really think it was because he felt that they were getting close.

One of the things that showed up is that each one of these places was not far from the highway where if he had five minutes before anything happened, he could be in traffic on the major roads and nobody would notice him. He would park his vehicle in such a way when we had bloodhounds follow and find out where he had parked, we found that he parked the vehicle between the houses.

The types of homes were middle class and well-built and set up so that he could prior to his attacks go into that area and wander around and not be seen or at least not noticed. He would be near an area where he could escape in a hurry. One of the things that we noticed was that when he went into a place he would open the gate going into their backyard, and he'd leave the gate open. He'd never closed them, and we never figured that out as to why either. What we did figure out is that his first rape, he had a plan and he stayed with that plan.

Because of that I felt that he couldn't possibly be a young teenager. I know you'd have to start with looking in windows and maybe killing dogs or pets or whatever. He had a plan that he followed and because of it—he's got to have a record before this, so I went up, and I got all parolees from different areas, and I got 6,000 parolees out of a six-month period prior to his first attack that we knew about. I eliminated a lot by age and the fact that they were in prison and finally got it down out of that to about forty-one that we could never contact, never locate.

Despite having the knowledge that the East Area Rapist was now in Contra Costa County and being on high alert, the police couldn't stop him, and he would attack less than a week later in the same city only a quarter mile away.

SEASON TWO, EPISODE NINE

Larry Crompton and his team didn't have to wait long for the East Area Rapist to strike in their county again because it would happen only six days later. Once again it would be in Concord on the 2700 block of Ryan Road, only a quarter mile from his attack less than a week earlier. At around 4:30 a.m., a 29-year-old woman and her 27-year-old boyfriend were fast asleep when their bedroom door burst open, waking the woman immediately. She screamed loudly waking up her boyfriend.

Standing in front of them was a man shining a flashlight in their eyes. The stranger warned them, "Don't scream. If you scream again, I'll kill you." The man told the couple that if they cooperated, they would be all right and that he just needed money for him and his girlfriend. He ordered the couple to roll over face down on the bed before throwing a shoelace to the female victim, ordering her to tie up her boyfriend. The assailant ordered her to tie her boyfriend's hands tightly behind his back. After she tied him, the assailant ordered her to lie down and tied her hands behind her back and then her ankles. He then retied the male victim's hands behind his back, even tighter.

The attacker placed the gun to the head of the male victim and was in the middle of threatening to blow his head off when the female victim's seven-year-old daughter walked into the room after being alarmed by the events. When the young girl saw the attacker with a gun, she started to scream. The assailant warned the woman to shut the little girl up, and the terrified mother told her daughter to get in the bed with her, but the attacker didn't like this idea, and he told the child to come with him. He forced her into the bathroom and then placed items against the door to keep the youngster from getting out.

Once the intruder had everyone secured, he started to search through items in the couple's bedroom. He left the room for a short time but returned and placed the gun to the male victim's head saying, "All we want is food and money, and then we'll get the hell out of here." He pulled blankets over the man's head and then placed plates on his back. The assailant warned the couple that he would use a knife on them if they tried anything.

He then went back to rifling through their drawers. He left the room but returned later on and ordered the female victim out of the bed, he removed her ankle bindings and forced her to walk into the living room. Then he forced her to lay face down on the floor. He put towels over her face.

As she lay helpless on the floor, the attacker continued to look around for stuff, going in and out of the garage. He wasn't gone long before he returned and asked the woman a question, "Do you want to live?" The woman said, "Yes." The intruder's reply let her know what was going to happen when he told her, "Then this had better be the best fuck I've ever had or I'm going to kill all of you." The attacker then sexually assaulted the woman.

After the assault was over, the rapist left the female victim lying on the floor and started to once again go in and out of the garage. It sounded like he was handling trash bags full of items. At one point, she heard the attacker in the garage say, here, put this in the car. The victim lay there on the floor straining to hear anything she could, but she didn't hear much, and, in fact, she never heard her attacker again as he quietly had slipped away.

The bound pair managed to get themselves loose of their bindings using a pair of scissors. Then they let the 7-year-old girl out of the bathroom before calling police at 5:32 a.m.

This was just an hour after the intruder had initially attacked the couple. Police took a description of the assailant, and the couple was able to tell police that the man was an adult male wearing gloves and a ski mask. He was about fife feet, ten inches and the female victim added that he had a very small penis. Of course, this is one of those little tidbits that comes up over and over again.

As police searched the home, they found several shoe laces. They also found an empty box of trash bags in the garage. They discovered metal shavings in the living room near the front door, and the police noted in their report that a TV set had been unplugged, and the cable wire had been ripped out of it.

The victims were able to determine that the assailant had made off with about eight dollars in cash, an alarm clock, and two cartons of cigarettes. This was hardly the kind of stuff a desperate burglar would seem to want. At this point, the male victim relayed something of interest to the police. He told them that on the day before, he had heard the neighbor in the house behind him pounding on his fence. When he went out and talked to the neighbor, he learned that the fence had been damaged, and a board was knocked off. Police went out and checked this fence and found strange gouges and markings on the victim's side of the fence.

While investigators looked outside of the home, they found that the screens for some of the windows had markings and gouges in them, but there didn't appear to be any pry marks. The point of entry was likely through the garage or one of several windows that was left open for ventilation, and dust on at least one of these windows seemed to have been disturbed.

The police wanted to question neighbors to see if they could glean any helpful info. They heard that almost twenty-four hours before the attack, at around 7:00 a.m. on October 12, a nearby neighbor on Ryan Court discovered her gate was open, and her bike was missing. A few neighbors reported hearing noises in their backyard overnight leading up to the attack.

Some of them said that they had heard similar sounds over the previous month.

Other residents reported receiving obscene and hang-up phone calls during the weeks prior. One homeowner's window screen had been removed, and an attempt was made to get into her house via the window. There was a lot of strange activity in the small section of the neighborhood leading up to the attack. On October 16, three days after the attack, the bike stolen out of the neighbor's backyard was found near an apartment complex on Ryan Road. Police concluded quickly that this was definitely the East Area Rapist.

These are two attacks, days apart, and less than a quarter mile away from each other. This shows that the East Area Rapist was not afraid to stay in a small area, even if police were focusing on him. After the second attack in this Concord neighborhood, police were not taking any chances. They stepped up patrols in the area, and in the city of Concord in general. The East Area Rapist would strike again, but it wouldn't be in Concord.

San Ramon is a town about twenty miles south of Concord, and the East Area Rapist would choose that town for his next attack in the early morning hours on October 28, 1978. This was just over two weeks since his last attack in Concord. This attack would happen on Montclaire Place. The victims would be a 23-year-old woman and her 24-year-old husband. While we will go into some details of this attack, we wanted the victim of this attack to tell her own story. Her name is Michelle, and she has only recently decided to come forward and tell her story. In fact, we're the first people to record her account of the event that happened almost forty years ago.

My name is Michelle, I was the victim number forty of the East Area Rapist. My week started, we were in the process of moving, and had that afternoon began moving boxes, furniture, et cetera, from our current residence to our new residence. I had been moving boxes in my vehicle with my son who was three years old at that time. My husband had been moving more furniture, larger items using a friend's truck, along with a couple of his friends.

As the evening progressed, I came home around 10:30 that evening with my son to put him to bed, and my husband, they continued moving. They finished moving apparently around 1:30 and got back to the house. They were sitting in the driveway, talking to each other, when our porch light went on. They had been discussing whether or not to come into the house, and when the light went on, they decided that would probably be a bad idea since clearly, I was awake. I was probably upset because it was so late, so they just dropped my husband off and left.

As it turns out, I was not awake when he came in. He came to bed at 1:30, it was approximately, I'm taking wild guesses here, around 2:30 when I was awakened with the flashlight in my eyes. The EAR was standing at the foot of the bed at the end of a hallway that entered into our room. He threw, I believe it was shoelaces at me and instructed me to wake up my husband and tie him up. I did that. He tied me up and then he began wandering around through the house. He was asking for money, insisting we had money, where was it. I told him I had money in my purse, and where it was located.

He went and got that money, and came back and said no that's not enough, I need more money. I instructed him that they were some silver dollars, and some two-dollar bills on a box, on our dresser. He continued wandering through the house, continuing back and front into the room. At one point, he grabbed me, had me get out of bed, walked me out of the room, down the hall, and into the family room. He pushed me onto the family room floor. He moved around quite a bit in the house, sometimes outdoors, sometimes it sounded like out through the garage door, back and forth.

He came into the kitchen and turned on-- He actually opened the refrigerator. There are a couple of things that have been reported, that I don't believe were quite accurate. There was an empty Coors twelve pack on the kitchen counter. The beer cans that were located on our property, we believe were just from my husband and his friends having some beer while they were packing.

As Michelle mentioned, she had been moving from one home to another, so the theme of real estate comes up again here in the East Area Rapist case. The East Area Rapist went through all the usual script routines in Michelle's attack. Waking her and her husband up, binding them, separating them, stacking dishes on her husband's back, and then sexually assaulting Michelle in another room. During the attack, the East Area Rapist told Michelle that he had seen her at a lake, and when she asked him which lake, he angrily cut her off and said, "Whisper, whisper or I will kill you."

During the assault, Michelle asked the rapist if she could have a drink of water, and he walked to the sink, and filled the glass of water, and brought it back to her. Instead of allowing her to drink it, he threw the water in her face. When the East Area Rapist left Michelle's home, he took a couple of her rings and about sixty-four dollars in cash and coins.

Police at the scene had noticed the empty beer cans in the yard, something that was not out of the ordinary at East Area Rapist crime scenes. But, according to Michelle, those cans were from her husband and his friends. Michelle and her husband have described the rapist's mask as being one that covered his entire head. He was about five feet, nine inches to six feet tall. She told police that he took breaks, walking outside through the sliding glass door and out to the patio.

Michelle heard the East Area Rapist going through her refrigerator and drinking. It was about 4:30 a.m. and Michelle had someone coming to pick her up at 5:30 a.m. She told the rapist that somebody would be there any minute. He must have been spooked by this because he left the home almost immediately. Police looked around Michelle's home and yard, and they discovered that the fence in her backyard had been damaged. Size nine and a half footprints, with a herringbone pattern, were also discovered in the backyard. Multiple witnesses saw a man dressed in dark clothing walking away from the area of Michelle's home between 4:45 and 5:20 a.m.

Contra Costa County did a great job in preserving her evidence, including the rape kit evidence. They carefully bagged and stored what they collected from Michelle's crime scene, and while they had no way of knowing what they had in 1978, well over a decade later, Michelle's case would be the first of the entire series to yield DNA, linking the East Area Rapist to other crimes, both in northern and southern California.

Michelle's attack had been the third Contra Costa County attack in the month of October. The East Area Rapist task force there was on high alert, as residents talked about the attacks, and fear spread through the community, the way it had done back in Sacramento county. We asked Larry Crompton how vigilant people were in Contra Costa County during this part of the East Area Rapist series.

> They were really worried, and one had a friend that was in Sacramento, was a victim. Every night, she and her husband would check all their windows, check their doors, and check under the bed and check under the cushions. And this one night, they checked under the cushions and found a rope, and it scared them to death, so they called us. Deputies responded and went through and those of us from the task force, me and one other, sat in the house that night and thought that he would come back.

> He may have seen the deputies that day because he didn't come back. While I was there in the house and heard dogs barking, I had my gun out, and I was waiting, but he never showed up. I think by them

finding that and him possibly seeing the deputies that got there that checked it out, he didn't hit there.

As Larry Crompton mentioned, the East Area Rapist task force from Contra Costa County was not taking possible East Area Rapist activity lightly, and they wanted to prepare for any other possible attacks by them. The East Area Rapist would attack again in less than a week, after Michelle's attack on November 4, 1978. It wouldn't be in Sam Ramon. In fact, it wouldn't even be in Contra Costa County. The East Area Rapist had his sights set on a new hunting ground, San Jose.

San Jose is a historic city, forty miles south of San Ramon, in Santa Clara County. In 1978, the city consisted of about 600,000 residents, and many areas in San Jose were middle or upper class. There were some pockets that were wealthy. One of these pockets included the section of Havenwood Drive, which today boasts million-dollar homes all along the street. On November 4, on the 130 block of the street, the East Area Rapist would target his next couple.

At about 3:45 a.m., a 34-year-old woman was asleep alone in her bed when she felt pressure and weight on top of her. She opened her eyes to find a man pressing down on her. It was dark, and she couldn't see the intruder clearly, but she felt him pressing something sharp against her. The man spoke in a harsh whisper, "Don't make a sound. If you do, I'm going to kill you. I have a knife." The man forced her face down and tied her hands behind her back using heavy string, and then her ankles were tied.

The terrified woman's thoughts then turned to her baby who was sleeping in another room.

The dark figure whispered to the woman that he was hungry and wanted food. After she had been fully secured, the attacker stood behind her and started making weird sounds. The victim thought he was masturbating. She started to cry, and the man put a knife to her temple. He walked out of the room and into the bathroom but returned after a few moments, blindfolded her and gagged her using ripped up towel pieces. He untied the woman's ankles and sexually assaulted her.

After the sexual attack, the assailant walked out of the room and looked around her house. He came back and asked her where her money was. He spent time looking through her house and then once more raped the woman before vanishing from the house. Shortly after the man left, the victim made it to a push button phone and used her toes to dial for help. Police got the call at 4:35 a.m.. They arrived at the woman's house before 5:00 a.m.

The woman had freed herself by the time police arrived, and she checked on her baby who was unharmed. Authorities questioned her about the rapist, but she couldn't provide very much in the way of details as it was very dark. She said he was approximately five feet, eleven inches, but other than that, she really couldn't add much more. Police discovered that both the entry and exit was made through the sliding glass door, which the victim felt had been unlocked. There were no signs of it being tampered with.

She told police that the rapist originally used gloves but had removed them during the attack. Police dusted for prints but didn't find any. Outside, they looked around the yard and determined that the suspect had likely entered the victim's backyard via a nearby schoolyard, but they didn't see any scuff marks on the fence. Additionally, the windows and doors to the home were checked, and there were no signs of prying or damage.

It seemed as if the San Jose Police Department didn't initially link this case to the East Area Rapist. After all, they had not had an East Area Rapist attack prior to this. In hindsight, we can look back and see how much of this attack matches the M.O. of the East Area Rapist, but this was a new area for him. Also, he chose a two-story home in this attack, something that he normally steered clear of. Even though this was the first East Area Rapist attack in San Jose, it would not be the last.

The next attack by the East Area Rapist wouldn't come for almost a month, but when he struck again, it would be back in San Jose on the 2700th block of Kesey Lane in the early morning hours of December 2. Like many of the East Area Rapist attacks on couples, this attack started out in a similar fashion. At around 2:00 a.m., a 27-year-old woman awoke to the light of a flashlight beam in her eyes. She screamed, and her 32-year-old husband woke up. A voice in the darkness hissed, "Don't look at me or I'll shoot you. All I want is some fucking food and money and then I'll leave." The man mentioned that he had a van waiting. He ordered the couple to lie face down.

The intruder threw white shoe laces to the female victim and told her to tie her husband's hands behind his back. Once the husband was tied, the attacker tied the female victim's hands behind her back and tied the feet of both victims. Once he had secured the couple, he walked off and started to go through the home. The couple called out to the man telling him that there was food in the fridge and cash in a linen closet in the hallway. The intruder found the cash and scooped it up. He then came back into the bedroom where he used torn strips of towel to blindfold and gag both victims. He left the room but returned after a few minutes.

When the attacker returned, he placed plates on the male victim's back, and he forced the female victim off the bed. He made her walk to the front room of the house. He shoved her down on the floor. After a moment, she could hear the intruder masturbating. He called out to the woman saying, "I've been watching you for a long time, and I've been wanting to fuck you for a long time." He then placed his penis in the woman's bound hands. After a moment, he held a knife to her throat and threatened her. He told her that she had better make him feel nice, or he would cut her throat. The woman was then sexually assaulted.

During the assault, the rapist held what felt like a gun to the woman's head and told her not to make a sound, or he would blow her brains out. After the rape was over, the attacker got up off the woman and walked into the kitchen. She was still blindfolded, but she could hear the intruder going through the cupboards and the refrigerator. She heard the man walk out of the house through the sliding glass door, and for five minutes, there was silence. Thinking that the rapist was gone, she tried to get up to move closer to her husband, who was still tied up in the bedroom. Then all of a sudden, the attacker stepped back into the house and told the woman to lie still, or he would kill her.

The horrified woman lay still on the floor, while the rapist once again looked around the kitchen. She could hear him talking out loud. It sounded as if he was sobbing. He said, "You motherfucker," and repeated it over and over. Once again, the man exited the home from the rear sliding glass door. This time, he didn't come back. After several minutes, the female who was still bound, crawled to her husband who was in the bedroom. They were able to knock the phone off the receiver and call police.

Police received the call at 4:30 a.m. and raced to the house, arriving in just a few minutes. Police quickly saw that the attacker had gained entry through the rear sliding door. He had broken out a nearby window, and then, reached in and unlocked the slider. The screen covering the window was lying against the house. Outside in the yard, police found a box of crackers and a Coors beer can.

The couple were able to determine that the attacker had gotten away with the husband's gold nugget wedding band, a digital clock radio, and about sixty dollars to seventy dollars worth of cash and change. The man had also made off with six packs of Coors beer. The victims couldn't describe the intruder in great detail, but felt he was between twenty and thirty years old, and he sounded somewhat educated.

Police asked neighbors if they had seen anything unusual, but the only thing that was reported was by a neighbor who found one of their flower pots broken in their yard. This was the second attack in San Jose in a month, and these would end up being the only two attacks committed there by the East Area Rapist. Now, one thing to mention is that, both the San Jose rape victims were Asian. Typically, it seemed as if the East Area Rapist targeted Caucasian females. Not always, but the majority of the women that he targeted were Caucasian. It also seemed as if the East Area Rapist targeted areas, and neighborhoods, and not necessarily people.

The two attacks in San Jose had brought Santa Clara County into the East Area Rapist mix. It was now anybody's guess where the East Area Rapist would strike again, and when. At around 2:00 a.m. on December 9, just a week after the second San Jose attack, a 32-year-old woman was asleep on Liberta Court in Danville, Contra Costa County. Suddenly, she was jolted awake by the feeling of somebody on top of her. She opened her eyes only to find a man holding a long but blunt object to her throat. The intruder told the frightened woman that he just wanted money for his van, and that she had better not make a move or a sound. He forced the woman to turn over on to her stomach, and then tied her hands behind back with white shoe laces before also tying her ankles.

The man left the room and went to the kitchen where he went through drawers and cabinets. He made his way back towards her room, stopping to go through a hall closet. When he arrived back in the woman's bedroom, he asked her if she was expecting anyone. She wasn't, and she told the man no. The intruder asked her if she liked to fuck. This terrified the woman even more. She didn't answer him. He then asked her if she liked to raise dicks. The woman blurted out, no, emphatically. The man said with a very smart tone, "Then, how come you always raise mine?"

The conversation with this woman seemed to imply that the rapist had seen her or knew her from someplace, but as we've seen in other our East Area Rapist cases that we've talked about, there were times when the victims felt that he was lying to them, and he didn't really know them.

The assailant used an orange towel to blindfold the woman. He walked into her bathroom and then returned a minute later. It sounded to her as if he was masturbating. She caught the smell of lotion that she kept in her bathroom. The man untied her feet, and then he raped her. Afterwards, he retied her ankles before leaving the room and headed back to the kitchen, where she could hear him looking for something.

After a short while, the man once again appeared in the bedroom. He untied the woman's ankles and raped her again. Afterwards, he tied her feet again, but very tightly. In a moment, he walked out of the room. A few minutes after that, she heard the sliding glass door on the back of her house open. She felt that the rapist had left her house but laid still for a while just in case. After what seemed like an hour, she finally tried to get free and using a serrated kitchen knife, managed to cut herself free. She tried to call police, but her phone cord was cut, so she ran out of the house to the neighbors across the street. They called police just after 5:00 a.m., and police were there within minutes.

Police jumped into action immediately thinking that the woman was probably a victim of the East Area Rapist and they didn't want to waste any time. They immediately ordered bloodhounds to be brought to the scene, and while they waited for the dogs to arrive, they questioned the victim about the attack. Several investigators including Larry Crompton were at the scene. The woman told them that her attacker was about five feet, nine to five feet, eleven and weighed somewhere around 150 to 160 pounds. He also wore a ski mask.

Investigators noticed how cold the residence was and discovered that the thermostat had been turned off by the rapist. A stereo that had been left on by the victim was unplugged, and one of her rings was on top of it. She discovered that her driver's license and some cash were missing from her purse. The victim relayed to police that her home had been broken into about six weeks earlier. She was then taken to John Muir Hospital. Police took notice that the home was currently for sale, and later found out that it was listed with a real estate agency in Davis, California.

As she was being taken away, the bloodhounds arrived on site. Their handlers brought the dogs into the home and let them work their way around. They allowed the dogs to become familiar with the items that the rapist had handled, and then they brought the dogs outside. The dogs started following the rapist's scent outside of the home. As they made their way, the dogs paused and sniffed a Schlitz Malt Liquor bottle that was lying on the ground in the victim's yard. The dogs tracked the rapist to the backyard fence, and the handler was sure that the assailant had gone over that fence. It led into another neighbor's yard. It appeared that there were scuff marks on the fence, perhaps from a tennis shoe.

It was now around 7:30 a.m. While the dogs worked the scent, police knocked on doors to see if neighbors had seen or heard anything unusual. They started with the resident who lived on the other side of the fence. Although they had not seen anything specific, they did relay that their young child had woken up screaming hysterically around the time the victim was attacked. Another neighbor reported that a few hours before the attack, just before midnight, a van was parked in the victim's driveway. Another resident on nearby El Capitan Drive reported that her driver's license went missing from her purse, but she wasn't sure if it was related to the attack.

As police talked to neighbors, the dogs continued to track the rapist's scent. They made a beeline towards a railroad and followed a trail parallel to the tracks heading south. Then they suddenly came to a stop. It was as if the scent trail ended abruptly. The dog's handler felt that the attacker most likely had gotten into a car at this spot and drove off. The handler later noted that the bloodhounds were acting very erratically during the search, and this was something that they typically only saw in the dogs when they were tracking someone who was either on drugs or had some sort of disease.

Police fanned out and searched the area closely where the scent had ended. It didn't take them long to find evidence where they felt the rapist had been parked. On the ground were three pages of paper torn from a spiral notebook. Police looked over the papers briefly, and then carefully placed them in evidence bags. At the time, they didn't know that they had found possibly the largest clues in the East Area Rapist case up to that point.

One of the pages contained a hand drawn map of a community or development on one side, and on the other, some words or phrases that were scrawled and scratched out. The second piece of paper contained an essay about General Custer, and the last piece of paper contained a ranting essay or letter about how badly someone hated their sixth-grade school year. The three pages seemed almost unrelated to each other but had obviously come from the same notebook. No prints were found on the pages and nothing that could identify the author was included. The pages were booked into the Contra Costa County Sheriff's Department evidence room where they would sit for years, until investigator Paul Holes decided to look through the evidence room in an effort to dig up something on an East Area Rapist suspect he was looking into. Paul sat down with us to help fill in some of the details and his personal opinions on this evidence.

> *I think it's important to understand how I came across that evidence. I was actively investigating a suspect that was what I consider a prime suspect back in 1979. He was a railroad guy out of Sacramento that could be put in every single location in the Northern California series at the same time those attacks were occurring. Back when he was contacted by Larry Crompton and Larry Crompton's partner, the guy immediately lawyered up, he was uncooperative, everything was suspicious about that individual.*

> *During that investigation, I found that the original investigators had recovered a ski mask that this*

suspect had worn back in 1978 or 1979 and had put it into Sheriff's property. I went after that ski mask, trying to get that suspect's DNA to compare to see if he was the East Area Rapist. When I'm in the box at the property room that had that ski mask, at the bottom of that box and there's many items in each box that's inside of a property room. At the bottom of that box I just happened to see a plastic bag, evidence bag, that had a tag on it that said collected from railroad right of way.

Well, since I was looking at the suspect that was a railroad worker, he was a brakeman for the Western Pacific Railroad, that really caught my eye. So, I dug down to that little bag and pulled it out, and it was folded pieces of torn out spiral notebook paper that was in that plastic bag. When I pulled that out, what I saw was rudimentary essays, the Custer essay, the Mad is the word essay, and then this hand-drawn diagram. I almost just folded it back up, put it back in the plastic bag, sealed it up, and put it back into property without thinking about it, but that diagram caught my eye because it was something unusual.

My initial thought, as many people who first see that diagrams initial thought was, "Oh, this could be somebody who is out prowling a neighborhood and trying to make a map of where he's prowling, and possibly where he wants to attack." Fortuitously, I decided I better take this back to my office and look at it more closely. That's what I did. I took it back, and I read the essays and was looking at the diagram, and I realized that the diagram contained a lot more detail than what somebody needed to put into it to just be a prowling map.

Then on the back of the diagram there was some female names; Melanie scratched out, Jen or Jerry scratched out, the words come from and then maybe smellany. Some people think it's snelling which I don't think so. That caught my eye and then there's this big bold word scrawled diagonally across the back of the diagram, and I was struggling to try to figure out what was written there, and my clerk came in and I said, "Hey, what does this say?" She immediately said, "That says punishment." I was like, "What?"

All of a sudden it became very obvious what that word was, and then I started looking at it and I'm going, "That is entirely consistent with who the East Area Rapist was. He's punishing his victims." Then when you start looking at the Mad is the Word essay and the psychology behind the person who wrote that essay, I started to see that well, that is entirely consistent behaviorally with who our offender is.

As Paul mentioned, the *Mad is the Word* essay was a bitter recounting of someone's, quite possibly the East Area Rapist's, sixth-grade year of school, and it gives you an insight into how his mind may have worked. The essay reads:

Mad is the word. The word that reminds me of sixth grade. I hated that year. I wish I had known what was going to be going on during my sixth-grade year, the last and worst year of my elementary school. Mad is a word that remains in my head about my dreadful years as a sixth grader. My madness was one that was caused by disappointments that hurt me very much, disappointments from my teacher such as field trips that were planned but canceled. My sixth-grade teacher gave me a lot of disappointments which made me very mad and made me build a state of hatred in my heart. No one ever let me down that hard before and I never hated anyone as much as I did him.

Disappointment wasn't the only reason that made me mad at my sixth-grade class, another was getting in trouble at school, especially talking. That's what really bugged me was writing sentences, those awful sentences that my teacher made me write, hours and hours, I'd sit and write 50, 100, 150 sentences day and night. I wrote those dreadful paragraphs which embarrassed me and more importantly it made me ashamed for myself, which in turn deep down inside made me realize that writing sentences wasn't fair.

It wasn't fair to make me suffer like that. It wasn't fair to make me sit and write until my bones ached until my hands felt every horrid pain I've ever had. As I wrote, I got madder and madder until I cried. I cried because I was ashamed. I cried because I was disgusted. I cried because I was mad, and I cried for myself. A kid who kept on having to write those damn sentences. My angriness from sixth grade will scar my memory for life, and I will be ashamed for my sixth-grade year forever.

There are some possible clues in the essay that might narrow down who the East Area Rapist was. One of the clues is that the sixth-grade teacher referenced was a man. Assuming that the East Area Rapist attended sixth grade approximately between 1960 and 1970, based on his age description, there were not nearly as many male elementary school teachers back during that time. Another clue mentioned were field trips and punishment dished out by the male teacher, which included writing sentences. Very recently a teacher who had taught in Sacramento County who may be the one mentioned in this letter was identified. Efforts are underway by investigators to look back at male students who came through his classroom during that time-frame. Perhaps one of the students went on to become the East Area Rapist. Paul Holes helped us break down the Mad is the Word essay:

The assignment the mad is the word, most certainly there is the one person who called in, who felt that what was written in that essay described her father who was a teacher in the Rancho Cordova area. That was very interesting in that she recognized that as a possibility, and that is something that investigators we've definitely taken a look at to the best we can with the records that exist many, many years later. You talk about our offender's age and back calculating to when he was in the sixth grade. We're approaching fifty years later, and many school districts don't have good records as to what was going on at that time. Some do. I've been very successful in tracking down sixth-grade teachers on some suspects. That is one possible avenue that could lead to identifying our offender.

Paul went on to tell us more about his research into the map that was found at the scene.

I recognized that that diagram was not done by some middle school kid. It was much more sophisticated and possibly was unique enough to lead me to identify the occupation of the person who dropped it. Ultimately, I came to believe that it was the East Area Rapist that dropped that diagram based on where it was found and the circumstances that it was found at the crime scene along his escape route. Initially, as I was talking to people, I formed the opinion based on these various experts across many different disciplines within the development industry, that this individual was somehow affiliated with the development field.

I marched down that path because I thought, well, that really limits the population base, and I should be able to find somebody who's a developer. As I continued with my investigation I found that there are additional occupations, somebody within the development, building, real estate arena that most certainly would have a reason to draw that type of diagram. I thought I was narrowing the scope and then eventually that scope started to broaden as I continued with my investigation, which was very disheartening.

Relative to anything else, I believe that it is still unique enough that it is a limited population that would have reason to possess that particular diagram. In the lake, there are two sets of handwriting. There's the upper handwriting that's cursive that says "lake spope" or "lake spape." Then there is a printed set of handwriting underneath that that says "lake", and its S-U-P-R, for maybe lake super, not sure.

It's possible that it's two different individuals that are writing the lake spope or lake spape in cursive. That handwriting is the same handwriting that is present in the essays. I believe that handwriting is our offender's handwriting. The printed handwriting could be our offender who just decided to print there, but I think that it is possible that you have a second person that is collaborating with our offender and has written the printed writing lower.

There are other markings on that diagram that also show the possibility that you do have some collaborative effort going on. You have some pencil marks that are on some of the buildings that tend to indicate that somebody is talking to another individual, and they're swirling the pencil hovering it over a particular location saying "Here, this is what I'm thinking, and then over here this is something else that I think we can do at this particular location."

Now, it's very subjective interpretation, and I can't be conclusive that this diagram is demonstrative of a collaboration, but I think it's a possibility. What excites me about that, is that whoever our offender was possibly collaborating with that diagram, maybe that person will remember that, see that diagram and call in. I pass that diagram out like it's like candy in the various jurisdictions where I'm walking. I'm literally boots on the ground walking through these jurisdictions where our offender was, passing that diagram out to developers, to real estate agents, to builders. I'm talking to them, I'm e-mailing that diagram out, so yes, I am distributing it far and wide as I go through my investigation.

We asked Paul if there's any possible solutions as to what community the map diagram might represent.

It's interesting because depending on the person's own background, where they're from and what they're familiar with, they place the possible locations for that diagram within their own experience. Individuals out of Stockton, for example, are placing it and recognizing it as a Stockton development. People in Modesto recognize it as possibly a location in Modesto, the same thing for Davis, et cetera.

That's part of the complexity when you start looking at such a large geographic spread that our offender covered. We have kind of built-in biases both as investigators as well as people that we are talking to because they have their own world concept that they're trying to relate that diagram to. Based on what I have come across in terms of talking to individuals and experts, professors of landscape architecture, practitioners in the development field, surveyors, civil engineers, you name it I've talked to them. I believe the diagram is a brainstorm session.

To date, the homework, as these three pages of writing has come to be known, has not lead to the East Area Rapist being identified, but perhaps maybe the right person has not yet seen it. Someone may eventually recognize the writing. Perhaps the East Area Rapist realized he had made a huge mistake by dropping the homework evidence or maybe he just needed a break.

Whatever the reason, he wouldn't strike again until March 20, 1979, four months after dropping the homework evidence. The March attack would be the beginning of the end of his attacks in Northern California before heading to Southern

California where his already sadistic and brutal attacks would turn deadly. This serial rapist would become a serial killer.

SEASON TWO, EPISODE TEN

Rancho Cordova had not suffered a confirmed East Area Rapist attack in two years, and it had been over a year since the murders of the Maggiores in February of 1978. Residents were likely relieved that the East Area Rapist was gone, but on March 20 of 1979, he returned, and this time it would be in an area of Rancho Cordova that he had not struck before. The 2300 block of Filmore Lane. Filmore Lane consisted of several homes which were three years old or so.

While it was not an area with confirmed East Area Rapist attacks, there had been various prowlers and burglaries reported in the area since the East Area Rapist crimes started in 1976, and this area was less than a mile from the botched 1977 stakeout at the 7-Eleven.

Around 2:15 a.m., a 38-year old woman awoke to find a man on top of her, he was holding down her arms. She immediately started to struggle with the intruder, and he punched her in the face four or five times with his right hand. In his left hand, he was holding an object that he pressed against the woman. The man who was wearing a nylon stocking over his face spoke to the woman through clenched teeth, warning her, "All I want is your fucking money; I won't hurt you if you shut up."

The intruder then turned the woman over so that she was lying face down, he gagged her with the white scarf and then tied her hands behind her back using the white cord. He threw a comforter over her head and then told her not to look up. She heard the bedroom light flip on, and then she heard the man moving the jewelry in her dresser. It sounded to her as if he were scraping across the dresser and then into a paper bag.

Afterwards the man left the room and started ransacking the rest of the house. She suddenly became frightened that the sound of the man going through her stuff would wake up her two children who were sleeping elsewhere in the house.

The man returned a few times to the woman's side and checked on her bindings. During these visits he whispered in her ear, "Where's the fucking money?" She told him that she had money in her purse that was in the kitchen, but the assailant lost interest in the money at that point and began to pull her pajama bottoms off her, getting them down past her buttocks. Suddenly, the alarm clock in her daughter's bedroom went off. The girl had set the alarm for 6:00 a.m.. The attacker called the bound woman a bitch before throwing the covers over her and bolting from the house.

The woman waited for ten minutes to make sure that the man was gone. She was able to easily get the cord off her wrist as it had been, according to her, more wrapped than tied. She called police at 6:10 a.m. and they arrived at her house within minutes. The woman described the attacker as being about six feet tall and perhaps 180 pounds. She was able to gather that the man had made off with a bunch of her jewelry which included a Jewel Box brand women's watch valued at $700, a sterling charm bracelet, and several other pieces of jewelry. The attacker had also gotten away with her purse, credit cards, driver's license, and house keys. She estimated the value of everything to be around $3,000.

As police looked around the home, they couldn't find any obvious point of entry. There were no pried windows or doors, no damaged locks. The woman told the police that she had only been living there for about four months after moving from Petaluma, California. The previous owners of the home had been an older couple, and, to her knowledge, they had never had any trouble before.

Police also talked to the victim's son and daughter, who had been unharmed, and they learned that about five hours before the attack, around 12:30 a.m., the woman's son had been awakened by the sound of someone moving around outside of the house, but he didn't think too much of it, and he had gone back to sleep.

Police also questioned neighbors of the victim. Most of them had not seen anything unusual, but a few reported a dog barking around 5:00 a.m., which was unusual for the area. Another neighbor reported that his CB radio had been stolen a week earlier, but overall, things were normal leading up to the attack and immediately afterwards. Now, this attack is listed as to confirmed East Area Rapist attack, but it's a bit different too. The attacker never did mention needing food or money for his van, and he barely tied the victim at all. His mask appeared to be a stocking mask, and not the ski mask typically worn by the East Area Rapist.

If this was the work of the East Area Rapist, it showed that he still had ties to the Rancho Cordova area. Even though, this was an area east of his known attacks. This is considered an official East Area Rapist attack, but there are some individuals who have their doubts. Either way, people in the area once again had their guard up. They were on edge in the Rancho Cordova area, but the people in the city of Fremont, located in Alameda County, which is about 100 miles southwest of Rancho Cordova were not. Just south of Contra Costa County, Alameda County is home of the prestigious UC Berkeley University and had a population of about 1 million residents in 1979.

On April 3, a 27-year-old woman and her boyfriend, also 27, returned to their home to unwind after a night out. They had driven to San Jose to check on some rental properties that one of them owned. While in San Jose, they had dinner and then drove home. It was around 9:10 p.m. when they arrived home. When they walked into the house, they noticed that one of the spare bedroom doors was closed, which was noticeable as they normally kept it open. Unfortunately, they dismissed it. They went into their bedroom where they were intimate with each other, and then they went to bed at around 10:30 p.m.

It was after midnight, around 12:20 a.m., we're into April 4 now. The couple woke up to find a masked man holding a flashlight. Their eyes were blinded from the flashlight beam. Once their eyes adjusted to the light, they could see that the man was holding what appeared to be a semi-automatic handgun. The couple heard a quiet, raspy voice from behind the flashlight say, "Don't move, or I'll shoot your fucking head off." The intruder ordered the pair to turn over and lie face down.

He threw shoelaces to the 27-year-old woman, ordering her to tie her boyfriend's hands behind his back. As she finished tying up her boyfriend's hands, she looked up towards the light, and the dark figure hissed, "Don't look at me." He once again told them not to make any moves, or he would shoot their fucking heads off. On top of that, he mentioned to the couple that he would cut their heads off.

Once the male victim was secured, the attacker turned his attention towards the female victim, and tied her hands behind her back, as well as her ankles. Once she was secured, the assailant tied the male victim's ankles as well. The masked man then asked the female victim where her purse was, and she told him that it was in her car parked in the garage. The man then left the room and went to the garage to find her purse.

He soon returned and told the helpless couple that he wanted to separate them. He then ordered the female victim to come with him, helping her to stand up. He walked her out of the room and down the hall. She noticed little details about the man. He was white. She could see brown hair on his legs. The man's shoes were white tennis shoes, and he had checkered socks on. When they got to the front room, the man laid the victim down gently on the floor. He adjusted her ankle bindings and then covered her head with a blanket for blindfolding her.

The man made his way into the kitchen, where he grabbed some dishes and then walked back to the bedroom where the male victim was tied. The dishes clanged as the man carried them down the hallway, he stacked the dishes on the male victim's back, and warned him not to move. The attacker made his way back to the female victim and stood over her. He whispered something into the woman's ear, but she couldn't hear what he was saying. When she told him that she couldn't hear him, the man became angry, and hissed at her to whisper. He once again whispered into her ear and told her, "If you do what I want, I'll take food and money and leave without hurting anyone."

The woman knew at that moment that the masked man was going to sexually assault her. He walked over and turned on the television set and turned the volume down. He placed his penis in the woman's bound hands and told her to stroke it. After a few moments, he stopped her and untied her ankles, and then raped the helpless woman. After the sexual assault was over, he retied the victim's ankles together and tied her to a bookcase before turning off the television set.

He then walked out of the room, and she could hear him moving through the house. It sounded as if he was digging through change or moving keys around. After a short time, the house was silent. She thought the rapist was gone but waited for five minutes before making a move. She was able to make her way into the kitchen, where she used a knife to cut her bindings off, before freeing her boyfriend who was still tied in the bedroom. They immediately called police.

Police received the call just after 1:30 a.m. and they were on scene by 1:45. The couple detailed the events of the attack and replayed for police what the rapist had said and done. They remembered that he mentioned wanting food and money for his van. The couple felt that the voice he used was put on, and not his everyday voice. They described the man as sounding as if he was in his twenties, with a medium build, about five feet, eleven inches to six feet tall and weighing in the range of 170 to 180 pounds.

It was then that the couple realized the significance of the closed bedroom door, and they told police about it. When police checked out the room, they found that the bedroom window was broken around the latch area. As police searched the home, they also found that the dining room window was open, and there were muddy footprints underneath. The window's screen was found outside about five feet from the house. After checking the perimeter of the house, police discovered that multiple windows and two sliding glass doors had fresh pry marks on them, indicating that the rapist had tried to enter the home via multiple entry points.

The couple told police that in the previous two months, on two separate occasions, they had witnessed a prowler in their yard, and both times they had called police, but nothing came from it. Police questioned the victims' neighbors to see if they had seen anything unusual, and one of them had, or at least had heard something unusual. At about 7:40 p.m., around five hours before the attack, a neighbor heard the victims' gate open. Then they thought they heard breaking glass, they shined a light out into the victims' yard but didn't see anything unusual, and they dismissed it.

The victims determined the rapist had made off with the male victim's keys and had taken jewelry and cash from the female victim's purse. Oddly, he had only taken half of her cash and left the rest. This was a one-off attack in Fremont. The East Area Rapist never struck here prior to this attack and wouldn't strike here again.

It's also worth expanding on the fact that the male victim had rental properties in San Jose, and the couple had driven to these properties hours before the attack. It turned out that at least one of the properties was very close to the San Jose attacks committed by the East Area Rapist. It was only about a mile away. While that could just be a coincidence, to put things in perspective, the city of San Jose is about 180 square miles, so maybe there's a little bit more to it.

At the very least, it's another real estate clue in this case, but as we said, this attack in Fremont was the only attack that occurred there. One area that had been struck multiple times was the heart of Contra Costa County. The East Area

Rapist had struck there in Concord, San Ramon, and Danville. These were all along the I-680 corridor. It appeared that he had skipped the city of Walnut Creek, which was in between Concord and Danville, but that would change on June 2, 1979, when the East Area Rapist would attack his next victim there in the city of Walnut Creek.

At around 10:00 p.m., on the 200 block of El Divisadero Drive, a 17-year-old girl was babysitting for her neighbor. She often babysat at this home on most Saturday nights. The children she was babysitting for were sound asleep in their bedrooms, and the teenager decided to relax at the kitchen table. As she sat there, something caught her attention in the hallway. She looked up and saw a man in a white mask standing there with a large knife protruding from a leather sheath in his hand. Before she knew what was happening, he raced towards her and pushed her head down to the table.

The girl couldn't move. Her head was pinned down to the table. She couldn't look up even if she wanted to. The man hissed angrily to her, "Shut up and don't make any noise." The intruder pulled the girl up by her left arm and forced it behind her back. He started to walk her down the hallway before leading her into the master bedroom. The attacker forced the girl face down on the bed, and using nylon bindings that were similar to flex cuffs, he tied her hands behind her back tightly. He then tied her ankles together loosely. After she was bound he used a towel to gag her and placed her halter top over her face.

After the teenager was secured, she could hear the man digging through the bedroom closet and then through drawers. It sounded to her as if the man was sorting through clothes. She then heard him handling the TV set and clock radio that were next to the bed. After a few minutes the man opened the sliding glass door leading from the bedroom to the backyard and walked outside. The terrified young girl hoped that the man was gone, but after a minute or two, he walked back inside. The man then warned the girl that if she was still he wouldn't kill her. He turned the girl over and started to remove her clothing and untied the bindings on her ankles.

Although her face was covered she could tell that the man had pulled his pants down and was masturbating. He asked the teenager if she had ever fucked before. The young girl was horrified, and she knew what was about to happen. The man sexually assaulted her, and during the attack, he placed his penis into her bound hands. At times she could feel what felt like a knife still in the sheath at the side of her neck.

After the sexual assault was over the rapist warned the girl that if she moved, he would slit her throat. She heard the man once again start rampaging through the room before exiting through the sliding glass door. This time he didn't return. After several minutes the victim thought it was safe, She started to work on getting her bindings off. As soon as she got free, she raced to the phone and called the parents of the children she was babysitting but during the call had trouble talking with them and finally hung the phone up. She next called a friend of the family, who in turn, called the Walnut Creek Police Department at 10:34 p.m.. A nearby police officer arrived at the home just seconds later.

Police first called an ambulance and then the girl's parents. They discovered that the children in the home had slept through the attack and were unharmed. Before the victim was taken away to John Muir Hospital for treatment, she was able to describe her attacker as being white, about five feet, six with a medium build. She described her attacker in detail adding how angry the man seemed at times.

The rapist had lightly bitten her breast a few times during the sexual attack, and then at one point had bitten it very hard. This was something that the East Area Rapist was not known to do even though false rumors had circulated since the early East Area Rapist attacks that he was cutting off the nipples of victims.

Police at the scene immediately began squashing talk that this attack was the work of the East Area Rapist, but Contra Costa County investigator Larry Crompton was called in to investigate, and he didn't share the Walnut Creek Police Department's opinion. One of the first things that stood out was the 'for lease' sign on the garage door of a vacant house directly south of the attack.

While investigating the exterior of the home where the rape occurred, the police didn't find any footprints, but they did find the gate open. When they talked with the home owners, they learned that the gate was always kept closed, and they had shut it that night before heading out. Police determined that the suspect had entered the home through an unlocked sliding glass door.

Bloodhounds were brought in to work the crime scene. They picked up a trail that led from the yard to an area near San Jose Court and San Carlos Drive. This was about half a mile southwest of where the attack occurred. The trail ended near a home that had a swimming pool currently being built. Investigators felt that the rapist had likely parked there and then walked to the scene of the attack. Coincidentally or not the victim of this attack lived on San Marino Court just a two-minute walk from where the trail ended. That night police caught a break that sounded very promising when they heard about a suspicious car that had been pulled over about two and a half miles from the crime scene.

The Pleasant Hill Police Department had stopped the car at about 1:46 a.m. just off I-680 near Geary Road and North Main Street. They suspected that the man who was driving may have been intoxicated. After questioning him, the man gave them permission to search his car. When the police did, they found a large knife and a sheath under the driver seat and a pair of underwear. They noticed that the man fit the physical description that had been broadcast that night about the rape suspect.

Police were excited because they thought that they may have caught the attacker before he got a chance to make his getaway. They brought in the bloodhounds that had tracked the rapist's scent earlier that night to see how they responded. Based on the dogs' response, their handlers felt that the driver's scent was consistent with the rapist's scent, but further investigation would later rule the suspect out, first through an alibi and then years later through DNA.

Back at the crime scene, investigators started to turn their attention to neighbors hoping that they could shed some light on the attack. It was discovered that on the night of the attack, sometime between 9:30 and 11:30, a bicycle had been stolen from a home on Los Banos Court about a five-minute walk northwest of where the dogs had lost the scent. The bike would later be found on El Divisadero Court, a few homes down from the scene of the attack.

Other neighbors reported prowlers in the weeks leading up to the attack, and a few of them reported receiving hang-up phone calls. The 17-year old victim herself had received hang-up phone calls during the month of May, both at her home and while babysitting on El Divisadero. Women who lived at a residence nearby reported that someone had broken into their home and the only thing that they seem have taken were pictures of them. They too received hang-up phone calls, and just a couple of days after the attack, the mother of the victim saw a maroon colored El Camino parked near her house. She thought that it seemed out of place, so she walked towards it to investigate, but as she did, the car sped off. The only description that she could give of the man driving the car was that he was a white male.

With this attack, it was clear early on that the Walnut Creek Police Department didn't think that this rape was the work of the East Area Rapist. There were some differences to support this notion. The attacker was described as about five feet, six, a couple inches shorter than most East Area Rapist descriptions.

He also bit the nipple of the victim. Something that the East Area Rapist didn't normally do.

There were also some similarities that made investigators like Larry Crompton feel that this was the work of the East Area Rapist. The way in which he ordered the victim to lie face down and placing his penis in her bound hands were indicators that this was likely the East Area Rapist. In the end, this victim would officially be classified by the East Area Rapist task force as the rapist's most recent victim. But the East Area Rapist was not finished with Contra Costa County. In fact, he returned to a city there that he had struck in before, Danville.

On June 11, only nine days after the attack in Walnut Creek, the rapist would strike on the 1000 block of Allegheny Drive. This area was very close to the scene of the last Danville attack on Liberta Court. In fact, the homework evidence that was recovered was found very close to Allegheny Drive. At 4:00 a.m., a husband and wife, both 33 years old, were asleep when something caused the women to wake up. When she did, there was a man with a flashlight at the foot of the bed. She sat up and grabbed her husband causing him to wake up. They both looked towards the man holding the flashlight.

At that point, the intruder whispered through clenched teeth, "Neither one of you motherfuckers move, or I'll blow your heads off." They then noticed the gun he was holding. He started to walk closer and told the pair that he just wanted their money.

Once the man started walking and the flashlight wasn't as blinding, they could see he was wearing a mask. He stepped very close to the husband's side of the bed and raised the gun to his head and cocked it, and he said, "One move and I'll kill every motherfucker in the house." The victims had been totally surprised. They were not able to resist. Add on top of that the fact that they were worried about the safety of their daughters who were asleep in their bedrooms. The intruder ordered the male victim to roll over on his stomach before ordering the man's wife to tie his hands behind his back using shoe laces that the man had thrown to her. The shoe laces were from the victim's shoes that were in their closet.

After the husband was secured, the assailant ordered the female victim down face first and tied her hands as well. He then tied both victims' ankles. After the couple was secured, the attacker told them that he only wanted their money. He said, "All I want is the money and then I can get back to the city, or I can kill every motherfucker here and then leave." The entire time the stranger talked, it was through clenched teeth. The women volunteered that her purse was in the kitchen under the bar, and her husband's wallet was in his pants pocket in the den.

The intruder left the victims to retrieve the money and warned them not to move. He was only gone for a few minutes before he returned, and when he did, he accused the couple of moving around. He yanked the female victim out of the bed and forced her to walk with him out of the room. He stopped for a moment to gag the male victim with a yellow towel that had been in their bathroom. The attacker marched the woman into the living room and threw her to the floor. He went back in to where the male victim was and covered him with a sheet. He removed several glass bottles from the dresser and placed them on the victim's back warning him, "If I hear these bottles jingle, I'll blow your fucking head off."

The assailant then made his way back to the female victim in the living room to check on her but found her to still be in the same spot. He then started rummaging through the house checking mirrors, drawers, closets. Every few minutes he would check on the male victim to make sure he was still secured. As he passed by the wife during the ransacking, he told her he was hungry and needed something to eat. She heard him walk into the kitchen and grab a beer from their refrigerator. He then came back and told her that he wanted to fuck her. He referred to her by her first name. He approached the victim from behind and placed his penis into her bound hands and told her to play with it.

At this point, the attacker untied the women's ankles and sexually assaulted her but after just a few minutes he stopped and tied her ankles together again. He walked off into the kitchen once again going through things, and it sounded like he was placing items into paper bags. This was around 4:30 a.m. and the husband, who was still tied up in the bedroom, heard what sounded to him like a small truck race up the street and stop in front of his house. It sounded as if the truck idled there for almost a minute, then it raced off again towards El Capitan.

The house was silent, and the male victim started to move a bit after waiting just a few minutes, and then suddenly the man realized that the intruder was standing in the doorway watching him.

The assailant walked back into the living room, and as he walked by the female victim, he told her that he was going to go out and put some stuff in his van. After a few moments of silence, the male victim peeked at his clock and saw it was 4:45 a.m. and both victims felt that the man who had terrorized them was finally gone. They started trying to free themselves. The male victim hopped to his oldest daughter's bedroom and found her safe in bed. He woke her up and told her to call police who arrived at the scene at around 5:00 a.m.

Police questioned the victims and got a description of the man who had attacked them. He was in his twenties, around five feet, five inches to five feet, nine inches. They felt that he had a heavier or stockier build than most of the previous East Area Rapist descriptions, but this could have been due to a bulky or heavy sweater they described him as wearing. The point of entry was determined to be a bedroom window, and muddy footprints were found in that room. The exit point was the sliding glass door that was standing wide open. Footprints were found outside the victim's home. They came from a size nine and a half shoe with a herringbone patterned tread. Similar footprints were found in other nearby yards.

Police questioned neighbors to see if they had seen anything of interest. One neighbor reported that his gate was standing wide open, and it had been closed the night before. Another resident had heard a noise at around 2:30 a.m. and had looked outside through the window but didn't see anything unusual. Still another neighbor saw a newer, dark colored van parked near El Capitan and Camino Ramon. Bloodhounds were brought in to try to follow the rapist scent. They tracked the scent to the intersection of El Capitan and Delta Way. Then the scent vanished.

Like in the previous Danville attacks seven months earlier, the theory was that the East Area Rapist had escaped in a car that he had parked nearby. But, unlike the previous Danville attack, there were no homework pages left behind. Fortunately, the rapist did leave his DNA behind, and it wound up being well preserved and was the third DNA sample of the East Area Rapist that would later be used to tie his crimes together.

Two weeks later, on June 25, the East Area Rapist would strike on San Pedro Court in Walnut Creek. As he had done early in the series in Sacramento County, he demonstrated a pattern of bouncing back and forth between towns in the same county keeping police guessing in the process. At around 4:15 a.m., a 13-year-old girl woke up to find an intruder with his hand over her mouth. She opened her eyes and tried to make sense of what she was seeing in the darkness. The assailant spoke through a forced whisper, "Don't say a word. I'm not going to kill you. All I want is money." But as he said these words, he pressed the tip of a knife against her.

The man started tying the girl's wrists and ankles together. As he did, he warned her that he would kill her if she made a sound. He then gagged the girl with a bra. The attacker pumped a bottle of lotion into his hand and started to masturbate in front of the girl. He turned her over and pulled her clothes off and blindfolded her. The girl was terrified, and she imagined what would happen if her 17-year-old sister or her father woke up and came into her bedroom. The man addressed her by her first name and told her, "Let it drop easy. Give me a good drop, or I'll kill you." She didn't know what that meant, but she knew what was about to happen. He then sexually assaulted the teenager.

After he was done with the assault, the man told the girl that if she made a sound, he would kill her. He said to her that he had to "looky looky" for money. She could hear the man moving around in the darkness, and then he left the room. The house fell silent, and after a couple of minutes, she struggled to get up and hobbled out into the hallway. She started crying out, "I've been raped." The girl's father was awake. Although his alarm had been set for 4:45, he woke up for some unknown reason, just a moment before he heard his daughter. He stared at the alarm clock that was due to go off in ten minutes. When he heard his daughter, he jumped up out of bed and met her in the hallway.

The young victim's father found her partially bound in white twine. The commotion woke up the older girl. The father called out to the older daughter to grab something to cut the bindings. She brought back a knife, and they freed the 13-year-old victim before calling police. Police received the call at 5:00 a.m. and an officer was at the scene within a couple minutes. Police first questioned the victim, and she told them the details of the attack. She described her attacker as being a white male close to six feet tall and weighing 150 to 160 pounds. He wore some sort of mask.

The police questioned the victim's father and sister, but neither of them could add much since they had both slept through the entire attack. The father did tell police that they had all gone to bed the night before at around 10:00 p.m. Before they went to bed, he had walked around and made sure that the house was locked, but he also added an important detail. He mentioned that at 9:00 p.m., shortly before they had all gone to bed, the phone rang. His youngest daughter answered it, and there was silence. After the young girl said hello a couple of times, her father took the phone away from her and said hello, and at that point, the caller hung up.

Police didn't find any evidence of windows being pried, but they did find that the chain on the front door had a lot of slack, so much so that it was obvious that somebody without much skill could disengage the chain with minimum effort. Police brought in bloodhounds, the same bloodhounds used to track the East Area Rapist previously. The dog picked up the rapist's scent quickly and followed it around the outside of the home and then north on San Carlos before finally losing the scent near San Jose Court. This is the same spot where the dogs had previously tracked the rapist to when he had struck three weeks earlier in Walnut Creek.

Apparently, he had once again parked in the same location and had made his escape undetected. This left little doubt that this 13-year-old was an East Area Rapist victim. It turned out that she was the second youngest rape victim of the entire East Area Rapist series second to Margaret, who was 12 years old. Like Margaret, the East Area Rapist had attacked her while a parent was home. Out of all the East Area Rapist attacks, only two involved victims whose parents were home at the time, and they just happened to be the youngest victims.

The East Area Rapist Task Force in Contra Costa County was on high alert over the next week, but when that next week came and went with no attack, they turned their attention to the Fourth of July holiday. But, the Fourth came and went as well with no attacks. In the early morning hours of July 6, 1979, the East Area Rapist would strike in Contra Costa County once again. This time back in Danville on Sycamore Court just over two miles from his previous Danville attack. The victims in this attack would be a 33-year-old woman and her 32-year-old husband.

Just before 4 a.m., the husband who was a light sleeper awoke to a rustling sound. He opened his eyes and across the bedroom near the master bathroom, he saw the outline of a man who was slowly pulling a ski mask down over his face.

Unfortunately for this intruder, this couple had formulated a plan should the East Area Rapist ever show up at their home, and they immediately sprang into action to carry it out.

The plan was for the husband to rush the attacker no matter what and confront him while his wife escaped. Sticking to the plan, the husband jumped out of bed and raced towards the intruder who looked shocked to see the man confronting him. He didn't have a gun in his hand yet, and the husband yelled obscenities at the intruder saying, "Who the fuck do you think you are?" In part because his adrenaline had kicked in, but also to ensure that his wife had been alerted. The husband stood in a fighting stance between the doorway leading out of the bedroom, and the man who was near the bathroom. This plan went smoothly because the wife ran by him and out of the bedroom door into the hallway.

Once the husband saw that his wife had made it out, he turned again towards the intruder, who meekly stared back at him and just stood there blinking like a kid who had been caught putting his hands into the cookie jar. The husband raced out behind his wife never turning back to see if the intruder was following them. They escaped through a sliding door. Unlike past instances, when a neighbor heard the couple screaming in their backyard, they picked up the phone and called police just after 4:00 a.m. and police were there within minutes. They entered the home, searching it to ensure the intruder wasn't inside. He wasn't.

Police took notice that the victim's residence was a condominium. Although the East Area Rapist had struck a condo or apartment before, it wasn't his usual style. Police wanted to identify the entry point as well as the exit point, so they could start searching for him. The front door was locked from the inside with a deadbolt. The only way the intruder could have escaped through that door was if he had a key for it and locked it as he left. They also checked doors in the garage. The entry door leading into the garage was usually kept unlocked because there was something wrong with the lock mechanism, and it was extremely hard to lock. When police examined the door, it was locked. The only other way out through the garage was through the powered garage door, which was closed.

Police did notice that the driver's door to the victims' car, a Porsche, was ajar but they weren't sure if the intruder had entered the vehicle or if the owner had not closed it all the way when he parked it. The neighbors who called police immediately looked out their window and into the victims' front yard upon hearing their screams, but they didn't see anyone moving. Like they had done before, police brought in the bloodhounds. It took the bloodhounds a little bit of time to pick up the scent, but when they did, they picked it up in the hallway, and that led them out into the backyard. The dogs tracked the scent through a large open field in the area behind the condos, but they lost it on the other side of the field.

Back at the crime scene, police questioned the couple to get specific details of the intruder. The pair described the man as being about five feet, ten to six feet tall and weighing about 160 pounds. They felt he was in his mid-twenties. He was wearing a ski mask that looked homemade and didn't come down over his entire chin. They also noticed that he was wearing a dark windbreaker with lettering on the left side of the jacket. The lettering appeared to be gold or white and started with a C, it was a short word perhaps course, coach, or corn something along those lines, but they couldn't be sure. Since the male victim had seen him before he pulled the mask down, police felt that this was the best chance they had to find out what the East Area Rapist looked like, assuming that this was him. They later put the victim under hypnosis, and he further detailed the intruders face. A partial sketch was made from the description but has not been released publicly. After seeing this sketch, I can tell you that I don't fully agree with the description that accompanies the sketch, but it reads as follows, "Iris is large, possibly hazel colored eyes, possibly a small thin mouth, possibly a square shaped chin."

While walking through the area searching for the suspect, police discovered a man who fit the general description of the intruder. He appeared to be living out of his car. They walked up on him as he was using a pair of pants to clean off his back window. They questioned him and felt that he didn't belong in the area. They arranged for the victims to see him, and they felt that based on his build, which they described as a wiry football player, he could have been the man they saw. Later, however, police would rule him out as being the East Area Rapist.

As police questioned residents in the area, they discovered that there were a couple homes for sale. In fact, a home very close to the victim had an open house a couple of weeks prior to the act, and it attracted many people. Police continued to check with other neighbors, and they found one on nearby Thornhill Road who had reported a prowler six days earlier on June 30. Her home was currently up for sale. A resident reported that some of the buildings nearby were in the process of being painted around the time of the attack. This is an interesting detail as we mentioned before there were blue paint flakes found at several crime scenes during the East Area Rapist series, perhaps he could have been involved in the painting project.

Other neighbors reported receiving hang-up phone calls in the days prior to the attack, and one reported that someone had opened her sliding glass door. But, despite all the activity and the quick response by police, the intruder slipped through the dragnet. Police came to believe that this intruder was the East Area Rapist, and this was considered an official East Area Rapist attack.

The most crucial thing to come out of this attack was that it was the first time that the East Area Rapist had been witnessed without his mask on. Police now had something to work with, and they felt that this might be the clue that could help solve the case, but just when the investigators felt that they had gotten their best break up to that point, the East Area Rapist vanished.

Days turned into weeks and weeks in the months. Summer passed and turned to fall, and there was not another crime attributed to the East Area Rapist in any of the Northern California counties that he had struck in. Some theorized that being seen without his mask on sent the rapist into a panic, and then he feared he might be identified, which forced him to stop attacking. For investigator Larry Crompton, not catching the East Area Rapist weighed heavily on him.

Well, when you get into incidents like this where they are so violent, and you talk to the victims, and you find out what's going through their mind, and you get it in your head, I have a job to do, my job is to catch this person before he hurts anybody else. It just gets worse as you don't catch him, and then after it was over, and he left our area, I would wake up at three o'clock in the morning, and I would say, what did I do wrong? What did I miss? What did I do? What should I have done? It took many years before I got it in my head this wasn't about me, this is about the victims and the victims' families, and it made it a little easier, but I never did get it out of my head, it's still here.

Larry Crompton would go on to retire, and he would write a book about the case called *Sudden Terror*, which we highly recommend. Even though Larry had retired, he wasn't done with the case, and, in fact, he would be instrumental in linking the East Area Rapist to a new set of crimes.

SEASON TWO, EPISODE ELEVEN

While Larry Crompton and the rest of the Northern California residents wondered where the East Area Rapist had gone, residents in Southern California were about to deal with a deadly predator of their own. He would become known as the Night Stalker. We're not talking about Richard Ramirez; this Night Stalker was before Ramirez. Years later, this offender would become known as the original Night Stalker.

In Santa Barbara County in Southern California, Goleta was an unincorporated town in 1979. Boasting temperatures that average 70 degrees year-round, it was close to the beach and home to a lot of surfers. The town itself was quiet, laid back, and the crime rate was very low. Things were quiet, and that was perfectly fine for residents there. In September of 1979, a strange incident occurred that seemed to mark the beginning of a troubling period in Goleta.

In late September, a woman was in her home on the 5400 block of Berkeley Road one evening, when a man knocked on her door. He told her that his dog had been hurt after running between her house and the one next door. After the dog ran off he had called for it, and the dog hobbled back to him and fell on the ground at his feet.

He first knocked on the door of a neighbor of this woman but did not get an answer. Then he found this woman at home. He asked her if he could use her phone to call a friend to come pick up him and his dog. She allowed the man in and let him use her phone. A few minutes later, a vehicle pulled up and took the man and his dog away.

Later that evening, the next-door neighbor who wasn't home when the injury occurred to the dog arrived home and found that somebody had turned her faucet on and her front yard was flooded. The next day, the man with the injured dog returned and caught both neighbors outside talking to each other. They discussed what had happened the day before.

The man told the women that he had rushed his dog to the veterinarian, and it required nearly seventy stitches, for what the vet thought was a stab wound. The three of them walked to the area between their homes, in the rear part of the yard, looking for something that could have injured the animal, but they didn't find anything of interest. Following the dog incident, there were various reports of people being seen walking through residents' yards at night, prowler incidents, as well as fences and gates being disturbed.

A week later, on the 5400 block of Queen Ann Lane just a mile north of where this dog incident occurred, a couple was attacked while they slept around 2:00 a.m. on October 1. A 33-year-old woman and her 32-year-old boyfriend, both computer programmers, were fast asleep when the female victim woke up to find a man at the foot of her bed. He was shining a flashlight in her eyes. She grabbed her boyfriend, waking him up. The pair could not see if the intruder was wearing a mask or not.

The man hissed from behind the light, "Don't move fucker. I got to have money." He instructed the pair to turn over on their stomachs and then threw pre-tied lengths of nylon twine to the female victim. He ordered her to tie up her boyfriend's hands behind his back. After he was secured, the attacker tied the female victim's hands behind her back. Their hands were tied very tightly and both victims immediately began losing circulation in their hands. The intruder then tied the woman's ankles together loosely. Without the light in their eyes, they finally saw that the man was wearing ski mask.

The stranger reiterated that he had to have money. He warned the terrified couple that he wouldn't hurt them if they gave him money. The female victim volunteered that there was money in her purse in the kitchen. The assailant began looking around through their belongings and going into their closet. He then returned, stood over the pair, and hissed, "I'll kill you fuckers." He walked out of the room and started to ransack the rest of the home.

After a few minutes, the man came back and told the female victim that he couldn't find her purse and ordered her to come with him to show him where it was at. He untied her ankles, allowing her to walk by his side. He dragged her roughly towards the kitchen where she told him where her purse was. When they got to the living room on the way to the kitchen, the man forced her down on the floor, and then retied her ankles.

The attacker left the room and returned later with shorts that he threw over the woman's head. Although her head was covered by the shorts, she could see that the attacker was shining his flashlight up and down her naked body. She then heard him breathing heavily, and she could tell that he was masturbating. As he masturbated, he told the woman, "Now am going to kill you by cutting your throat."

The masked intruder walked away from her and went into the kitchen, and she could hear him saying out loud over and over," I will kill him, I will kill him." She immediately got the sense that the man did plan to kill her and without hesitating she jumped to her feet and started hopping down the hallway towards the front door. She had trouble seeing clearly with the shorts on her head and tripped near the front door. She stood up and with her bound hands struggled to open the door, but she somehow did get it open and hopped outside. Once she was outside, the bindings on her ankles came loose, and she tried to run and scream. She didn't make it far before she felt the attacker's hands on her back pushing her down on the ground. The masked man held a knife to her throat and told her that she had better be quiet.

He scooped the woman up and escorted her back towards the front door of the house. When they got inside, he threw her down and tied her ankles once again. He went to the bedroom to check on the male victim and found that he had escaped through a sliding-glass door into the backyard but was trapped by a wooden fence. The male victim started to smash against the fence with all his weight, screaming as he did this, but eventually he realized he couldn't get through. He couldn't get away, so he hid in some bushes. The assailant ran out of the house into the backyard looking around for the male victim, but he didn't see him in the bushes, and then suddenly the attacker could hear the female victim screaming from the front yard. She had once again gotten to her feet and made it out the front door screaming. The intruder ran back inside through the house towards the front door.

As the attacker made it out the front door, he saw the terrified woman racing away from him screaming. Luckily for this couple, the next-door neighbor was an FBI agent who was awake and heard their screams. He grabbed his gun and raced outside. As he neared the driveway of the victims, he saw a dark figure race by on a bicycle. The FBI agent ran to his car and jumped in to pursue the man on the bike. When he tried to start it, the engine wouldn't start, something that wasn't out of the ordinary with his car. After a couple of tries he started the car up and raced off in the direction of the bike rider. He lost sight of the cyclist but turned left on North Kellogg and cruised quickly but kept his eyes open, heading south towards San Patricio. At that intersection, he once again caught the sight of the man on the bike who was peddling for his life.

The FBI agent floored his car, gained on the suspect, getting within about 100 yards of him. At this point the fleeing assailant had to know he could not outrun this car, so he jumped the curb, bailed off the bike escaping on foot into some bushes. As the FBI agent stopped near the spot where the suspect ditched the bike, he caught sight of him scaling a fence and jumping into a backyard. At this point the FBI agent didn't know who he was, or exactly why he was chasing him, and he doesn't have back up, so he ends up giving up the pursuit. He drove back to the victims' residence, and he found the pair outside half naked and scared. By this time neighbors had called the police, and they arrived on the scene within minutes.

The FBI agent walked the officers through what had happened and then led them to the spot where he had chased the suspect to. When they arrived on the scene, they found the bike, which was a ten-speed. It was later determined that the bike belonged to a probation officer on the 1000 block of North Patterson Avenue just north of the victims' home and that it had been stolen earlier that evening. The probation officer who owned the bike was not a suspect.

Meanwhile, the police had also found a black steak knife that the assailant had wielded during the attack. Shoe prints left by the suspect indicated that he was wearing Adidas running shoes approximately size nine. The tracks seemed to indicate that he had left on foot heading back towards the direction he was chased from. Back at the crime scene the victims and the FBI agent described the fleeing attacker as being white, about five feet, ten inches to five feet, eleven inches with a medium build. The victims described the attacker's voice as being soft spoken, but it appeared as if he was trying to make it sound deeper. The point of entry appeared to be a pried sliding glass door, possibly pried with a screwdriver. Police discovered footprints in the victims' yard. The attack seemed random, it wasn't typical of the area, and police didn't find any additional leads. Although being out of the ordinary, it wouldn't be the last unusual event in that area of Goleta.

Almost three months later, on December 29, 1979, there was a burst of suspicious activity and burglaries. In the early evening, someone attempted to enter a home on the 5300 block of Parejo Drive using a screwdriver, but they were not successful. The attempted burglary at this address stood out to neighbors because just a few homes away an elderly woman in her seventies had been bludgeoned to death in 1974. The woman whose name was Eva Taylor was recently widowed at the time of her murder. She had married her husband Grover in 1970, but he passed away in 1972. Her daughter at the time of the murder lived in Santa Barbara, but the rest of her family lived in Sacramento County.

Investigators on the Eva Taylor case determined that there was no sexual attack on the woman, but there was a sexual component possibly to the attack. It seemed as if her killer had gone through her undergarments. There was also evidence that Taylor's killer may have prepared a meal and ate it at her kitchen table. When he left, it appeared that he tried to set the home on fire by leaving the gas stove flame on low. Her killer made off with a few pieces of jewelry that were not very valuable. The sliding-glass door on Taylor's home had been pried open with a screwdriver that was found at the scene and was traced to Raytheon, a company in Santa Barbara County.

A young girl had been babysitting next door that night, and she had received a couple of hang-up phone calls. Earlier in the day, she had seen a suspicious man watching her, possibly driving a news or a cable truck. The police received a break during a neighborhood canvas when it was learned that a resident had seen a young man possibly in his late teens or early twenties jumping over Taylor's fence. A sketch of the suspect was made, but it didn't lead anywhere, and four decades later, the Taylor murder remains unsolved.

Other incidents were reported on the night of December 29, 1979. On Hannah Drive, just south of the attempted burglary on Parejo, thieves entered a home and made off with cash and jewelry. The jewelry itself wasn't very valuable. Possibly the most interesting event or burglary that night happened on the 5400 block of Queen Ann Lane, the same street only two-tenths of a mile from the early morning attack on the couple three months earlier.

A woman who lived next door to the home that was burglarized recounted what she had witnessed shortly before the burglary occurred. It was about 6:10 p.m. when she saw a woman standing near the front pouch of the property. The home owner wasn't home, he had gone to see a movie. Later, around 7:00

p.m., she saw a man that she didn't recognize on the porch ringing the doorbell to the home. Again, she knew these people were not the residents of the home, but she didn't pay much attention, and she went inside. A half hour later around 7:30, she had to run an errand and left her house. As she left, she once again saw the same man she had seen earlier. He appeared to be ringing the doorbell as she drove off.

At about 9:30 p.m., upon arriving home, the homeowner entered his house and discovered that he had been robbed. Investigators discovered that the point of entry had been a pried garage door. Inside, the thief had made off with several pieces of jewelry and had also pried open a safe.

Later, the eyewitness who had seen people on the porch would describe the male she had seen as being about five feet, eight to six feet tall, 25 to 30 years old, with a mustache, and wearing a knit cap. The female that she saw was described as in her twenties and about five feet, four and having a large pointed nose.

The property that was burglarized backed up to a school and directly across the schoolyard was Windsor Court. Around 6.00 p.m., on the same night of this burglary, a family on Windsor Court left the house for the evening before returning at 9:45 p.m.

As they pulled in, their headlights shined into their living room, and they saw a man inside crouched down who took off across the room towards the back of the house. The man exited their house through the back door and ran through their backyard over their fence into the schoolyard. As he crossed the fence, automatic sprinklers on the school property came on. The couple immediately called police who arrived quickly.

Police searched the home to make sure it was safe to enter. Nothing seemed to be missing, but the family's poodle had been struck in the eye with some sort of object. We've read conflicting reports about this dog. One report said the dog was injured, and the other one stated that it was killed. The witnesses described the man they saw fleeing as being in his late teens to 30 years old.

He was wearing what looked to be something like a fisherman's hat. Police found the sliding glass door had been pried open. As they looked around the yard, they discovered footprints, which they later cast and photographed. They matched the footprints found at the Queen Ann attack three months earlier. Given the timing of these two occurrences and the fact that only a schoolyard separated them, it's very possible that these two burglaries are related.

The flurry of events on the night of the twenty-ninth continued. On the 700 block of Avenida Pequena at a condo complex, a bike was stolen sometime that evening after midnight around 1:30 on the morning of the 30th. A woman who lived just a few doors down from where the bike was stolen, woke to the sound of someone trying to get inside her home.

The prowler left after not having success. Her sliding glass door was partially open, and she thought that the person coming in might be her son. She called out to him, but her son answered her from upstairs, and then a dog started to bark. She heard the person outside of her home run off. Another nearby condo, which was vacant, was broken into. This condo was at 769 Via Pequena.

A man named Doctor Robert Offerman, an orthopedic surgeon, lived next to the vacant condo that had been broken into. He and a woman he had been seeing, Doctor Debra Manning, a clinical psychologist was scheduled to play a game of tennis with friends of theirs. The friends arrived to pick up Offerman and Manning at 11:00 a.m. at his condo located at 767 Avenida Pequena.

They rang the doorbell but didn't get a response. They noticed that a sliding glass door was open, so they decided to go inside. When they did, they found two dead bodies. They raced out and called police.

The Santa Barbara County Sheriff's Department arrived soon after. They entered the home and checked the scene out. The two bodies were in Offerman's master bedroom, and they would quickly verify that the bodies were that of Drs. Offerman and Manning. It was easy to see that the pair had been murdered, and police secured the crime scene and started to examine the single story, two-bedroom condo that was attached to the vacant condo next to it.

Police examined all the entry points into the condo and found that the front door was locked and secure with no evidence of pry marks or tampering. A green Christmas wreath hung on the door, and the porch light was on. When they checked the south side of the residence, police found three different sliding glass doors leading into the home.

One led to the living room, one to the dining room, and the other to the master bedroom. They found that the one leading into the master bedroom was closed, but it was not locked, and there was no evidence that it had been broken into or pried. The dining room door was closed and locked, but the one that led to the living room stood wide open.

There were noticeable pry marks found on this door, and the door had been partially pulled away from the wall, leaving plaster residue on the floor. Outside of the home on the ground, four feet away from this door, was a plastic bag that contained cooked turkey meat and bones. The turkey remnants were determined to have come from the leftover Christmas turkey in Offerman's refrigerator.

As they walked around the yard, investigators discovered footprints. The footprints were from an Adidas running shoe and were later found to be consistent with prints found at the scene where the intruder bludgeoned a poodle. They were also consistent with the footprints found at the home of the couple who were attacked on Queen Ann Lane.

These prints indicated that the killer had likely climbed the fence where a scuff mark was located and walked along the edge of the house, stopping and looking through partially open shutters that allowed him to see into the master bedroom. It appeared that the killer lingered in this area of the yard for some time. In addition to the footprints at the scene, police also discovered dog tracks.

However, neither Offerman nor Manning owned a dog. After examining the area, they found that the vacant condo next to Offerman's condo had been broken into. Police found the same shoe prints in the yard of the vacant condo that they had found in Offerman's yard. They found a piece of twine under the bathroom sink in the vacant condo.

Investigators carefully sifted through clues inside the bedroom and examined the bodies of Offerman and Manning. Robert Offerman was found on the floor of the master bedroom on his knees with his buttocks in the air. He was clutching a piece of twine in his left hand that was wrapped around his wrist.

He had been shot once in the chest and three times in the back. Debra Manning was found nude in the bed a few feet away. She was lying face down. Her hands were tied behind her back, and she had been shot once in the back of the head execution style. Both victims had been shot with the same .38 caliber gun. Cash and credit cards were found in her purse nearby. The initial police theory was that this was a robbery gone wrong, but since Manning's purse and its contents were found, there was some reason to doubt this. However, they did discover that Dr. Offerman's medical bag and a Minolta camera were missing.

Neither victim had been sexually assaulted, but evidence showed that the pair had sex with each other that night. On a dresser, detectives found a business card for Apollo Airlines, but they had no idea if it had been placed there by the killer or if it belonged to one of the victims. They also noted in the report that the thermostat had been turned to the off position.

Based on all the evidence at the crime scene, police theorized that the couple were in bed when an intruder gained entry through the sliding glass door in the living room and took the couple by surprise at gunpoint. He may have told the couple that he was going to rob them because Manning's two valuable rings were stuffed between the mattress and headboard. This was probably an effort on her part to keep them from being stolen. Since Manning was still bound and Offerman had a partial binding on his hand, the investigators felt that the murderer thought that he had both victims secured. But, Offerman somehow broke free, charged at the intruder before he was shot multiple times. It seemed likely that the killer walked over to Manning who was lying face down and shot her once in the back of the head execution style.

After a canvas was completed of people who lived near the crime scene, police found people who had heard the gunshots just after 3:00 a.m. One neighbor heard what he thought was a gunshot followed by three more gunshots, and then a slight pause, followed by a final gunshot. This was approximately 3:05 a.m. on the morning of December 30.

One neighbor heard what he described as being firecrackers and went out into the parking lot but didn't see anything unusual. He assumed that the sounds were firecrackers since it was almost New Year's Eve. Another witness heard tires screeching and looked out their window around 3:15 a.m. When they did, they saw what looked like a white boxy car driving through the parking lot without its headlights on.

None of these neighbors and potential witnesses reported seeing a person in the area, so there were no descriptions of the killer. The bike that had been stolen that night was later found on Crown Avenue, less than a mile northwest of Avenida Pequena. The location where the bike was found on Crown Avenue was just southwest of the 1000 block of North Patterson, and this was where the bike had been stolen from in the Queen Ann Lane attack three months earlier.

Based on where the bike was found, investigators searched the area for clues or evidence over the following two days. On the 800 block of North Kellogg, police found twine in two different yards. This was the same twine used to bind Offerman and Manning, as well as the twine found in the vacant condo next door to them. Police retraced the killer's likely steps from Avenida Pequena to where the bike was found, and they crossed over Windsor Court and Queen Anne Lane along the way. Both of those streets had homes that were burglarized in the preceding three months. The couple who were attacked three months earlier were attacked on Queen Anne Lane.

Near North Kellogg and Normal Way, police found footprints that matched those found at the Offerman/Manning crime scene. Alongside the footprints were dog tracks. These prints led down to the San Jose creek bed. Police tracked them for a while but lost the trail in the creek bed. Pieces of twine were also found in this area. It seemed as if the killer walked or rode a stolen bike from the crime scene, then ditched it where it was found before walking the rest of the way into the creek bed.

Whether or not the killer rode the bike or walked the entire way, it seemed as if the dog accompanied him from the murder scene. The area of the creek that the killer walked through to make his escape led up to North Patterson to the approximate location where the bike had been stolen from the probation officer three months earlier. Since all the prowling and attacks during this three-month period took place very close to the San Jose creek bed, the offender would later be dubbed, "The Creek Killer."

Investigators turned the lives of Offerman and Manning upside down searching for answers. Robert Offerman was in the process of a divorce at the time of this murder and had been separated since 1978, Manning had just completed a divorce two days before the murders. Her ex-husband, like Offerman, was an orthopedic surgeon. As is typical in most murders, those closest to the victims or people with obvious motives are looked at first. Offerman had an estate consisting of millions of dollars' worth of holdings and investments.

Manning's ex-husband took and passed a lie detector test and investigators quickly ruled out those closest to the victims as being involved in their murders. Detectives looked at the timeline leading up to the murders to see if any clues could be found that might lead to the killer. They discovered that Manning, who worked and lived in Santa Maria, California, had been receiving hang-up phone calls shortly before her death. In addition, someone had tried unsuccessfully to force entry into her residence on Stansbury Drive. She was involved with the rape crisis hotline, was an avid jogger, swimmer, and tennis player, and she had moved to Santa Maria in 1976 from Boston.

Robert Offerman had a successful medical practice in Santa Barbara. He had been married in 1964 and had one child. Like Manning, he was an avid jogger and tennis player. Both victims were also dating other people at the time of the murders. Deborah Manning was a very private person, so friends and co-workers didn't know much about her private life. Robert Offerman was a member of a Porsche club in Santa Barbara. Both victims were friendly and well respected in Santa Barbara County without any known enemies.

Authorities found one witness who was able to provide important details that may have been directly related to the Manning/Offerman murder. The witness reported that around midnight on December 30, just three hours before police believe the murders happened, he heard what he believed was Offerman's Porsche pull into his normal parking spot near his condo.

The witness heard the voice of two men talking, one he was sure was Offerman's, but he didn't recognize the second voice. The witness also heard a woman's voice talking but didn't know Manning well enough to say whether it was her voice.

Police continued to backtrack to the days before the murders but didn't see anything out of the ordinary. Police did find that Offerman and Manning had attended a party on December 28 in which several doctors and lawyers were present. The party was held at nearby Toltec Place, and that street will be significant as we move along to some of the Southern California cases.

There have been rumblings that Manning's office janitor had a run in with a young man who was a patient of hers, and the janitor was badly beaten by this youth. The young man, with ties to Sacramento, was no stranger to police. In fact, his name was one of several that had come up as a possible suspect in some of the burglaries going on in Goleta. It wouldn't be until two years later when he would be connected to this case.

That young man was a neighbor of a man who was heavily involved with real estate in Santa Barbara County. This man, who was involved in real estate, owned a dog that supposedly only had three toes on one of its paws, and one of the rumors was that the paw prints found at the Manning/Offerman crime scene only had three toes on one paw. It was more likely that the dog's prints were only partial prints. That didn't stop investigators from talking to several veterinarians in Santa Barbara County to see if they had treated any dogs recently with three toes on one paw.

Another rumor that circulated in the Offerman/Manning murders was that Robert Offerman himself was sexually assaulted. This isn't true, and it's likely that this rumor started after his body was found nude face down, with his buttocks in the air. After the murders, the suspicious activity in Goleta died down. Police were stumped as to why anybody would want to kill the doctors.

Police did, however, investigate two suspicious rapes of young girls in 1979 along the San Jose Creek by strangers, but they couldn't connect them to the Offerman/Manning murders. A few months after their murders, the Sacramento Sheriff's Department caught wind of the double homicide and felt that based on initial reports that the East Area Rapist might have gone down to Goleta and had been responsible for the attacks. The Santa Barbara Sheriff's Department didn't think so and dismissed the theory. Goleta once again was quiet, and the Creek Killer seemed to have vanished, but he would return.

SEASON TWO, EPISODE TWELVE

Almost forty miles Southeast of Goleta, lies the city of Ventura, California, situated along Highway 101 between scenic and easy going Santa Barbara County and the hustle and bustle of Los Angeles. In 1980 Ventura had a population of just under 75,000 people. For the most part, it was a middle to upper-class area and home to many attorneys, physicians, and other prominent citizens. Lawns were well-manicured, and the streets were peaceful. Ventura was not the place where you would have expected a horrifying double murder of a respected couple to occur, but in March of 1980 that's exactly what happened.

On Sunday March 16, 12-year-old Gary Smith made his way to his father's home on 573 High Point Drive to cut the grass. This was something that he did on a regular basis. High Point Drive was in the prestigious neighborhood known as Clear Point. Although his parents had been divorced for some time, the young man frequently visited his father, 43-year-old Lyman Smith, who was a well-respected attorney in Ventura County. At the time, Smith was being considered by the governor for an appointment to the County Superior Court.

Gary along with his two siblings were close with their father and their step-mom Charlene. Though as with any relationship that mixed teenagers and step-mothers, there were moments of anxiety and times when members of the family would butt heads, but for the most part, they all got along. Charlene, who was 33, had been married to Lyman since mid-1976. She was a home decorator, dabbled in making jewelry, and everybody that knew Charlene thought of her as a beautiful woman. The pair seemed to have everything going for them, which is what made what happened next even more shocking.

Gary arrived at his father's home just before 2:00 p.m. When he rode into the yard, he dropped his bike and made his way to the front door. He noticed two gardeners working in the backyard which overlooked a lush green belt area. Gary didn't have a key, so he knocked on the door and rang the doorbell, but he didn't try opening the door. After not getting a response from Lyman or Charlene, the 12-year-old walked around to the back yard. He noticed that both Lyman's and Charlene's cars were parked in the driveway.

He stopped and asked the gardeners if Charlene was home, and the two men told him that she should be in the house. He checked the door leading into the garage, but it was locked. He didn't know what to think.

Gary walked around to the front door once again, and this time he turned the doorknob and found that it was unlocked. He opened the door and stepped inside, and as soon as he stepped inside the house, he noticed that two large pillows were not in their proper spots on the couch. Instead, they were lying on the floor, and Gary knew this was something that Charlene would never allow to happen. It was then that a repeated buzzing noise from the back bedroom caught his attention. He realized that it was the buzz of an alarm clock going off.

Gary was very nervous at this point, but he wandered back to the master bedroom where the alarm clock was going off. As he made his way, he noticed shreds of wood bark fragments leading down the hallway toward his father's bedroom, and again you have to think of this as something highly irregular in what Gary knows to be a very clean well-kept home. This is the way that Charlene kept her house, she would not have stood for all these things out of place.

As Gary arrived at the doorway of the bedroom, he looked into the room towards the alarm clock, which was located near the bed. The only sound he heard was the buzzing from the clock, other than that, there was complete silence. The scene was quite eerie. He noticed a sheet on the bed and could see that it was covering what appeared to be two people whom he presumed were his father and stepmother.

He inched closer to the bed and reached out for a corner of the sheet slowly pulling it back, what he found was something horrible, something no child should have to find. He had discovered the lifeless and bloodied bodies of Lyman and Charlene Smith. Horrified, he picked up the phone that was next to the bed and called his mother, but she didn't answer, he then called the operator and told her what he had discovered. The operator relayed the information to the Ventura Police Department, and they were dispatched to the scene.

Ventura Police arrived at the scene of the crime around 7:12 p.m. and they found the badly shaken boy Gary Smith outside on the front lawn waiting for them. The first officer arriving on scene called for backup because he knew that they had a very serious situation on their hands and an obvious crime scene. The property was closed off with police tape, and detectives soon arrived on the scene. Investigators noted the condition of the bodies and the home. It was obvious that both victims had been brutally bludgeoned to death. Detectives quickly determined that the murder weapon was a fire-log taken from the wood pile near the garage. There was blood spatter all around the victims and on the walls, and as they examined Charlene's body they found the right side of her face resting gently on the pillow. Her ankles were tied together with what appeared to be drapery cord. The bed sheet and blankets had been pulled completely over her entire body. She was found wearing no rings or jewelry and the only thing she had on was a T-shirt.

The coroner would later rule that she had been dead for about three days before her body was discovered and that she'd been killed with one or two strikes to the left side of her head from a blunt object, likely the log. It was described that this log would have come down with such force that it would have been in excess of six hundred pounds per square inch.

Police then turned their attention to Lyman Smith's body. Lyman was nude and lying face down in the bed. Like Charlene, his head was also resting on a pillow, and also like Charlene, Lyman's ankles were bound with a drapery cord. In addition, his hands were bound behind him with the cord. There were two very distinct and very difficult to tie knots in the bindings. These knots would later be determined to be diamond knots. The coroner would determine that Lyman was killed the same time as Charlene, and the cause of death was at least one savage blow to the right side of his head with a blunt object causing a brain-stem injury and almost instantaneous death.

Near the head of the bed, investigators found a bloody piece of firewood. The log measured about twenty-one and a half inches long, and it was about three inches around on one end and four to five inches around on the other. Scattered around on the floor at the foot of the bed, detectives noted large amounts of bark. Mixed in with this bark were twenty-one polished stones. These stones were found to belong to Charlene and were part of a business she was working on involving jewelry. Officially, the coroner concluded that the Smiths had been murdered while they laid in bed on the evening of Thursday March 13. Police examined the rest of the home, and they found a piece of black cloth and some pine needles under one of the cushions on the living room couch, but they weren't able to find any signs of forced entry.

At first, robbery didn't seem to be a motive. There was an assortment of jewelry, guns, and other valuable items that were left undisturbed. The victim's wallets, credit cards, and driver's licenses weren't touched. Due to the lack of forced entry, no initial signs of robbery, and the frenzied bludgeoning of the victims, investigators started to think that this may have been a crime of passion or jealousy or revenge committed by somebody who knew the Smiths. However, the coroner found evidence that Charlene Smith had been raped, and they were able to gather physical evidence and semen from the killer. At the time, DNA was not something known to investigators, but luckily they did properly preserve all the evidence and years later it would reveal the killer's DNA.

Police discovered that on the night of the murders, the last known person to speak with the couple was Charlene's former mother-in-law who spoke over the phone with Charlene. They had remained close, and she described Charlene as sounding happier than she ever had before. This call was made at around 7:00 p.m. Establishing a timeline was important to the investigation. Police wanted to piece together, if they could, what happened between the phone call to Charlene's ex-mother-in-law and the time of Gary finding the bodies, but after that phone call the events of that night remained unknown.

Detectives fanned out to canvass the neighborhood to see if they could find any valuable information that might point to the killer or killers. One neighbor reported that a few days before the murders, they heard a prowler in their backyard. This person had tried unsuccessfully to enter the home through a bathroom window. Another resident on El Malabar Drive which was just a few homes away from the Smiths, noticed an out of place white car on the evening t the couple was killed. It was parked there for several hours but was gone the next morning.

Another nearby resident thought that they heard a couple of screams the night of the murders. The first one was louder, and the second one was possibly muffled. They couldn't pinpoint where the screams had come from but felt they were likely from the Smiths' home. Still another neighbor was awakened by what they felt was a scream at around 2:00 a.m. but as they listened in the darkness, they didn't hear anything else and went back to sleep.

At around the same time the Smiths' next door neighbors were awakened by their dog. They got up and let the dog outside and watched as the dog went over to the fence along Smiths' property and stood there looking into the Smiths' yard for several minutes before returning into the house. Police found yet another neighbor, who in the overnight hours, had been awakened by some noise coming from downstairs in her home. Her dog went downstairs and was growling, and the woman sensed that there was somebody trying to get into her home. She raced back up to her bedroom and woke her husband up, and he went down to investigate, but if there was somebody trying to break in, they had vanished.

While it seemed as if there was a prowler or maybe even multiple prowlers in the area leading up to the murders, police still felt that the killer may have been known by the victims.

As investigators do in most murder cases, they started looking at the people closest to the victims and worked outward from there. They started with Lyman's oldest daughter Jennifer who like many typical teenagers didn't always get along with her father. Police quickly ruled Jennifer out as well as the rest of the family.

As they started to build some background of the Smiths' lives they uncovered some interesting details that seemed like possible motives for the murders. Investigators found that Lyman Smith had moved from Sacramento years before and still had family there at the time of the murders. He established himself as a successful attorney and businessman before he divorced his first wife and married Charlene in 1976. He dabbled in various business ventures including land development and trucking and had an airline business, most of which were successful. Charlene had been divorced twice prior to marrying Lyman. Although they seemed like the perfect couple to outsiders, detectives found signs of trouble in their marriage. The couple had briefly split, and Charlene had considered a divorce, but they reconciled.

It was also discovered that Charlene had been having an affair for some time. Detectives learned that the man she was having an affair with was one of their own a police officers. While the affair piqued their interest, they quickly were able to rule out this man as having anything to do with the murders. After further investigation and initially suspecting that robbery wasn't a motive in the murders, police learned that there was several thousand dollars worth of jewelry missing. They estimated that perhaps twenty pieces of jewelry including rings, necklaces, and earrings had been stolen from the bathroom counter that Charlene normally kept them on.

After the investigation was in full swing, a neighbor of the Smiths' contacted police to tell them of an incident that grabbed their attention. The neighbor reported that although he couldn't remember if it was Saturday or Sunday, someone had tried to enter his home prior to the bodies being found. It was early in the morning hours between midnight and 3:00 a.m. when his infant son woke up screaming.

His wife went in to check on the child but found nothing unusual. Later that day he was walking around his house when he found that his son's window had been tampered with. The screen was missing, and he saw that there was a one and a half inch diameter hole in the area of the window adjacent to its latch. There was also a crack running down the right side of the window. He had the window replaced but later after hearing about the murders, he contacted police who came and checked it out but like with many things, in this case, nothing came out of that. Investigators soon turned their attention to Lyman Smith's business dealings, which led them to one of his business partners.

They suspected that this man may have soured over some business dealings with Lyman or perhaps maybe even secretly coveted Charlene. Investigators felt that they might have found the killer when they discovered a fingerprint that belonged to this business partner on a glass in the Smith home. They started to look closer at the business partner, and they questioned people that knew him. A church associate of his told investigators that he had confessed to being the killer, and police wound up charging the business partner in the murders of Lyman and Charlene Smith, and this guy was imprisoned for almost a year.

In a preliminary trial, the accusations of the church associate proved to be false, and the case against him fell apart. He was released soon after that, and he left the state. His reputation was obviously tainted at this point and this didn't stop police from suspecting him of the murders. Years later they would test the crime scene DNA against his, and it was not until that point that they found no match, and he was finally ruled out once and for all.

After the case fell apart against Lyman Smith's partner and with the subsequent investigation not leading any real direction, police were left without much to go on. There seemed to be no real motive for the murders, and people that may have had one were ruled out. Perhaps after all it really was a case of two people in the wrong place at the wrong time. Maybe they were victims of a random act of violence. Besides some marital volatility, both victims seem like upstanding people. Neither was involved in any illegal activities.

A thorough investigation revealed that Charlene spent money quickly, and without hesitation, racking up large amounts of credit card debt. At the same time, Lyman was always striving to be successful and to make more money both in his legal career and through his business ventures. The Smiths seemed like so many other married couples in California, good times and bad, ups and downs. They weren't the perfect couple, but they were far from the people you'd expect to be victims of such a heinous act.

Investigators in the double murders of the Smiths would wind up comparing notes with investigators on other murder cases that occurred in Southern California. Comparing notes in their cases, they concluded that these attacks were committed by different people, but this is a conclusion that would be proven wrong many years later.

One of Lyman Smith's family members is Ann Penn, and as a direct result of the murders, she was motivated to write a book called *Murder on His Mind*. Lyman Smith's daughter Jennifer joined us to talk about her recollections of the murders of her father and stepmother.

My name is Jennifer. In 1980 I had just turned 18 years old in February, and in March of that year, Sunday afternoon, I was in the house with my brothers. It was a Sunday afternoon in March; my mom came into the house and looked shell-shocked. She had my little brother who ran into his bedroom with her, and then my other brother and I were there, and she told us that our father was dead. At first, I thought possibly he had been in a fight with my step-mother and I knew he had a gun, and I was afraid that maybe something happened with that, but in fact she said no. Both my dad and Charlene were dead and that they had been murdered.

As you can imagine, I still can remember that moment so distinctly like where I was seated, where my mom was standing, how my brother reacted and how it just didn't even make any sense at all because I couldn't imagine, other than in the heat of passion like a fight. I couldn't imagine anybody wanted to kill my dad. It just blew my mind. In those days in the 1980s, the newspaper came at the end of the day. This means it was breaking, but it was breaking among neighbors. Essentially, my dad was very well-known in Ventura County and so was Charlene.

Some good friends of theirs had come across my brother, who was 13 at the time, and had discovered their bodies that Sunday. The judge and his wife had stopped and had taken care of my brother. They were neighbors that lived up the street from my dad. With that, the word started getting out, but again remember, we didn't have mobile phones. We didn't have any way to communicate, so this was something that was happening from people going home and making phone calls and talking to one another. There was a lot of activity, and it was all kind of hard to take in.

We knew they had been killed with a log which is so strange. We found out later, the log had been taken from a wood pile outside their home and essentially, their skulls had been smashed with this log. It was brutal, and a lot of folks have asked how much my little brother saw but he did not see that much. When he had gone to the house, he had gone to mow the lawn. When he walked in the house, he had heard an alarm clock going off, and it seemed so strange to him, and so he walked back to their bedroom and then kind of stopped kind of went like, "Maybe I'm waking them up, maybe I shouldn't go back there." But the alarm didn't go off, so he walked into the bedroom, and the comforter had been pulled up over them so that they were both, including their heads, underneath this comforter.

My brother walked around to the side, my dad's side of the nightstand and pulled back the cover. My dad had a skin cancer, and he had a very definite scar on his right shoulder. My brother saw that and knew it was my dad and put the blanket back up. The blanket was kind of stuck in his skull. As you might imagine where the wound was, it had dried, and it had just been there, and he put the blanket back, and then he called 911. It was right when 911 had just started. They had him go out to the street and wait for the police, and that is when our friends saw Gary outside waiting.

As the days passed, it was a freak murder. It just didn't make a lot of sense to anybody. Of course it is a small town. Ventura was a fairly small town at the time, and like I said, everybody knew my dad and Charlene. My dad had been a lawyer there for many years, and my stepmom had worked in law enforcement and as a *legal secretary. She'd been my dad's legal secretary for as long as I had known her. She joined my dad when I think I was five years old. She had been a part of our lives, just like anything else, from essentially as far back as I could remember Charlene had been part of our lives. To have them both be dead, it stunned the whole community.*

For me, I had graduated from high school early. I had started junior college and essentially ended up dropping out because it was so stressful. There were so many things that happened because I just turned 18, there were some things I had to do as an adult child that kept me pretty involved with the activities. Then the crime happened. I was a suspect essentially because I had not been getting along with my dad that well for quite a while. He and I really were too much alike, but I had just gone to see them a week before they were killed.

I had gone up to their house to see them, and it was the first time I got to see both my dad and Charlene as an adult. It was a pretty awesome time together, and I think probably a lot of folks can relate to this. When you are an adult and you have that conversation with your parents where you find out, "My goodness. They've tried marijuana." That was a big deal then. My dad and Charlene had tried marijuana. I also found out they had tried cocaine. It was the first time I felt like peers. I felt like I was hanging out with my peers as adults, and they were finally sharing information with me that was adult information.

We spent a lot of time that night just sitting around the table, which now kind of freaks me out. It faced the glass doors and it faced the greenbelt, where the police suspect that the killer sat and watched my dad and Charlene night after night as he was casing the house, which was what he tended to do. As you know, he planted ropes and things in other people's houses because he had been there before. It's a little freaky now to realize he could have seen me in their house that night a week before the murders.

We're not exactly sure when they were killed. From what I understand from the report in Orange County, he was in the house a long time with them. A very long time. We've never been able to really understand when they died; though we always think of it as during the three-day weekend 13th, 14th and 15th of March. I tend to think of them every year because it happened some time that weekend.

When the murder happened in Ventura, as it started to play out, a business partner of my dad became a suspect, and they did have a hearing, a preliminary hearing, to see if there was enough evidence to hold him over. It turns out eventually that there was not and of course he didn't do it, but we didn't know that at the time. It was interesting to go through that. One of the things you find out when you are a victim of a serious crime when you are a kid is that it does influence your life.

I became caught up in trying to understand murders and crime scenes. I know that I read the autopsy, at that time, the autopsy report that was put out as his business partner was arraigned and went through the preliminary hearing. Ever since then, I've been interested in forensics. It's nothing I've ever done as a career, but it's been very interesting to look at the forensics and how much information they have on that. This is again before DNA. I mean, the most interesting part of the forensics for me was understanding what they had eaten the night before. I was very interested in trying to figure out when they had died because again at that time it was still kind of vague.

It wasn't until right around 2000 that I went to the police station, and I was just checking in saying, "Hey, where are we? twenty years have gone by is there any news on this case." I remember I've never had anybody say this to me. I remember a police officer said, "I'm going to need you to sit down." I did and then he explained that Lyman and Charlene's murder had been connected to a set of murders in Southern California to the Orange County closed case office, which is where we met Detective Ray Paul, who has just been amazing as far as I am concerned. You never think you are going to know a detective for forty years, and I have known this man at least for twenty, I met him in the 2000's.

He had put together the connection, and I am sure he had help, but as far as I knew, Detective Paul put together these murders and found the connection among them. I know now watching even these reports that a lot more people were involved behind the scenes, but he was my point person. We went down to Orange County and talked to the cold case folks. There have been two times in my life where I have been just blown away by something I've seen in the prosecution of this massive case. The first time was when I walked into the cold case office and saw the list of the victims. They had had the victims on a big sheet, almost like butcher paper, that went from the ceiling to floor with victim names on it. It just shocked me.

I must have gone down to Orange County a little bit after they had put together the DNA with the East Area Rapist because that happened a little bit later. There was a giant butcher paper with a list of all the victims of all the crimes, and I just stood there like it almost took my breath away. It just was astounding to see so many names on a piece of paper, and I have to say that the cold case crew, they had so much respect for those victims, there was a sense of reverence about it, and it felt very respectful.

It didn't feel in any way – sorry, I kept thinking of the right word, but it didn't feel like they were doing anything bad. It felt very respectful to see this list on the wall. Like I said, it just took my breath away. After then, we understood the connection among all the crimes based on this DNA, which for me, made me happy to know in a really weird way, we had caught the guy. We may not have the person, but we have the DNA, and we specifically know who it is. It's the person with this DNA. It's very good to know that those murders could be connected to him because if we could get the person, we would have the easy conviction, not even a question.

We asked Jennifer to tell us about any suspicions that her family had at the time of the murder.

Right when the murders happened, gosh, there weren't a lot of suspicions. There was a lot of talk. My dad had a lot of business deals, so there were a lot of folks that could be suspects. He had also been an active attorney. He had done some defending of criminals that were possible suspects. My stepmother had worked in law enforcement and as a legal secretary and had been married to a former sheriff. There were so many suspects.

Our family did not have any sense of who it could be. Actually, my dad and Charlene were pretty good at fighting, so that's why I actually thought it could have been a fight that gotten out of control, because we're an extroverted kind of people. I thought it could have been a fight that had gone wrong. It was really hard to think of people outside of that other than business contacts. To find out later, the probability of a murder being someone you know is so high, or heat of passion or somebody that felt like they were somehow wronged.

To find out it was random, I remember it was extremely hard for me personally, and I think also as a woman, to find out that this was random, that my stepmother was brutalized.

Especially as I've grown up and really understood crime, that has been one of the hardest things for me. Even watching Unmasking a Killer and some of the other shows, it has made the crime visual in a way that I think is different than when you just grow up with it and know it, and it's been part of your life, but it's been how you know the story. Not seeing it acted out or seeing folks play out how it might have happened. It's also really hard to see the pictures and the guy in the stocking cap. I'm an old lady and it's hard for me to see that still. It takes my breath away when I see those things.

Jennifer discussed the possibility that the killer somehow knew her father from his background in Sacramento.

Our suspect has been all over California, and our family had been all over California. My dad was raised in Sacramento, so was my mom. My stepmother was raised in Southern California, and I didn't think of a connection specifically between the suspect and my family in terms of where we had lived. I actually often think that the suspect very much paid attention to my stepmother. She's very attractive. Very attractive and was out about town. It's so random it's hard to think that there was any intent. I didn't particularly think that he knew them other than he picked them randomly.

Jennifer explained to us how her family has dealt with the murders after almost forty years.

I have two brothers that are younger than I am. One was 15 and one was 13, and both of them have done really well, I choose my mom that in spite of our upbringing and all those things that happened, she's lucky she's got three great kids who have done well for themselves and have families and are pretty much regular members of society. Nobody went into law-- actually, my youngest brother did go into law, but he does it much more from a business standpoint, not from trying cases and litigating and that sort of thing.

Everybody's turned out pretty remarkably normal. There are things that change you when you have that – there are things that change about you when there is a murder in your past. Like for me, I keep bells on my doors, and I've been fairly obsessed as a side interest in serial killers to crime that pathology, the sociology of it and all of those things, I'm very interested in the pathology and what makes these kinds of people tick and why they choose to hurt other humans. That's hard for me because it's not just the person they hurt, we all are in our own ecosystems. You hurt everybody associated with the person. It's amazing the level of hurt.

In fact, even a person on Twitter said, "Would you buy a house if somebody had been murdered in it?" The poor guy, he was just joking, but I replied to him and I said, "Interestingly enough, that happened to us, and we had a house we had to sell after a murder." The other thing is people didn't think about it. Like they just got so many things in your life, so anybody who's thinking of hurting somebody else, I'm going to tell you to stop because you wind up hurting so many more people and have such a deeper impact than you think, and it's just awful.

I think for us, closure is a weird thing. I really would like closure for rape victims because they live with the different kind of horrors than I do, I know what happened, but it ended with them dying. They at least, for my dad and Charlene, there was a break. For the rape victims, I feel horrible because they've lived with this their whole lives, and I understand what a huge earthquake this is in your life when it happens. They are remarkable, remarkable men and women to me that they got through this and that they're still willing to talk and share and be brave because it is scary. I mean he's still out there. That part is scary. Like those victims, I think none of us are choosing to live in fear. We're choosing to stand up and fight, be heard, and to work hard to catch this guy.

We did this interview with Jennifer just a couple weeks before Joseph J. DeAngelo was arrested in this case. She had no idea at the time that we talked to her that in just a couple of weeks, she would learn the identity of the man dubbed the Diamond Knot Killer, who had murdered her father and stepmother.

SEASON TWO, EPISODE THIRTEEN

The next set of murders occurred in Dana Point about 130 miles east of the Ventura murder of the Smiths. Dana Point is an affluent neighborhood with many upscale homes nestled inside gated communities. On August 19th, 1980, newlyweds Keith and Patrice Harrington were murdered. The families were at a complete loss to find answers in the shocking and senseless murders of the two newlyweds. Keith and Patrice, or Patty as she was known to friends and family, were good people with bright futures. There murders happened in an area where violent crimes of this nature were almost nonexistent.

Keith, 24, and Patty, 28, had gotten married in May of 1980 in Orange County. Keith grew up in Los Angeles, was the youngest of four children, all boys, and was close with his older brothers. The family by all accounts were go-getters and worked hard for their successes. Keith was no exception. He wanted to be a doctor and following college at the University of Irvine, Keith got into medical school at the University of California Irvine Medical Center. He was seeking his residency in emergency room medicine. Keith was quite athletic and an avid jogger. He ran five to six miles a day. He was also into skiing and sailing, and he drove a sporty orange 1970 MG.

Patti Harrington had been raised in an Air Force family and traveled frequently growing up. She had previously worked as a pediatric nurse and at the time of her murder worked on-call for a nursing registry. She met Keith while working at the UCI Medical Center. Like Keith, Patty was active too and enjoyed roller skating and jogging. In the month leading up to her murder, Patty had taken a calligraphy course and just prior to the murders had started taking an aerobics class. Keith's father, Roger Harrington, owned multiple homes and allowed Keith and Patty to live rent free in one of these homes, until they got their feet on the ground following their marriage. The home they lived in was at 33381 Cockleshell Drive in Dana Point. The home was just over five years old and was in a gated and guarded community known as Niguel Shores.

Keith and Patty were a young, successful, and happy couple. They seemed to have a beautiful future ahead of them and didn't have an enemy in the world. But on August 19, 1980, their lives were cut short leaving their families and investigators to ask why. On that day, at around 5:00 p.m., Keith arrived home from work and was pleasantly surprised to see his father Roger there talking to Patty. Roger had been there all day installing a sprinkler system.

Patty, who had worked the overnight shift was very tired and was asleep in bed most of the day. At 2:00 p.m., Roger ran out to get sprinkler parts while Patty was asleep. He came back at around four and found Patty awake reading a book. She seemed fine, only mentioning that she was really tired. At five, when Keith arrived home, the three of them talked for a while, and Roger mentioned to the young couple that his coffee pot at home was broken and that he was going to have to replace it. Nothing seemed out of the ordinary to Roger. He left around 6:00 p.m. and headed back to his home.

The events later that day would be partially determined through the investigation, but the next person known to have contact with the pair was Patty's sister who called at 11:00 p.m.. Keith answered the phone, and according to Patty's sister, he sounded sleepy. He passed the phone over to Patty, and the two sisters spoke for about five minutes. Patty told her sister that she was tired and had to go to sleep because she was expecting a call from the nursing registry at 5:00 a.m.. Nothing seemed out of the ordinary to Patty's sister, and they ended their call.

The next day, Wednesday, August 20, Keith and Patty were set to have dinner at 7:00 p.m. with Keith's father, along with family and friends at Roger's home. They didn't show, and that was very unusual for the couple. But Roger and his company went on with dinner. But the next day, Thursday, August 21, as dinner time approached, Roger still had not heard from either Keith or Patty, and he decided to drive to their home to check on them. He arrived at their home around 6:30 p.m., and when he got there, he noticed that their mailbox was packed with what looked like more than one day's worth of mail. He saw that both of their cars were still in the garage. Roger tried to enter the front door but found that it was locked. He walked around to the back of the home, tried to enter through a sliding glass door but found that locked as well.

Using an extra key, Roger Harrington let himself into the house. The home was very stuffy and hot. Roger opened the window to circulate some fresh air. There were no lights on. In the kitchen, on top of the counter was a new Mr. Coffee brand glass pot, still in the package. Roger immediately thought of Patty and that she likely had run right out and bought a coffee pot for him after he had told them that his was broken. That's the kind of person she was. Nearby, a grocery bag sat on the counter. The home was quiet. Roger walked slowly down the hallway to the bedroom that the young couple slept in, which was not the home's master bedroom. They preferred a smaller bedroom on the southeast side of the home.

Roger peeked into the bedroom, but it was just as dark as the rest of the house. The bedroom's window shutters were closed. As Roger made his way to the bed, he could see the outline of two bodies covered by a comforter. He slowly pulled back the comforter and found his son Keith dead in the bed. Patty was lying next to Keith and she was also dead.

Roger raced from the room horrified at what he had found and used one of the homes two phones to call one of his other sons. Roger was devastated upon finding the bodies. His son urged him to call police. After hanging up with his son, he immediately called the police, and they arrived within minutes.

Detectives were called in for what was, obviously, a case of double murder. The immediate cause of death for Keith and Patty appeared to be bludgeoning. Both had severe head wounds, and it appeared that the blows to Patty were savage. There was no sign of a weapon near the bodies. The bodies were lying face down on the bed. The comforter that covered the bodies had been pulled up over the heads of the victims, which minimized blood spatter. But there was a small amount of spatter on the headboard and the wall. Both of the victims' heads were on pillows. Their faces looking away from the center of the bed, away from each other.

They were both found with various pieces of jewelry on, including wedding bands, earrings, and necklaces. Police noticed that the victims' hands were positioned behind them as if they had been bound, but they were not found with any bindings on. After examining their wrists, authorities found the telltale signs that their wrists had been bound. So, they knew that the killer had removed the bindings before leaving the scene. They did, however, find three pieces of brown macramé type cord. A coroner would later determine that both victims had died as a result of massive head trauma caused by a blunt object. Their time of death was estimated to be sometime during the evening, two days earlier on August 19.

Police would later find out that Patty's sister had talked to Patty and Keith around 11:00 p.m. that night. So, they theorized that the murderer or murderers attacked them soon after. The coroner also concluded that Patty had been raped. They collected physical and biological evidence including semen. At the time, they were able to determine that the semen samples belonged to two different men, but it wouldn't be until years later that DNA technology linked one of the samples, the smaller of the two, to Keith. The larger sample belonged to the killer. The killer's DNA sample would also be linked to other crimes years later.

Police turned their attention to the rest of the house looking for clues. Keith's home office was a mess, and police thought that it may have been ransacked. But people who knew Keith told investigators that, "No, this was not out of the ordinary." There were no signs of robbery and no signs of forced entry. Both Patty's and Keith's cars were found undisturbed in the garage. In the kitchen, investigators found a single burned wood match. One of the victims had a lock of hair cut off, and it was found on the entryway floor. Unfortunately, the police reports don't specify whether the lock of hair came from Keith or Patty. The lock of hair may have been a memento taken by the killer and possibly dropped on his way out of the house. But all in all, there really was not much evidence from the crime scene, and there was no sign of a struggle. It seemed as if the killer had gained access to the home and completely surprised the couple. They never had a chance. Due to the lack of forced entry, police suspected that Keith or Patty had left a door unlocked and that the killer simply walked through it.

Based on the shopping bag and coffee pot being found on the kitchen counter, police thought that either Keith or Patty or both of them had left their home the night of their murders and gone shopping. Later in the investigation, based on three canceled checks that cleared their bank account, police learned that Patty had signed for purchases at three different stores that night. The three stores that Patty had visited were Best Products on Marguerite Parkway in Mission Viejo where she purchased a coffee pot with check number 1296; the May Company in Laguna Hills, where she bought baby gifts with check number 1303; and a local Alpha Beta market, where she bought groceries with check number 1304.

These purchases were made between 6:00 p.m. when Roger last saw the couple and 11:00 p.m. when Patty's sister called her. Police further narrowed down the time frame to between 7:00 and 9:00 p.m. It's unclear if police were able to determine if Keith accompanied Patty to these stores. The shopping and phone call from Patty's sister helped the investigators set up a timeline.

Police wondered if the couple was killed by someone within their gated community or had an intruder somehow breached the security? They quickly found that there were areas in the back of the gated community where people could come and go. There were no guards there and they discovered that the fence that surrounded the community was not very tall. It could easily have been scaled. Police canvassed the area, questioned neighbors and residents, but no one saw anything unusual. Then, three days after the murder, it was discovered that a jogger had found a left-handed leather motocross glove covered in blood.

The area where the glove was found was on the freshly graded hills of a new housing project. This area was about three-quarters of a mile east of the Harrington's home. Tests were done at the time that it was found, and the blood was found to be human. Later in 1998, as DNA was coming on the scene, further testing was attempted on this glove, but due to the degraded condition of the evidence, no new clues could be gained from it.

As with most investigations police started with family, friends, co-workers, and associates of Keith and Patty but found no viable suspects. The case seemed like a random rape and double murder. The investigators wound up talking to close to 250 people ranging from ex-boyfriends and girlfriends to friends, car repairman, and people who worked for the gated community. They also identified and questioned men who had previous arrests for cat burglaries, prowling, and sexual assaults. On September 11th 1980, investigators in Patty's and Keith's murders met with investigators from Ventura County, who were digging for clues in the double murder of Lyman and Charlene Smith.

Neither department had any strong suspects and worked hard to see if their cases could be related. Over 100 miles separated the murdered couples, but there were many similarities. The two departments also reached out to Santa Barbara County detectives to see if the unsolved double murders of Robert Offerman and Deborah Manning could be related, but the Santa Barbara Sheriff's Department was skeptical of a connection. Their victims had been shot. Investigators in the Harrington murders also reached out to police in San Diego to compare notes on a double homicide that occurred there but found no connection.

On September 18, 1980, to mark the one-month anniversary of the murders, the Harrington family held a press conference. At this press conference they announced that they were offering a $25,000 reward for information that led to the identification of Keith's and Patty's killer. The Harrington family for years tried to spread word about the murders of Keith and Patty, but in a time before social media, their efforts fell on deaf ears. The reward they offered was never claimed, and no one ever came forward with info about the killer. Keith was due to graduate from medical school in 1981, and that year his father Roger accepted on Keith's behalf a diploma that the school gave to Keith posthumously.

If there was any good that came from the case of the Harrington murderers, it was the hard work that Keith's brother Bruce did at his own expense in getting Proposition 69 passed. Prop 69 as it's known, is a law in California that requires convicted felons to hand over their DNA, so that it can be entered into a database. As a result, California today has one of the largest state databases in the country. As new felons come into the system and their DNA is entered into the database, the authorities can see if they get any matches to DNA that's on file for unsolved crimes. It doesn't have to be a direct hit. It simply needs to be a family member in the felon database that links to unsolved crime. The law went into effect in 2004 and was tweaked until 2009.

Prop 69 has undoubtedly led to cases being solved and suspects being cleared. But there's a catch. There's no grandfather clause. So, anybody with felony convictions prior to 2004 did not have to give DNA samples. Investigators searched this database for years waiting and hoping the Golden State Killer or a relative of his would be convicted of a felony in California. But that never happened. There was no match. However, had the law been around the 1990s, the Golden State Killer would have been identified long before now.

We've talked about the murders of a couple in Santa Barbara, the Offerman-Manning murders. We talked about Lyman and Charlene Smith in Ventura, and now we've talked about the murders of Keith and Patty Harrington. The details in each of these double murders were very similar in many ways. But there were slight differences, and they were spread out over almost 200 miles. Still, there were rumblings in some jurisdictions that investigated these crimes that a single killer may have been responsible. And some of the East Area Rapist investigators from up in northern California including guys like Larry Crompton from Contra Costa County, were starting to catch wind of these attacks in southern California. To them the M.O. seemed a lot like the East Area Rapist. The main difference was that these victims were being murdered. But notions that the East Area Rapist had moved to southern California and had started to kill people seemed to be dismissed by investigators in southern California. There was nothing that the East Area Rapist investigators could really do.

Orange County had suffered its first brutal double murders with the Harrington murders, but the killings in the area weren't over. To some, the murders of the Harringtons and the Smiths were reminiscent of the Bedroom Basher, a rapist and killer who struck in Orange County from 1970 to 1980, murdering five different women. The Bedroom Basher had killed using hammers and lumber to bludgeon his victims. But there were differences between the Bedroom Basher's M.O. and signature and that of the murder of the Harringtons. Eventually, DNA identified the Bedroom Basher as Gerald Parker who was convicted of the basher murders and sentenced to death by lethal injection. His DNA did not match the murderer of the Harringtons.

Police continued to investigate the Dana Point murders of the Harringtons in Orange County into 1981. Then, almost six months after the Harringtons were murdered, police in Irvine, which is located in another part of Orange County, were called to the scene of a horrific murder. The victim in that murder was 28-year-old Manuela Witthuhn. Her body had been discovered by her mother at Manuela's residence located at 35 Columbus in Irvine on February 6th. Manuela was a junior loan officer at California First Bank. She was married to David Witthuhn who worked in the auto parts industry. The pair had been married for just over five years and didn't have any children. David had been hospitalized with a viral infection that required him to stay in the hospital for a few days. This left Manuela alone in their single story three-bedroom home. Manuela didn't like being alone without David. Her father had offered to let Manuela have his large and protective German Shepherd until David was out of the hospital, but she turned him down.

On Thursday, February 5, 1981, Manuela finished work and headed home. At about 6:00 p.m., she stopped to talk to a neighbor across the street from her home. She had given them some unopened cartons of milk that she had in the refrigerator. Since David was away in the hospital, she knew she wouldn't finish the milk on her own before it went bad, so she offered it to her neighbors. She seemed to be in a rush as she gave the milk to her neighbors but was in good spirits.

She next stopped at a neighbor a few homes down and had a short conversation. She told these neighbors that David was away in the hospital and that she got cold at night all by herself, and she had resorted to sleeping inside a sleeping bag on top of her bed. These neighbors also stated that she was in good spirits and that she had told them that David would be out of the hospital the next day Friday, the 6. At dinnertime these neighbors noticed that Manuela's Mercedes was parked in front of her house between 6:00 p.m. and 6:30 p.m. But when they looked again around 7:30 p.m., it was gone.

Around 7:00 p.m., Manuela had driven to visit her parent's house on Loma Street in Irvine, a little over two miles from her home. After visiting with them she headed to the hospital to see David. She visited with David for a while and then headed home telling him that she planned to read a book once she got home. From his hospital bed, David called Manuela at home around 11:00 p.m. and spoke to her for a few minutes. The next morning, he tried to call Manuela at home a few times, but she didn't answer. He called over to her parents and asked them if they would make the short drive to check on their daughter. They said they would and headed over there arriving at the Witthuhn home at 35 Columbus at 12:00 p.m. When they got there the couple entered the home and soon found Manuela's lifeless body on her bed in a sleeping bag. There was blood everywhere on the sleeping bag and on the wall nearby. It was a terrible moment for Manuela's parents to experience. They called police who arrived on the scene shortly after noon.

Investigators assessed the scene. Manuela's body was lying face down inside of her sleeping bag. She had been struck on the head and, based on a tear in the sleeping bag, police felt that the sleeping bag was over her head when she was bludgeoned. Most of the blood was contained inside the sleeping bag, but there was some blood spatter on the wall behind the bed. When police examined her body after removing it from the sleeping bag, they found that she was dressed in a black velour robe. They discovered that there were deep indentations on her wrists and ankles, an indication that she had been bound. But as in the previous Harrington case, the bindings were not left at the scene.

A coroner who examined Manuela's body determined the cause of death was the massive head injury, which resulted in a cerebral contusion and hemorrhage. Her time of death was estimated to be approximately 2:00 a.m. Friday, February 6.

The coroner also determined that Manuela had been sexually assaulted. Semen samples from the rapist and murderer would years later reveal DNA that would be linked to so many more shocking crimes.

Police looked around the home for any indication of forced entry, and they found that the rear sliding glass door had been pried. One interesting thing that stood out to police was that most of the pry marks were on the inside of the door. A flat-head screwdriver was found nearby, and it was covered in various types of paint. Police felt that the killer likely had pried open this sliding glass door with the screwdriver. Police were also looking to see if anything was missing from the home and, later aided by David Witthuhn, after he was released from the hospital, determined that a few things were indeed missing. A distinct crystal ball and a lamp with a cannonball-like shape were both missing. Both of these objects had some weight to them. They were solid and, either one may have possibly been the murder weapon. Neither item has ever been found.

As they made their way around the home, they found several burnt matches in various locations. A television set that was kept in a back bedroom was found outside of the house on the patio. Police thought that the killer intended to take it with him but maybe was interrupted and abandoned it or that he planned to step on it to help him get over the Witthuhns' fence. In the yard investigators found very distinct tennis shoe prints from a shoe style that was commonly worn by racquetball players. It would come out that the Witthuhns had seen mysterious footprints in their yard a few months before Manuela was murdered, but they didn't pay very much attention to them.

Perhaps one of the most interesting things reportedly missing from the Witthuhn home was the tape out of the answering machine. I've heard two different accounts about the tape, one that it was removed from an old answering machine that was kept under the bed and another account that the tape was removed from the one currently used by the Witthuhns at the time of the murder. Either way it's interesting because of the possibility that the killer took it perhaps to listen to Manuela's voice as a souvenir, or he took it because his voice was on the tape perhaps as a caller to the home.

For years after the murder, David struggled with the loss of Manuela right up until he passed away in 2008 at the young age of 55. For a period of time some people even suspected him of the murder, which had to be awful for David. But he seemed to have the most ironclad alibi in the world. He was hospitalized at the time of the murder, and on top of this alibi. his DNA didn't match. So that would have been something very tough to go through. Something that he had to endure for the rest of his life.

TThe Orange County murders of the Harringtons and Manuela Witthuhn were shocking and horrifying, but they wouldn't be the last murders in Orange County with a similar M.O.

SEASON TWO, EPISODE FOURTEEN

The 1981 double murders of newlyweds Keith and Patty Harrington in Dana Point and the murder of Manuela Witthuhn in 1981 in Irvine were terrible bludgeoning murders. These murders, coupled with the 1980 murders of Lyman and Charlene Smith in Ventura and the 1979 murders of Doctors Robert Offerman and Deborah Manning in Goleta, left many investigators in Southern California in fear, that there was a maniac running around crisscrossing Southern California.

Many residents of these areas where these crimes happened took notice as well. Some people thought there was a single predator at large. He had been known in the Goleta area as the Creek Killer, in Ventura as the Diamond Knot Killer, and in Orange County people started calling him The Night Stalker. This moniker is not to be confused with Richard Ramirez, the Night Stalker who raped and killed in the mid-1980s. The Original Night Stalker in this case never got the same type of coverage that Richard Ramirez did and maybe that's what allowed him to go undetected. Years later, Larry Poole, an Orange County investigator who was an expert on this series of crimes, coined the phrase original night stalker. Someone asked Poole if this night stalker was related to the Richard Ramirez night stalker case. Poole was very quick to correct them. He said, "No, this was the original night stalker," and the name stuck.

It had been over a year and a half since the Creek Killer in Goleta had taken the lives of Drs. Offerman and Manning before vanishing into the night. Things had quieted down and people in the quiet community got back to their normal routines. In July of 1981, less than a mile away from the 1979 Offerman and Manning crime scene, another brutal murder of a couple would rock the quiet community in Goleta. An older homeowner at 449 Toltec Way had decided to put her home up for sale in May of 1981, after her husband passed away. She invited a relative to live in the home until it sold while she moved to another part of California. The relative she invited to stay there was 35-year-old Cheri Domingo. Cheri had been living in Montecito, California, about thirteen miles away in another part of Santa Barbara County with her teenage daughter Debbie. Cheri welcomed the move. As a divorcee, she had her hands full with her daughter Debbie, who had reached the age where she knew how to push buttons. She knew how to test limits. On top of everything that she is dealing with, Cheri had just been terminated from her job as a corporate manager. Cheri thought that the move might be a fresh start and might make things easier between her and Debbie. It didn't. In fact, things got even worse. Cheri would tell people that she just couldn't handle her daughter. They had shouting matches, and, in July, Debbie left her home and stayed with friends. Cheri stood strong and chose not to cave in to her daughter's teenage rebellion.

Instead she focused on trying to relax. Everybody who knew Cheri described her as extremely attractive. She was a five feet, four inches tall, 120 lb. brunette, who loved the beach and sunbathing. Cheri's ex-husband had remarried, but she had not. But, she was looking for a special someone. Cheri had placed some personal ads in local Santa Barbara County newspapers.

Despite apparently being lonely, Cheri did have a man in her life. Twenty-seven-year-old Gregory Sanchez, who was eight years Cheri's junior, was a strapping athletic man. Standing six feet, three inches and weighing 180 pounds. Sanchez was an imposing figure to most. But to Cheri he was kind and attentive. The pair dated on and off since 1975 when they had met at a company they both worked for in Santa Barbara

County. Their relationship had ups and downs, but they seem to get along. Even strong-willed Debbie approved of Greg and got along with him as well.

But Cheri seemed to have some doubts. She felt he was too young. At times Greg seemed committed to Cheri. He had even proposed to her but never followed through with it. At other times, like most single 27-year-old men, he seemed to enjoy his life the way it was, driving a sporty car and dating other women. The pair had lived together for a while in 1980 but broke up in December of that year.

Despite the hesitation and doubts on both of their parts, the pair stayed close, and they spent a lot of time together. On July 26, 1981, Cheri was home alone at the Toltec Way residence when she apparently missed Greg enough to call and invite him over. Greg took some directions from Cheri on how to get to her house. He wrote them down on a piece of paper. He climbed into his car, and he drove to 449 Toltec Way that evening. He didn't bring anything with him, as far as a change of clothes or toiletries. Greg may not have planned on staying overnight with Cheri.

The next day on July 27, 1981, between 10:30 and 11:00 a.m., the listing agent for the house called Cheri to make arrangements with her to show the home. She didn't answer the phone. The agent decided to drive to the home and using his realtor's key let himself in the front door but found the door was secured by the safety chain. He decided to walk around the kitchen side of the residence and found the sliding glass door open. He had brought a family with him that was interested in the home but asked them to wait in the kitchen while he went to see if the home was free to show.

The agent called out as he walked towards the back of the residence. The home was quiet and dark. He got to the master bedroom and on the floor saw the body of a nude man. Horrified, the realtor raced back to the family that was waiting for him in the kitchen, and he told them what he'd found. He picked up the phone and dialed 911. Deputies quickly responded to the scene. They found the body of the male lying on the floor but also found the nude body of a woman lying face down on the bed. Santa Barbara County Sheriff's detectives were called to the scene, and they quickly identified the two victims as Cheri Domingo and Greg Sanchez.

There was no doubt they had a double murder on their hands. They started their investigation inside the home while outside curious neighbors on the quiet cul-de-sac were gathering around to see what was going on. One of the people there immediately thought of Cheri's daughter, Debbie, and felt that she needed to contact her as soon as possible. She didn't want Debbie to hear the news that her mom was dead from someone else.

Back at the crime scene, investigators were examining the bodies of Cheri and Greg. Greg had sustained a gunshot to the face that was not fatal. What killed Greg was blunt force trauma to the head from a blunt object. Clothing from the bedroom closet was laid over Greg's face.

In examining Cheri's body, investigators found that she had been completely covered with bedding. Both of her arms were behind her back as if they had been tied behind her. But there were no ligatures. However, there were marks on her wrists indicating that she had been bound. Ligature marks were also found on her ankles. A coroner would later conclude that the cause of death was a result of massive cerebral injuries due to blunt force trauma and that death was instantaneous. The weapon was likely the same one that killed Greg. Although she had not been raped, there was semen found on Cheri from her killer.

As they looked around the bedroom, the detectives found a piece of hemp twine on the right side of the bed that was about ten inches long. They also found a bloody footprint from a herringbone pattern shoe on a bathrobe. Working their way through the home, investigators found a piece of cake on a plate in the kitchen alongside a partially drank can of soda. Detectives found other clues as they scoured the house, including partially burned matches that matched similar matches found in other Southern California murder scenes.

There was no obvious point of entry into the home, although a small bathroom window was open. Investigators felt that although the window was too small to fit through, it was not out of the question for someone to have reached in and opened a door that led from the bathroom to the outside of the home. There was evidence that the killer had spent a good amount of time in that bathroom.

Police theorized that in the early morning hours of July 27, 1981, the killer entered the home and may have interrupted Cheri and Greg during a moment of intimacy. They were likely confronted with a gun, and the murderer forced them to lie down face-first on the bed. Cheri was completely immobilized, but somehow Greg possibly escaped and charged the attacker and was shot in the face with a .38-caliber bullet. Again, this shot was not fatal but undoubtedly hurt Greg bad enough to incapacitate him. The killer likely masturbated on Cheri before or after killing her. When he bludgeoned Cheri, the killer made sure the bedding was completely over her head to minimize blood spatter.

At some point Greg came to and tried to stand up, and he was likely met by the murderer as he was getting to his feet. This was probably the point where Greg was bludgeoned. When his body fell to the floor, it landed partially in the closet. The killer removed some clothing that was hanging in the closet and covered Greg's head with it. Police used luminol at the crime scene to bring out areas of blood not seen with the human eye. They were able to see a trail leading down the hallway away from the bodies.

Outside of the home, police found a tool shed that appeared to have been tampered with. One of the tools that may have been the murder weapon was missing. Police also found wadded up pieces of toilet paper around the exterior of the home and in nearby yards. A large amount of toilet paper was found next to a wooden footbridge on Berkeley Drive, a very short walk away.

Police canvassed the neighborhood, questioning residents in an effort to piece together clues. A neighbor who lived next door reported that around 2:15 a.m. he woke up due to his dog barking. He and his wife sat up in bed but didn't hear anything else unusual, and then they went back to sleep. Another resident woke up around 4:00 a.m. that morning hearing what they thought was a single gunshot. The gunshot was followed by what sounded like a woman's voice, but then there was silence. The resident didn't report the incident to police at the time, thinking that it was probably teenagers setting off firecrackers.

Another neighbor close to the crime scene added that at about 9:45 p.m. the night before on the twenty-sixth, they had seen the outline of a man standing on the boundaries of properties close to the crime scene. They could only see him in the shadows, and he seemed to be angling himself behind a large tree. They never did get a closer look at him and didn't stop to investigate him.

Police next talked to a mother and daughter who had been out jogging in the area of Toltec Way along the trail and wooden footbridge where the large amount of toilet paper was found. The two women recounted for detectives that on the night of the twenty-sixth around 11:00 p.m., they saw a man in an area directly to the rear of the crime scene. This man had a German Shepherd with him and what stood out to them was that as they jogged by, the man and the dog didn't flinch. They stood perfectly still. The women described them as looking as if they were almost frozen. They immediately got the feeling that this man was out of place, and they headed back to their home nearby. They described this man as being in his late twenties or early thirties, standing about five feet, ten inches, weighing in around 190 to 200 pounds. They said that he had a husky build and neatly combed blond hair.

Another strange incident happened at a home close to the murder scene. At about 10:00 p.m. on the night of the twenty-sixth, a resident heard their doorbell ring and went to the door to answer it. When they did there was nobody there. They dismissed it as a prank. However, about five minutes later they looked outside again and found a bunch of wadded up toilet paper on their front lawn that wasn't there before. One couple reported that they were walking along Berkeley Street, close to the crime scene on the night of the twenty-sixth when they saw a young man in his twenties who seemed to be following them. He gained quickly on them as they walked faster at one point coming within ten feet of them. But they made their way to the other side of the street, and the young man continued walking and disappeared. This is a large amount of odd activity going on in the area around this cul-de-sac, and this cul-de-sac is less than a mile from the burglaries and the murders in Goleta. It's also very close to the area where the man found his dog stabbed in a yard on Berkeley in 1979.

During the neighborhood questioning, one name came up from residents repeatedly as somebody who might be responsible for the crimes. It was a name that was familiar to police. Brett Glasby was a 19-year-old man in Goleta who had a reputation for being involved in burglaries and drugs. Several people reported that he had a short temper. It was also reported that he had once punched a janitor who worked for Deborah Manning, who was killed in the 1979 Goleta attack.

Police wanted to question the youth to see if he knew anything about the crime. Glasby was an interesting guy. He came from a good family, but he seemed to have gone down the wrong path, turned away from a military career, and opted instead to become a criminal. He once got in trouble for a fight, and his parents felt that he needed a change of scenery. They decided to send him to Sacramento to stay with someone that the family knew who worked in law enforcement. But that didn't help. Glasby returned to Goleta and continued down the wrong path.

Glasby was questioned by police and denied being involved with any murders. Two different witnesses to some of the events that happened the night before the murder, including the daughter who was jogging with her mom, knew Brett Glasby. Both of these people were positive that he was not the man they saw. Police remained suspicious of Glasby and kept an eye on him. One interesting thing about Glasby was that he lived next to a well-known real estate professional in Goleta. This real estate man supposedly had a German Shepherd with three toes on one paw. We had talked about the possibility of a three toed dog print found at the scene of the Offerman-Manning murders in 1979. However, it's more likely that the prints of the dog were like the only partial prints and that it wasn't really missing toes. But that's just the kind of strange rabbit holes that this case presented.

In February of 1982 Brett Glasby and his brother Brian traveled to Mexico. While they were there they participated in a drug deal that went bad and both brothers were shot to death. Their father went to Mexico to retrieve their bodies and immediately had them cremated. Years later based on tips and interesting connections, some investigators felt that Glasby may have been involved in the murders. But another murder would happen in 1986 and would be attributed to the same killer. At this point in time Glasby was dead, so it couldn't have been him. But to rule out any crazy theories that Brett Glasby was still alive, investigators years later used other investigative techniques to once and for all rule out Glasby. This left the Santa Barbara County Sheriff's Department with no real suspects in the case. The normally quiet and peaceful neighborhood of Goleta experienced from 1979 to 1981 a series of brutal attacks, burglaries, and murder. But once again the killer vanished and was never heard from again in Goleta.

We interviewed Debbie Domingo for the podcast, and she told us about growing up with her mother and what it was like that awful day that she found out her mother had been murdered. Debbie detailed the difficulties the pair had in getting along.

Police questioned Debbie about her mother's murder and even had her take a polygraph test. She spoke well of Greg and was not surprised that he had tried to fight the attacker.

We conducted this interview with Debbie in January of 2018 and to wrap up the interview we asked her one last question. Do you think 2018 is the year the killer will be identified? This was her response.

> *Well, I certainly hope so. However, I thought it was going to be 2017. I thought it was going to be last year. I was so ready. I think so many of us were just poised and ready and waiting for the day that a headline comes out that says we got him. Am I disappointed that 2017 wasn't the year? A little bit. Do I think 2018 can be the year? Absolutely. I think that it's just a numbers game right now. I think every day that goes by we get closer and closer to an identity. I think technology is on our side. I think the hardworking detectives are on our side. I just really feel like it could be any day now.*

None of us knew at the time of the interview that any day now wasn't very far off and that the Golden State Killer would be caught just about ninety days later.

After the latest murders of Domingo and Sanchez, the press was beginning to notice that Southern California may have a serial predator on its hands. On August 2, 1981, the *Los Angeles Times* ran a lengthy and detailed article speculating that all of the 1979 to 1981 murders we have discussed might be the work of one man. It was titled, "Night Stalker theory connecting eight Southland slayings disputed." In the article it detailed how similar the crimes were and how investigators from various jurisdictions theorized that the murders may have been the work of one man. They began to pay attention to all crimes in Southern California bearing similar patterns or M.O. But for weeks and then months, no similar crimes were committed. Months turned into years, and the mysterious killer seemed to have vanished.

In the killer's wake, other notorious killers grabbed the spotlight and attention from investigators. The Scorecard Killer and the Grim Sleeper were roaming Southern California and committing brutal murders. Then in 1985, the Night Stalker, Richard Ramirez, was captured after his own sadistic rape and murder spree. But the original Night Stalker alluded capture, and it seemed as if he might fade into history as yet another uncaught serial killer. Then, in May of 1986, a murder of an 18-year-old in Irvine, California, once again piqued investigators' interest.

Eighteen-year-old Janelle Cruz was a beautiful young woman who was working hard towards a bright future for herself. Her parents had divorced, and it had been very hard on Janelle. She was very close with her younger sister, Michelle. In March of 1986, just over a month before Janelle was murdered, The *Los Angeles Times* ran an article about the Job Corps, which offered young people a fresh start towards a better future. The article featured Janelle and detailed her accomplishment of completing the Job Corps training in Utah. Janelle had signed up for Orange Coast College and was working part-time at a local pizza shop in Irvine. It seemed as if she had a plan in place and was ready to work hard as she moved into adulthood.

But late on the night of May 4, or in the early morning hours of May 5, 1986, those plans came to a shocking and violent end. We spoke with Janelle's sister Michelle, who told us about her life with Janelle prior to her murder. She detailed for us the events leading up to the murder and its aftermath.

Hi, I'm Michelle Cruz, and my sister Janelle Cruz was the last victim of the Golden State Killer. We were very carefree. We had a lot of friends and a lot of fun. Went to the beach a lot. We went to the mall. Always had our friends over. We had a group of people we hung out with. We were all real close. Janelle and I pretty much did everything together because we had the same friends and life in Orange County, it was just a really nice area to be brought up, very manicured. It was a new area. Irvine was being developed. Everything seemed really new and fresh and clean and you didn't hear about a lot of problems. You just didn't hear a lot of crime or anything like that there.

We lived in Irvine for about eight years. Prior to Irvine, we lived in Newport Beach. Prior to Janelle being killed, I had moved to Mammoth Mountain for the winter. I was gone for three months. In three months, I did not know what Janelle was doing. The only thing that I knew was that she had met a guy at Laguna Beach, and we had a conversation on Friday about that. It was our last conversation. She just was very happy. It's like she really liked this guy. The last thing she said was, "I love you," and we hung up the phone. But for the three months that I was gone, I don't know what she was doing.

At the time Janelle was killed, my stepfather and my mother were talking about maybe getting back together, rekindling. My stepfather was going to Cancun. He invited my mom to go. The reason my mom went is because my little brother was going, and she didn't want him to go alone with my stepfather. She said, "Let me go," so she can keep an eye on him. He was five years old at the time. They went to Cancun. When my mom was saying goodbye to Janelle that day, maybe that morning, and I think it was a Saturday morning, my mom had these red earrings, and they made her feel very uncomfortable. She felt like they were blood spots because she didn't want to wear them. She decided not to and she just gave them to Janelle. "I don't want these, they bother me." My mom looks back on that now and it's like, was that something of a feeling that she was getting that something was going to happen to Janelle? We don't know. She left for Cancun. Janelle did not want to be there by herself. She tried to get friends to come over. I don't know why she tried to get friends. I don't know if she felt uncomfortable. Maybe she had heard something the prior evening. She called multiple friends trying to get them to come over, and none of them could.

I know that one of her friends that she was reaching out to, he was at a convention, and so he called her back around midnight, and Janelle didn't answer. He said, "I remember calling her back, and it was around midnight, but she never answered." He didn't think anything about it. But now you look back, and that was the time that she was probably getting killed or was killed at that time. Just crazy that he calls right at that time when she couldn't get to that phone. I don't know if Janelle worked during the day or not, but she had gone to her work and was hanging out there. I think she may have got something to eat or drink and was sitting down the table talking to her other co-workers, and she invited one of her co-workers to come hang out with her for a little bit because she didn't want to be by herself. He agreed and then when he got off work, he followed her home, and they were hanging out there for a little bit. Then it came to about 10:00, 10:30-ish, and he says he had to go because he was using his mom's car. They both left. She left in her car. He left in his, and then Janelle came back about fifteen minutes later and walked into the house, and I guess that's when the killer was hiding and got her when she came back in.

That door on the outside is actually really close to our bedroom window. So, if he came in, he came in through the garage into the laundry room because I heard noises in the laundry room. Well, Janelle disregarded that noise as maybe the dryer, and it wasn't too long after that noise, that he had left, when they both actually left, and then Janelle came back. The killer could have been in the house when they left. She came back home, went into the house and from what I found out she was in the kitchen when he first got to her and maybe hit her in the back of the head. She struggled and put up a fight, a really good fight, but she ended up in her bedroom.

She had been raped, and bludgeoned and killed pretty bad. She had lost all her teeth from him hitting her. My stepfather had lost a pipe wrench in the backyard, and that pipe wrench was missing. So, they were assuming that that could have been the weapon used to kill Janelle. The night before, Janelle had three friends over. I guess they were her guy friends. Again, these are guys we hung out with. We were raised in the area, so we knew these people, and they lived in our area. They came over and they were hanging out with Janelle, and they did hear some noises in the backyard. Janelle was on the phone at the time talking to her friend, and these guys ran outside to see what that noise was.

When they ran outside, they did not see anything, so they came back in the house, and, I guess, disregarded it. But it must have been a noise loud enough for them to all run out there and see what it was. When I left for Mammoth, our house was not up for sale. During the few months that I was gone, they had put it up for sale. It couldn't have been up for sale for too long, and that is actually how Janelle was found by a realtor who was showing the property to a prospective buyer. The realtor walked into the bedroom and saw Janelle lying there on the bed. She called the broker who had our house for sale, who listed it, and then they ended up calling the police. That is how she was found through the realtor. From what I know she did not hear anything or she was not getting any phone calls. My mother did not get any phone calls either and, remember, my mom at that time was a really pretty young beautician. So,

I always wondered, was it Janelle that he was after, or my mother? Because she was really popular in the Irvine area as a hairstylist.

The other thought was maybe it was a real estate agent because when you go out of town, they mark that in the database, saying the owner won't be there, so you can show the property. So maybe somebody in real estate knew. I don't remember when the police reached out to me. I know that when they found out that Janelle had been killed, and my mom and my stepfather were in Cancun, they did call all the hotels in Mexico trying to locate my mom. They finally located her, and my mom and my stepfather took the next flight out, came back home, and I'm sure they were interviewed.

Like Debbie Domingo, Michelle had no way of knowing that her sister's killer would be identified just a few months after we talked with her. Michelle laid out what police think happened to Janelle. She had a friend over the night of her murder, and they both heard some noises, but when they investigated there was no sign of anybody. When this friend left, Janelle also left for a short time but returned to her home soon after. Police think that the killer was in her home waiting for her. She was attacked in the kitchen and fought a losing battle where she wound up being raped and murdered in her bedroom.

After police arrived at the home at 13 Encina following the call from the real estate agent, they examined Janelle's body, which was on her bed. She was partially nude, and a blanket had been placed over her head. They also noted blades of grass on the bed. Janelle had been savagely beaten. Her teeth had been knocked out. The coroner would find that she had actually swallowed them. The wounds were so severe to the front of her head, that she was unrecognizable. This was a brutal crime. Michelle touched on it a bit. Janelle had a lot of friends, and police wound up finding them all and questioning them, and this included her friend who was at her house that night. He was not initially truthful with police because he was afraid that they would accuse him of the murder. He was initially a suspect, and it wouldn't be until years later that he was cleared by DNA.

While investigating the crime scene, police found a radio playing, and it was tuned to a channel that Janelle often listened to. They found blood spatter all over Janelle's room, on the shutters and at the head of Janelle's bed. There was also blood found in the kitchen. Police were sure that the attack had started there before concluding in Janelle's bedroom. Janelle's stepfather owned a pipe wrench that was missing, and police believe that it was likely the murder weapon. Police didn't find any signs of forced entry, but people who knew Janelle reported that she often forgot to lock the doors to the home.

When police searched outside of the home, they found a piece of patio furniture had been moved to enable the murderer to climb over the rear fence. The most important clue found at the crime scene was the killer's semen, which would later reveal his DNA. That DNA would later be matched to the DNA from the Manuela Witthuhn murder scene two miles away, and the other Orange County murders of Patrice and Keith Harrington in Dana Point. It would also be connected to the 1980 murders of the Smiths in Ventura. There was no doubt about it. There had been a single Night Stalker moving through areas in Southern California and killing lone women and couples.

In 1986, after the murder of Janelle Cruz, the original Night Stalker seemed to vanish. No other crimes with similar M.O. would be attributed to him in Southern California. Like Northern California's East Area Rapist, a prolific serial offender had seemingly slipped away from detectives who were working hard to identify and apprehend him. But back up in Northern California, investigators there had not forgotten the East Area Rapist. Some of them were convinced that he had made his way to Southern California and became a full-fledged serial killer.

Larry Crompton was convinced that the original Night Stalker was also the East Area Rapist and that he had also been responsible for the Goleta murders and attacks as well.

You get it in your head, I have a job to do. My job is to catch this person before he hurts anybody else. It just gets worse as you don't catch him. After it was over, and he left our area, I would wake up at three o'clock in the morning and I would say, "What did I do wrong? What did I miss? What did I do? What should I have done?" It took many, many years before I got it in my head that this wasn't about me. This is about the victims and the victims' families, and it made it a little easier. But I never did get it out of my head. It's still there, and that's why I wrote my book. It was to get this investigation going.

I started writing it when I was still in Contra Costa. I didn't want to put it out because at the time, even though I knew about the murders, and I knew the murderer was the same, at that time, we hadn't proven it. Nobody would believe Sergeant Bevans and I once we heard about the-- we hadn't heard about the double homicide that was down there with Robert Offerman and Alexandria Manning. Jim Bevans heard about it first, and he called them, and they said, "No, don't know what you're talking about." He called me and went over with me and I called them, and they told me the same thing.

Then I was sent to a school down in San Diego, and there happened to be a deputy from Santa Barbara there, and I got talking to him about the double homicide. I said, "We have gone over this and nobody will believe us, but he's a rapist." He said, "We had an attempted rape where the people got away." I said, "What?" We got those reports, and we looked them over and said the murderer and our rapist, it definitely is the same person. Again, nobody would believe us.

Sacramento said he's out of our area, Contra Costa said he's out of our area, and you have to let it go. Well, Paul Holes called me after I retired, and he said that he was told that I was on the task force.

He said, "I'm a DNA expert," and he said, "If you can give me some names of the rape victims," he said, "I'll do the DNA on it." I gave him three names from our area. He called me back a few months later, and he said, "Yes," he said, "I joined two of those," and he said, "I'm working on the third one, I'll call you back." He did, and he said, "Yes," he said those three matched with the DNA, which we knew that they would anyway. We knew all of these were by the same rapist. I said, "Paul, I know of five murders down in Southern California," and I said, "I can't get any cooperation at all. Nobody will believe me. I know it's our rapist."

I said, "If you can get a criminalist down there to work with you, I know it's the same." He called me back about seven months later. He said, "No, they didn't have five homicides." He said, "They had ten. We just joined six of them with the DNA." I was contacted by Orange County, or Paul told me Orange County wanted me to contact them. I did, and they flew me down there. It was very fortunate that I had kept all the reports of all of the rapes, all of the attacks from the first through the last one in our area. I took those down with me. Had them boxed up and took them down. They knew nothing about the rapes. They had already done DNA on some of the homicides, six of them. That really, really put the investigation together.

Paul Holes followed up on Larry Compton's suspicions, and although it wasn't overnight, Paul would go on to link the East Area Rapist crimes in Northern California with the original Night Stalker crimes in Southern California by DNA. This would earn this predator a new moniker: EARONS. We talked with Paul Holes about two months before he retired.

I was initially hired on with the Sheriff's office as, believe it or not, a forensic toxicologist, which was a civilian position. I worked for about three and a half years doing controlled substance analysis and alcohol analysis, but I always had my eyes set on this Deputy Sheriff Criminalist position because I really wanted to do crime scene investigation. That was my passion. Finally, in 1994, I got hired on as a Deputy Sheriff Criminalist. The serology unit was the old-time enzyme typing that we used to do in forensics before DNA. But I just happened to come on board in the crime lab when the very early DNA technology was starting. I started getting trained in that and I had a passion for serial predators and cold cases. Very shortly after seeing the potential of this early DNA technology, I decided to see what I could do with this DNA technology on some of these unsolved cases. That's how I started working on various cold cases in Contra Costa County. The very first one that I pulled out was the East Area Rapist case. Unbeknownst to me, at that time, I had no idea the magnitude of that particular series. All I had access to was a handful of the East Bay reports that were present within the library. My former chief of the lab was on the original Contra Costa County task force with Larry Crompton. He told me all about the East Area Rapist, and I said, "Well, that sounds like a good case to see what we could do to solve it using this DNA technology."

At that point in time, the only thing we knew about that series was it was a series of sexual assaults which were far past the statute of limitations, and that was in 1994. More just out of curiosity than anything else, I decided, well, I'm going to proceed to see what I can do with the East Area Rapist evidence and found three cases in the Sheriff's property room, two Danville attacks and one San Ramon attack that still had the sexual assault kits that were collected from the victims back in 1978 to 1979. I was able to get those assault kits, identified that there was semen present in each of those cases and then proceeded to use this old DNA technology. I generated three DNA profiles across the three cases and all three profiles were the same. That was like, okay, the original investigators who had linked these cases together based on M.O. were right. At that point, that's when I decided to reach out to Larry Crompton and ask him if he had any primary suspects, so I could try to get their DNA to see if one of those primary suspects would be the guy. When I called Larry up, he told me, "We looked at a lot of guys, and I can't say that there was one that really stood out." He told me that back in the day, they thought the East Area Rapist had possibly shown up down in Santa Barbara. But when he had called Santa Barbara, Santa Barbara told him, "No, our case is not related to yours," and he ran into a brick wall. At that point, and this is now 1996-1997-time frame, I decided well, I'm going to call Santa Barbara. That's what I did. I called Santa Barbara, and I got pretty much the same message from the investigator I talked to, and he said, "No, we've got some cases here, but nothing related to Northern California. However, Irvine has some cases in which they're doing DNA on, so you might want to call Irvine PD."

I ended up calling Irvine PD and spoke with an investigator there and that investigator said, "Yes, we have two cases in which the Orange County Sheriff's Office has linked with DNA. You might want to call them and see what you can do with the DNA profile." That's what I did, I called the Orange County Sheriff's crime lab, spoke with a DNA analyst there named Mary who had done a lot of work on the original Night Stalker series. Unfortunately, Orange County Sheriff's lab and the Contra Costa Sheriff's lab had different DNA technologies, and it was because we were at the *very beginning stages of DNA coming into forensics. Things weren't quite standardized. In fact, Orange County was a little bit ahead of Contra Costa County. Mary's profile for the original Night Stalker series was different. It was a different profile, different technology than the one I had generated for the East Area Rapist. However, we had one marker that was the same and the type at that marker, this DQ alpha marker was the same. It wasn't an elimination. It was still a possibility. However, it wasn't a very strong association. It was better than an ABO blood type, but not much better. I told Mary back then in 1997 that when Contra Costa County had the newer DNA technology on board, I would be calling her back. It took Contra Costa County four years to get that newer DNA technology on board. At that point in time I had promoted up, I was now managing the lab, so I assigned a DNA analyst to run the East Area Rapist DNA in the new technology. He did. All three cases out of Contra Costa County still had the same DNA profile with a much more discriminating DNA technology. Then I had him call Mary. When he did, they literally read the DNA profile to each other over the phone. It was at that point, which was in March of 2001 when the East Area Rapist was linked to the original Night Stalker cases in Southern California. We knew at that point that all fifty attacks up in Northern California, plus or minus, were committed by the same individual who killed ten people down in Southern California.*

As I say, in this case, I've been involved in this case for twenty-four years. There's no questioning my persistence. There might be questioning my competency because I haven't solved it in twenty-four years but at least I'm trying. Probably the most significant difference between this series and the Zodiac series is we have the evidence to solve this case. When we find the guy, we will know it for sure. There isn't going to be any hemming and hawing and justifying why this guy is a suspect versus somebody else. We will know it. I do believe that we will identify him. Now, will we identify him while he's still alive? That's really the big question. But, ultimately, I do believe that as DNA technology is progressing, as DNA genealogy aspects are expanding that eventually he will be found and hopefully he's found while he's still walking and upright. But if he's found and he's six feet under and he has a tombstone, I'm going to be there with a shovel. I'm going to dig him up.

The frustration at times has caused me to push the case away saying I'm done only two weeks later the itch comes back, and then I'm back reading the case files and reformulating and redirecting and making another effort at it. It is frustrating because I think at this point if he were in a crowd I could pick him out of that crowd. That's how I feel, and I have failed to do that yet. How is this guy eluding us? I think he obviously is a more intelligent offender than the average guy out there. I think he's fairly sophisticated. He likes to portray himself as being something like the troll under the bridge, and he's not. He did a good job at his self-preservation and protecting his identity. But then he's also had luck on his side. That, I think, is what's frustrating. Eventually that luck is going to run out, and I think it is going to run out sooner than later.

Paul predicted that this killer and rapist's luck was going to run out sooner rather than later. It turned out Paul was right. Just after Paul retired, police arrested Joseph J DeAngelo as being East Area Rapist/Golden State Killer.

SEASON TWO, EPISODE FIFTEEN

Once the East Area Rapist and the Original Night Stalker were linked by DNA, this killer then earned the nickname EARONS. You can see how all these monikers all over the State of California refer to the same deadly predator. But residents in the State of California, depending on where you went or whom you asked, were not aware of this rapist and murderer. They only knew him by whatever moniker he had locally where they lived. These multiple names led to a lot of confusion.

The late California true crime writer and blogger Michelle McNamara had become obsessed with this case. She was shocked that despite being from California and having her own personal interest in true crime, she had not heard about this killer until she saw a segment about the case on a TV show. She immersed herself in the case and became obsessed with it. In 2013, Michelle penned an article for *LA Magazine* titled *In the Footsteps of a Killer*. In that article, she discussed EARONS in great detail. She felt that she needed to rebrand the killer with a moniker that would encompass all of his crimes in California, and she gave him the name The Golden State Killer. The name was memorable, and it stuck.

Over the past two years or so, through social media campaigns, TV shows, and podcasts, people all over California and then throughout the country finally learned about this killer and the horrible details of the fifty rapes and at least twelve murders he committed. The spotlight was finally on this offender, and law enforcement was working hard to identify him. In April of 2018, all of that work finally paid off with the arrest of Joseph

J. DeAngelo. We are going to break down as completely as possible his timeline and background. Joseph James DeAngelo Jr. was born on November 8, 1945 in Bath, New York, to Joseph J. DeAngelo Sr. and Kathleen DeAngelo. He has three siblings: an older sister Rebecca, a younger sister Constance, and a younger brother John.

The DeAngelo family was an Air Force family, and they spent time overseas before returning to the States in the mid-1950s. It has been reported by some news outlets that while he was in Germany, DeAngelo Jr. witnessed his sister being raped by a group of older men. You just have to wonder what, if this is true, what seeing this happen as a young kid may have done to his psyche. The DeAngelo family moved out to California, and, from 1960 to 1963, we know that they lived at various addresses in Rancho Cordova on Portsmouth Drive, Abington Way, and Olson Drive. While there were never any East Area Rapist attacks on these streets, they are not very far from many of the East Area Rapist attacks.

In 1964, Joseph DeAngelo Sr. divorced Kathleen, and he went back to Korea, where he remarried. Something that seems very odd is that it was reported that he had children with his second wife, and he named the children that he had with her the same names as his previous children. During the early 1960s, Joseph J. DeAngelo Jr. attended elementary school and junior high school in Rancho Cordova. From 1961 to 1963, he attended Folsom High School in Sacramento County. In 1964, DeAngelo dropped out of school and got his GED.

In September of 1964, DeAngelo join the Navy and from October to December of that year, he was stationed in San Diego, where he went through training. From 1965 to 1968, DeAngelo served on two ships. He served on the USS Canberra and the USS Piedmont. During this time, he saw some action in Vietnam. It's been reported that he lost a finger or maybe even parts of multiple fingers in action. Now what's interesting is that his younger brother John joined the Army in 1969, and in 1971 he lost a finger in action in Vietnam. We haven't been able to verify that DeAngelo lost a finger in action, but we know for sure that his younger brother John did. That is very strange. Two brothers both losing a finger or possibly parts of fingers in battle. In February of 1965, DeAngelo's mother Kathleen remarried Jack Bosanko in Tulare County. By 1968, DeAngelo was out of the military and attended college at Sierra College in Rocklin, California. Rocklin is in Placer County about twenty miles from Sacramento. In May of 1970, an engagement announcement for DeAngelo and his fiancée Bonnie Colwell appeared in the *Auburn Journal* newspaper.

The announcement read as follows: "Colwell, DeAngelo pair announce engagement. Announcement has been made of the engagement of Bonnie Jean Colwell and Joseph James DeAngelo Jr. No definite date has been set for the wedding. The bride-elect is the daughter of Mr. and Mrs. Stanley B. Colwell of rural Auburn and the future bridegroom is the son of Mrs. Jack Bosanko of Auburn and Joseph J. DeAngelo Senior of Korea. Miss Colwell graduated from Del Oro High School and Sierra College where she is a lab assistant in the science department. She is affiliated with the Life Science Club, the Honor Society and the President's Honor Roll. Young DeAngelo is a graduate of Folsom High School and Sierra College. He is employed by Sierra Crane and Hoist Company of Newcastle. He is affiliated with the Vets Club, the AGS, the President's Honor Roll and the International Diving Association."

There were some really interesting things in that article. The biggest one was the name Bonnie. In multiple East Area Rapist attacks, the victims felt that the rapist had mentioned Bonnie or mommy. The victims recounted how the rapist sobbed in a corner making statements like, "I hate you mommy," or, "I hate you Bonnie." But at least one victim was adamant that the East Area Rapist said Bonnie, not mommy. We also know from that article that DeAngelo at the time was working for the Sierra Hoist and Crane Company in New Castle, California, in Placer County. It's also interesting that he was mentioned as being associated with the International Diving Association. As it turned out, Bonnie broke off the engagement and never married Joseph DeAngelo. Instead, she went on to marry someone else. As a result, a lot of people think that in DeAngelo's mind, Bonnie may have driven him to his crimes. Obviously, she's not responsible, but he may have thought so in his mind. Investigators are in the process of trying to learn any details from Bonnie to help shed more light on DeAngelo's background.

In December of 1970, DeAngelo got an associate degree in Police Science. In 1971 he went on to attend college at Sacramento State University, and while there, he obtained a bachelor's degree in Criminal Justice. From 1972 to 1973, it's reported that DeAngelo did a thirty-two week internship for the Roseville PD, essentially where he's playing a ride-along cop after taking his Criminal Justice course. Roseville is in Placer County about thirteen miles from Rancho Cordova. During the time that he was there is when the Cordova Cat Burglar was striking in areas of Rancho Cordova. So, it's highly likely that DeAngelo could have been the Cordova Cat Burglar as well. This part of the timeline reveals some major clues. In May of 1973, DeAngelo started a job with the Exeter PD. One of his duties for the Exeter Police Department was part of the burglary task force. Essentially, his job was to help curb burglaries. But it's in May of 1973, ten miles away in Visalia, that the Visalia Ransacker crimes began.

It's later in 1973, in November, that DeAngelo married Sharon Huddle in Placer County. This article is from the 1973 *Sacramento Bee:*

> *The Auburn First Congregational Church served as a setting for the marriage of Sharon Marie Huddle and Joseph James DeAngelo Jr. She is the daughter of Mr. and Mrs. Clarence M. Huddle of Citrus Heights and his parents are Mrs. Jack Bosanko of Garden Grove and Joseph J. DeAngelo of Korea. She is a graduate of San Juan High School and American River College.*

Her husband was graduated from Folsom High School and California State University in Sacramento. Honor attendants were Patricia Huddle of Citrus Heights and Larry Schneider of Rancho Cordova.

There are additional clues in this article. First, it mentioned that DeAngelo's mom is living down in Orange County. It also mentioned who Sharon's parents were and that they lived in Citrus Heights. They were still living there at the same address in 1976 when the East Area Rapist attacked Jane Carson Sandler. DeAngelo's in-laws' house was one mile from Jane Carson Sandler's house. Additionally, like Sandler and her husband, DeAngelo's father-in-law was in the Air Force. So maybe there's some connection there. One final clue in that article was the mention of Larry Schneider of Rancho Cordova being an honor attendant. Schneider lived very close to Dawes and Dolcetto, close to where many confirmed and suspected East Area Rapist attacks happened. This included the October 1975 attack of a mother and daughter near that intersection. In 1974, DeAngelo was living at an unpublicized address in Visalia. Being a police officer, it wasn't uncommon for his address and phone number not to be published in the phonebook. But it's a Visalia city directory, so it does seem as if he lived in Visalia. His occupation is listed as City Police Department, but we definitely think this is for the Exeter PD and not the Visalia PD.

During 1973 and 1974 the Visalia Ransacker crimes were in full swing in Visalia. There were dozens of burglaries. In 1975, things turned deadly and the burglaries turned to murder. In September of that year, Beth Snelling was the victim of an attempted kidnapping and her father Claude tried to come to her defense, but he was shot and killed. Then, three months later in December, Officer Bill McGowan was shot at by the Ransacker. McGowan only received minor injuries, and he was able to give a description of a round baby-faced Visalia Ransacker. A sketch was circulated in the area and immediately after dozens of burglaries the Ransacker vanished from Visalia. The VR vanished from Visalia in December of 1975, and in 1976 DeAngelo took a job as a police officer with the Auburn PD. This was just about twenty miles from where the East Area Rapist began striking in June of 1976. While DeAngelo was on that police force, the East Area Rapist attacks happened all over Northern California. In July of 1979, DeAngelo was caught stealing dog repellent and a hammer from a hardware store in Sacramento County. It's also been said that he got into some sort of altercation with the store clerk. What's extremely relevant is that after his arrest, the East Area Rapist crimes stopped in Northern California. The next month in August, DeAngelo was officially fired from the Auburn PD. In October, just a month later the East Area Rapist attacked in Goleta, in Santa Barbara County. In December he allegedly murdered Offerman and Manning in Goleta, and this is one of the things that is now being investigated. Why was DeAngelo in Goleta? In fact, after he was fired from the Auburn PD, his movements are hard to track.

We do know that DeAngelo and his wife, using a VA loan, bought a home in Sacramento County in 1980. In March of 1980, the Smiths were murdered in Ventura. In August of 1980, the Harringtons were murdered in Dana Point. In February of 1981, Manuela Witthuhn was murdered in Irvine. In July of 1981, Cheri Domingo and Greg Sanchez were murdered in Goleta. Then, in September of 1981, DeAngelo had a life-changing event when his first child was born in Sacramento County. That's something that profilers predicted might mark an end or a pause in the killer's activities, and they were right. The Golden State Killer did not kill again for five years. During that time in 1982, DeAngelo's wife was admitted to the Bar to practice law. In May of 1986, Janelle Cruz was murdered in Irvine. Six months later, DeAngelo's second daughter was born in Los Angeles County. After the Cruz murder, there are no additional murders officially tied to the Golden State Killer. There are several murders in Southern California that have been thrown out there by various people and sources as possibly being connected to the Golden State Killer.

Dorothy Jane Scott went missing in May of 1980, in Orange County. She had been receiving taunting calls prior to vanishing and was afraid for her safety. She once found a dead rose on her car. The mysterious caller threatened to cut her into little bits. She vanished after taking a friend to the UC Irvine Medical Center for treatment. We've mentioned that hospital before in relation to Golden State Killer victims Keith and Patty Harrington. After she vanished, her parents received taunting calls from somebody that said they killed her. In 1984, her body was discovered by a construction worker in a shallow grave. Mixed in with her remains were the remains of a dog. Because of the taunting phone calls and a history of violence against dogs by the Golden State Killer, this case may be worth a closer look. At the time she went missing, Scott was living in Stanton, California. DeAngelo's brother had lived in Stanton at some point as well. At the time of her murder, he lived three miles from her parents.

Julia Wilkinson, a nurse, was found bludgeoned in her garage in San Diego in December of 1980. Witnesses saw a suspect around her home, and a sketch was generated. Police theorized that she interrupted a prowler, or a burglar. Police are also looking into whether or not the Golden State Killer may be responsible for a 1978 double murder in Simi Valley, which is in Ventura County. Twenty-four-year-old Rhonda Wicht was found brutally beaten and raped, and she had been strangled to death with a macramé rope. Her four-year-old son was also found dead in the home with a pillow over his head. Rhonda's boyfriend was convicted of the murders and sentenced to life without parole. But he has always denied killing Rhonda and her son. Recently, DNA evidence found at the scene was examined and found not to match up. He was released from prison after almost forty years. Police are examining the DNA evidence, and they plan to compare it to DeAngelo's to see if it is a match. The timeline of DeAngelo during the 1980s and his movements are puzzling, and investigators will be digging hard to see what they can find. One thing we know for sure is that DeAngelo had family all over Southern California and that he and his wife may have lived down there for a stretch, perhaps with her parents. DeAngelo did have relatives in the 1980s who lived in the middle of the two-mile section of Irvine between the Witthuhn and Cruz murders. It will be interesting to see how the dots connect.

In May of 1989, DeAngelo's third daughter was born in Sacramento County, and in August of that year, DeAngelo started working at the SaveMart in Roseville, where he worked up until 2017 when he retired. In 1991, it appears as if DeAngelo and his wife separated, but they never officially divorced. There has been a lot of speculation around this. Some people have theorized that they may have remained married due to the fact that one spouse cannot be compelled to testify against the other in court. It's been widely reported that she has not cooperated with police since DeAngelo was arrested in April of 2018.

We talked about DNA being DeAngelo's downfall, and investigators in the Golden State Killer case always felt that DNA would nail him. They monitored DNA databases and continued to look for possible connections to the Golden State Killer. They uploaded the Golden State Killer's DNA into GEDmatch, a public DNA database, and found multiple distant relatives. From there, his days were numbered. A forensic genealogist tracked several generations of family members until they found DeAngelo. Although he was a bit older than the estimates, they felt they had their guy. They retrieved an item discarded by DeAngelo in public and tested it for DNA. It matched the Golden State Killer perfectly. Police put together a plan to take down DeAngelo. They knew he was dangerous, and they wanted to take him alive. On April 24, in the early evening hours, a team of specialized tactical officers from the FBI in Sacramento County staked out DeAngelo's Citrus Heights home. He came out of his house, and an undercover officer walked up to DeAngelo in his yard pretending to be lost. DeAngelo apparently became confrontational, but the tactical team rushed him, and they took him into custody.

As they loaded him in the car, DeAngelo said, "But I've got a roast in the oven", as if he were in complete shock. Just imagining this guy who is being arrested for some of the most heinous sexual assaults and murders in history saying, "But I've got a roast in the oven." It has been reported that one of DeAngelo's daughters was inside the home, and apparently all of this happened so quickly that she didn't immediately realize that he was gone. Unknown to anyone, police questioned DeAngelo for hours.

The days after the arrest were obviously very hectic, but police didn't waste any time charging DeAngelo. He was charged with the Ventura murders of the Smiths, as well as the murders of the Maggiores. Then the dominos started to fall, and he was charged with the Goleta murders of Greg Sanchez and Cheri Domingo as well as those of Drs. Offerman and Manning. Finally, he was charged with the murders of Janelle Cruz, Manuela Witthuhn, and Keith and Patty Harrington. He received twelve murder charges in all. We can't forget that Claude Snelling from Visalia is likely a Golden State Killer victim as well, but, as of yet, DeAngelo has not been charged in his murder. DeAngelo has made multiple court appearances, but it remains to be seen if he will enter a plea or try to avoid a trial. It's also unclear what, if anything, he has admitted to. Cameras, for at least one court appearance, were barred from the courtroom. His public defender is trying to keep details of the warrants used to arrest DeAngelo sealed. The press is going to fight to have those warrants unsealed because they want to know details, and so do we.

We earlier mentioned Proposition 69, the California law that requires felons to give their DNA. That law didn't go into effect until 2004. The Golden State Killer case is a great example of why that law is so great, and, in fact, if the law was in force ten years earlier, DeAngelo would have likely been identified much earlier. DeAngelo's brother had a felony arrest in the 1990s before Proposition 69 went into effect. Had the law been in place and worked as it was designed to, his

DNA would have been uploaded to a central law enforcement database, and it would have been matched as a familial hit to his brother's DNA, and no doubt this case would have been solved much sooner.

Paul Holes had a big hand in solving this case using DNA. Our first interview with Paul was done about ten weeks before he retired. We were able to interview Paul after the arrest, and we asked Paul to share with us a little about the work he did with the DNA database match that led to the suspect in the case, Joseph DeAngelo.

> *Well, there really isn't a way to sit there and watch the databases to see if there's a relative. The big issue with exploiting that type of technology is first to generate the type of DNA profile that is compatible to search the databases. There's been times over the years I have been looking at, well how can I search ancestry. com to look for relatives of the Golden State Killer or 23AndMe, or My heritage, these various genealogy databases. What you have to understand is that law enforcement crime labs do not produce a DNA profile that is compatible with that type of genealogy search, and the genealogy laboratories do not work with law enforcement to produce that type of profile nor do they necessarily have the capability to work with forensic samples.*

> *I think a lot of people out there don't realize the type of evidence we're dealing with. When we talk about, well, we've got DNA from the Golden State Killer, well what we've got is, we've got a swab that was typically collected from the female victim that has the female's DNA and the offender's DNA mixed and that's a problem. If you were to take that sample and send it into a typical genealogy lab, they wouldn't know what to do with it because they don't know how to separate out the male DNA from the female DNA.*

The big hurdle was trying to find DNA evidence in our case in which we could adequately separate the male DNA from the female DNA. We had enough of the DNA to be able to use this technology on and have a lab that would generate a genealogy type profile. There were multiple steps that were needed in order to get to that point, and so that was what I was working on. I started working on that around April or May of 2017, in terms of identifying a suitable sample. I had consumed all the DNA in the Contra Costa County East Area Rapist cases years ago pursuing what's called the YSTR technology. That's the paternal DNA, it's inherited from father to son through the generations.

Six years ago, I was pursuing that genealogy work, and I had consumed all the DNA I had in my possession in order to get a good extended 67 marker profile for the East Area Rapist. Now I'm looking at this new autosomal DNA technology that all the genealogy companies are now using such as Ancestry and 23AndMe, and I didn't have the DNA. I now had to convince somebody down in Southern California, where they still had Golden State Killer DNA, to basically allow me to take some of that valuable DNA and generate this genealogy profile to search the genealogy databases. That is the big hurdle, and that's what took so long. People from the public calling up and saying you know me and my wife are watching a show, and we both turned to each other and said they should just search ancestry.com. It's not that easy when you are dealing with a forensic sample. Once we got to where we could generate a genealogy compatible DNA profile, then it was, "What databases are we going to search?" The obvious one was the open source public facing database GEDmatch and that's what we did.

I uploaded it into GEDmatch, I got a list of relatives, and then we started doing traditional genealogy to try to figure out if we could ultimately land on who the Golden State Killer was from that list. The way it works is that, it's not like the FBI's CODIS system where you're uploading the offender's DNA, and you get a hit, a one-to-one hit. This is a genealogy match so what you're doing is, you're uploading the profile and the genealogy website is searching for the people that share the most amount of DNA. Some people would share 100 centimorgans of DNA with your offender's DNA. Then there is another person that shares 95 centimorgans and there's another person that shares 65 centimorgans, and it goes down in diminishing amounts. The smaller the amount of DNA the person shares, the more distantly related they are. When we got the results back out of GEDmatch, searching the Golden State Killer's DNA, what we got was a list of individuals that the best match that we got was on the order of a third cousin, and we had roughly fifteen, twenty-third-cousin level matches before we started dropping down into the lower level of a fourth cousin or worse so that's what we had to start with. There wasn't just a person, it was multiple people that were very distantly related. They're so distantly related, they don't even know that the person that's a relative DNA wise, such as Joe DeAngelo, even exists.

We got down and I'll say just roughly a handful of individuals of males that kind of checked the boxes of being the right age, that were living in California in the 1970s, but only two were close enough to Sacramento. There is this one other individual that we focused on first who's had two uncles that lived right in the heart of Cordova Meadows in 1975-1976, where the East Area Rapist first started attacking. Because of that connection, and one of those uncles ultimately moved to Stockton and bought a house from the company that employed the second Stockton victim, that particular person that we were looking at rose to the top of the *pile because there was a geographic connection with that person their relatives and what we knew about the Golden State Killer. Ultimately, we were able to eliminate that person and that person has no idea they were even looked at as maybe being associated with the Golden State Killer case. That's when we focused on DeAngelo because he did have the Auburn connection. He was close enough, and yes, he was a little bit older than what most people thought, but we thought well he's at least in the Sacramento region at the right time frame.*

We knew that he attended Folsom High School back in 1962, so it appeared that his family was down in the Rancho Cordova area because those that were in Rancho Cordova were bused to Folsom High School during that time frame. We thought we need to start looking at him, and that's when I started reaching out and talking to people who knew him. As we got more information that's when he became much more interesting.

Paul mentioned talking to people who knew DeAngelo, and we asked him about the challenge of reaching out to people to investigate him but doing it in a way that would not tip him off.

Well, that's part of the investigative strategy. You have to assess the relationship of the person you want to talk to and DeAngelo what it was back in the day and then what it is today. For example, everybody is aware of this Bonnie. We had a newspaper article that we found early on, DeAngelo had been engaged to a Bonnie back in 1970. Then of course, if there's an engagement then you'd expect to see a marriage license and possibly children and everything else, but there was nothing. There was no indication that the couple had ever been married. You start investigating who Bonnie is, and you start seeing that she's remarried and has been married for a long time and obviously there's no shared children with DeAngelo. The chances that Bonnie and this Joe DeAngelo today after more than forty years from that engagement, the chances of them being friendly with each other and in constant communication is low. It's not impossible but it's low so you have to roll the dice, and so I did, I rolled the dice. I ended up calling Bonnie, left her a message and unfortunately, she was out of the country, and she never heard my message. On the other side, his wife Sharon, you start looking at that relationship, and you recognize that they have three children together.

There's no divorce on record, you have one child that is living with him and two children that are living with her. There is a potential friendly relationship there and there is no marriage. They were still married on paper. There was no relationship in between the time that you see the separation to the current date, and then you back away. I never contacted Sharon because of my fear that those two were still talking to each other. It really is you have to assess the circumstances back forty years ago to the current day in order to determine how you want to approach somebody, and that's what I did. When I found that he was an Auburn PD officer, the logical thing is to call up Auburn PD and say, "Hey, do you have any personnel records?" Then one thing led to another, and the next thing I know I'm talking to the former chief of police who fired DeAngelo and when talking to him, he goes, "I remember him well, I was his sergeant when he was in patrol." He told me all sorts of stuff that just notched DeAngelo up as being a much more interesting person as the Golden State Killer suspect than what we knew previously.

We wanted to know if Paul had any interaction with DeAngelo personally before the arrest.

The closest that I came is the last day before I retired. I drove out and parked in front of his house. He was interesting enough where I needed to start doing what I typically do when I call a prime suspect, where I start really digging into somebody. I went, I wanted to see where he was living, see if I can see him out in the yard or what was going on around his house. I wasn't thinking that he's the guy at the time. He was just an interesting individual. I even considered that, I should probably just go up and knock on this guy's door. What's the likelihood that he is really the Golden State Killer? You get so jaded after having so many prime suspects be eliminated by DNA, you almost let your guard down. That's what I did. I got to a point where I thought I was going to go and just say what I've done many times, this is who I am. I'm looking into an old case. Do you mind if I ask you a few questions?" Once I established a rapport with the person, "Do you mind if I get your DNA sample? That way, once you're eliminated, you don't have to worry about anybody ever contacting you again on this case." Most people readily agreed to providing a DNA sample. I backed away from that because I realized that I just didn't know enough at that point in time. It was too early, I thought I might be pressing, I'm going to be retiring in a day, I don't want to just let the fact that my job was ending was going to cause me to make a rash decision. That's when I put the car in drive and drove away. At that time and day, I just drove straight home. During the drive I'm just beating myself up going, "Maybe I should just go talk to that guy. Maybe I could help the investigation if I get his DNA because then we could see are we closer in the genealogy standpoint with DeAngelo, then we would know that we were in the right family branch of the genealogy work." I said, "I should do that, but just never turned the car around to go get that done." In retrospect, that really turned out to be the right decision.

Even though I retired, with this team, we knew we were close at that point. Fortunately, the guys that were still active embraced me as retiree, just basically it was a seamless transition. My email address changed from a ContraCostaCounty.org type of email address to a gmail.com email address. We were still emailing back and forth like nothing had changed. We were still talking to each other on the phone like nothing had changed. My role really did not change even though I just was not going down to Martinez, California, and sitting in my district attorney's office. I was sitting at home talking to them on the phone and continuing to move forward with the strategy. I was never in the interview room with him. The way things worked out is he was brought in, Sacramento Sheriff's homicide detective Ken Clark was the primary interviewer of him, initially. Ken and I were supposed to go in and talk to him about the Central Valley and East Bay, East Area Rapist attacks before Southern California agencies were to take their turn. I can't get into specifics, but the way that the interview worked out and how he responded, basically we had to skip the sexual assaults in Northern California that couldn't be prosecuted to get the investigators with homicides in there sooner than later. I did not get the chance to sit in the room with DeAngelo and talk to him, but I watched through the monitors seven hours of him being interviewed. I do have a good feel on how he responded to the various people that were talking to him and how he answered, or I should say didn't answer for the most part, any of the questions that they were asking him. To my knowledge he has not admitted to anything.

We asked Paul how surprised he was, personally, that DeAngelo was a father, a grandfather, and an ex-cop.

I wouldn't say any of that was surprising. The fact that he was a law enforcement officer -- It's not surprising. Though I will say that when I was evaluating the case, this guy being a law enforcement officer was something that would come up from time to time over the course of the 1970s to the current day. I took the position that this guy is an intelligent offender. He is somebody that would naturally do some of the things that we are seeing because he's all about self-preservation. It doesn't mean he has law enforcement training. Now, we know DeAngelo was a law enforcement officer, then of course, now you see, "Okay, this guy did have law enforcement training, and he capitalized on that training to do the things that he was doing." He was doing other things that you generally don't learn in law enforcement. It again speaks to DeAngelo as a sophisticated and an intelligent offender who also learned from his mistakes. He adjusted his M.O. to suit the situation and continuously improved upon his abilities to avoid capture.

Paul had been on record as thinking the Visalia Ransacker and East Area Rapist were likely not the same person. We wanted to see if this opinion had changed.

With Visalia Ransacker, I took the position that I did not think that the East Area Rapist and the Visalia Ransacker were the same person. Now, I'm not surprised that they were, and I do think circumstantially that DeAngelo is likely the Visalia Ransacker, though it still needs to be proven. I do think that's what it's looking like. It's not surprising. It's more of how he changed his physical appearance and his skill sets and even his behaviors in those six months from when he shot officer McGowan to when he is showing up and becoming the East Area Rapist. This is where from evaluating the series and this is getting into that academic mode, what you're looking at, again, it speaks to this guy's intelligence. He's recognizing his faults as the Visalia Ransacker. He was not good at getting inside houses. He often would pry or attempt to pry multiple windows and multiple doors before getting in. He was not good at staying hidden. Multiple people in that town saw him and what turns out to be spot on composites were generated. When he leaves Visalia, he recognizes he made mistakes.

Now, he is modifying his skill sets, he is modifying his M.O., and he's even modifying his behaviors with the victims in order to prevent his mistakes from Visalia from occurring again. It is very interesting to watch the evolution of an intelligent offender who does have elevated skill sets as a result of his law enforcement training and how he adjusted in order to be able to continue to offend, to continue to satisfy those compulsions that he had. You would think the average person with the scares down in Visalia would say, "I'm done, they got too close to me," and they wouldn't continue. He just got better as a result because he wanted to continue.

I do believe that he purposely physically transformed himself. Again, he was seen as the Visalia Ransacker, and he is described as kind of this heavier sat rounded shoulder, thick hipped, thick thighed, short fat feet, and a very pudgy round face to all of a sudden having a slim athletic build six months later. I was thinking well maybe he went to the academy where he was doing a lot of physical fitness, he's burning a lot of calories but at least as of right now with the records that I've seen, that's not the case. He did the Academy way back in 1974, and when he transfers up to Auburn PD, he's just taking classroom training; he's not actually doing any physical training. I believe that he recognized that he had been seen, a composite showing him how he looked heavier was out there, and he decided I've got to lose weight in order to help hide my identity. In addition, he takes additional steps. He's making sure he always has a ski mask on, he's making sure he's blinding his victims with a flashlight. Even with taking those two steps, when he's inside the house dealing with the victims he's telling them, "Don't look at me or I'll kill you," even though he's got a ski mask on. He is taking it many steps down the road of preserving his identity because he knows that he sucked at preserving his identity as the Visalia Ransacker.

We asked Paul if he still thought that the homework evidence that was attributed to the East Area Rapist actually could be linked to DeAngelo.

At this point in time I still think it's possibly related, but my confidence is not as high as it used to be. I was inside DeAngelo's house and walked through his house and I saw numerous examples of his writing. I even saw a hand drawn diagram that he had generated, and after observing that I walked away going, "I can see enough overlap between what was present in his house and the homework evidence where I think it's still in play." We don't know enough about DeAngelo at this point in time, he most certainly is going through school. The homework evidence, the two essays, appeared to be school assignments, so I'm very interested to see what coursework, besides criminal justice, he took when he was at Sierra College or when he was at Sac State. The hand drawn diagram I think is a bit more perplexing, and I've said that I see evidence that there is a collaboration between two people with what's going on in the markings in that homework evidence. It's possible that you have another individual that is drawing that diagram and is talking to DeAngelo about that, but I don't know, it's speculation at this time. Did he take drafting or landscape architecture at Sierra College or Sac State, and this was merely a homework assignment? The experts that I put that diagram in front of are pointing out industry specific symbols that generally practitioners would use, not something that you would learn in a classroom. That's why I've always leaned towards this is somebody who's actually out at the job site.

What's really resonated with me since DeAngelo was identified, is I had a guy online who had been in law enforcement for forty-five years say, "Hey, back in the day we used to moonlight as security guards on construction job sites in order to make a little bit more money because we weren't paid very good back in the day." When you look at the prevalence of where this guy is attacking, especially after he moves out of Sacramento, when he gets into Stockton or when he's in Davis even Modesto and out in the East Bay in Concord, even down in Danville, Fremont, and San Jose, he is attacking either in or immediately adjacent to active construction. When I see that pattern and that's where a job site security guard makes sense to me. Why would a security guard have that hand drawn diagram? I can't really answer that at this point in time, and so I'm really interested to find out is there a reason for him to have drawn that himself either through classroom training or through maybe interactions with people who were in the development building industry. Or was I spinning my wheels following a red herring for several years, diving down on that diagram, I just don't know at this point.

We wanted to know if the reality of DeAngelo being identified had sunk in for Paul yet.

I'm feeling good that the case is solved. There's still sort of an uneasy feeling because I have so many unanswered questions about who this guy was, and

I want those questions answered just in my mind, so I can better understand this offender and how he committed these crimes. Another part of it is I've been so busy since we announced DeAngelo as the Golden State Killer. I still, to this day, haven't really been able to just sit back, push away, and start contemplating the magnitude of the closure to this case.

We definitely wanted to get Paul's take on DeAngelo's first court appearance.

That was all an act. We know he was under surveillance for a week, and he was directly observed to be very physically capable, very physically mobile. He was riding a motorcycle at high rates of speed down the freeway, he's moving around his house, he's doing mechanical work on his daughter's car, and making trips to an auto parts store. He is getting around, the guys that had directly observed him while he was under surveillance are saying this guy does not move around like a 72-year old. He's moving around like a 50-year old, so seeing him get wheeled into court in a wheelchair to me it was a bunch of BS. I saw his wheel spinning sitting in that interview room, and him starting to implement his strategy. This guy is a tactician, and he was all about self-preservation when he was out there committing his attacks, and now that he's caught, once the shock of, "Oh my God they caught me," wore off, he's now in that mode of how can I minimize the impact to me of being in this situation. I believe that wheel chair and kind of being the feeble old man was he was trying to get sympathy from the court and setting up a strategy for a defense down the road. He's thinking ahead and doing that.

We reached out to Sacramento County District Attorney Anne Marie Shubert before Joseph D'Angelo was arrested. She was able to give us a bit of insight about how the prosecution against the Golden State Killer might go once he was arrested.

Clearly, he's responsible for a dozen murders and many of those murders are connected by DNA. Those crimes span several jurisdictions. There would be several jurisdictions, if he's caught, when he's caught, if he's still alive and all those kinds of things. He could be prosecuted for the murders. The rapes as everybody knows, the individual is responsible for upward of fifty rapes in Northern California. The rapes would be barred by the statue limitations, now that doesn't mean that those crimes would not be admissible in a courtroom because they would be likely to be used to show his M.O. and his intent and all those kinds of things. My honest answer would be that there are several jurisdictions that have murder cases including Orange County, Santa Barbara County, and Ventura County. Sacramento has a double. but that is not connected by DNA. When the person is caught, if he's alive, then the decision would have to be made by presumably the various elected DAs. which is the most appropriate jurisdiction to proceed.

We asked DA Shubert how it would be decided which jurisdictions would prosecute?

That's a factor, another factor would be how many murders occurred in that jurisdiction. There's a number of different things and can you prosecute them all in the same jurisdiction. Can you prosecute all twelve in one jurisdiction? Those are a variety of different questions that have to be answered, but obviously, the counties that have the ones that are connected by DNA and the probably the highest value would be prime considerations.

DA Shubert explains some of the details about the relatively short statute of limitations.

What I can tell you is that, in 1976, it was probably no more than six years, but it may have been even less. It's quite fascinating actually to look back in history at what happened as a result of these rapes in Sacramento. It's funny because we've pulled all the news footage from that time period in the hopes that maybe it would give us some tip or something. At that time in 1976, at least based upon the news footage, rape was not even a crime that would mandate state prison, and so there was a lot of protesting by women at that time basically saying that these individuals should be sent to prison, if they're apprehended, to protect rape victims.

Setting that aside, the law now in California is far different in terms of prosecuting sexual assault cases. Essentially if you have DNA on a rape case, there's virtually no statue limitations anymore, assuming you follow certain rules, but the rights that people have now with respect to prosecuting those types of crimes are far broader than they were at the time of 1976. That just is a testament to how we have evolved as a society to make sure that one, we protect people's rights, but, two, that we are able to apprehend people for crimes that they committed even long ago.

She went on to talk about the potential things that they have to consider in a prosecution against the Golden State Killer after he was arrested.

I spent many years doing cold cases, and cold cases present their own challenges in many ways because time has elapsed, but you put it in front of a jury, and a jury is going to judge you based upon today's kind of standards which is very different you know with a kind of CSI standard nowadays. But we have to put an old case in front of a jury, not talking about this case in particular, on a cold case murder that we might have had when we have DNA. A rape-murder of a let's say it's a woman that gets raped and murdered, we question so then you get a hit on it when you match it to somebody then when you start going through the questions. "Okay, is he from that neighborhood? Why would he have contact with that victim? What is his prior history? Is he from Sacramento?" For instance, we had a double up here, a very famous case called the sweetheart murders, where a guy, two young college kids from UC Davis were kidnapped and horribly murdered and ultimately that individual was apprehended through DNA, and it was the same kinds of questions you're asking. "Why were their bodies dumped in this area? Did he have a reason to be in that area? What connection did he have to Sacramento?" In that particular case his brother happened to live within a mile of where these bodies were dumped. As a DA or an investigator, you're always trying to figure out what is the reason for where the crime occurred, where the bodies were found, and just building the same investigative information that you would on another case but understanding that it's a crime that is forty years old.

Sometimes that's harder, it's much more difficult to find information from 1976. You get a hit today, and it's a John Smith and then we're saying okay, does John Smith have a connection to Sacramento? Does he have a connection to Orange County or Ventura County or Santa Barbara? Why was he there? What kind of job did he have? Those kinds of things that would help us try to answer those questions.

We wanted to know specifically if there are any crimes associated with the rapes that could still be prosecuted such as any kidnapping charges.

It could be kidnap-for-purposes of rape. What I learned about cold cases is that you are bound by the law that existed at the time. I would have to go and pull my 1976 penal code and say, was kidnap-for-purposes of rape a crime at that time? If it was a crime, what was the statute limitation? It gets interesting, and sometimes at the end of the day for this particular case, because he's connected to so many murders, I don't want to say that the rapes don't matter, they very much matter, but our goal is to prosecute the individual and make sure that they are never able to hurt anybody again. All those crimes matter, but there's no question there's a sufficient number of crimes to make sure he's going to be held accountable.

DA Shubert was able to tell us what kind of sentence the East Area Rapist might face if he had committed those rapes in the present day.

That could be a life term now, a lot of that has come over time through various ballot initiatives that were passed by voters to get tough on sex offenders. In 1994, if my memory's right, California passed what's called the one strike for the sex offender. If he committed a sex crime with certain kind of circumstances, if he broke into a house, committed residential burglary for the purposes of committing a rape you can get life but again that was '94. We have very tough laws since then but the question, what existed in 1976 at the time, that's what we have to look at. I mean this case obviously spanned four decades, and there's been tremendous amount of effort and renewed efforts over time to solve it. There are a lot of very dedicated folks, law enforcement and non-law enforcement that want it solved. My philosophy has always been about this case that it may be that it's a needle in a haystack, but the needle is there somewhere, and we need everybody possible to help us find that needle. It may be law enforcement, it may be somebody that just happens to know about the case and suddenly finds out that they have some strange jewelry in their Uncle Bob's possession, and they don't understand why. But, it's just being vigilant and being informed that might often lead to that tip that identifies this person. I say this often, the answer's out there, it's just a matter of our persistence in finding him.

We knew that the Criminology podcast that spawned this book would garner interest from a lot of people. When we began the research for the podcast, the case of the Golden State Killer was starting to become more well-known throughout the United States and the rest of the world. But, we could never have known that in the middle of the podcast, there would be an arrest in this case that was over forty years old. And that arrest sparked a huge wave of interest in the case. We were fortunate to get so many people connected with the case, both past and present, to talk with us for the podcast. We spoke with the investigators who worked the case back in the 1970s, victims and family members of victims of this monster, and with some of the investigators who were working the case and had a hand in the arrest of Joseph DeAngelo. We have presented as many of those interviews as we could in this book. The majority of the interviews took place many months before the arrest was made. We would like to thank everyone who took the time to contribute to the podcast and to this book. It will be interesting to see how things pan out in the case against DeAngelo, but we, like the rest of the world, will be watching as it unfolds.

PHOTOS AND DOCUMENTS

Composites of the Visalia Ransacker circa 1974-1975

Claude Snelling, murdered in his Visalia home in
December of 1975 trying to defend his daughter, Beth

1. 06/18/76: Rancho Cordova, 0400 hours, lone female, 24 years old, asleep. Ski-masked male, naked from waist down, standing in bedroom doorway, erect penis, ran to victim and put knife to her temple. Suspect attempted to make it appear as two suspects were involved. On 01/02/78, victim received phone call threatening to kill her. Victim states it is the suspect who raped her.

2. 07/17/76: Carmichael, 0200 hours, two sisters home alone. Woke one sister, tied her up, then went to second bedroom and woke second sister and tied her up. Second sister tried to fight and suspect hit her in back of head. One sister, 15 years old, was raped; one sister, overweight, 16 years old, not touched. Suspect wearing full mask.

3. 08/29/76: Rancho Cordova, 0320 hours, 41-year old mother, 12 and 15 year old daughters. Youngest daughter told mother she saw a man with a ski mask outside her window. Mother got up to look and saw suspect, dialed operator. Suspect entered through bedroom window wearing ski mask and no pants. Mother fought suspect, who beat her with a club. Mother and daughter eventually escaped. Suspect fled, no rape.

Fall of 1976, A portion of a police report detailing the East Area Rapist's first 4 confirmed 1976 attacks

Suspect's Description	WMA, 23, 5-10, 165, Brown hair, very pale legs, brown leg hair. Very bad odor about him possibly his breath.
Voice Characteristics	Talked in a whisper through clenched teeth.
Clothing	Coat, possible fatigue pants, possible zip-up sweatshirt with front pockets and a hood. Hood was worn over his mask.
Gloves	Tan leather gloves.
Mask	Leather hood, extending beneath his shirt, slits for eyes and mouth.
Shoes/Boots	Black square toed shoes
Lighting	Small flashlight - in left hand.
Weapons	Small wooden handled knife.

Portion of a police report from a November, 1976 East Area Rapist attack

Composite of the East Area Rapist from a March 1977 attack

Type of Location	Single Family Residence - One Story
Suspect's Description	5-9/5-10, 160-170, slender to medium build Very small penis
Voice Characteristics	Spoke with a whisper - stuttered on letter "L". Harsh, raspy whisper. Hyper - loud breaths in and out.
Clothing	Dark colored - bulky waist length jacket. Dark trousers.
Gloves	Black leather gloves.
Mask	Red knit ski mask with oval eye and mouth holes.
Shoes/Boots	
Lighting	Small 2-cell flashlight. Small bright beam.
Weapons	Large caliber semi-automatic pistol, blue steel, possibly 45 caliber, military type

Portion of a police report from a May, 1977 East Area Rapist Attack

Katie and Brian Maggiore killed by the East Area Rapist February 1978

Crime scene evidence photo from
Maggiore murders Feb 1978

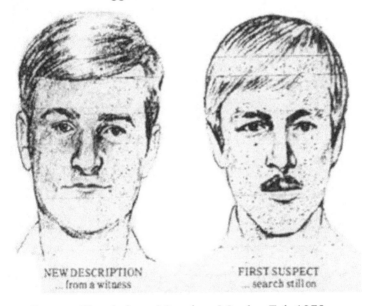

NEW DESCRIPTION
... from a witness

FIRST SUSPECT
... search still on

Suspect Sketch from Maggiore Murder, Feb 1978

1. (CV) ████████
   ████ Belann Court ████
   Concord, ████
   DBA: Housewife

   WFA ████

   (V-2) ████
   ████ Belann Court ████
   Concord, ████
   DBA: ████████

   WMA ████

   (S) Male person, believed to be white male adult; believed to be in his
   twenties or early thirties years of age; approximately 5-11 to 6-0;
   medium build; wearing dark color clothing; possibly wearing some type
   of corduroy pants; wearing a dark color ski mask with the eyes and mouth
   cut out; wearing brushed suede type gloves; shoes believed to be of soft
   sole. S's speech described as being very distinct, not fast speaking.
   CV said S had a musty type smell about him. V-2 described S's smell as
   similar to cinnamon.

Portion of Police report from October, 1978 East Area Rapist attack

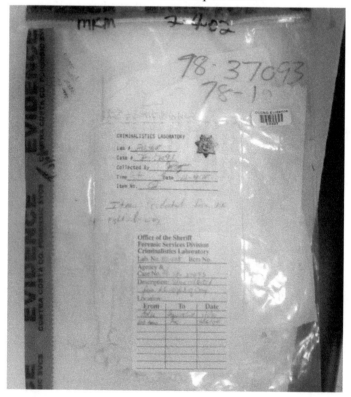

Evidence photo of 'The Homework' papers dropped by the East Area Rapist at a December 1978 crime scene

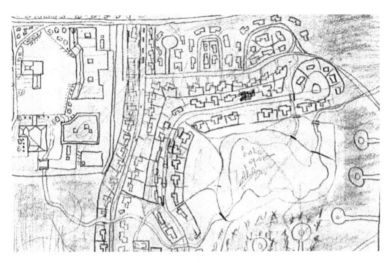

Part of a handwritten and drawn Map found as part of 'The Homework Evidence' at a December, 1978 East Area Rapist Crime scene

Sketch circulated July 1979 of East Area Rapist at a Danville attack

Sketch of suspicious man seen around the
July 1979 attack in San Ramon

Doctors Robert Offerman, and Debra Manning murdered in
Goleta CA by the Original Night Stalker in December, 1979

Charlene & Lyman Smith, murdered in Ventura CA
by the Original Night Stalker in March 1980

Patty & Keith Harrington, murdered in Dana Point,
CA by the Original Night Stalker in August, 1980

Manuela Witthuhn, murdered in Irvine, CA in
February 1981 by the Original Night Stalker

Cheri Domingo, and Greg Sanchez murdered in Goleta,
CA in July 1981 by the Original Night Stalker

Janelle Cruz, murdered in May 1986 in Irvine
CA by the Original Night Stalker

Police evidence photo of a shoe print found at an
unknown Golden State Killer crime scene

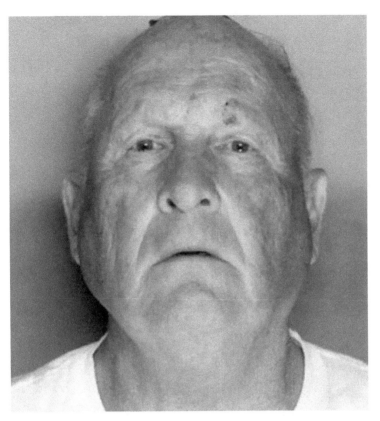

Mugshot of suspect, Joseph J. DeAngelo Jr taken after his April, 2018 arrest. He is believed to be the Visalia Ransacker, AKA East Area Rapist, AKA Original Night Stalker, AKA Golden State Killer. He is currently awaiting court proceedings and has not entered a plea.

BONUS MATERIAL

After Joseph J. DeAngelo was arrested in April of 2018 as the suspect in the Golden State Killer case, details soon emerged on just how the arrest came and at that moment, a new age in crime fighting was born.

After only having access to so many private DNA databases, and not getting any hits, investigator Paul Holes had something in mind. He decided to upload the Golden State Killer's DNA to Gedmatch, a public DNA database in which its users can add their DNA profile to connect with others who shared that DNA. The site was primarily used for genealogy purposes. Its privacy policy was very clear to its users, that by uploading and sharing their DNA, that it was opensource, and anybody that wanted it had access to it. This is the complete opposite of premium private pay databases like Ancestry.com or 23andme.com who have a very tight, and protective privacy policy. Paul Holes knew that entering the Golden State Killer's DNA into this database would likely provide close genealogical links to his suspect, and from there, the family could be sorted through until the right suspect was found. But the challenge was getting access to those premium private databases. They would not willingly let Paul Holes, or his fellow investigators enter their suspect's DNA into that database. It would require a search warrant, and getting a search warrant would be hard as it would likely be too broad a request asking for such unlimited access.

Paul Holes knew that since Gedmatch did not have these same privacy restrictions, that he would not need to get a warrant to search the DNA profiles looking for familial links to his suspect, so he entered the DNA into a database and got a distant familial hit. But that was just the beginning; a lot of work remained ahead of him. He needed to enlist a professional forensic genealogist to trace the family tree from the relatives connected to the suspect's DNA. It wasn't a fast process, but it was a fruitful one. A handful of likely male suspects were developed, and it soon became evident that DeAngelo was the most likely suspect, although he was slightly older than expected. Once they closed in on him, they collected his DNA via an undercover method, and it turned out to be a 100% match to the Golden State Killer's. From there, DeAngelo was taken into custody, and is currently awaiting court process to determine his guilt or innocence.

There was no doubt, this new process worked. The Golden State Killer had been unidentified for over 40 years, and the advent of new and emerging DNA technology mixed with good old-fashioned police work and determination, led to his capture.

As news of the arrest, and how it came to be made national news, police agencies all across the country took notice. Whether they had well preserved DNA evidence from a decades old cold case, or fresh DNA from a recent case, they knew that they could solve cases using this same method. But, it turned out that many of these police across the country were thinking along the same lines as Paul Holes, and they had enlisted the help of Parabon NanoLabs. Parabon is a lab that specializes in DNA phenotyping services for law enforcement. They had already been generating composites of what a suspect in a crime might look like based on their DNA profile. Soon after the DeAngelo's arrest, it was reported that Parabon was working on 100 or more criminal cases that contained DNA. They would do the DNA work, and then a professional genealogist would track the family members of the DNA contributor in these crimes back to the right suspect.

It didn't take long for the dominoes to start falling. Several cold and high profile murder cases have been solved, and the perpetrators identified using this same method in 2018. These solved cases include the murders of Christy Mirack murdered in 1992, April Tinsley murdered in 1988, and Virginia Freeman murdered in 1981. These are just a handful. Additionally, the process also helped to identify the true identities of two men who had assumed false identities, and whose cases were very familiar in true crime circles. The true identities of 'Lyle Stevic' and 'Joseph Newton Chandler' were learned, and their backstories are now being examined. And this is only the beginning. This same technology can and will be used to identify not just the perps in murder cases, but also the remains of unidentified bodies and victims of crimes, or disasters, etc.

The sky truly is the limit with this entire process and technology. But it's not without its critics. Some people fear for one reason or another, that law enforcement having access to so much information is dangerous. It will be interesting to see what legal challenges the process faces moving forward. But despite being frowned upon by a few, it seems that the technology and crime solving method is indeed being embraced by many. GedMatch has seen an influx of people racing to input their DNA into the database, vs a small number of people removing it. This could be the beginning of a long and valuable road to fighting and solving crimes, and we can look back at the Golden State Killer case and remember where it all began.

For More News About Criminology Podcast,
Signup For Our Newsletter:

http://wbp.bz/newsletter

Word-of-mouth is critical to an author's long-term success. If you appreciated this book please leave a review on the Amazon sales page:

http://wbp.bz/goldena

Season One, Episode One

MIKE FERGUSON: You're listening to the premiere episode of *Criminology*. I'm Mike Ferguson and with me, as my co-host on this journey, Mike Morford. Mike, I know we did this on the introduction episode, but I also know there's a lot of people that don't listen to introduction episodes, so I think we need to take just a moment and introduce ourselves to the audience before we jump right in. So, like I said, my name is Mike Ferguson. I host a couple of other podcasts: *True Crime All the Time* and *True Crime All the Time Unsolved*.

MIKE MORFORD: Everybody, my name is Mike Morford and you can call me Morf. Since there are two Mikes on the podcast we don't want to confuse you, so I'm Morf. I'm a true crime blogger and researcher.

MIKE FERGUSON: And this is going to be a big departure, Morf, from what I'm used to. You know on *True Crime All the Time* and *True Crime All Time Unsolved*, we do a different case every week and we're gearing up that week and the weeks leading up to one single case in a short period of time. Now, what you and I have chosen to do is take the deepest dive possible on some of these unbelievably fascinating cases and to do that it's going to take us six, eight, ten episodes depending on the case, but that's how much time that we believe it takes to give every single detail, not to leave anything out. And for our first season, we chose the infamous Zodiac case, and Morf, I think we have to talk a little bit about why we chose it.

MIKE MORFORD: So, this is a case that Mike and I know a lot about. You know, as far as myself, I've been researching the case for over a decade. I run a site called *zodiackillersite. com*, and to do it justice, to really explore the case and find out why it's one of America's biggest true crime mysteries, it's good to take a number of episodes to really explore this case and try and get to the bottom of it and we're hoping that the listeners out there can go along with us on this ride and see why it's such a fascinating case.

MIKE FERGUSON: And I'm really looking forward to it Morf, and I'll tell you why. There's a lot of great podcasts out there. Some of them have done Zodiac but nobody has done the number of episodes that we're going to do. And as good a job as they may have done in one episode, two episodes, three episodes, there's just no way that you can get all of the pertinent information about this case. It's just too big. So for anyone that's not familiar with the case, let's just do a quick synopsis.

The Zodiac was a serial killer operating in the late 60s and early 70s in the San Francisco Bay area of California. But Zodiac is not your typical serial killer because he becomes a publicity seeker, interacting with the press and the police. So what ends up happening is that the crimes themselves become just one part of the story of the Zodiac. We're going to look into the entire story of the Zodiac. Not only the crimes, but we're going to be talking about his communications with the police, we're going to be talking about the possible suspects, we're going to dive into the clues that surfaced along the way. But by the end of this season, our hope is that you're able to form your own opinion, draw your own conclusions about this Zodiac case. So Morf, we have to start at the beginning, right, where else would you start? This case is going to start out in 1968 on the outskirts of Vallejo, California. About thirty miles northeast of San Francisco, it's a blue-collar town. Back then, had a population of about 65,000 people. It was home to a lot of military personnel, retired military, ship workers, welders, oil refinery workers. It doesn't get much more blue-collar than 1968 Vallejo. Like a lot of other towns, Vallejo had its good sections and it had its bad sections, but the crime rate overall in 1968 was pretty low. They didn't have a lot of major crimes. What the town did have was some light gang activity, they had a lot of fights, some burglaries and drug busts, but very few murders. Now compare that to today, Vallejo has a lot more crimes involving murder, but in 1968, this was a pretty peaceful town. And this was also an era when life was a little bit easier, a little more laid-back compared to today's fast-paced life. But Morf, all of that was about to change on December 20, 1968. Just a few days before Christmas, two young local teenagers, they were on their very first date, were found murdered without any apparent motive. And at the time, nobody realized what was at hand, and that these murderers would begin one of America's greatest and most puzzling unsolved mysteries.

MIKE MORFORD: So the two teens that were killed on December 20, 1968, were seventeen-year-old David Faraday and sixteen-year-old Betty Lou Jensen. David was a senior at Vallejo High School and Betty was a junior at nearby Hogan High. David was a good kid with a good reputation and he was active in the Boy Scouts. David was the oldest of three kids and his parents were Thomas and Jean Faraday. Betty was the daughter of Vern and Virginia Jensen, and she had an older sister Melodie. The two teens had met at a party and had been seeing each other, unknown to Betty's parents who didn't want her to date yet. Betty's parents had finally given her permission to go out with Dave, so they were both excited to go on their first official date. Betty's parents gave the two an 11:00 p.m. curfew and the pair told her parents they planned to go to a Christmas concert, but they skipped the concert and wound up out on secluded Lake Herman Road on the outskirts of Vallejo. Dave had told friends that on that night he planned to ask Betty to go steady with him and he wanted to give Betty his class ring.

MIKE FERGUSON: And Morf, if you think back to the 60s, that was a big deal to give your class ring to a girl. That really meant something. I think at this point we need to talk about Lake Herman Road. It was a six-mile stretch that connected the towns of Vallejo and Venetia. It was a lightly traveled road; it didn't have many streetlights. On top of that, there were not many homes on the road, with the exception being a few ranches and farms. Now there was one particular parking spot along Lake Herman Road and this was a spot where teens would park to have some privacy, make out, hold hands, smoke pot, whatever teens were doing back in 1968. Now I say parking spot but it was really a turnout from the main road. It turned onto a dirt road that led to the Venetia pumping station. And this dirt road was blocked with a locked gate to ensure the cars could not enter, and teens would park right in front of this gate. On the night of December 20, Dave drove Betty in his parents' 1961 Rambler and they arrived around 10:00 p.m.. It was a very cold night for that area. Temperatures dropped into the low 20s so, because of that, Dave left the motor running and he and Betty sat talking, enjoying their privacy.

MIKE MORFORD: Normally Lake Herman Road was a quiet road, but on this night several cars were driving by, and they took note of the Rambler parked and the silhouettes of the two teenagers inside the car, sitting close to each other. Not far from that parking spot, a red truck sat parked up the edge of the road. There were no passengers inside of it. There were no other cars around. A married couple would drive by and see the Rambler around 11:00 p.m.. Now remember, Betty was due to be home by this time. The married couple could see the two in the car move apart when their oncoming headlights shined on the Rambler. The married couple was out looking at pipework on the side of the road that the husband's company had recently done. They drove down the road a bit and turned around at the entrance of a ranch. While turning around, the couple saw two men walking with rifles. The two men were raccoon hunters that were walking back to their red truck. The married couple headed back down the road and then again drove by David Faraday's Rambler, still parked by itself. A couple minutes later, the raccoon hunters drove by the Rambler and they also took notice of it. They did not see any other people or cars around. It was estimated that the hunters drove by the Rambler at around 11:10 p.m..

MIKE FERGUSON: Around 11:14, there's another car traveling on Lake Herman Road to Venetia and this car is driven by a man that's on his way to the midnight shift at Humble Oil. And he drives by the Rambler but he notices that there's another car sitting to the right of the Rambler at this point in time. So the man notices this car to the right of the Rambler but all he could tell police later was that it was dark and it was lacking in chrome. The other thing that this man would tell police is that he didn't notice any people either inside or around either of the cars that he saw. About this same time, a woman named Stella Borges leaves her home on Lake Herman Road, along with her mother, to go pick up her son. And her house on Lake Herman Road is about two to three miles from where the Rambler was parked. And the route that she takes leads her right by the spot where Faraday and Jensen are parked. So Stella and her mom are driving down the road, they come around a big curve right in front of the turnout, and it's about 11:20 as their headlights shined on the turnout around the bend. And it's at this point that the two women see a horrible sight. Betty is lying on her side on the edge of Lake Herman Road, twenty-eight feet from the Rambler which is still parked in the same spot. Now the other thing that they see is Dave lying on the ground close to the car, but what they don't see is any other car in the turnout. As you can imagine, these two women are horrified and Stella takes off speeding down the road headed toward Venetia and she's able to flag down a police car within five minutes. So we're at 11:25 now, and they race behind her in their patrol car and they all arrived back at the scene at 11:28. So the two officers on the scene are Officer Pitta and Officer Warner of the Venetia Police. And they get out of their patrol car and they start to examine the scene. What the officers see first is Betty Jensen lying face down and they would note this in their report. It was evident that Betty was dead; she was lying in a large pool of her own blood. Now Stella Borges is still at the scene, she's talking to officers, and she explains to them that when she had first driven by what she had seen Betty was on her side. The most likely explanation for this is that Betty was still alive when Stella Borges first drove by and that's why she was on her side. But by the time that the police get to her she has passed and is now face down.

MIKE MORFORD: It turns out Betty had been shot five times in her back. Pitta now went over to look at David and although it seemed like he was dead, Officer Pitta detected breathing. Pitta got on the radio and called EMS and anybody else that could get out to the scene to assist. Other Venetia officers arrived and eventually an ambulance. They loaded David into the ambulance and raced to the nearby Vallejo Hospital, but he would be pronounced dead on arrival. The Solano County Sheriff's Department actually took the lead in this case as the crime happened in their jurisdiction, and they showed up to investigate. As in typical crime scenes involving bodies, they drew white chalk outlines around the spots where the bodies had been. They examined the scene, and found several shell casings. They had come from a .22 caliber Winchester Western Super-X long rifle ammo. The scene was handled by Officer Russ Butterbach and Sgt. Les Lundblad, who was in charge.

KRON NEWS REPORTER: Sergeant, could you briefly describe what apparently happened last night?

SGT. LUNDBLAD: Yes, we had a double homicide that took place out on a county road about sometime after 11 o'clock last night. A double homicide involving victims ... were a sixteen-year-old girl and a seventeen-year-old boy.

KRON NEWS REPORTER: How did this incident occur apparently?

SGT. LUNDBLAD: Well, they were shot.

KRON NEWS REPORTER: What were the circumstances involved?

SGT. LUNDBLAD: Possibly they were ordered out of the car by the responsible ... and the boy was shot right at the side of the car and the girl apparently tried to run and she was shot and found twenty-eight feet further on.

KRON NEWS REPORTER: There was one bullet hole that penetrated one of the windows of the car. Was this a stray bullet or was this one of the bullets that hit the victim and went on through?

SGT. LUNDBLAD: This could be a stray bullet or a warning bullet of some sort. We can't connect it with the bodies, but it's the same type of shell.

KRON NEWS REPORTER: You have any idea what the possible motive might be for this?

SGT. LUNDBLAD: We have no motive at this time.

MIKE FERGUSON: When Dave's body was unloaded at the hospital, the ring that he had planned to give to Betty was found wrapped tightly in his fingers. Back at the crime scene, it was discovered that a shot had been fired through the roof of the Rambler and police theorize that this shot was fired in an effort to get the kids out of the car. It appeared that both kids were forced to exit out of the passenger side of the car. Betty would've exited the car first, as she was sitting on the passenger side, with Dave behind her. When Dave stepped out of the car, he was shot very quickly at almost point-blank range behind his left ear. At some point, Betty took off running towards the road and was shot five times in her back as she ran. As police investigated, they saw no signs of sexual assault. There were no signs of robbery. Investigators would secure the crime scene for the night and it would not be until the next morning that the timeline of the murders would start to become clear.

http://wbp.bz/zodiaca

1.

July 25, 2003

The monster stirred inside him. Most times, he could tame it. Keep it hidden. Silence its screams. But tonight, the beast demanded release.

She lifted her head up. "You're taking too long. I'm done."

He pressed her head back down. "You're done when I say you're done ..."

She wriggled beneath the firmness of his grip. "No!" she protested, forcing herself up from his lap. She stared him straight in the eyes—defiant and unafraid. "That's all I'm doing for you, Devin."

His calloused fingertips nervously tapped the upholstered backbench and his spine tingled with an odd mixture of excitement and fear. The beast was rising. There was no going back. Not now. Not ever. "Rape her," the monster instructed. "Rape the whore!"

*

It had been a long night of hustling for Nilsa Arizmendi and Angel "Ace" Sanchez. Maybe it was the hot weather, but the regular johns were being especially cheap and irritable, and Nilsa was forced to negotiate smaller fees. Ordinarily, she charged $30 for a half hour, but tonight's tricks were turning a maximum of only $20 and some demanded blowjobs for a measly 10 bucks. Like shrewd customers at a turn-of-thecentury street market, the johns knew that the vendor in question was desperate for cash.

Ace loitered around the corners of New Britain Avenue, where his girlfriend worked. He stared glumly at the filthy surroundings, trying not to think about Nilsa's activities. He did not like their lifestyle. In fact, he despised it. But how else could he and Nilsa score drugs? The couple's shared habit was not cheap. In July 2003, they were each smoking about 20 to 30 pieces of crack per day and shooting up a bundle-and-a-half of heroin, which translated to about 10 to 15 bags on the streets. Sometimes, Nilsa used up to three bundles of heroin a day, depending on the amount of crack she smoked. It was a nasty cycle. The crack got Nilsa and Ace ramped up and wired and the heroin brought them down. They needed both to survive.

Without the drugs, sickness set in. Being drug sick was terrible—worse than having the flu. In the darkness of their motel room, the childhood sweethearts huddled together in sweat-soaked sheets, shivering with nausea and chills. Every joint and bone ached as invisible bugs furiously crawled beneath the surface of their skin. In between fits of vomiting, their bowels loosened and the bed became soiled. Nilsa kept the curtains drawn and placed the Do Not Disturb sign on the outside door handle for days at a time. The room was a mess. Their lives were a mess. Besides the incessant and all-consuming craving for heroin, she felt shame.

"This shit has to stop," Ace thought as he watched Nilsa emerge from the back seat of an old man's car. She walked toward him, tucked her tie-dyed T-shirt into her dungaree shorts and offered a faint smile. Normally 140 pounds, the 5'2", dark-haired woman was now only skin and bones. "I'm tired," she said. "Let's go home."

On the walk back, Nilsa briefly disappeared and scored a blast of crack at Goodwin Park in Hartford. She returned to Ace and attempted to take his hand. He pulled away. "I'm done with this shit. You gotta go to rehab, Nilsa. We both gotta go."

She acted like she did not hear him. It was usually the best way to avoid a fight.

But tonight, Ace would not let up. "I'm done with the fucking drugs," he mumbled, running his hand through his greasy dark hair. Normally, he kept it long, but a few days before, he had cut it short. "Done with the hustling. Fuck. Fuck this shit."

Their shadowy figures forged into the night, softly illuminated by the neon lights of outdated motels. Rolling hills of forest stood far in the distance, strangely comforting and yet somehow sinister. When Nilsa's high wore down, they started to quarrel. This time, Ace would not take no for an answer. They both had to go to rehab in the morning.

Nilsa was reluctant. She had been in and out of rehab for years and it never did her any good. Still, she loved her four children and desperately wanted to be done with the drugs and get clean forever and for good. Overhead, the night sky opened and a warm drizzle began to fall. The blue rock watch on Nilsa's frail wrist ticked into the early morning hours. They walked southbound along the pike, past Cedar Hill Cemetery containing the corpses of Connecticut's affluent class, including legendary actress Katharine Hepburn, and then a smaller cemetery containing the remains of lesser-known citizens.

Ace gently elbowed Nilsa. "You gonna start singing?"

She sometimes sang Christian hymns that she learned in childhood as they walked along the pike. It passed the time and gave them both a sense of comfort in the midst of all the pain. She smiled beneath the foggy moonlight. "You want me to?"

"You know I like your voice," he replied.

Her smooth, clear voice chimed like a bell into the darkness of the night:

O Lord my God, When I in awesome wonder,

Consider all the worlds Thy Hands have made;
I see the stars, I hear the rolling thunder,
Thy power throughout the universe displayed.

By the time they reached the parking lot of the Stop & Shop in Wethersfield, Ace had persuaded Nilsa to agree to the plan. Nilsa was worthy of a long and healthy life. After all, Ace needed her. Her mother needed her. Her children needed her. She vowed to never turn another trick again or inject poison into her veins. The party was over and fuck her if it had not been the party from Hell.

Nilsa eyed a lone vehicle parked in the far corner of the store's lot. "That's Devin's van."

"Let's get back to the motel," Ace said.

"I'm just gonna say hi."

Nilsa walked across the lot to the beat-up blue van owned by their mutual acquaintance, Devin Howell. They had met Howell a few months before. At the time, he was pumping gas at the Exxon gas station on the corner of Broad Street and New Britain Avenue. The rain was heavy and Ace and Nilsa were soaking wet as they approached Howell's van and asked for a ride to their motel room on the Berlin Turnpike in Wethersfield. "We'll give you five bucks," Ace said.

Howell had to go to Lowe's to price out some supplies for an upcoming job. He was driving in that direction anyway, so it was not a problem to assist two near-strangers who appeared down on their luck. "Yeah, sure. The door's unlocked."

Nilsa and Ace squeezed into the bucket seat on the passenger side. Nilsa used her street name, Maria, when she introduced herself to Howell. As they drove to The Almar Motel, Howell told the couple in his mild Southern drawl that he had a lawn-care business. Ace glanced over his shoulder at the back of the van. The space was large, with a long bench sofa littered with lawn service tools and clothing. The stench of body odor pervaded the vehicle's interior.

When they arrived at the motel, Ace and Nilsa invited Howell into their room to hang out. Howell brought some beer and marijuana. Nilsa and Ace offered to share a little crack, but Howell refused. He was a weed and booze guy. Together, the three got high on their poisons of choice. Howell told them that he was living in his van and he often parked it at the Stop & Shop parking lot in Wethersfield. He left the motel less than an hour later. As he drove back to the Stop & Shop lot to bed down for the night, he glanced at the open ashtray and saw that a $20 bill rolled up inside of it was gone. "No fucking good deed goes unpunished," he cynically thought. Ace and Nilsa had ripped him off.

In the months that followed, the occasional contact with Howell proved beneficial to Nilsa and Ace. The couple had lived on the Berlin Turnpike for the last 18 months or so, first at The Elm Motel and then at The Almar. Their daily routine involved walking from the motel on the pike to the familiar section of New Britain Avenue in Hartford where Nilsa turned tricks, about 1½ miles from The Almar. Ace had not worked a job for seven or eight months and he no longer had a vehicle of his own. Especially in the cold weather, Nilsa and Ace relied on acquaintances to spot them walking along the busy roadway and offer a lift. Occasionally, they had money for a cab, but that meant less money for drugs.

Howell also proved useful in assisting Nilsa and Ace to cop drugs. He did not mind driving them to local dealers living 15 to 20 minutes away. He would not get high with them when they scored. He seemed content to do them a favor by giving them a ride in exchange for a few dollars. All told, Howell served as the couple's makeshift Uber driver on about five occasions over the course of one month.

At approximately 2:45 a.m. on July 25, 2003, Ace watched Nilsa's skeletal form traipse across the empty parking lot. It was hard for him to believe that this was the same woman whose weight had sky-rocketed to 180 pounds when she was last released from federal prison—all beefed up by the cheap, starchy food. Nilsa stopped at the van and appeared to talk to Howell, who sat in the driver's seat. Then she walked around the van and got into the passenger side. Howell turned on the engine and slowly drove away. It was the last time Ace would see Nilsa alive.

*

When Christ shall come, with shout of acclamation,
And take me home, what joy shall fill my heart.
Then I shall bow, in humble adoration,
And then proclaim: "My God, how great Thou art!"

Nilsa "Coco" Arizmendi, Jan. 29, 1970–July 25, 2003
Rest In Peace

http://wbp.bz/hisgardena

AVAILABLE FROM BRIAN WHITNEY
AND WILDBLUE PRESS!

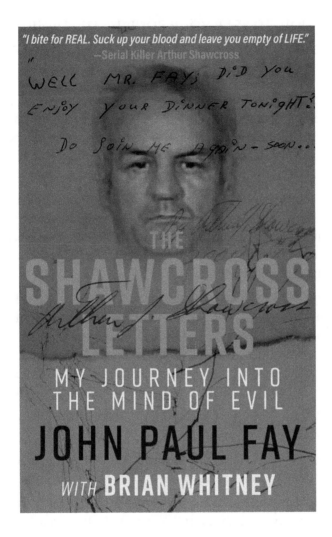

THE SHAWCROSS LETTERS by John
Paul Fay and Brian Whitney

http://wbp.bz/shawcrossa

Chapter One

HOW TO SELL YOUR SOUL TO THE DEVIL
(AND LIVE JUST LONG ENOUGH TO TELL ABOUT IT)

When God died, the world went berserk.

As a directly connected note and, perhaps, a warning before proceeding, the almost familial relationship I had with Arthur Shawcross, one of history's most terrifying serial killers and admitted (often, boastfully so) cannibals, was a decidedly unholy one.

My relationship to Arthur Shawcross was the closest to a wholesome relationship I've yet had. It has continued to be so. Of course, let it be noted, "wholesome" is a relative designation, as I don't abide the concept of human relationships the way an average individual does.

Not only did I swan dive into the rabbit wormhole, I demolished the only way in or out. Through either willful incompetence, or concentrated free will and accord, to open a vein to attempt an under-the-radar flight from the profanity of a monochrome existence, I made it a preposterous impossibility to reverse course. Whatever, I'm here now, just swinging at the ball as it comes.

The grit.

The grime, the slime, the crime, and the grim, seductive sublime.

The night-washed alleys and sleepily-lit hallways where the dreary, weary, and shady ride out a nod, disguised by their own layer cakes of filth, one get-well-soon spike or dope-sick robbery from overdose or a life sentence.

The backrooms, basements, bunkers, and burnout bachelor pads quietly hiding odd little men who own one too many axes. The secret places unobtrusively blending into the background just out of sight, out of mind.

This is where I live; this is what I live for.

I was playing peek-a-boo with the Devil long before I began my tumbles, fumbles, and stumbles through the brambles of Wonderland and the eerily precarious shores of the abyss led me to Shawcross. Or, perhaps Shawcross, the proudly self-appointed "mutant," was led to me. After all, he reached out to me first.

I'm not entirely certain what this says about my character, but I could never have dreamed how important a figure, at a deeply personal level, Arthur Shawcross was about to become for me. It went well beyond our business arrangements and book agreement. I became dependent on his presence to validate my own minefield of a mind, which was already uniquely primed and wired as unspecified bipolar with antisocial traits. According to a myriad of rather unfortunate psychiatrists I have seen, I am also afflicted with PTSD, OCD, and, occasionally, a psychotic episode to keep people around me on their toes.

There's no denying that inside of me, as my own descent into a Hell-spun lunacy was just getting underway, Shawcross grew roots, integrating into my life as a surreal, symbiotic, perversion of the surrogate father-son dynamic.

Shawcross was the quintessential enabler, a recurring echo goading me into more and more misadventurous indulgences of my tendencies for exorbitantly bizarre behaviors, an ever-present voice interwoven into the hallucinatory soundtrack of my life, founded on the fallen, twisted trees of a ceaselessly treacherous forest.

One or two sharp, brief breaths of counsel here. Don't play with black magic, demons, or, indeed, the Devil Himself, unless you want what you're calling. In other words, do be careful what you wish for. Be dedicated or just be dead. And if you're insane, don't take said insanity lightly. Though, it can, and does, keep life engaging.

Whether ritual magic brings madness or madness leads one to find such things appealing in the first place, I couldn't aptly uncover. In either case, I have my suspicions that Shawcross might have been the ultimate embodiment of my blindly pursuing the darkest of occult sciences, arts, and necromancy, dredging devils from the Pit just to keep me company.

The same reason that I chose, in my drunken hazes, to keep certain friends around for longer than maybe they'd intended. Although the law calls it "false imprisonment," it was real enough for all involved. Certain key details might not be recalled entirely due to chronic alcoholic blackouts, but some graciously administered prescription sleeping medication somehow being mixed into drinks and guests coming out of deep, deep rest the next day or two later, shackled to their bed, may possibly have been an odd phase I went through. No allegations have been made, so this might all be strange delusion. What I can recount clearly was that I was a captive of myself as well, cuffing and shackling my own hands and feet many times over, long before my actual arrests, to get acclimated to moving about with such restrictions. A self-fulfilling prophecy, I suppose. Certainly, I didn't help it not to happen.

When I was ten, my parents pulled their worst off-balancing act up to that point, separated and shuffled their children to any family members who would take us out of pity more than graciousness, establishing us as what my maternal grandmother called "latchkey kids." I felt lost, needing connection to something, someone, anything, anyone. Auntie Lorraine, my father's sister who assumed the role of unofficial surrogate mother, used to take me out for daytrips into witch territory Salem and occasionally treated me to lunch with the witches (I met world-renowned witch Laurie Cabot once at one of those lunches and she very respectfully advised me on a dream potion I'd wanted to try), palm and tarot card readings, life-altering Ouija board sessions, and bought me an elaborate library of books on occult magic and Satanic sciences. My intrigue with the practice of magic took hold of me the way that hard drugs would later. For certain, it was addicting, but it kept a lonely boy busy. My occupation was self-destruction right from the beginning.

Digesting each book, I was especially drawn to the revelation that one could call entities over from wherever they resided. In my reeling desolation, with such an emotionally confused barrier between myself and most everyone else, I thought of it as a friend-on-demand (or more realistically, demon-on-demand). It was hope for something different, something better. My life from the beginning had been a daily carpet bombing of behind-closed-doors abuse and dread, so there really wasn't much to lose.

Experimenting with spells seemed like something over which I could have relative control. It was only the clueless summoning of a randomly chosen demon from a book of black magic incantations, invocations, evocations, provocations, irritations, and optional mutilations. The book was a no-special-occasion gift from Auntie Lorraine, who my parents took full advantage of as far as dumping their children onto, as my "mother" had only had her three children for cosmetic purposes, a sick façade of normalcy, and a pathological need for attention. In the moment, as a child playing with devils beckoning just where Earth and Hell converged, while other children wrapped themselves up in what I considered the most mundane and bloodless of activities, I thought I'd not performed the ritual correctly, or that it simply didn't work.

Much later, I agonized over whether I engaged in an invocation rather than an evocation, or some magical mash-up symbiosis of spells. The summation of said summoning, an invocation is inviting a spirit or demon/jinn into yourself, an evocation is calling these forces outside of yourself at a relatively safe distance. Decades later, emptying bottle after bottle of rum, chasing nearly every mind-altering alchemical substance known to humankind, I wondered if maybe I had not failed at summoning something after all. Particularly, on cocaine I tend to do a lot of wondering aloud. And, may the late-to-the-party Lord help me, I have a racecar-in-the-red proclivity for other radically morbid musings of possibly interdimensional proportions. But it doesn't become overtly dangerous until I remember where I hid the knives. Of course, crazy saves me.

My curiosity came from a deadly serious place. It wasn't only the possibility of having brought an incarnate demon, in the form of Arthur Shawcross, into my life, but some intangible, churning fog rolling with a speed of driven determination, of the most exotic tint of the macabre into myself.

For the uninitiated, the otherwise profane, and those not well rooted to the Underbelly--where even the air is not for the faint of heart: when the wolves are at your door, it's best not to answer. You can't tease demons, who command full-bore commitment. The Devil won't slip a ring around your finger but around your neck. And these forces from well over the rainbow will drag you through the mud like a dumbfounded dog if you're not mindful and always respectful. Candidly speaking then, DO NOT do what I did. Not only did I answer the door, I invited the Beast in with the morbid giddiness of some mad occult scientist. Though, this seemed to be my nature anyway, however unnatural it may be.

Looking back now, that first piece of mail from the Sullivan Correctional Facility was a slow-motion spark heading into a sea of gasoline and dynamite.

6-25-00

Mr. John Fay,

Are you by any chance known by the handle, SAWMAN?

Sometimes I examine who is who on the market. I've quite a list of buyers and sellers. The sellers I stop writing to! That is if the sell my letters to others!

I am leery of who I write to in the mail.

Do you know a Melissa from Ripon, CA? I've a few photos of her. I can say MUCH on that one.

Let's talk for a while truthful to each other.

A.J.S.

Another rule to pay mind to: NEVER take a human skull to a job interview with you. That being noted, it was during the "Golden Age" of eBay. For me at least, but I was bootlegging every imaginable genre of film and auctioning sideshow curios and gaffs including the perennially popular shrunken heads, back when any perfectly sane enterprising capitalist could auction the artifacts of murderers (aka Murderabilia).

For someone like me, who was not all that employable, mainly because of my penchant for trying to strangle bosses, this was a respectable supplemental income. I managed to get my hands on several pieces of Shawcross's artwork (some meticulous 8" x 10" pencil drawings of birds) in a quite amusing trade with a fellow eBayer. She was a female fan of Shawcross and other serial killers throughout the country. I'd traded her a number of homemade video compilations of serial killer interviews, documentaries, and news footage, which I had put together. This kind of subject matter is, as I empirically observed, far more popular than a society of people wearing masks of normalcy might want to know, admit, or admit to knowing.

Financially, it was sensible and sound to auction the drawings of Shawcross' blue jays, cardinals, and seagulls in flight. I figured I would just wait and see whose attention might be piqued, confident that there were other collectors into these unusual acquisitions; people whom let their personas down in the privacy of their hideaways from the world as they tentatively trawled the depths for brushes with evil at a safe distance.

That strange day in June of 2000, when I discovered the unexpected letter from Arthur Shawcross, was, as usual, a grindingly lonely one. Living alongside a shattered and scattered family, it made no difference. We were never on eye-to-eye terms and it's still impossible to imagine how I share blood with such a deranged example of humanity. Taken completely by surprise, after hesitating for half an hour or thereabouts before opening the mail, I had the distinctly alarming feeling that I might be in some kind of trouble. Like the time I was apprehended shoplifting, finally, at one of the nearby malls when I was fifteen. Wrestling ferociously with five security guards, I was eventually half carried and dragged into the department store's tight quarters of a security room. I'd been sloppy that day.

This began with the first mistake of taking my cousin Raymond instead of my usual partner-in-grime Mike, which makes for really bad luck. Apparently, it poisons the dynamic to break that connection. That had been the first apprehension I had the pleasure to experience. What this store essentially did was to extort me for two-hundred-fifty dollars rather than prosecute. So, my first actual arrest wouldn't happen for another twenty-one years, despite many police detainments, interactions, and escorts with ambulances to one hospital or another. With any situation such as this, though, one has an uneasy sense of having the cloak torn off and suddenly realizing how visible you actually are.

As for Shawcross, I worried that I hit an unfortunate nerve with this convicted serial killing cannibal. I also was moderately apprehensive about his having my home address.

A year or two later, chances are I would've taken a blackout cocktail before reading the ice-breaking letter. As it was, I was sober as a judge is supposed to be in most modern American courtrooms, my mind sparking with apprehension, excitement, and, curiously enough, the faint hope that I'd found a new friend off the beaten path.

My policy being to keep as much to myself as was possible, I said nothing about the letter to anybody. It was none of their business. As my divorced parents, who, through some abortion of logic, were still residing in the same ass-backward household, going about their daily scenarios of monotony (my dad continued to stalk my mother even after their divorce, despite sharing the same house), and my two younger sisters impetuously pursued their strapped-for-intelligence boy toys of the month, I went ahead and opened the note. Peeling the envelope, there was a sudden concussive shock that slammed my senses. It was like some innate understanding that I had just then broken the seal on a portal into a deathly pale landscape which should not have been breached and certainly never explored. It was an expression of destiny as tailored in Hell, rising ominously as a duo of the damned and doomed.

Something I have stringently kept to myself was that my usually deadened instinct for brotherhood was buoyed to the surface by Shawcross. It was validation from the pinnacle of we, the soldiers of the macabre; a stamp of approval by one of the world's most unrepentant cannibal compatriots. Could I really have shared that with anyone of sepia-tone sensibilities with the vapid values of a plate of bacon and eggs? Dr. D, my psychiatrist, was already itching to bury me even before things really got out of control. She was a quirky doctor of psychiatry indeed, a straitjacket framed above her desk.

Not that I hadn't recognized it as an especially delicate situation. After all, I was dealing with an openly evil man whose skeletons were so out of the closet that they were re-inventing the cemetery business, handed down a two-hundred-fifty-year bid for a pastime I'd only been experiencing as phantasms, internally toying with for eight or so years at the time, as astounding and frightening in its implications as that is. What mostly concerned me was the prospect of Shawcross being unreasonably challenging. All the other male figures and ass-sideways "role models" in my shit-com of a life certainly were. Exceedingly brutal and mean-spirited men, every one of them. Of course, Shawcross wouldn't be entirely different with his own brand of brutality and intolerance, even toward me on occasion (especially near the end). But we had something in common that I characterize as the "affliction."

How in the arcane name of the devil-headed god Jahbulon of Babylon would I, or could I, respond? Play our words backwards and you'll understand that grim minds think alike, no matter what we try to say in the mundane world to diminish who we really are. I realized later that I only worried because of that often-crippling lack of self-confidence that stays on me like a perpetually wet blanket, sewn to my soul and not quite locking on to who and what I actually am. I believe that I was groomed for this sinister season, which has really been the only thing in my life I've carried a passion for that was never exhausting to me. The only thing that doesn't feel like work to love. After all, lovers quite literally come and go, whether through boredom or death, but the pursuit of subterfuge sin just doesn't seem to grow old. And it certainly won't die.

I became increasingly indignant as I processed the letter's contents, and lamented that even a habitually murdering maniac wasn't quite catching onto the gist of where I was coming from. A horrible and horrific disconnect, I felt. I did realize how careful I had to be and not write back with a psychotic's abandon. My rants have ruined me for long-term friendships before. So then, I took the path of indignation but ever so delicately. The intentions were to clear up what I believed was a misalignment of communication. If I wanted anyone to understand me, it was Arthur Shawcross. The two of us were companion madmen of the Outskirts; a netherworld director's cut of society, which I had no inclinations of departing anytime soon. As Shawcross had crossed precipices I had yet to, there was something morbidly spellbinding about him. Dare I admit, it felt like an almost inside-out romance. We weren't necessarily on the same page and wouldn't always agree on everything, or ever have perfectly matching personalities, but we were at least on the same bookshelf. An odd camaraderie, I'm the first to confess. These psychedelic shades of gray were never an easy topic to cover with the uninitiated. Not that I wish it on anyone; it skins the spirit bare.

At the beginning of it all, I pitched Shawcross a business arrangement. If he were amenable, wonderful! If not, I'd either get a response spattered with a serial killing cannibal's strain of hate or just never hear from the Genesee River Killer again. Either way, I was a battered lifetime veteran of bad starts and unhappy endings, so what would be the loss? Still, there was hope, muddied and bloodied as it was.

7/6/00

MR. FAY,

What was the drawing of mine that you sold? What did you sell the item for? I can use a money order -- only if it does not put you out! May I ask who bought said item? Can you send addresses of people who are collectors?

Where might you be moving to? Now that you have parted with one item of mine, here are two more to help you on your way, Mr. Sawman. Some handle you have there! It was the handle, Sawman, that got my attention.

I have used a MACHETE on a few...Head come right off! Vietnam will do that to you!

Mr. Fay, I hear about letters being sold all the time. The people who do that I generally leave alone. I dislike writing to someone and have them sell a letter because I have said things that are not cool for the eyes of others!

Wish I was in Boston again. Last time I was there. I was a teenager.

Melissa of California, I'd like to rattle her bones a few times for real... she would not be the same afterward. HAHA

Mr. Fay, you now have her photos. Do as you wish with them.

Stay cool.

Later,

Arthur S.

http://wbp.bz/shawcrossa

See even more at:
http://wbp.bz/tc

More True Crime You'll Love From WildBlue Press

A MURDER IN MY HOMETOWN by Rebecca Morris

Nearly 50 years after the murder of seventeen year old Dick Kitchel, Rebecca Morris returned to her hometown to write about how the murder changed a town, a school, and the lives of his friends.

wbp.bz/hometowna

THE BEAST I LOVED by Robert Davidson

Robert Davidson again demonstrates that he is a master of psychological horror in this riveting and hypnotic story ... I was so enthralled that I finished the book in a single sitting. "—James Byron Huggins, International Bestselling Author of The Reckoning

wbp.bz/tbila

BULLIED TO DEATH by Judith A. Yates

On September 5, 2015, in a public park in LaVergne, Tennessee, fourteen-year-old Sherokee Harriman drove a kitchen knife into her stomach as other teens watched in horror. Despite attempts to save her, the girl died, and the coroner ruled it a "suicide." But was it? Or was it a crime perpetuated by other teens who had bullied her?

wbp.bz/btda

SUMMARY EXECUTION by Michael Withey

"An incredible true story that reads like an international crime thriller peopled with assassins, political activists, shady FBI informants, murdered witnesses, a tenacious attorney, and a murderous foreign dictator."—Steve Jackson, New York Times bestselling author of NO STONE UNTURNED

wbp.bz/sea

CPSIA information can be obtained
at www.ICGtesting.com
Printed in the USA
LVHW032327040420
652230LV00006B/2289